KHADIJAH ELSHAYYAL is a postdoctoral research fellow at Edinburgh University's Alwaleed Centre for the Study of Islam in the Contemporary World, where she also teaches courses on Islam and Muslims in Britain at undergraduate and postgraduate levels. She holds a PhD in History from Royal Holloway, University of London, and her research interests lie in the representation, political and cultural engagement of Muslims and ethnic minorities in the UK.

'*Muslim Identity Politics* is a hugely welcome contribution to an evolving field of social science and humanities enquiry. Using a historical analytical framework, this book charts the complex nature of the reality of Muslims in Britain since the postwar migration phases of the 1960s, carefully dissecting the layers of social and religious representation since then. It ultimately argues that the British Muslim space has been subject to internal as well as external pressures, which are growing considerably in the current climate. Populism, xenophobia, the rise and fall of Islamic State, and virulent Islamophobia blight Muslims from without, while internal theological fissures, class distinctions and the shutting out of key organisations by the government has banished the Muslim voice from the top table of high politics from within.'

Tahir Abbas, Professor, and Fellow of the Royal Society of Arts, is Visiting Senior Fellow at the Department of Government at the London School of Economics

'A welcome contribution to a growing collection of academic literature that is concerned with uncovering the overlooked history and heritage of Muslims in the UK... Elshayyal shows that Muslim activists, while sometimes overlooked, have been neither quiescent nor peripheral within the wider British political sphere.'

Carl Morris in *Religion, State and Society*

'An absolute must-read ... for anyone trying to appreciate the particular struggles and tensions in Muslim political engagement'

Hira Amin in *Islamophobia Studies Yearbook*

'This timely, nuanced study of identity, Islamophobia and emancipatory politics in contemporary Britain deploys historical insight combined with a socio-legal perspective to critically explore what "freedom of expression" means for early twenty-first century British Muslims. As well as identifying the "equality gap" that lies at the heart of much of what British Muslims experience, Elshayyal also – importantly – shows how this fracture can be addressed and narrowed, and thus her work prompts essential rethinking in relation to the contested place of Muslims in Britain today.'

Humayun Ansari, Professor of the History of Islam
and Cultural Diversity, Royal Holloway,
University of London

'This book breaks new ground and will be an important contribution to the place of Islam in public life in the UK. It is an interesting and valuable addition to a subject that is likely to remain relevant for years to come.'

Sadek Hamid, Senior Research Assistant,
University of Oxford; Author of *Sufis, Salafis and Islamists:*
The Contested Ground of British Islamic Activism

'This is a book to celebrate: with Elshayyal's considerable expertise, wisdom and even gentle humour, we gain a better understanding of how "identity politics" can be understood in a positive way. Moving us away from the well-worn sketch of identity politics as a fissiparous impulse that leads groups away from the national interest, she creates a fine framework for constructive discussion of the identities of British Muslims and of others. We benefit from her clear analysis of evidence-based arguments that show how Muslims have been, and still are, treated differently and in discriminatory ways from other British minority groups. Elshayyal invites us to identify arguments that can be set against polemical security rhetoric; she shows us how rich the cultural imagination of Britain really is, if we accept identity politics as a fast-evolving phenomenon, and finally she facilitates a coherent understanding of what it means for us all to be living with an equality gap that takes different forms and deserves to be tackled in a unified manner.'

Alison Scott-Baumann, Professor of Society and Belief,
the School of Oriental and African Studies (SOAS)

MUSLIM IDENTITY POLITICS

Islam, Activism and Equality in Britain

KHADIJAH ELSHAYYAL

I.B. TAURIS

LONDON • NEW YORK • OXFORD • NEW DELHI • SYDNEY

I.B. TAURIS
Bloomsbury Publishing Plc
50 Bedford Square, London, WC1B 3DP, UK
1385 Broadway, New York, NY 10018, USA

BLOOMSBURY, I.B. TAURIS and the I.B. Tauris logo are
trademarks of Bloomsbury Publishing Plc

First published in Great Britain 2018
Paperback edition published 2020

Cover design: www.paulsmithdesign.com
Cover image: Nahella Ashraf, anti-racism and women's rights activist, speaks
at an anti-Trump 'Muslim Ban' demonstration on Saturday, 4 February 2017 in
Manchester, United Kingdom. Jonathan Nicholson/NurPhoto/PA Images

A catalogue record for this book is available from the British Library.

A catalog record for this book is available from the Library of Congress.

ISBN: HB: 978-1-7845-3779-1
PB: 978-1-8386-0204-8
ePDF: 978-1-7867-3353-5
eBook: 978-1-7867-2353-6

Series: Library of European Studies 23

Typeset by OKS Prepress Services, Chennai, India

To find out more about our authors and books visit
www.bloomsbury.com and sign up for our newsletters.

For my parents

Contents

Preface to paperback edition

In the year and a half since this book was first published, the political landscape of Britain has been held hostage by the continuing fallout from the Brexit referendum of 2016. Here we are, over three years after the vote, mired in deadlock and uncertainty, and with no clear political resolution or way forward. Whilst there are a great many urgent and pressing implications of this crisis, most relevant to this book has been the sharp and sustained rise in xenophobia, nativism, and Islamophobia that we are currently witnessing.

Only a few years earlier, obituaries were being written for the far right's political fortunes in the UK. Electoral gains in local council and European elections that were made by the BNP during 2009-11 had proved short-lived, and ongoing internal conflicts compared favourably with worrying electoral patterns which had delivered far-right candidates to government positions on the continent. Liberal commentators then considered the steady rise of UKIP as a moderate right-wing vehicle for the expression of growing anti-immigration anxieties and disillusionment with mainstream political parties.[1] Yet the Brexit referendum threw the nation's highly polarised political climate into sharp relief, as anti-immigration rhetoric gave way to outright and unabashed racism – not only from the likes of UKIP, but also from key Conservative Party figures and the 'Leave' campaign, who competed in employing anti-Muslim and anti-immigrant tropes during a tense and heated campaign period, which peaked with the murder of Jo Cox MP. As Nesrine Malik has noted, rather than take caution from this deeply tragic incident, Cox's assassination has been irreverently and repeatedly instrumentalised by the pro-Brexit right.[2] We saw this demonstrated most recently by the current Prime Minister Boris Johnson, who rather perversely defended his own use of populist and divisive rhetoric by claiming that delivering Brexit would be the most appropriate way of honouring Cox's memory.

This mainstreaming of far-right rhetoric and policy cannot be understated. We are now at a place where the scapegoating of minorities is thinly veiled as resistance to 'political correctness' and free speech has become more of a political football than ever. One now infamous example which illustrates this is Boris Johnson's persistent and unapologetic defence of his use of insulting language to describe Muslim women's attire in a 2018 *Daily Telegraph* article.[3] Despite statistics demonstrating a sharp spike in targeted attacks on Muslims in the wake of the article,[4] critics have been dismissed as 'snowflakes',[5] and are 'gas lit' by claims that the piece was a 'strong liberal defence' of women's rights.[6]

Far-right actors including violent and violence-inciting street movements are emboldened by mainstream politicians riding the Brexit wave, seeking to sustain and to be sustained by appealing to populist nostalgia for imagined bygone days of an unencumbered and self-sufficient UK. Yet this image could not be further from the daily lived realities of those minorities and disadvantaged groups for whom the political and cultural histories of the UK have been replete with experiences of structural exclusion, injustice and oppression.

So how has this volatile political landscape, developing alongside a relentless austerity programme, impacted Muslim communal activism and its pursuit of equality? In what follows, I will highlight and consider some of the main issues relating to the Equality Gap, and the changing terrain within which British Muslim advocacy and activism now operates.

(RE) CONSIDERING THE EQUALITY GAP:

In my concluding chapter, I reflected on the Equality Gap, and how it has fared over the course of the past few decades. I argued that the foremost initial claims advanced by Muslim advocacy groups during the 1980s and 1990s had largely been incorporated into legal developments over the years, delivering some measure of access to equality for Muslims in the UK. However, I noted that this progress had laid bare deeper issues around persistent Islamophobia and inequalities at a structural level. My revised articulation of the Equality Gap described how Muslims can face serious and substantive inequalities *despite* the streamlining of equalities legislation that was spearheaded by New Labour during the noughties. This streamlining *has* delivered formal protections against religious discrimination in public life, protections which pioneer Muslim activists had so passionately campaigned for. However, although the specific claims that were put forward to the state by UKACIA and the MCB in the 1980s and 1990s regarding parity of access to equalities provision under the law have largely been met, the implementation of such legal provisions continue to happen against the backdrop of public institutions and structures that centre whiteness, or the 'dominant background culture' as normative, and treat minority religious and cultural markers as peripheral outliers.

I want to examine how this conclusion has panned out by homing in more closely on perhaps the most heated site of Muslim identity politics at present – namely, the securitisation agenda. In the second half of this book, I discuss at length the unimpeded encroachment of state securitisation measures. These measures have been consistently shown to be founded on an anxiety about a predisposition of Muslims, and by extension, ethnic minorities in general, to extremism and violence.

My discussion in Chapter 6 unpacked the state's two-pronged approach of 'hard' and 'soft' counter-extremism initiatives. In recent years, there has been a significant convergence of these two approaches, through blunt legal tools seeking to exert influence on public spaces and civic bodies. The Prevent Duty of 2015 is the most potent illustration of this development, with its requirement for frontline personnel in public institutions to actively promote a prescriptive formulation of 'fundamental British values' (FBV). Much has been said already about the problematic nature of prescribing such values, burdening ill-equipped professionals with the active promotion of these values and, more worryingly, the 'detection' and referral of those judged to be breaching them.[7] But aside from this, as Breen and Meer show, the very articulation of these FBV is 'forged on (uncontested) latent assumptions of whiteness', any 'misalignment' from which, carries 'specific implications and specific risks' for Muslims.[8]

Of further relevance to the Equality Gap has been the increasing reliance of the government's counter-extremism strategy on the Equality Act 2010 to represent FBV.[9] As John Holmwood has noted, the coupling of FBV with the Equality Act via the work of the Commission for Countering Extremism (CCE) encourages compliant civil society groups to weaponise the very characteristics specified for protection in the Act against Muslim community practices that are deemed to be in contravention of FBV. This dynamic has been at the heart of the ongoing and very unfortunate saga in several Birmingham primary schools around the 'No Outsiders' programme which frames LGBTQ+ inclusive education as a tool with which to tackle extremism in (Muslim-majority) local communities. This framing has been roundly repudiated by activists and academics, including Judith Butler, whose own research had constituted the theoretical underpinning for the programme itself.[10] Though purportedly an independent body, the CCE itself has given explicit and passionate backing to this problematic framing of FBV, to the extent that its Lead Commissioner, Sara Khan, went as far as criticising the Department for Education for not pursuing a 'strong enough' line with protesting families, who she described somewhat pathologisingly as a 'mob'.[11]

In Chapter 6 I used case-studies to demonstrate ways in which freedom of speech was being curtailed by counter-terrorism legislation, highlighting how it was being used by the state to police political and theological opinions, and to delimit which were 'acceptable' and which were not. If we return to the CCE, we see how its approach has been continuously aligned with that of the state. On one hand, the Commission has been vocal about a professed concern with protecting civil liberties and freedom of expression.[12] However, one specific incident in its recent evidence-gathering process has drawn attention to a rather more draconian approach – in what became something of a public spat concerning the social media activity of two academic specialists employed to write papers for the CCE, both of whom had been highly critical of the government's counter extremism strategy.[13] In an unambiguously heavy-handed inquisition-style disciplining, the CCE issued ultimatums to these individuals, seeking to censure their comments and making their continued involvement conditional upon a renouncement of alleged anti-Semitic views, and on their compliance with the demand to attend an educative meeting with Jewish communal organisations.[14] The Commission's eventual decision to reject their contributions on flimsy grounds of poor quality,[15] whilst publishing other pieces that would unquestionably fail any credible peer-review process[16] served to cement the impression already harboured by many that the CCE's data gathering operation was only seeking to generate amenable research to justify pre-determined policy recommendations.

Furthermore, this incident exhibited with clarity that the theme of conditionality which I discuss in Chapters 7 and 8, remains a firm and consistent feature of any state engagement with Muslim actors. It is not just reserved for advocacy groups like the MCB, but also extends to Muslim individuals engaging on a professional basis with government-established independent bodies. Such an approach lacks even-handedness on the part of the state, since no other religion is subjected to similar levels of stringent scrutiny or conditionality. It also demonstrates how, with the blunt tool of FBV, the silencing of dissenting voices has become integrated into the cost of engagement. Consequently, the deeply problematic 'good' and 'bad' Muslim binary is sustained, and academic freedom is undermined.

Effectively, these cases, which are prototypical of the Conservative Party's assimilationist brand of 'muscular liberalism' (see p.181), constitute a serious regression in the path of narrowing the Equality Gap through a politics of recognition. Thus, the situation is now one whereby an ever more pervasive state security apparatus is severely undermining gains towards greater equality that had been made during the 1990s and early 2000s. There is provision for equality and protection from discrimination in the *letter* of the law. However, structural issues around privileging of a specific, biased reading of FBV, and the use of legal measures to enforce compliance to this reading means that the equality which may be procedurally enshrined in the law, does not obtain *in practice* for Muslims. Further, the cynically expanding reach of counter-terrorism into community spaces creates additional obstacles hindering authentic communal activism and representation, both formally and more informally. Resultantly, dissension from state security strategy has become hazardous to the survival of any initiative, as we shall see in the next section.

ACTIVISM, ADVOCACY AND ENGAGEMENT:

Although grassroots activism and organising has been a constant feature of British Muslim communities, on a national level it has historically tended to be overshadowed, in some cases, with its own willingness, by the work of communal 'umbrella' groups. This was motivated to a large extent by a yearning to have centralised spokespeople as a show of power and unity, and as a necessary strategy for making gains from engagement with the state. Two main factors have in recent years led to a shift from this situation. Firstly, as I discuss in Chapter 6 and 7, discontinuation of formal government engagement with Muslim communal representation, and secondly, the democratisation and opening-up of activism, which has been significantly expedited by the proliferation of access to interactive digital spaces and social media.

In Chapter 5, I discussed how the engagement and leadership of Muslims in causes such as the anti-war movement signified a confident and evolving activist scene. In my concluding chapter, I considered several further examples of Muslim activism in 'mainstream' spaces, including the role of Muslims in grassroots coalitions, such as those seeking justice and providing support for the Grenfell community in West London after the atrocity of June 2017 which killed 72 and displaced hundreds. This trend of social justice activism – framed in broad and inclusive terms but strongly underpinned and inspired by spiritual foundations – is one which is expanding and thriving. It is a turn which is often fluid, and difficult to define, but it also offers greater avenues for inclusion, transparency and accountability – features that have long been points of weary contention among critics of formal representative groups. Yet despite these positives, this very same trend has revealed new challenges on several fronts. Among these, has been the vigorous intrusion of state counter-terrorism into community spaces, leading to a blurring of how such spaces and initiatives are perceived and delineated. This has in turn exacerbated existing mistrust and animosity among Muslim activists and groups, and between them and the state, as they question just how safe and autonomous their community spaces really are.

In a development which all but acknowledges the failure of old-style Prevent with its overt profiling and targeting of areas with significant Muslim populations, the state and its delivery partners in the corporate and third sectors have turned to the technical repackaging and rebranding of the strategy. This has included a range of highly questionable methods, such as the deliberate engineering of civil society responses to crisis moments through pre-planned social media hashtags, campaigns and vigils,[17] to the subcontracting of public relations companies to run pseudo-grassroots initiatives exploring topical religious and social issues whilst delivering 'on-point' messaging in conformity with the counter-extremism agenda.[18] In redoubling its focus on such spaces, the security state itself is ironically recognising the importance of grassroots activism as a rich arena from which they can sustain counter-terrorism activity including monitoring and surveillance. With the severe dearth of funding options available to any small- or medium-scale community initiative during current times of austerity, this state of affairs poses particularly troubling and urgent predicaments for individuals and collectives struggling to stay viable while preserving their authenticity, independence and integrity. The recent public debate around the Bradford Literature Festival's acceptance of counter-extremism funding is aptly illustrative of this dilemma.[19]

Concurrently, within and between Muslim communities, the burgeoning of grassroots activism has allowed for the nature of relations between community groups and collectives to shift and mature. Whereas in the past, formal representation occupied a position of primacy over public spokesperson roles, changing dynamics within Muslim communities have combined with the impact of disengagement by government to prompt a recalibration of focus. Digital platforms, and particularly social media have afforded expanding opportunities for freer expression, networking and accountability – quickening the pace of communication and coordination, and playing a vital role in further democratising community organising and representation. Fluid and open collectives seek to disrupt received narratives *within* and *about* their communities, using focuses such as cultural production, political organising or spiritual learning and expression to underpin their activism. Whilst these tools have allowed grassroots organising to spread and thrive, these same tools have similarly begun to be utilised by the very same organisations which activists have shunned or disengaged with for their rigidity and opacity, or their (actual or perceived) closeness to the state. Representative bodies including the MCB and its precursors had for decades been critiqued for an aloof, stagnant leadership style and unwieldy, often out of touch procedures and priorities (see Chapter 7). With the most diverse and youthful leadership team in its 22-year history now at its helm, the MCB has invested heavily in developing the clarity and accessibility of its online presence, and in taking its flagship community projects to locations across the UK through listening exercises and interactive conferences and workshops. In the words of Hassan Joudi, Deputy Secretary General at the MCB:

> we have to think hard about how are we as Muslim communities (are) communicating with our young, and interacting with them to make our organisations... fun to engage with, to be involved with, (and) to attract the right people (rather than being) something stale and just what our uncles and aunties do... I think we see the danger that we have if we don't think about that now, and identify practical ways and solutions to the lack of engagement we see.[20]

Thus, while persistent disengagement from successive governments has forced the MCB to divert its predominant focus away from seeking to directly influence state policy (though this does remain an important if somewhat more peripheral ambition), changing community dynamics have coaxed its hand towards investing far more resources into capacity-building initiatives. These have included institutional and leadership development schemes, consulting widely through a National Listening Exercise to respond to damaging counter-extremism strategies, and streamlining its day-to-day operations to become more accessible and inclusive. Whereas in its early years, the MCB portrayed an image of itself very much as *the* vanguard of British Islam, representing and speaking for an entire community, its current mode of representation is presented in a more conciliatory style, of listening to seek consensus and understanding, and casting a wider net to engage beyond its formal affiliate base with diverse and even oppositional views.[21]

Having said this, the MCB continues to voice a deliberately and self-consciously more measured stance, still harbouring aspirations that it can regain consultative status with the state when an opportunity arises. As such, it remains distinct from community voices that are unbridled by similar hopes, and therefore find that they are free to express bolder, more outspoken and radical positions. These latter voices are in one sense proving the most impactful when it comes to garnering the state's interest and attention, as evidenced by explicit attempts at the demonisation of the Islamic Human Rights Commission, MEND and Cage by the previous Home Secretary, Sajid Javid.[22]

As I touched upon in Chapter 7, successive Conservative administrations since 2010 have chosen to engage differentially with communal representation from minority faith communities. This discrepancy is most starkly evident when considering the state's approach to the BOD, and Jewish communal groups more generally, in comparison with its approach to the MCB, and Muslim communal groups. The example I explored in this book related to the 'places of worship security funding scheme'- which leaves mosques and Muslim community spaces at a pronounced disadvantage in their access to state-funded security protection, as compared with synagogues and Jewish community spaces. In view of this context, it is worthwhile to consider briefly one of the MCB's most distinguished areas of consistent focus over the past couple of years: compiling and disseminating evidence to highlight endemic levels of Islamophobia within the Conservative Party, and campaigning assiduously for the government to formally recognise this problem and address it by initiating an independent inquiry.[23] The response from the Conservative Party has been an emphatic refusal of officials to acknowledge the gravity and extent of the problem at hand, or indeed a denial of it altogether.[24] Receiving this reaction alongside the government's rejection of the All Party Parliamentary Group on British Muslims' recently proposed definition of Islamophobia, Muslim advocacy groups might be forgiven for sensing discrimination, as they witness meetings between cabinet ministers and the BOD being presented primarily as reassurances of solidarity and concrete pledges of support in addressing anti-Semitism.[25]

It seems appropriate to close this reflection by noting that this state of affairs only serves to corroborate my first point: that despite a streamlining of equalities now being enshrined law, access to equality for Muslims continues to be restricted and conditional in significant areas. Today, the notion of identity politics is overwhelmingly characterised as divisive and damaging in a mainstream political landscape that is at the mercy of populism and polarisation. With Muslims often being at the forefront of those negatively impacted by these trends, it should come as no surprise that a changing and evolving constellation of British Muslim activists, collectives and formal organisations is more committed than ever to a collaborative and defensive identity politics referencing their faith.

Notes

1 Goodwin, Matthew 'What lies behind the spectacular collapse of the British far-right' *New Statesman*, 10 February 2014.

2 Malik, Nesrine, *We Need New Stories: challenging the toxic myths behind our age of discontent* (Weidenfield and Nicolson, 2019), pp.137-8.

3 Johnson, Boris, 'Denmark has got it wrong. Yes, the burka is oppressive and ridiculous – but that's still no reason to ban it' *The Telegraph* 5 August 2018.

4 'Normalising Hatred', Tell MAMA Annual Report 2018, p. 48.

5 Jacob Rees Mogg MP in interview with *ITV News*, 13 June 2019.

6 Johnson, Boris, speech at Conservative leadership election hustings in Nottingham, 6 July 2019, available at: https://www.theguardian.com/politics/video/2019/jul/06/boris-johnson-i-compared-muslim-women-to-letterboxes-to-defend-their-right-to-wear-burqas-video [accessed 10 September 2019].

7 Sian, Katy, 'Spies, surveillance and stakeouts: monitoring Muslim moves in British state schools', *Race Ethnicity and Education* 18:2 (2015) pp.183-201.

8 Breen, Damian and Nasar Meer, 'Securing whiteness?: Critical Race Theory (CRT) and the securitization of Muslims in education' *Identities* 26:5 (2019) pp.595-613.

9 Holmwood, John, 'Fundamental British Values, Religion and Inequalities' *Discover Society*, 4 September 2019, available at: https://discoversociety.org/2019/09/04/fundamental-british-values-religion-and-inequalities/ (accessed 5 September 2019).

10 Butler, Judith, *et al* 'The government is hijacking LGBT+ sex education to bolster its counterterrorism strategy – it must stop now' Letters, *Independent*, 5 September 2019.

11 'Sex Education: the LGBT debate in Schools' *BBC Panorama* 15 July 2019.

12 Khan, Sara, speech delivered at Coin Street Community Centre, London, 19 July 2019. Transcript available at: https://www.gov.uk/government/speeches/lead-commissionners-speech-on-a-positive-vision-for-countering-extremism [accessed 9 September 2019], where she says: '…we must guard our right to debate and speak our minds. Our right to be radical'.

13 The row arose after the publication of a sensationalist piece in the *Sunday Times* portraying the academics as 'extremists' with anti-Semitic sympathies - Gilligan, Andrew and Richard Kerbaj 'Muslim advisers hit by anti-Semitism row' *The Sunday Times*, 5 May 2019.

14 Author's personal conversations and correspondences with Sadek Hamid and Tahir Abbas, May, July and October 2019.

15 CCE, 'Our academic papers on extremism' *CCE Blog*, 7 October 2019, available at: https://extremismcommission.blog.gov.uk/2019/10/07/our-academic-papers-on-extremism/ (accessed 7 October 2019).

16 For one example, see Hasan, Usama *et al.*, 'Mainstreaming Islamism: Islamist institutions and civil society organisations' (September 2019), available at: https://assets.publishing.service.gov.uk/government/uploads/system/uploads/attachment_data/file/836965/mainstreaming-islamism-islamist-insitutions-and-civil-society-organisations.pdf (accessed 7 October 2019). I will refrain from commenting on the strength of the argument presented in this paper – suffice to point out that it is essentially a weakly framed compilation of narratives, and reads much more as a dossier of 'evidence' rather than a coherent or robust piece of academic research.

17 Cobain, Ian, ''Mind control': The secret UK government blueprints shaping post-terror planning' *Middle East Eye*, 22 May 2019, available at: https://www.middleeasteye.net/news/mind-control-secret-british-government-blueprints-shaping-post-terror-planning (accessed 10 September 2019).

18 Birt, Yahya, 'Astroturfing and the rise of the secular security state in Britain' Medium, 17 August 2019, available at: https://medium.com/@yahyabirt/astroturfing-and-the-rise-of-the-secular-security-state-in-britain-cd21c5005d43 (accessed 28 August 2019).

19 Atkinson, Nathan, 'Bradford Literature Festival has 15 withdrawals over fund source' *Telegraph and Argus*, 26 June 2019.

20 Author's interview with Hassan Joudi, Deputy Secretary General of the MCB, 2 August 2019.

21 Author's interview with Samayya Afzal, Community Engagement Manager at the MCB, 26 July 2019.

22 Javid, Sajid, speech delivered at Coin Street Community Centre, London, 19 July 2019. Transcript available at: https://www.gov.uk/government/speeches/confronting-extremism-together [accessed 9 September 2019].

23 See letter from Harun Khan to Brandon Lewis, Chairman of the Conservative Party, 30 May 2018. Available at: https://mcb.org.uk/wp-content/uploads/2018/06/BrandonLewis_ConservativeChair-Islamophobia_30May2018.docx.pdf (accessed 10 September 2019).

24 Shah, Naz,'Dear Sajid Javid, Denouncing Accusations Of Islamophobia In The Tory Party Doesn't Mean It Doesn't Exist' *Huffington Post*, 3 June 2018, available at: https://www.huffingtonpost.co.uk/entry/dear-sajid-javid-denouncing-islamophobia-in-the-tory-party-doesnt-make-it-untrue_uk_5b1428d1e4b0d5e89e209832 (accessed 10 September 2019). This article cites then Home Secretary, Sajid Javid, using his position to justify his claim of an absence of an Islamophobia problem in the Conservative Party.

25 Two examples of statements addressing the BOD and reaffirming a commitment to tackling anti-Semitism include this tweet from Robert Jenrick MP, Secretary of State for Housing, Communities and Local Government: https://twitter.com/mhclg/status/1173114376473255936?s=20 and this, from Priti Patel MP, Home Secretary: https://twitter.com/patel4witham/status/1166404236659367936?s=20 (both accessed 7 October 2019). There have been no comparable statements made to the MCB or any Muslim communal organisation.

List of Illustrations

Acknowledgements

It is a privilege to record my thanks here to all the people who have helped and assisted me in the process of writing this book. My interest in Muslim identity politics developed during my time at the UCL School of Public Policy, where Cecile Laborde was influential in offering guidance in developing the initial stages of my research – in particular the sections on political theory. Much of the material on which this book is based has been drawn from my PhD thesis, and I thank Humayun Ansari for his invaluable role as a mentor and supervisor during the PhD and beyond. His advice, comments, insights, questions and support throughout have been immensely beneficial as well as motivational. I also thank Dan Stone and Francis Robinson for the helpful feedback they gave on my early writing.

I am indebted to the large number of individuals from British Muslim communities and organisations, as well as some from the Jewish communities with whom I held formal interviews and informal conversations, and who provided me with vital access to sources. Their generosity with both time, information and occasionally hospitality was deeply touching and much appreciated. Many have requested to remain anonymous, so I will respect their wishes by simply acknowledging them collectively, heartfelt thanks to you all! During the research period, Jasmine Gani was a constant sounding board and a haven of friendship and wisdom, as she continues to be today.

I completed the book during my time at the Alwaleed Centre in Edinburgh and would like to thank all my colleagues there for making it such a pleasurable and supportive environment. In particular, thanks to Hugh Goddard for encouraging me to pursue separate research on Muslims in Scotland, the process of which has broadened my perspective and enriched the analysis in this book. Thanks to Giulia Liberatore for her generous willingness to provide valuable comments on parts of the manuscript, and to David Warren for his perceptive and extremely helpful observations as I prepared to go to print. The students on my Muslims in Britain course at the University of Edinburgh between 2015–2018 have been a stimulating source of insight and debate.

I am grateful to Lubaaba Al-Azami, Samia Bano, Ron Geaves, Sadek Hamid and Fatima Rajina for their helpful comments and words of encouragement at various stages, and also to my anonymous reviewers for their thoughtful and meticulous feedback.

An earlier version of Chapter 5 was previously published as 'From Crisis to Opportunity: 9/11 and the progress of young British Muslim political engagement' in Timothy Peace's (ed.), *Muslim Political Participation in Britain* (Routledge, 2015), pp. 174–192, so thanks to the publishers for permission to reproduce some of the material here.

Sophie Rudland, Lisa Goodrum and Angelique Neumann at I.B.Tauris have been wonderful to work with. Thanks also to Nick James for his attention to detail in editing and indexing.

Special thanks are reserved for my family, without whom I am nothing. My parents – Fatma and Farid – provided that compelling parental combination of encouragement and expectation that was crucial to the completion of this project. My mother in particular has been my role model in more ways than she can imagine. Basma, Abdurrahman, Abdulkhaliq and Jamal – thank you! Hany has been a source of unstinting support and encouragement and Yusuf and Kareem have given me endless joy and hope.

Abbreviations

AYMs	Asian Youth Movements
BCM	Bradford Council of Mosques
BMF	British Muslim Forum
BMI	British Muslim Initiative
BMPA	Bradford Muslim Parents' Association
BMSD	British Muslims for Secular Democracy
BNP	British National Party
BOD	Board of Deputies of British Jews
CCE	Commission for Countering Extremism
CEF	Community Engagement Forum
CENTRI	Counter-Extremism Consultancy, Training, Research and Interventions
CRC	Community Relations Council
CRE	Commission for Racial Equality
CST	Community Security Trust
DCLG	Department for Communities and Local Government
DI	Dawatul Islam
EDL	English Defence League
EHRC	Equality and Human Rights Commission
EIWG	Engaging with the Islamic World Group
FBV	Fundamental British Values
FCO	Foreign and Commonwealth Office
FOSIS	Federation of Students' Islamic Societies
HT	Hizb-ut-Tahrir

ICIT	Institute of Contemporary Islamic Thought
IFE	Islamic Forum Europe
IJV	Independent Jewish Voices
IPB	Islamic Party of Britain
ISA	Information Sharing Agreement
ISB	Islamic Society of Britain
JFS	Jews' Free School
JI	Jamaat-e-Islami
JIMAS	Jam'iyat Ihyaa Minhaj Ahlus Sunnah wal jama'a
JLC	Jewish Leadership Council
LMI	Liverpool Muslim Institute
MAB	Muslim Association of Britain
MB	Muslim Brotherhood
MCB	Muslim Council of Britain
MEND	Muslim Engagement and Development
MET	Muslim Educational Trust
MINAB	Mosques and Imams Advisory Board
MP	Muslim Parliament
MSS	Muslim Students' Society
NICMU	National Interim Council for Muslim Unity
NMWAG	National Muslim Women's Advisory Group
OASIS	Organisation of Ahlus Sunnah Islamic Societies
PBM	Progressive British Muslims
PET	Preventing Extremism Together
PVE	Preventing Violent Extremism
RMW	Radical Middle Way
SMC	Sufi Muslim Council
StWC	Stop the War Coalition
Tell MAMA	(Tell) Measuring Anti-Muslim Attacks
TJ	Tablighi Jamaat
UKACIA	United Kingdom Action Committee on Islamic Affairs
UKIM	United Kingdom Islamic Mission
UKIP	United Kingdom Independence Party

UMO	Union of Muslim Organisations
YMAG	Young Muslim Advisory Group
YMO	Young Muslim Organisation
YMUK	Young Muslims United Kingdom

Glossary of Non-English Terms

(ARABIC, UNLESS OTHERWISE INDICATED)

Al salaf al salih	the pious predecessors
Al wala' wal bara'	loyalty (to Islam/Muslims) and disassociation (from disbelief/disbelievers)
Ashkenazi	(Hebrew) Jews who trace their origins to the indigenous Israelite tribes of the Middle East, generally used to describe present-day descendants of Rhineland Jews
Baitul mal	treasury
Bani Ibrahim	children of Abraham
Banlieues	(French) suburbs, with connotations of low-income populations and social housing
Biradari	(Urdu) clan-like network, 'brotherhood'
Da'wa	call or 'invitation' to Islam
Dar ul Islam	realm of Islam
Dar ul kufr	realm of disbelief
Darul Uloom	house of sciences (in the UK used for Islamic seminaries in the *Deobandi* tradition)
Du'at	'callers' to Islam/proselytisers (singular: *da'iya*)
Eid	bi-annual Muslim festival
Ghira	jealous guarding or protection of honour
Hadarim	(Hebrew) traditional Jewish religious schools (singular: *heder*)

Haham	(Hebrew) Rabbi of *Sephardi* congregations
Halal	permitted under Islam, e.g., *halal* meat
Hijra	migration. Capitalised form, *Hijra*, generally refers to the migration of the Prophet Muhammad from Mecca to Medina
Illa rasulallah	(anyone/thing) except the messenger of God
Isa'ah	insult, offence
'ird	honour, dignity
Janaza	Muslim prayer for the deceased
Jihad	struggle, greater *jihad* being the individual's everyday struggle with her desires, lesser *jihad* is the armed struggle
Jihadi	broadly descriptive of support for violence/armed fighting in the name of Islam
Khilafa, khulafaa	succession, successors (of the Prophet Muhammad). Singular: *khalifa*. Used in reference to an 'Islamic state', and its ruler/s
Kuffar	disbelievers
Kunya	Arab-style paedonymic
Madhab	school of thought in Islamic jurisprudence
Madrassa	school. Generally used in the UK to refer to those providing supplementary Islamic education
Milad ul nabi	birthday of the Prophet Muhammad
Mujahideen	those engaged in *jihad*
Nasheed	songs, used to refer to Muslim religious/devotional singing
Sabb an nabi	insulting the Prophet
Sephardi	(Hebrew) descendants of Jewish settlers originally from the Near East, who settled in the Iberian Peninsula
Shahada	Islamic declaration of faith
Shalwar Kameez	(Urdu) traditional South Asian dress consisting of a tunic over loose-fitting trousers
Shari'a	the path to water (old Arabic), the (legal) path of Islam

Shaykh ul Islam	title denoting religious leadership of a Muslim community
Shechita	(Hebrew) method of ritual slaughter according to Judaism
Shi'a	group/party (of Ali, the fourth *khalifa*), the minority denomination within Islam. Singular: *shi'i*
Sunnah	the recorded tradition of the Prophet Muhammad and, along with the Qur'an, a primary source of Islamic teaching
Sunni	of the *sunnah*, the majority denomination within Islam
Tajdif	blasphemy
Tawheed	the oneness/unity of God
Ummah	nation – used to refer to the worldwide Muslim community

Chronology of British Muslim Identity Politics: Incorporating relevant domestic and international historical events

Eighteenth, nineteenth and early twentieth centuries various waves of Muslim (mainly male) immigrants arrive in the UK to work as labourers, forming communities in UK port towns including Cardiff, Liverpool, London and South Shields.

1887 Liverpool Muslim Institute (LMI) established by Abdullah Quilliam.

1889 Quilliam's LMI sets up a prayer hall at Brougham Terrace in Liverpool; Woking Mosque (later the Shah Jahan Mosque), is constructed, the first purpose-built mosque in Britain.

1910 London Mosque Fund opens with the aim of obtaining donations towards the establishment of a mosque in London.

1913 Woking Muslim Mission established by Khwaja Kamaluddin, reviving the Woking (now Shah Jahan) Mosque, which had fallen into a period of disuse after the death of its founder Gottleib Wilhelm Leitner in 1899.

1914 British Muslim Society founded by Lord Headley.

1940 East London Mosque opens on its first premises on Commercial Street.

1944 King George VI donates 2.3 acres of land in Regents Park for use as the London Central Mosque. This is in return for a similar donation of land in Cairo for use as an Anglican cathedral.

1962 UKIM formed.

Circa. **1962** MSS formed.

1963 FOSIS established.

1964 The Labour Party comes to power under Harold Wilson, beginning an 11-year stretch of Labour governments, ending in 1979 (interrupted by Edward Heath's Conservative administration between 1970 and 1974).

1965 First Race Relations Act introduced, along with the Community Relations Commission, the precursor to the CRE.

1966 MET established.

1968 YMO formed as the youth wing of UKIM.

1970 UMO formed; Muslim Welfare House established in London.

1971 *Impact International*, Muslim news and current affairs magazine launched.

1973 Islamic Foundation established in Leicester.

1975 The East London Mosque opens in its current location at Whitechapel Road.

1976 Race Relations Act; CRE established.

1977 The London Central Mosque and Islamic Cultural Centre at Regents Park is opened.

1978 Dawatul Islam formed.

1979 Conservative government of Margaret Thatcher is elected.

1980s HT arrives in Britain; IFE formed.

xxx   *Muslim Identity Politics*

1984 Honeyford Affair; YMUK established as UKIM's youth wing; JIMAS formed.

Late 1980s YMUK breaks away from UKIM.

1987 First Palestinian Intifada.

1988 *The Satanic Verses* published by Viking Press; UKACIA formed.

1989 *The Muslim News* first published.

1990 Fatwa issued by Ayatollah Khomeini calling for the death of Salman Rushdie; ISB established; the Muslim Institute established; First Gulf War commences with the invasion of Kuwait by Iraq and the allied intervention which ensued.

1992 John Major is elected leader of the Conservative Party after Margaret Thatcher's resignation, and thus replaces her as prime minister; Muslim Parliament of Great Britain launched; Bosnian War breaks out and continues through to 1995.

1994 NICMU initiative commences; YMUK merges with ISB to become its official youth wing.

1996 Al Muhajiroun formed by breakaway members of HT.

1997 MCB established; MAB formed; Labour Party comes to power under Tony Blair; Runnymede Trust report on Islamophobia is published.

1998 First two Muslim schools granted voluntary aided status (and state funding) by the Education Secretary.

1999 Macpherson Report is published.

2000 Terrorism Act 2000; Second Palestinian Intifada; Race Relations Amendment Act 2000.

2001 9/11 attacks; revised anti-terror legislation; an optional religion question included in the national census for the first time; British forces sent to Afghanistan as part of the US-led coalition; Stop the War Coalition formed to oppose Britain's involvement in the 'War on Terror', MAB is a key partner in the coalition.

2003 Allied invasion of Iraq (Second Gulf War), as part of the War on Terror.

2004 Respect Party formed, it fields a number of high-profile Muslim candidates in the European Parliament and local council elections that summer.

2005 7/7 attacks; Preventing Violent Extremism working groups convened, producing extensive recommendations to the government; BMF and SMC launched; Respect Party leader George Galloway wins Bethnal Green and Bow seat (a constituency with a large Muslim population) in the General Election, on an anti-war platform, and with endorsement and support of many Muslim groups and figures.

2006 Terrorism Act 2006 passed; Racial and Religious Hatred Act passed; Prevent strategy initiated; Danish Cartoon Crisis (the cartoons were actually first published in *Jyllands Posten* in September 2005, but international awareness picked up by the end of the year, reaching its peak by Jan/Feb 2006).

2007 MINAB launched; NMWAG launched; Equality and Human Rights Commission (EHRC) comes into being, replacing the CRE and other statutory bodies to form a single equalities body dealing with discrimination on grounds of age, disability, gender, race, religion and sexual orientation.

2008 Blasphemy laws abolished; YMAG launched; Quilliam Foundation formed; start of protracted public stand-off between MCB and government ostensibly over Daud Abdullah's position regarding Gaza.

2009 Resumption of formal MCB-government relations, but this time as part of open engagement with much wider spectrum of Muslim groups, which included those emerging post-2005; EDL formed.

2010 Labour defeated in the General Election, and a Conservative-Liberal Democrat coalition forms government with David Cameron as Prime Minister, review of the Prevent strategy commences; Conservative Party demonstrates its antipathy towards 'Islamism' by instructing its politicians to boycott the Islam Channel's annual Global Peace and Unity event; Home Secretary Theresa May uses 'exclusion powers' for the first time, to refuse Indian TV preacher Dr Zakir Naik entry into the UK after a right-wing campaign, on grounds of his 'unacceptable behaviour'; meanwhile, Geert Wilders, a far-right Dutch politician known for his inflammatory anti-Muslim views visits UK after successfully overturning a ban imposed during the previous year.

2011 Review of Prevent strategy published; Sayeeda Warsi's speech on Islamophobia.

2012 MCB constitutional reforms passed, including a female quota in its National Council and a directly elected Secretary General; internet film, *Innocence of Muslims* reignites debates on free speech and Islam, and provokes heated protest across Muslim world; Muslim Leadership Panel initiated; Tell MAMA UK launched.

2013 Murder in Woolwich of an off-duty member of the armed forces, Fusilier Lee Rigby, by two Muslim men claiming to act in retaliation for 'anti-Muslim' British foreign policy. This was followed by a spate of 'revenge' arson attacks and vandalism on mosques and Muslim schools, apparently carried out by the EDL or their sympathisers, escalating to the murder in Birmingham of pensioner Mohammed Saleem by Ukrainian far-right terrorist and PhD student, Pavlo Lapshyn. Lapshyn had also planted explosives near various mosques around the Midlands.

2014 Rise of 'Islamic State'; a number of high-profile migrations of British Muslims to Syria, including Welsh students Reyaad Khan, Nasser and Aseel Muthanna, as well as Scottish schoolgirl Aqsa Mahmood and Zahra and Salma Halane from Manchester; Britain First stage a number of aggressive 'mosque invasions' in different areas of the UK as part of a self-styled 'Christian crusade'; 'Trojan Horse' affair in Birmingham – the Department for Education accuses the (largely Muslim) governing bodies in a raft of Birmingham schools of subversively promoting an agenda of 'Islamisation'.

2015 Murder of pensioner Muhsin Ahmed in Rotherham, assaulted as he walked to mosque for morning prayers; RAF drone assassination of Reyaad Khan in Raqqa, Syria – the first HMG extrajudicial killing of a British citizen abroad; Prevent becomes a statutory duty in the public sector as part of the Counter Extremism Act 2015; announcement that anti-Muslim hate crime will be recorded under its own category in England and Wales.

2016 Sectarian murder of shopkeeper Asad Shah in Glasgow by Tanveer Ahmed from Bradford, who claimed he was acting in defence of Islam and the Prophet Muhammad; Malia Bouattia becomes the first Muslim (and female of an ethnic minority background) to be elected to the position of president of the National Union of Students (NUS). She stood on a 'Preventing Prevent' platform and has been highly critical of government counter-extremism policy; Sadiq Khan wins the London mayoral election for the Labour Party, after an acrimonious campaign run by his rival from the Conservatives, Zac Goldsmith; review of Shari'a in the UK announced, as part of the government's counter-extremism strategy; murder in Birstall of MP Jo Cox by far-right terrorist Thomas Mair; National Action becomes the first extreme right wing group to be proscribed under counter-terrorism legislation; EU membership referendum takes place with a majority voting in favour of Brexit; publication of the 'Casey Review' into 'opportunity and integration'.

2017 Independent review of hate crime legislation in Scotland initiated by the Scottish Government; a series of four terror attacks in London and Manchester carried out by individuals who were (in some cases) known to the intelligence services leads to political debate about the efficacy of counter-extremism, including a commitment in the Conservative Party manifesto to establish a Commission for Counter-Extremism. A further attack on Muslim worshippers emerging from a mosque in North London by an alleged far-right terrorist prompted high-level government responses; proscription of National Action extended to related neo-Nazi groups, Scottish Dawn and NS131.

CHAPTER 1

Introduction

The Muslim presence in the UK can be traced back many centuries, with the earliest record of Muslim influence appearing to be the inscription of the *shahada*, the Muslim declaration of faith, on a coin issued by the eighth-century Anglo-Saxon king, Offa of Mercia.[1] There are extensive records of interactions between the British Isles and Muslims, through politics and warfare, as well as through culture and trade.[2] In modern times, various waves of immigration from Muslim countries have resulted in the settlement and development of communities in various, mostly urban, areas of the UK. To a large extent, immigrants from the Muslim world during modern times arrived for economic reasons.[3] The nineteenth and early twentieth-century settlement of Somali and Yemeni sailors in Wales and South Shields respectively, and the later arrival of South Asian immigrants in the postwar period and beyond, were all cases of economic migration. Young men usually travelled first to seek employment, only later to be joined by their families, or (notably in the earlier periods) to marry locally and settle with their families. The latest census (2011) indicated that Muslims in Britain exceed 2.8 million in number, forming over 5 per cent of the UK's total population. Islam is the largest minority religion in Britain, and the fastest-growing one, with almost 50 per cent of Muslims being UK-born. The Muslim population is hugely ethnically diverse, and forms approximately one-third of the Black and Minority Ethnic (BME) population of

Britain. It is also a population that is significantly over-represented in deprivation indicators.[4]

The focus of this book will be the development of a formal Muslim identity politics during the latter half of the twentieth century, through to present times – a topic that has not received in-depth scholarly attention from an historical perspective. Historic surveys have generally had a broader remit than political engagement, including it amongst cultural dynamics and developments, institution building, social aspects such as education and family life, as well as covering much longer time-spans.[5] Some of these works have encompassed studies of the very earliest examples of Muslim identity politics in Britain, including the political activity of individuals such as Syed Ameer Ali,[6] Khwaja Kamaluddin[7] and William Abdullah Quilliam,[8] all of whom engaged with the state on behalf of Muslim 'community interests'.

There have been numerous studies of contemporary British Muslim political engagement as part of European surveys,[9] or as single chapters within wider collections.[10] There have also been studies that have looked at political engagement and community organisation on a regional scale, such as Philip Lewis' *Islamic Britain*, which specifically focuses on the Muslim communities of Bradford during the 1990s,[11] studies of identity and political awareness among young Muslims,[12] and studies that centre around single events, and their impacts and reverberations.[13]

The work of Tariq Modood has been seminal in discussing structural disadvantages that Muslims have faced in the political landscape, as well as understanding the experience of anti-Muslim racism and discrimination, and how British Muslims have responded with a politics of identity.[14] However, his approach has been from within the disciplines of political philosophy and sociology, thus highlighting the opportunity and need for an historical analysis of the subject. With such an analysis, this book brings to the fore the central role played by identity politics in British Muslim activism and political engagement – both in the past and as it has shifted over time – demonstrating its continuing relevance.

While there have been innumerable instances of political engagement and community organisation amongst Muslims in Britain during preceding periods, these were largely concerned with setting up basic community institutions such as mosques, and other community support services for recently arrived immigrants. My focus in this book will be on the phase that was distinguished by its concern with coordination and representation on a national level. There were emergent elements of this concern from the early 1960s, however it was the Rushdie Affair during the late 1980s that really set into motion a drive for a formally instituted and widely recognised national body for the communal leadership and representation of Britain's Muslim communities.

I begin by tracing the journey of British Muslim identity politics on numerous and sometimes rather disparate fronts, from the 1960s through to the 1980s, a period of over two decades that was marked by a preoccupation with identity preservation among immigrant communities that were coming to terms with their now-permanent settlement in the UK. I then survey the period from the later 1980s to 1997, a highlight of which was the Rushdie Affair of 1988/9, and the subsequent formalisation of Muslim identity politics. Following this, I proceed to examine Muslim identity politics from 1997 (a significant date marking the launch of the Muslim Council of Britain (MCB) and the publication of the Runnymede Trust's report on Islamophobia) through the New Labour period up until the present. With these two decades having been a period of remarkable flux on so many levels, I narrow my focus to the theme of freedom of expression.

This theme is of distinct interest for a number of reasons. Firstly, freedom of expression was a central theme in the events of the late 1980s (namely the Rushdie Affair), which propelled British Muslim communities to forge a path towards formal identity politics on a coordinated, national scale. Secondly, it is a theme that brings out very interesting points of historical, cultural and geopolitical contrast and comparison between the immigrant Muslim communities to Great Britain, and the public political culture of Great Britain itself. On a global level, there has been a continuing trend of Muslims having claimed that deep provocation and gratuitous offence had been caused by instances where aspects of their faith had been mocked and ridiculed by others. Such moments have invariably drawn heated and heartfelt protest from among Muslims worldwide

(British Muslims among them), as well as regularly prompting calls for censorship, and occasionally violent and even fatal incidents. Many on the right wing of politics have argued condescendingly that the Muslim reaction to such moments has consistently been an expression of exceptionally irrational and unfathomable, 'Muslim rage'.[15] Examples such as the extensive and often hysterical global reaction in 2006 to the Muhammad cartoons published by the Danish newspaper *Jyllands Posten*[16] through to the violent protests that took place against the 2012 amateur internet video 'The Innocence of Muslims', and the fatal terrorist shootings of 2015 at the offices of satirical magazine Charlie Hebdo in Paris have all been cited in this context.[17]

However, although there has been some consistency in the profound offence taken by Muslims and their intolerance towards mockery or ridicule of their faith, this trend cannot be understood *simply* by making reference to their faith, without taking into account a host of other explanatory factors, such as the legacy of colonialism in Muslim-majority countries, the role of international geopolitics and the local influences of culture, economics and social structures. Additionally, it must be acknowledged that while this reaction of anger towards religious offence, and calls for censorship, has continued to manifest itself at various moments over recent decades, it nonetheless is an approach that is experiencing significant adjustment and revision among many Muslims. This is indicative of wider change and development that is taking place within Muslim communities – *especially* in Western countries – and Britain is an apt example of this.

Finally, the theme of freedom of expression is one that has attracted a great deal of resurgent interest in the post-9/11 age of terrorism and securitisation. New-wave counter-terrorism laws continue to delve ever deeper into the area of expression, to the extent that they have been charged by their opponents with creating 'thought crimes'.[18] At the same time, 'soft' initiatives, run or funded by the government to combat radicalisation and violent extremism by 'winning over hearts and minds', have been associated with the targeted surveillance, harassment and excessive monitoring of Muslims, and as such have been accused of having a chilling effect on free expression within these communities.

We can understand contemporary British Muslim identity politics to have grown and developed around the broad notion of an 'equality gap'.[19] Taking my cue from the theoretical debates on 'equality as recognition', I define this gap as the idea (both real and perceived) that Muslims have not had recourse to the same level of equality under the law as other, non-Muslim, citizens. This has often been expressed with reference to discrepancies in specific anti-discrimination provisions, but also extended wider than this to include unequal access to blasphemy legislation.[20] Using free speech-related examples, I examine contemporary British Muslim identity politics, assessing at various junctures the successes and failures of the path that organised Muslim identity politics has followed, and concluding by giving recommendations for the future and offering a vision for how the Equality Gap can be effectively narrowed, if not closed.

This book draws upon a range of current and recently released evidence and source material, shedding unique light on the development of this identity politics using the lens of freedom of expression issues, adding a distinctive perspective and an in-depth analytical narrative to the growing body of academic literature that deals with British Muslim experience. It is a study based upon historical analysis, using a range of primary and secondary sources. These include a number of extended interviews and informal conversations that I have conducted with key figures within Muslim community organisations, as well as other relevant activists. Additionally, I have had access to documentary material from the various organisations and structures within British Muslim communities as well as the relevant material from government departments and structures – these include promotional documents, as well as internal membership communications, meeting minutes and correspondence. Newspapers, magazines and other forms of media including television and radio – both mainstream and community-based – have all also provided useful primary and secondary sources for events and perspectives.

In the course of this book, I look at some of the arguments about the validity of politics based around religious identity, as well as the practical meaning that Muslim identity politics has held for those engaged with it – including their key concerns and aspirations. However, at this introductory stage, I will briefly address some of the main charges that have been made against the impacts of identity politics on communities, society and the general political climate – charges that have been put forward by academics but also taken up in the world of policy-making, the media and general public discourse.

As a form of political engagement and lobbying, identity politics is nothing new, and it is certainly something that citizens of a liberal democracy have every right to engage in. However, it has been the subject of much contention over recent years, particularly in respect of Muslim communities and the debate on multiculturalism. Detractors argue that New Labour excessively fostered identity politics, and, in doing so, cultivated an unhealthy, divisive political landscape whereby minority groups competed with one another for the largest portion of official attention, funding and privileges. According to Amartya Sen, this climate should more accurately be described as 'plural monoculturalism',[21] since actual meaningful interactions between different communities are few. Rather, identity politics promotes the side-by-side existence of a diversity of discrete communities, to the extent that they 'might pass one another like ships in the night'.[22]

An additional charge that has been made against identity politics is that, rather than providing an authentic space for minority or disadvantaged groups to be heard in the public sphere, the types of community groups and forums that governments are likely to engage with have had a tendency to be hijacked by the more privileged, such as those individuals resembling the archetypal 'community leader'.[23] In such a scenario, there is a danger that minority voices within minority communities are overlooked and organisations become preoccupied with furthering the political agendas or pet projects of those at their helm.[24]

Moreover, the continued exercise of identity politics is blamed for encouraging governments to address communities, and communities to view themselves, in a compartmentalised fashion, through the lens of their identity, as opposed to simply as citizens. So rather than appreciating the diversity of perspectives and aspirations within communities, identity politics can generate and entrench reification.

This, in turn, promotes an inaccurate and unfair picture of the lived realities of citizens, as well as acting as a general barrier to integration and social cohesion.[25] There is some truth in this argument – no representative body can ever hope to accurately speak for its community. Indeed, the proportion of individuals who will identify with, let alone engage with, such organisations is a minority within the communities concerned.[26] However, in the case of British Muslims as with other minority groups, the growth and development of identity politics cannot be attributed to a desire to self-segregate, as much as to a deeply felt need to make their voices heard, against a background culture that had not taken into account cultural and religious differences, indeed, one that has been ingrained with the privileging of some cultural and identity markers over others, and thus not delivered equal treatment to these communities.

Finally, British Muslim identity politics and community representation developed in recent times in conscious emulation of previous paths that had been trodden by identity politics in the arena of both race relations, and the experience of the Board of Deputies of British Jews (the BOD). By this token, regardless of the flaws or merits of identity politics, in the interests of even-handedness, it is hardly fair to deny such an opportunity to Muslims. For better or for worse, it is indisputable that identity politics has been an absolutely crucial issue for British Muslims, in particular over recent decades. This has been so whether as a platform from which community concerns and demands for equal treatment have been articulated, as a site for intra-community interactions and the evolution of identity and political engagement through debate and disagreement, or, indeed, whether it has been as a government-driven strategy through which to more coherently and effectively engage in dialogue with Muslim communities. On each of these levels, Muslim identity politics has been a topic worthy of close examination and critical analysis.

I look chronologically at developments, introducing and discussing the myriad of groups that have played a role in British Muslim political engagement and representation, as they appear and feature. Britain's Muslim communities are exceptionally diverse in terms of culture and ethnicity, as well as religious practice and political perspectives. This diversity has been reflected in the countless organisations and platforms that, together, have made up Muslim identity politics in recent times. Each has engaged with the issues of the day in its own way, and approaches have ranged from political isolationism to active lobbying of the state, to involvement in party politics and standing for political office. They have included participation in state-sponsored schemes, the development of cross-community civic partnerships, but also a preoccupation with international affairs and a subsequent disengagement from an 'un-Islamic' British civic life. All of these facets of Muslim identity politics will be surveyed, and aspects of their interplay with each other examined. I devote some specific focus to the MCB since, as I demonstrate, it has proven to be more consistent, more long-lived and more representative than other Muslim advocacy or representative groups. Moreover, it enjoyed a short period of exceptional primacy in the field of Muslim representation from the late 1990s until 2005.

With this historical and theoretical background in mind, I proceed to chart how and why the preservation of religious identity became a central preoccupation for budding Muslim community organisations in the UK from the 1960s onwards. I then discuss how an idea of recognition as parity has developed in practical terms in the context of British race relations and integration policy – in the specific case of British Muslims and the arguments presented by them for parity of recognition. I look at how the Muslim identity politics that grew out of this call for parity of treatment and recognition has developed over the past few decades, which key moments have influenced and shaped it, its challenges, successes and failures, and finally its prospects for the future.

METHODOLOGY AND CHAPTER OUTLINE

This book is first and foremost a work of historical analysis, relying on a wide range of primary and secondary source material as the basis of its research. Working within a recent time-frame, I found that there was great benefit in utilising oral history as an important source of information, analysis and perspective. To this end, I conducted interviews with a number of individuals, some coming from the various community organisations that feature in my research, while others were selected on the basis of long-standing involvement in Muslim community representative and advocacy initiatives. I also spoke with people who have been part of government-sponsored Muslim community initiatives, as well as individuals with a background in the Muslim media sector. Additionally, I spoke with some individuals from British Jewish community groups, as part of my comparative research into communal organising among British Jews in Chapter 4.

The style and format of my interviews varied – from face-to-face interviews to extended telephone conversations, email conversations and more informal discussions. The type of approach I used depended on a number of factors, including the availability and preference of the interviewee, the level of involvement that the individual had in events that I was covering, and therefore the amount and nature of subject matter that I wished to discuss with them in an interview. I prepared for interviews beforehand by considering the topics that I wished to cover and preparing some central questions. However, I maintained a flexible approach, allowing space for my interviewees to speak openly and at length. Most of my interviewees were specifically selected on the basis of my background research and knowledge. Nonetheless, I occasionally used a 'snowball' sampling method, whereby interviewees recommended to me further people who I should approach for interview. When it was used, I found this method to be appropriate as it allowed me to hear alternative perspectives on issues or events, and to corroborate or verify information that I had obtained from other sources.

I benefited significantly from my own personal position with respect to the British Muslim community landscape. Being a British Muslim myself, and one who has experienced close interaction and engagement over a significant period of time with a number of the groups and individuals that I study, I had the important advantage of 'trusted insider' status, in the sense that I possess extensive familiarity with the context and development of British Muslim community organisations. I was also previously acquainted with some of my interviewees. In some cases, I did find this background to be of additional advantage, since a certain level of trust was already in place, interviewees did not find it difficult to 'open up'. However, once or twice I felt that my background may have contributed towards an atmosphere of guardedness, whereby interviewees were perhaps suspicious of my motives in conducting what may have been perceived as overly critical research about certain Muslim groups and organisations. It was evident to me that the harsh public spotlight under which so many Muslim organisations have been functioning in recent years has created an air of caution sometimes so overwhelming that it is extended even towards those who are familiar. Reflexivity was important to me in the course of my fieldwork, as my familiarity with the contexts and subjects that I was studying meant that I had to continually reassess my position in the course of my interviews. I therefore made a conscious effort to remain unbiased and objective in my approach to interviews, maintaining a level of detachment and allowing space for my interviewees' perspectives to authentically come through.

I should make mention of the specific parameters within which this study is located. In looking at the development of British Muslim identity politics, a central contribution of my book will be an articulation of what I term the Equality Gap, and its role in Muslim claims-making. To be clear, this gap has been defined specifically with reference to political engagement and political claims-making. That is to say that it refers to a gap in equality as perceived and articulated by Muslim communities and representatives, in terms of their public and political engagement. Needless to say, there are cases to be made for the existence of other equality gaps between Muslims in Britain and other sections of society, for example, in social and economic terms. It can also be argued that equality gaps exist *within* some of Britain's Muslim communities, most obviously perhaps relating to the considerable inequalities that are faced by some Muslim women. However, while each of these undoubtedly have the potential to generate highly viable and extremely interesting lines of research, this book will not delve into them so that focus can be maintained and space constraints observed.

Chapter 2 sets the historical and theoretical scene by reviewing a number of themes, including free speech, equality and identity politics, considering their varying definitions and meanings both in

Muslim religious and political history and in the tradition of western political thought. A consideration of the different expectations and approaches to these themes that different historical experiences have helped to engender in both 'Muslim' and 'western' traditions will be coupled with a look at the nature of contemporary legal and political debates on the limits and safeguards on freedom of expression and other civil liberties.

Chapter 3 charts a narrative of modern British Muslim political history by focusing on a selection of moments when significant strides in political interaction and engagement took place. Particular cases will include some political and social initiatives by Muslim convert communities and immigrants during the late nineteenth and first half of the twentieth century. I also look at the growth of national and regional organisation *as Muslims* among postwar immigrant Muslims, a development which featured with increasing prominence the notion of preserving and promoting religious identity, pointing out how many of these organisations later provided support as well as personnel for the Muslim representative bodies that were later formed.

This leads me to Chapter 4, which discusses the formalisation of Muslim identity politics during the final two decades of the twentieth century, through the institutionalisation of national communal advocacy and representative organisations. This phase is distinguished from the preceding one by the prominence of efforts that were made to coordinate Muslim communities on a national level with the ultimate purpose of actively *representing* them and securing their rights by vocalising their needs whether politically or in other aspects of the public sphere. Catalysed by what became known as the Rushdie Affair, it was marked by an unprecedented combination of each of the following factors: intra-community, national- and regional- level communal coordination among Britain's Muslims; high-profile and consistent media coverage and public interest in British Muslim affairs; serious conversation and negotiation with the state; as well as significant international attention and intervention. I argue that the central notion upon which Muslim identity politics was to develop can be described collectively as an Equality Gap – referring to the idea that Muslims in Britain were not treated equally to their fellow non-Muslim citizens. The issues which were taken up by Muslim advocacy groups (most notably at this stage, the MCB) were not limited to this gap, however, the gap encapsulates their strongest source of legitimacy and constituted a reference point which was consistently used to justify their continued work.

Chapters 5 and 6 each focus on specific time periods when significant change of thought, direction and method in the practice of Muslim communal organisation took place. In looking at each of these phases, I demonstrate the overall level of progress that has taken place in the field of Muslim identity politics since 2001, taking note of and analysing areas of regression, showing how the experience of each of these two turning points was different, and drawing out aspects of continuity.

Chapter 5 examines the period between September 2001 and July 2005, a time characterised by a sharp increase in the level and intensity of community organisation, much of which came about as a direct response to the rapid alterations which were taking place in the global, and national arenas in reaction to the terrorist attacks of 11 September 2001 and the subsequent fallout. The introduction of heightened security measures including controversial anti-terror legislation in addition to the discourse and thinking behind the 'war on terror' provoked concerns in many quarters about silencing, restricting and/or channelling of expression and dissent, and played a notable role in framing the relationship between the government and the MCB, which by now was the virtually exclusive contact point for organised communal representation of Britain's Muslim communities. A reactive drive among Muslims to denounce and state clearly their positions on terrorism and violence, issues of loyalty and citizenship and the notion of separate cultures and the irreconcilability of Islam with 'western democracy' led to a growth in Muslim involvement with broad-based social and political coalitions, such as the anti-war movement. A substantive 'mainstreaming' of Muslim community interests occurred, a development that was further reflected in the proliferation of the diverse choices and styles of self-expression that were utilised by young British Muslims. Even the renewed calls and campaigns for outlawing religious hate speech were framed around new terms to those that had been used during the

Satanic Verses crisis, with the focus more on parity of treatment with other minorities as a matter of rights within the race relations framework, and on Islamophobia as a real form of discrimination and prejudice, and less on the idea of blasphemy and offence to religious sensitivities. Coinciding with an increasingly vocal far-right, which exploited the law's helplessness against incitement to religious hatred by running 'anti-Islam' campaigns, coupled with a volatile backdrop of unease and community tensions that had been fed by the terrorist attacks, maturity and sophistication in political claims-making from a Muslim identity perspective could not have come at a better time.

In Chapter 6, I argue that the terrorist attack on London's transport system on 7 July 2005 constituted another important turning point for British Muslim identity politics. The 'home-grown' aspect of the attack was a significant reason for introspection of a new kind both in government circles and within the Muslim communities. The new realities posed by the threat of terrorism on home soil to the sense of everyday safety and security meant that fresh (some previously unaskable) questions were being asked. At the crux of these lay a debate on the success or otherwise of the way that multiculturalism had been hitherto understood, as well as the viability of the political goal of integration that was being pursued. The Labour government's policy from this point followed a two-pronged approach with regard to security and community cohesion – a 'hard' approach, consisting of new and updated anti-terror legislation, most notably what became known as 'encourage-ment offences', and a 'soft' approach of community engagement which endeavoured to 'win over (Muslim) hearts and minds' in the fight against terror, an approach now most readily associated with the Prevent strategy and a greater inclination towards linking the 'Muslim question' to the state's expanding securitisation agenda. Within Muslim circles, there was a stark and sudden realisation of the gravity of the radicalisation problem as one that could not simply be brushed under the carpet or explained away on media appearances by 'community leaders'. Denial and conspiracy theory-type explanations for radicalisation and terrorism which had been relatively widely expressed in the wake of 9/11 almost instantly held much less purchase. Among the significant implications of this mood change has been a more proactive readiness to engage in serious intra-community debate, dialogue and cooperation on the part of many community organisations, including the MCB. The stakes had become too high to squabble over the future, or to allow it to be decided externally, leading to a renewed drive for unity between groups of different political and theological leanings. Openness in some ways replaced the suspicion and scepticism that the establishment and members of other faiths may previously have been met with by Muslim organisations, since 'Muslim issues' now affected everyone, and the conversation about the future of Islam and Muslims should encompass much more than *just* Muslim voices. Moreover, this phase underlined the need for the younger generations to come to the forefront of debates and decision-making within Muslim organisations, which remain over-whelmingly dominated by older, first-generation-immigrant men. For many, this remains a source of the stifling stagnation or rigidity of Muslim identity politics, and younger generations have increasingly made their voices heard through new organisations and initiatives, some of them pushing received boundaries of convention and orthodoxy. Though some of these have been more pliant to the government's objectives of securitisation and its foreign policy ambitions, and others have taken a far more critical role than the MCB, ultimately this evolving landscape has contributed to raising the bar in the level of organisational transparency and efficiency across the board. As an ever-increasing range of voices emerged to speak for Britain's Muslims, not only did they have to learn to work with each other, but also to work on becoming more relevant to and more representative of those they sought to represent.

Chapter 7 offers a discussion of some of the most crucial current debates affecting British Muslim identity politics. I reflect on a number of relevant developments since the 2010 General Election, when 13 years of Labour administration came to an end. These include shifts and changes in state approaches to multiculturalism – specifically in state relations with religious minority advocacy groups, which themselves are responding to changing landscapes in politics and within the communities they seek to represent. Finally, I offer some comments on the most recent and critical challenge to face Muslim communal organisation – the emergence of so called 'Islamic State' or Daesh, its appeal to British (and Western) Muslims to travel or to carry out terror attacks at home, and impacts that this urgent and unprecedented development has had on British Muslim identity politics and community organisation.

I summarise the book's key findings in Chapter 8, offering assessments and recommendations – both those emerging from the study itself, and with respect to where it can potentially be taken further, for example, through policy recommendations and suggesting suitable pathways and strategies for community leaders, groups and advocacy bodies to follow. I also revisit my notion of an Equality Gap as a tool to understand the basis for British Muslim identity politics, arguing that a number of substantive developments, particularly since the 2000s, have considerably narrowed the initial extent of the gap. However, other factors have caused the gap to persist, albeit with a changed focus. Whereas in the 1990s the Equality Gap encompassed concerns around freedom of expression and the implementation of race relations policy, today inadequacies in the law relate not only to equalities but also to the application of security measures. Additionally, we can point to the impacts of official and political attitudes towards anti-Muslim popular discourse and sentiment, such as those espoused by the so called 'alt-right', as occupying increasing significance in the appeals to equality that are currently being made in the arena of Muslim identity politics in the UK.

In articulating a revised iteration of the Equality Gap, I argue that notwithstanding progress and lessons learned over the past 50 years, there remains a justification for the continuation of a Muslim identity politics in Britain. However, rather than the traditional model of communal organisations seeking group rights and exemptions, this should instead be an identity politics that is attuned to the present political and cultural landscape. This updated model of identity politics can and should encapsulate intra- *as well as* cross-community collaborative action not only on matters of mutual interest but, more crucially, in genuine expression of mutual empathy and solidarity. This has been shown to be possible by a number of recent grassroots initiatives, some of which I highlight.

In short, they demonstrate the appealing possibility of a move away from the corporatist, 'community-leader' model, and towards an activism that speaks to Muslim-specific inequalities but from the standpoint of being deeply rooted in Britain. This activism would be all the stronger for its embrace of and solidarity with a wide range of allies, and its deep appreciation of how inequalities experienced by minorities and disadvantaged groups so often intersect.

CHAPTER 2

Setting the Scene: Historical and Theoretical Contexts

This chapter outlines the context in which the book is set, and the key questions that it tackles. Taking the notion of social equality and justice as my starting point, I hone in on three important themes that have particular bearing on the integration and claims-making of Muslims as a newly settled minority in Britain.

The first theme is that of freedom of expression, and, more generally, of civil liberties – the lens through which the study as a whole will analyse the development and evolution of British Muslim identity politics. I begin with a survey of the Enlightenment roots of the historical development of these concepts in British political thought and their impact on constitutional and legal evolution. I then also look at the historical pathway that similar ideas have travelled in the Islamic theological and political past, and how they have fared in recent history, in Muslim majority countries, many of which are – in their present forms – relatively recent creations. This examination is important insofar as it sheds light upon the theme of freedom of expression and the understanding and approach to civil liberties as it unfolded in recent British Muslim history. It facilitates in the comprehension of the ensuing historical analysis – where causal factors behind moments of conflict and intractability can only be fully understood with an appreciation of these different historical pathways, and their role and place in shaping the mindset and perspectives of the political establishment, the media and the wider public on the one hand, and those of Muslim community groups and interlocutors on the other.

Before I do this, mention must be made of the extent to which there was an awareness of Islam, its scriptures and traditions among Enlightenment thinkers.[1] Occasional sympathy towards Islam demonstrated by many key figures of the enlightenment may be taken to contradict the popular impression that 'Islam' and 'the West' have long been the sites of rival or opposing value systems. Although it may be tempting to portray Muslim and British (Western) perspectives on free speech as two separate monoliths, this would be inaccurate, since the works of several Enlightenment writers express admiration towards and fascination with aspects of Islam, including the person of the Prophet Muhammad, of Muslim societies, values and government.[2] Similarly, Muslim thinkers have differed in their understandings of free speech, not least due to their own cross-cultural interactions. These interactions and exchanges between cultures and contexts continue to the present day and are visible in the developing perspectives of Western Muslims on notions of free speech and blasphemy, and their varied responses to instances of offence.

The second part of this chapter looks more closely at the idea of equality, in the way with which it has been used for motivating and justifying British public policy over the past four or five decades, specifically with reference to British Muslims as a religious minority. It engages with the themes of equality and justice, and discusses contemporary debates within political theory around how they can best be secured for minority communities. I argue that Muslim identity politics in contemporary British history has invariably been underpinned by a call to some understanding of 'equality as recognition'. This, coupled with an understanding of 'equality as redistribution', provides a theoretical basis from which attempts to redress imbalances in the type of access British Muslims have had to equality and justice can be understood. This theoretical survey, together with the preceding survey of historical and cultural background in Chapter 1, constitutes a comprehensive background to the remainder of the book, which traces and examines the development of British Muslim identity politics from the 1970s through to the present.

The third part of this chapter considers the idea of identity politics, and does so specifically in relation to Britain's Muslim communities. I look at definitions of the term, both in academic literature and as popular usage, examining the merits of academic arguments in support of a politics of recognition and difference for minority and historically disadvantaged groups. I also consider how the idea of misrecognition can be used to explain and justify the need for a politics of identity. Further, I note that Muslim identity politics has evolved alongside the evolution of British Islam(s) itself. I point out the impact of internal debates, disagreements and rivalries within Muslim communities, the influence of representative communication and negotiation – whether with the government or with other public bodies, and the role of wider contemporary socio-political debates in shaping the priorities, style and nature of British Muslim identity politics. This theme recurs throughout the book, as I trace and critique the simultaneous development of British Muslim identity politics on each of these three fronts.

FREE SPEECH IN BRITISH AND MUSLIM TRADITIONS

As with any immigrant population, there was a certain inevitability that areas of misunderstanding and even conflict between Muslims and wider society would arise, as efforts were made to settle, to come to terms with the new home, and to build relations of trust and friendship while looking to the future. Appearance, culture, tradition and language were obvious markers of difference for recent immigrants. This was true on a day-to-day level of course, but was sometimes particularly significant at moments of negotiation. Prejudice and xenophobia were also present in their various forms and did not fail to make their impact on the level and quality of relationships (or lack of them). This is not to mention the colouring of perspectives from both sides by the legacy of colonialism and the relationships of power that existed between the UK and countries of origin.[3]

But apart from the serious complications and difficulties in communication that these factors would cause, there were also obstacles in communication of a more nuanced nature, which affected the level and effectiveness of conversation. The Rushdie Affair shed light on one important source of dissonance in perspectives when it came to understandings and expectations around the freedoms and limits of expression. Even a cursory survey of the language and logic behind arguments used by Muslim activists and commentators, and responses that they received from the government and the 'liberal establishment', gives sufficient indication as to serious differences in the origin and nature of the cultural and political development that this value had undergone in British political and constitutional history on one hand, and in the political experience of the South Asian countries from whence a majority of Britain's Muslims traced their origins, on the other.[4] The latter is arguably more complex since it encompasses influences from Islamic theological tradition as well as political history and of course colonial influences which in many cases played no small part in shaping and formalising the constitutions and legal frameworks of many (then still relatively young) Muslim-majority nations. In the following section, I look briefly at each of these trajectories and refer where relevant to illustrative aspects of *The Satanic Verses* experience to demonstrate how a failure to grasp these different formative pathways led quite spectacularly to a sharp intransigence and unhelpful polarisation of positions.

The social contract, natural rights and freedom of expression

The development of the British constitutional political system and the highly valued place of freedom of expression as a fundamental liberty in British politics and thereby in the public mindset have important origins in the thinking of Enlightenment philosophers – notably Thomas Hobbes and John Locke. As contemporaries of the English Civil War, the short-lived Cromwellian republic and the fraught restoration of the Stuart monarchy, they witnessed a time when security and liberty as values were uppermost in people's minds, as they had recently experienced a great deal of instability in respect of both.

Hobbes and Locke had strong, if divergent, views about the place and proper extent of political authority. Hobbes argued in favour of the necessity of arbitrary rule, as a way of keeping in place a system that would control the innate tendency in individual human beings to pursue the satisfaction of their desires, and thus to, if left unchecked, fall into a 'natural state' of conflict and competitive destruction. Such was the nature of humanity that it could only be tamed by the force of a powerful civil-state entity. Hobbes recognised that religious and clerical authority had also sought to keep arbitrary control over mankind, but, rather than the separation of powers, he favoured the civil-secular model which, on the basis of a social contract, would provide citizens with order and protection and the scope for self-preservation, while they in return would accept its control and authority. Rights and freedoms were therefore enjoyed by individuals at the discretion of the ruler. While obviously this position does not sit at all well with the present-day understanding of freedom of expression, and indeed more generally, of freedom and the relationship of the individual with government, Hobbes has been credited for setting a foundational precedent for modern thinking on the nation-state and its functions. In addition, the staunch defence by Hobbes of centralised arbitrary rule can be understood to have set some momentum for the oppositional idea of natural rights and freedoms in the context of a more representative and more accountable style of government as elucidated by John Locke.[5]

From Locke's Protestant perspective, the Stuarts' unpromising interest in Catholicism – in particular the prospect of a Catholic James II succeeding Charles II to the throne – presented to him the unattractive image of a return of the sort of arbitrary monarchical power for which Charles I had been executed and the monarchy abolished. Thus it was something to be deeply wary of, since both Catholicism and arbitrary rule shared worrying propensities to impose undue restrictions upon the individual's liberty and to curtail the power of parliament, which, to Locke, represented the people's will.[6] Locke's view of the social contract that bound political communities together had as central to it the idea of individual natural rights. It was the sovereign's duty to safeguard these rights, and whilst there is some disagreement around where Locke placed the limit of the individuals' obedience to the sovereign,[7] he nonetheless advocated the necessity of protecting these natural rights, and the importance of accountability of the sovereign to the people (e.g. through parliament) when decisions about such rights needed to be made.[8] Such a position relies importantly on there being access to free expression, and this principle ties in with Locke's writings on the subject of toleration – which includes the toleration of religious and political dissent. Criticism has been levelled at Locke for his failure to go far enough in matters of toleration, for instance his view that government may not afford toleration to Catholics and atheists for reasons of the potential political damage that they might cause.[9] However, what is of more importance to the discussion at hand is the spirit of Locke's perspective on toleration and its longer-term impact on the evolution of British political norms and values. Locke's support for the notion of toleration and the right of resistance against tyranny gave reasons for the perspective that dissent and difference had a value and that the undue stifling of them may provoke legitimate responses of protest or rebellion. This notion of inviolable individual rights was later developed by thinkers such as John Stuart Mill, and can be seen to have been subsequently built upon and according to some accounts to have influenced the modern understanding of 'human rights', which, as enshrined in present-day international and European Union human rights agreements and instruments, includes the right to free expression.

Mill's writings on freedom of expression have proved both seminal and influential in the evolution of the English legal system. Mill defended the idea that expressive acts should be immune from restrictions on the basis of two main points. The first was the danger of 'assuming infallibility' – that as compelling and persuasive an opinion (or the falsity of an opposing opinion) might be, the curtailing of an opponent's free expression would amount to an assumption of infallibility.[10] Secondly, that the free expression of all opinions, whether true or false, was vital to the formation of an 'intellectually active people'.[11] However, he also articulated the exceptional grounds upon which he felt that restrictions to expression could be justifiably placed, and at the foundation of these grounds was his 'harm principle', which remains a legislative cornerstone as well as a widely accepted and hotly defended concept in British public political culture. To quote Mill: 'that the only purpose for which power can be rightfully exerted over any member of a civilised community, against his will, is to prevent harm to others'.[12]

This principle has continued to have a profound impact on the modern British political psyche and informs the spirited defence of free expression that has regularly been invoked to rebut calls from minorities for censoring or indeed censuring of material that has caused deep offence. However, what has often not been fully appreciated is the way in which the impact of offence caused by such material *can* have the potential to cause harm, and particularly because it is directed at aspects of identity that have *already* been subjected to some form of public disadvantage or misrecognition. Brown argues that there is some room for an effective response to racial and religious hatred that draws upon Mill's work. A political, even a 'sparingly used' legislative response that 'balances freedom of speech against future possible harms', can go some way towards redressing discrimination and the potential resultant inequalities, with minimal impact on freedom of expression.[13]

Of course, there are and always have been legal restrictions to freedom of expression in the UK – well known examples include libel, privacy and blasphemy laws.[14] However, these have not existed without contention and dispute over their validity or over the appropriateness of where exactly to place boundaries. More recently, anti-terrorism legislation has included controversial restrictions on speech that 'encourages' or 'glorifies' terrorism, or expresses support for proscribed terrorist groups. This last example is a case in point, as the unease with which it has been received by so many, from experts in law and civil liberties to ordinary members of the public, is demonstrative of just how cherished and sacrosanct freedom of expression is.

Freedom of expression in Islam and Muslim tradition

Many Muslim immigrant communities, whether arriving from the Indian subcontinent, other commonwealth countries or from areas in the Arab world and the Middle East, had experiences and expectations on the issue of freedom of expression that carried remarkably different historical and cultural meanings and often owed their provenance to a wholly different set of values.

In terms of faith and theology, there have been some characterisations of Islam that argue that the concept of freedom of expression is alien to Muslim tradition, and that instead a focus on the community as the source of individual identity and fulfilment is given far greater importance. The notion of Islam as a 'communitarian' faith suggests that greater value is placed on the protection of the faith community's honour, as well as that of its revered figures, than on the concept of individual freedom. Indeed, this has been argued by several authors, including some Muslims.[15] I contend that such a portrait is rather too simplistic to do justice to the reality of how choices are made and priorities are ordered by the 'average' Muslim citizen (if such a person can be said to exist). Even *if* all Muslims regarded their affinity to their faith as carrying such weight that it overrode their understanding of individual freedoms, this argument also assumes that, for all Muslims, their faith somehow automatically trumps other aspects of their identity, such as liberalism or even secularism, for example – values which hold freedom of expression in unquestionably high regard.

Yet while I accept that there may be *some* Muslims whose worldview closely matches the 'communitarian' characterisation mentioned above, it is important to also point out that, even so, the idea of free speech is itself not wholly absent from Islamic sources and tradition. Muhammad Hashim Kamali argues that freedom of expression is absolutely intrinsic to the Islamic faith as a right, and that on occasion its exercise also becomes analogous to a duty. Kamali cites two objectives that are directly served by the value of free speech – the discovery of truth and the upholding of human dignity.[16] These objectives mark out important distinctions in the conception of free expression from an Islamic theological perspective, and from the present day 'Western'[17] conceptions of free expression as a basic individual right and guarantor against tyranny, be it from a regime or from a religion, or, for that matter, from a theocratic regime. This last possibility carries acute resonance with Ayatollah Khomeini's fatwa sentencing Rushdie to death, which seemed to symbolise everything that was to be abhorred and feared about the arbitrary theocracy that the Islamic Republic of Iran was popularly perceived to be – the prioritising of religious dogma and obedience to a religious authority over freedom of expression and the life of an individual.

Kamali's two free speech objectives fit well with the overall project of the *shari'a*,[18] of which the ultimate objectives are the protection of belief, life, intellect, honour and property. From an individual perspective, these objectives can be approximated into the language of rights without much difficulty, in the sense that the individual has a right that the state should provide adequate protection of these aspects of their self. And while speech and/or expression are not individually mentioned, there is clearly scope for their inclusion in at least two of the above categories, namely belief and intellect. In fact, it could be said that any understanding of these two categories would be crucially deficient without provision for free expression.

A number of Western Muslim thinkers have taken these ideas further, and promulgated Islamically inspired cases in favour of free expression and critical thinking, defending the *rights* of others to criticise and even insult Islam, while at the same time insisting that such a right should be exercised in a multicultural, multi-religious society with caution and respect – indeed that it should not be wrongly construed as a *duty*. Usama Hasan has presented a theologically grounded argument against blasphemy legislation, which insists that Islam does not prescribe any earthly punishment for blasphemy. Violations of respect for sacred symbols are to be punished in the spiritual and other-worldly realms, not through any worldly legislation or penalties. Hasan observes that in the contemporary context it is extremely difficult to define blasphemy, especially on the type of global level that recent controversies have played out. Moreover, he notes that in the Qur'an and Sunnah, there is an absence of 'explicit sanction … for the criminalisation and punishment of blasphemy',[19] and that those sources which are used to support such measures are often 'misquoted', since they all refer to wartime situations.[20] In an appreciation of cultural nuance, Hasan acknowledges that instances in Islamic tradition of wartime retaliation against poets who had mocked the Prophet Muhammad had occurred, but that 'in the seventh century Arabian culture (was) dominated by an oral tradition (and) poetry was used for propaganda and psychological warfare'.[21] As a general rule, however, particularly in this globalised age, he maintains that blasphemy legislation is not called for, nor does it fulfil any specific role that is called for by Islamic sources and scriptures.

Interestingly, it is the potent impact of offensive speech freely expressed that has been the source of representations from Muslims for protection. The extensive reach of powerful media outlets and influential artists can encourage or give added legitimacy to anti-Muslim sentiment, and as a minority group, with a comparatively far more limited voice, there is less opportunity to counter such offensive speech on a similarly large scale. So while defending the right of free expression, some thinkers have called for caution, understanding and empathy in good measure, because of the potentially substantial harms that unfettered free expression in this area can cause.

Tariq Ramadan is one example. At a PEN International gathering in New York, he argued that freedom of expression should not be restricted by law to protect minorities from offence. However, he also acknowledged that this offence was often deeply and genuinely felt, and sometimes had complex and far-reaching consequences. Instead he called for sensitivity, and 'intellectual empathy' with those in the Muslim world who had been so deeply offended by recent controversies. Additionally, he argued that a commitment to consistency and even-handedness was needed when it came to free speech. It was inconsistent, he maintained, for certain European countries to continue to criminalise Holocaust denial, whilst simultaneously displaying incredulity at Muslim calls for censorship and complaints of offence at mockery of their faith.[22]

A similar position was taken by Tariq Modood in the wake of the Danish 'Muhammad cartoons crisis' of 2006. He argued that the cartoons occupied 'an entirely different league of offence', since they constituted a comment on Muslims as a whole rather than only the Prophet Muhammad as an individual. As such, the portrayal in one cartoon of the prophet as a terrorist was effectively a racist stereotype of Muslims collectively. But rather than banning or censorship, society should respond to such Islamophobic expressions with protest or censure, in a similar fashion to what has become the norm with most racist expressions.[23]

Talal Asad invites a critical consideration of secular liberal responses to Muslim offence, by asking whether 'modern secular aversion to the category of blasphemy derive(s) from a suspicion of political religion.'[24] This aversion, he argues, is specifically focused on Islam, and is combined with latent paranoia, 'loathing and fear' of Muslim immigrants, to manifest an intolerant hostility towards any (violent) protests against religious offence. Thus, 'aggression in the name of God shocks secular liberal sensibilities, whereas the art of killing in the name of the secular nation, of democracy, does not'.[25] Without absolving the violence perpetrated by Muslim protesters, Asad argues that the shrill defence of the value of free speech at all costs by vehement secularists against 'Muslim rage' might actually have more to do with their own prejudices than they might like to admit.

A substantial difficulty when it comes to reconciling the 'Eastern' and 'Western' traditions is the location of acceptable boundaries of free expression. I have already illustrated examples of where limits of expression in British legal and public norms lie. In the case of Muslim tradition, legal restraints have been placed primarily where the objectives of the discovery of truth and upholding of human dignity are deemed to be at threat of being seriously undermined. In particular, restrictions placed on expression that is considered to equate to apostasy or blasphemy have been notoriously troubling to the 'Western' mind, conjuring unpalatable images of violence and capital punishment. Notwithstanding the fact that there is a range of scholarly opinion regarding the applicability of any official punishments for either,[26] let alone any applicability of capital punishment, there has historically been a widespread sense of reverence and sensitivity around the character and person of the Prophet Muhammad among Muslims, a sentiment which to a large extent remains to this day.[27] It was this sensitivity that was aroused by the publication in 1988 of Salman Rushdie's novel, *The Satanic Verses*, and the nature of the reaction to it was to a substantial extent an expression of this reverence. The inviolability of honour (*'ird*) in *shari'a* is a concept which Shabbir Akhtar utilises to supplement the greater (blasphemous) charge of *sabb al-nabi* (insulting the Prophet) in his spirited case for the proscription of *The Satanic Verses*.[28] Interpretatively, this is something of an attempt to bridge the two pathways, by approximating the harm caused by blasphemy against the Prophet (which the 'Western' mind might struggle to understand the gravity of), with the more familiar charge of personal attack – libel or defamation.[29]

Apart from this cultural and religious reverence for the Prophet, there were other factors which caused reaction to intensify and escalate. Two of the most important include an international dimension, and the response and attitude of 'the other side' to initial objections. With respect to the international factor, this is best detected in the stance of the Muslim Institute and its leader Kalim Siddiqui, who positively celebrated the Iranian Revolution and argued that Muslims in the UK could draw strength and support from the new Islamic republic, as well as assurance from the defence that the fatwa provided in the face of Rushdie's 'attack'.[30] As for the second factor – the manner and tactics that were chosen by government representatives appear to have only fuelled resentment and frustration among Muslim protesters. Talal Asad remarks that they were both 'lecturing' and 'colonial' in tone and in content.[31] Judging by the correspondences and commentaries that were written during this period, this was certainly a widespread feeling.[32] And while the above at least explains the frustration of Muslim groups at the apparent futility of their efforts at explaining their position and defending their 'rights', it was perhaps this very insistence by Muslims on overwhelmingly using blasphemy as the main reason for their campaign for the book's recall which so riled the 'liberal establishment' and caused them to dig their heels in hostility further still. How could the precious and hard-won value of free expression, particularly of artistic expression, be permitted to be threatened with such tremendous force merely on the grounds that it offended the religious sensitivities of members of a minority faith?

In a sense, these different pathways so coloured attitudes and expectations on both sides that the dialogue which took place during and in the aftermath of the Rushdie Affair can very well be characterised as both sides talking *at* one another rather than *with* each other.

Why have Muslims taken such deep offence at attacks on their faith?

Differing understandings of rights and freedoms, and differing ways of relating to government, are not the only areas where culture and mindset between East and West can have their divergences. Communities who had arrived in the UK as part of the chain migrations from the mid-twentieth century onwards experienced major lifestyle changes on a number of levels. Apart from linguistic differences, there was the contrast between the close-knit rural life, which many (especially South Asian immigrants) were accustomed to, and the unfamiliarity of the more individualistic lifestyle of the city. More specifically, the role of religion and cultural influences in each of these lifestyles differed greatly. Many immigrants had come from environments where religion formed much more of an integrated, very spiritual backdrop to everyday life – a norm which contrasted with the ever more detached understanding of religion in relation to daily life that was prevalent in the urban contexts that they were joining. So while it may have been very natural in rural Kashmir, for example, to understand religion through its manifestation in day-to-day rites of passage, through family and tribal relations and folklore, in the new context of Britain, religion necessarily had to fit into not only a new template of meaning and even practice, but also had to deal with the fact that it (Islam) was a minority and perceptibly 'foreign' religion. As a consequence, the experience of adjusting and finding a place in their new home was made additionally unsettling when access to, and relationships with religion were abruptly altered.[33]

Even the very actions used to express feelings of dissent and protest were infused with cultural baggage. To return to the Rushdie Affair, the decision of a protester from the Bradford Council of Mosques to set fire to a copy of *The Satanic Verses* was intended to be a dramatic publicity stunt that would force the media and establishment to step away from their apparent lack of empathy and their disdain towards the deep offence and hurt of which Muslims were complaining. The idea was that by burning the book, the complaints and representations that had been made by Muslim representatives would finally be afforded the seriousness and attention that they deserved. Yet, as Zaiba Malik, a British-Pakistani journalist who grew up in Bradford, describes in her memoirs, while the book-burners certainly bagged countless newspaper headlines for the Bradford Council of Mosques, they weren't so successful at garnering compassion for their cause:

> Journalists, writers, commentators and thinkers were appalled and shocked at what had happened at the Tyrls [the location in central Bradford where the first book-burning took place]. Don't these Muslims understand that we believe in freedom of expression in this country, that free speech is a cornerstone of our democracy, that it is a right we have had to fight long and hard for and is one we will absolutely defend – even if it causes offence?[34]

She further quotes Eric Pickles, the then (Conservative) leader of Bradford Council who later argued that 'Of all the symbolic actions, setting fire to a book was probably the worst thing to do. It looked like something out of Nuremburg'.[35] Such was the centrality of the impact of culture on creating and sustaining a harsh dissonance between two parties that so desperately needed to be understood by one another. For the Muslim community, the book-burning was more than a plea to be heard by those in positions of power; it was a symbol of just how much the crime of *sabb an-nabi* was considered to be a red line that must not be crossed at any cost. Yet for the politicians and the media, who the Muslim community were so desperate to convince, the act of book-burning represented the epitome of backwardness and intolerance.

I would take this notion of cultural dissonance even further and argue that understandings of honour in many parts of the Muslim world are coloured more by traditional and cultural norms than by religion *per se*. Cultural practices and customs in many Muslim majority countries, and specifically the Indian sub-continent, are often infused with a strong understanding of familial or tribal honour and loyalty. These are historically enshrined values, which often enjoy a somewhat fabled status in public consciousness. Perhaps these have come to be most infamously (mis)understood in the West through the unfortunately titled 'honour' crimes. Acts of violence – often lethal – which have been rationalised or justified by perpetrators using the notion that the victims' 'sinful' or 'shameful' behaviours are directly linked to the honour and reputation of her family, clan or community.

But the 'Eastern' conception of honour that I refer to has wider and deeper significance than this. The dense literature and poetry of pre-Islamic Arabia is rife with references to tribal and familial honour, revenge on behalf of scorned or slighted fellow tribesmen and family feuds that continued for generations. The Arabic word *ghira*, which connotes an ardent or jealous protection of honour, is a central notion to be understood, and one which has a place not only in the Arabic speaking countries but in the Muslim communities of South Asia as well. It is most often expressed in connection with religion and familial honour especially relating to females. While clearly not something exclusive to the east, an appreciation of this aspect of cultural background and heritage can contribute to a more informed understanding of seemingly (to Western eyes) exaggerated Muslim responses to offensive criticism of their faith.

To illustrate, let us look at more recent controversies such as the 2006 Danish cartoon crisis and the 2012 'Innocence of Muslims' film. Both have drawn ire and criticism from western Muslims, but protests have not reached anywhere near the scale of those that took place in the Muslim world. Notably, any protests that *did* take place in Britain were peaceful and far removed from the violent mobs that took to the streets of various Muslim-majority countries.[36] A common refrain of protesters in Muslim-majority countries was the phrase *'illa rasulallah'*, '(anyone/thing) but the messenger of God', emphasising how the person of the Prophet Muhammad was directly and inextricably tied with their personal honour and reputation – they could bear any insult *but* criticism or ridicule of this most revered figure.

Finally, it would be short-sighted for us to fail to recognise the role that geopolitical factors have also played in exacerbating sensitivities and pushing many in the Muslim world to protest with such heated fervour at what are considered to be deeply offensive and sacrilegious depictions of their faith in the public sphere. To return to the 'Innocence of Muslims' film, angry, riotous protest in the Muslim world can only be comprehensively understood in its proper and complete context. For many protesters in the Muslim world, the film was indeed considered to be highly insulting, but as many have noted, it was often more of a final straw that set off riots that were waiting to happen anyway.[37] US military presence, political intervention and deadly drone attacks are just some of the reasons why ordinary people in countries such as Libya, Pakistan and Afghanistan have, in recent times, had plenty of reasons to harbour hostility and resentment towards Western countries, and the USA in particular (where the film originated). To quote the words of one commentator on the affair: 'Broken by poverty, threatened by drones, caught in the war between al Qaida and the US, to many Arab Muslims, the film represents an attack on the last shelter of dignity – sacred beliefs – when all else has been desecrated.'[38]

Additionally, the impacts of highly restrictive political regimes in many of these countries meant that mass dissent and protest directed at domestic issues such as political corruption and economic deprivation was often not a safe option, as opposition activists could suffer heavy penalties for their views. Instead, pent-up public anger was more readily vented against less locally contentious foreign 'enemies' who had slighted religious sensitivities.[39]

There were elements of all of these factors present in 1988 when the Rushdie Affair first broke out. Thus it was that while both the Muslim communities of Britain and the British political and media establishments of the time were not seeking to conflict or to clash with one another, a clash nonetheless occurred. I shall return to look at the Rushdie Affair in greater depth in Chapters 3 and 4, from the perspective of its role in igniting Muslim identity politics in earnest. For now, suffice to say that the affair offers a clear illumination of how significantly the different cultural and political experiences of British Muslim communities and British public and political institutions affected each of their respective approaches to communication, as well as their senses of priorities when it came to negotiation, with one another.

Moving on from the contextual background to Muslim claims-making and the development of their political agency, I will now look at some of the theoretical background to equalities policy, exploring the justifications from a theoretical perspective for Muslim identity politics, with a view to understanding the way in which it was articulated by Muslim advocacy groups, as well as the government's approach to Muslim claims-making.

EQUALITY IN THE THEORETICAL TERRAIN

A common motivating factor behind active political engagement for any individual or group is a sense that some form of injustice or inequality has been felt and is in need of being rectified. The case with minority communities is often that politicisation and political organisation is related to experiences of poor treatment or margin-alisation in different spheres of life, be they the economic, for instance through poor working conditions, or aspects of social and political life, where legal arrangements might affect minorities unfairly or disproportionately – either by deliberate design or through inadvertent omission of factors relating to difference. In what follows, I look at how this pursuit of equality on a policy level is justified through a theoretical framework, looking specifically at arguments for equality as recognition which have been the key theoretical underpinning for multiculturalism and race relations policy in the UK, and, more recently, for policy efforts to tackle Islamophobia.

Equality as recognition
The question of how to deliver equality through the law to all citizens is one that is of primary concern to any liberal society. The term 'equality' is both broad and contestable, and continues to be the focus of both agreement (in terms of its importance) and debate (in its definition). A major feature in this debate has centred on where

to measure equality. Should we be satisfied as long as equality of opportunity is available to all or is it also important to look at how 'equal' the outcomes of any institution or process are? The relevant distinction here lies in the first of these, equality of opportunity, being concerned with *redistribution* – how well the opportunity for equality is distributed among individuals; and the other, with *recognition* – an attitude that is concerned with aspects of social and political relations that cannot be 'quantified' in the same way that distributive and economic inequalities can, and which seeks to seriously incorporate into the political community, in a fair and sustainable manner, groups that visibly or perceptively differ from the mainstream.

I will concentrate on how the idea of *recognition* has come to be understood as a method through which greater access to equality can be secured, in particular for members of minorities within society, for whom there might be the experience of unjustifiable, added disadvantage. This could be either as a result of social norms, preferences and privileges being predominantly aligned in favour of (or shaped by) the majority, or it could be as a result of historical injustices (or, on some accounts, continued injustices) that they may have suffered. Additionally, these injustices could take the form of oppression or suppression on account of their difference or of their minority status. The concern of the state with these kinds of challenges can be informed by a broader range of matters, but the importance of seeking to eliminate inequality remains a valid and central justification that is used for public policy efforts to pursue measures that will target the particular disadvantages that are considered to disproportionately or specifically affect minority groups.

Before moving on to examine the trajectory of relevant policy that has evolved in the UK over the course of recent decades, I will first devote my attention to illustrating some key theoretical arguments. While there exist numerous disagreements and debates between recognition theorists as to the role and scope of recognition, all are identifiable by their advocacy of the idea that recognition is a crucial aspect of equality in a pluralist political community. A central feature of any politics of recognition is the idea that individuals are in need of a certain level of recognition from those around them in their communities and groups, and in wider society and the political domain, in order to fulfil their true potential and to be able to function on a satisfactory level – one which all individuals should be in a position to expect for themselves.

Speaking in positive terms, a politics of recognition espouses the principle that individuals are in *need* of recognition from those around them in order to fully function and truly realise themselves and their aspirations. Members of minority or disadvantaged groups who are denied such recognition are therefore seen to be lacking in necessary tools for attaining genuine equality with the mainstream, and are denied an important aspect of their personal well-being. Without adequate recognition, individuals are potentially deprived of the basic resources and opportunity with which to define and project themselves to those around them in a way that is aligned with their personal volition and self-understanding. Thus recognition is a fundamental and powerful aspect of an individual's relationship with themselves, and with society around them.

From recognition to parity – three approaches

The works of Charles Taylor and Axel Honneth have served as focal points for what is now a wide-ranging and extensive literature on recognition. Both are critical of what they see as the 'conventional' liberal framework's rigidity toward individuals and in particular those who are stigmatised or form part of a minority, and both take inspiration from the Hegelian tradition.[40] Taylor articulates a 'deeply rooted' desire, which all human beings possess, for recognition by others of their unique and distinctive identity. Difference-blind liberalism, in its insistence on overlooking diversity as either irrelevant or peripheral to the concern of the political community, does not deliver this. Instead, it invariably succumbs to the very state of bias or partiality that it avowedly shuns. This is because true (complete) neutrality does not exist in any political community since the political structures, institutions and the norms of public life of each are inevitably shaped by its historical experience as well as the culture, tradition and even preferences of the majority. In restricting itself to 'recognising' only those qualities that are universally shared among individuals, Taylor argues that there is a failing which renders 'difference-blind liberalism' incapable of genuinely accommodating the notion of authenticity. An individual cannot be true to herself if those around her in society do not give due recognition to aspects of herself that do not happen to conform to the predominant or preferred norms, practices and values in society.

Honneth, as a critical theorist, places emphasis on recognition less as an aspect of identity politics than as a tool with which to critique injustice that exists in the realm of communication, as observed in intersubjective relationships (as distinct from injustice in the realm of production, which redistribution seeks to put right). In focusing on intersubjectivity, he identifies three strands through which social attitudes and interactions can disrupt a subject's relationship to herself. These are love (where physical integrity is violated through 'practical maltreatment' such as physical abuse which can destroy a person's self-confidence and underlying trust in herself), rights (where basic respect or legal protection for it, on a level with that enjoyed by other members of society are denied, thus damaging a subject's moral self-respect by signalling that her status is somehow below that of others around her) and solidarity or esteem (denigration of a certain individual or collective ways of life as inferior or deficient, depriving the subject of social support and thus impacting eventually on the opportunities that she has for self-realisation).[41] These strands constitute a 'denial of recognition', and as such the injustice they cause is serious, 'not simply because it harms subjects or restricts their freedom to act, but because it injures them with regard to the positive understanding of themselves that they have acquired intersubjectively'.[42]

Anna Elisabetta Galeotti's 'toleration as recognition' thesis defends the view that, especially for minorities, recognition in the public sphere is the most effective and fairest way with which toleration (the widely cherished principle of 'live and let live') can be practised. That toleration itself is an essential value to be pursued, especially within a pluralist context, is a matter of broad general agreement.[43] The object of toleration as recognition is to achieve equal and fair treatment in the public realm for minorities that are (or have been) 'occupying unequal positions in relation to social standing, public respect, social and political power', due to the dominance and power of force and quantity that majority preferences can deliberately or inadvertently give rise to. What recognition achieves, either through gesture and symbolism or through 'literal' (actual) policy changes, is a readjustment of existing political arrangements in such a way that redresses the social and political marginality that some minorities would find themselves experiencing.[44]

At this point it is also important to note objections that have been made to the sometimes popular idea that recognition is profoundly in competition with or irreconcilably distinct from a politics of redistribution. In this respect, the later work of Nancy Fraser goes some way to showing how the idea of recognition is more closely connected with redistribution than is often assumed to be the case. In criticising Axel Honneth's account, she highlights how a politics of recognition implies and relies upon a certain understanding of redistribution as a partner in the same 'two-dimensional' conception of justice.[45]

Similar points are made by Bhikhu Parekh, albeit from a different perspective, when he asserts that 'the politics of recognition remains impotent unless it is embedded in the politics of redistribution'.[46] An important concern of his is to defend the idea that cultural injustice among and between citizens and groups (as distinct from the state-centred locus of justice and injustice that redistributive politics might tend to focus on) is of great significance. Parekh is of the opinion that the traditional preoccupation with a 'statist view' of justice has limited its own vision and scope in its disregard for the vital experiences of injustice that are suffered in the realm of inter-subjective relations. And so, while the emphases and preoccupations of their positions differ, Parekh, like Fraser, argues that both recognition and redistribution must be understood and deployed in tandem.

Misrecognition as a motivator for political agency

Another important factor to consider when discussing the theoretical foundations for Muslim political agency as a community in Britain is the notion of misrecognition, sometimes described as the 'sister concept' of recognition.[47] The experience of misrecognition for Muslims in the UK has been portrayed by Wendy Martineau as

> (having) to do not with overt forms of discrimination or prejudice that lead to explicit claims-making but involves a more subtle form by which the dominant social imaginary constructs some citizens' degree of 'belonging' in society as more complete than others, and that places subtle restrictions on some people's ability to participate equally in society.[48]

By this line of argument, the Equality Gap would not only be based on claims-making and actual changes to the law, but also a subtler complaint of misrecognition. Martineau follows Taylor, Honneth and other recognition theorists in arguing that misrecognition occurs as a failure in the 'communication of meanings' between 'ordinary agents'. This 'partial non-communication' is what causes a polarisation between cultural identities and can give way to a sense of conflict, as well as breeding feelings of defensiveness by those groups who feel that they are under attack. The impact of these processes leads to the oppression of the less-powerful cultural group by the one wielding more power, as exemplified by the feelings of acute powerlessness which, as I describe above, drove Muslim protesters to burn *The Satanic Verses* during the height of their frustration at the impasse they were experiencing with the British government and the disdain with which the media were treating their anguish.

Proponents of a Muslim identity politics, especially of the sort that emerged in the latter part of the twentieth century, would most likely have differed with Martineau on the appropriate solution to the problems caused by misrecognition. Martineau is wary of settling for a recognition of cultural identities as a solution to the harms caused by misrecognition, since 'conceiving multicultural recognition in terms of the affirmative recognition of identities both detracts attention away from the processes that produce misrecognition and may in fact be unhelpful in rectifying this'.[49] Instead she favours a 'hermeneutic approach' – one where calls for recognition are viewed within the context of the very struggles for recognition that are taking place. This, she contends, will allow for greater dialogue to take place, both between different groups (the majority and the minority/ies), as well as 'minority voices *within* minorities',[50] voices that can easily be drowned out or sidelined under the type of system that typically relies on 'community leaders' to represent the interests of minority groups.[51]

In contrast, the early pioneers of contemporary Muslim identity politics were very keen on securing group rights and exemptions, in addition, of course, to securing even-handed legal treatment when it came to recourse to certain legislation – specifically blasphemy and anti-discrimination legislation. This approach was primarily about group recognition. Muslim identity politics in Britain grew and evolved around a yearning to make Muslims 'count', calling for 'affirmative recognition' rather than a desire to 'fuse cultural horizons'.[52] Such an approach was in no small part influenced by the precedents that had been set by pre-existing models for identity politics, notably the arena of race relations and the representation of the British Jewish community. Successive governments have also themselves actively encouraged the 'affirmative recognition' model for their official dealings with minority groups.[53]

There are merits to Martineau's critique. Detractors of multi-culturalism policy often draw attention to the 'competition' for recognition and resources that it allegedly breeds.[54] By focusing on what she sees as the root causes of misrecognition – divergence and poor communication between different 'cultural horizons' – it would seem that, while Martineau does not rule out a place for recognition, her approach would at least lead towards a viable solution. In doing so, she theoretically avoids a descent into Nancy Fraser's 'practical recognition-effect',[55] where an official encouragement of individuals to self-identify with a group leads to a continual clamouring of groups, and groups within groups, for some elusive ideal of equal recognition, thus creating something of a self-perpetuating cycle that is never truly satisfied.

With respect to the specific case of Muslim identity politics in Britain, I contend that affirmative recognition on its own will not provide an adequately robust solution to the issues at the heart of Muslim political engagement. Martineau's notion of 'fusing horizons' offers a helpful and more nuanced way forward, and I argue that a combination of both can provide a chance for genuine progress. Having said this, there are other compelling reasons why there remains room for the continuation of a Muslim politics of identity, albeit in a revised form of the one that we have come to know over recent decades.

IDENTITY POLITICS – DEFINITION, THEORY AND PRACTICE

The term 'identity politics' has come to signify any political participation that is based around the self-interest, or the specific perspective, of a particular group within society. Usually this group will be a minority, or one that has suffered (or continues to suffer) particular injustice or inequality. Examples include disability, ethnicity, gender, race, religion and sexual orientation. Historically, the second half of the twentieth century has witnessed successive waves of political movements seeking to rectify injustices that had been suffered by disadvantaged or minority groups.[56] These have given rise to the practice of identity politics in various wide-ranging formats across liberal democracies, where it is sought to remedy perceived injustices or disadvantages, often through challenging the dominant culture's account of the inferiority of the identity in question, and redefining it on its own terms, often through raising consciousness within the various communities associated with the identity. Political claims are put forward to the state, proposing remedial measures to secure equality and tackle disadvantage. Alternative methods of campaigning and political action have also been pursued. The development of liberal democracies in modern times has been credited with enabling the rise of identity politics, in the sense that it provides individuals with the opportunity to freely group with those who share their identities and collectively put forward their claims.[57] However, proponents of identity politics have also criticised liberal democracy as being incapable of catering sufficiently to identity politics. This is because they have tended to be organised around a system of political parties, interest groups and lobbies that individuals can join or leave at will, rather than identity groups, for which membership is very often a fact of birth. Moreover, the conventional style adopted by liberal democracies in respect of interest groups, lobbies and political parties can easily overlook and thus exclude marginalised or minority (identity) groups, thus perpetuating their marginalisation and not allowing their minority views or preferences to be heard.[58]

CHAPTER 3

The Birth of Modern British Muslim Identity Politics: Identity Preservation in the 1960s–1980s

Some of the earliest examples of political awareness and organising among Muslims in the UK during the late nineteenth and early twentieth century show us that there was a varied degree of political activity encompassing individuals as well as institutions and communities. Here I discuss how this activism was to set the scene for the growth of centralised Muslim identity politics. I then analyse the history and development of race identity politics, alongside that of the UK's race relations strategy, following important features of their evolution over the second half of the twentieth century. Finally, after highlighting the major legal and institutional achievements that were made in measures to support race equality and outlawing race discrimination, I consider the later genesis and development of a distinct Muslim identity politics, which had been previously subsumed under the broad categories of 'race' and 'ethnicity'.[1] It wasn't until the 1980s, with the emergence of local Muslim campaigns and identity-focused organisations, that this began to be vigorously challenged and Muslim-specific demands were more assertively articulated.

A concern with 'cultural' identity preservation began to gain momentum in the early 1970s with the growth and development of community organisations, and reached a major watershed with the outbreak of the Rushdie Affair in 1988. With the increased permanence of their settlement, the identity politics of British Muslims came to mature, and underwent a process of refinement in terms of their attitudes and priorities. There was a notable growth and development of an array of different identity-focused Muslim community organisations from the 1960s through to the 1980s and beyond. These reflected and often replicated the spectrum of religious tendencies that existed in the 'Muslim world', and were responsible for a wave of community organising that was focused primarily on the preservation and revival of religious identity among Britain's Muslims. This was as distinct from previous efforts, which had been much more preoccupied with laying practical foundations for settlement and community infrastructure.

Another factor influencing developments in Muslim identity politics was the antecedent emergence of a (race-focused) equalities agenda, and the founding of an established place for multiculturalism in national politics and policy-making. Using case studies to illustrate how the trajectory of Muslim identity politics took its course, I will show how the race relations agenda paved the way for the shape that Muslim identity politics was to take.

MUSLIMS, IDENTITY AND 'BRITISHNESS'

In more recent decades, the idea of a British Islam has been highly topical, as Muslim communities of immigrant heritage have entered into their third and fourth generations, and public debates around loyalty, identity and integration have become more and more pervasive. Accompanying the increasing longevity of UK Muslim communal organisations, there was an ongoing evolution of structures, discourses and trends across social and political spectra. This, coupled with both local and international political priorities around terrorism and security, gave the impetus for a vocal, more mainstream conversation on British Islam greater urgency. Many British Muslim communities and organisations have tended to reflect religious, social, cultural and political trends from 'back home' – in some cases imitating their foreign forebears in structure, politics, language, aims and objectives. Inextricable from this phase was the experience of identity formation, which crucially included coming to terms with a new context and climate, an experience which is undoubtedly shared by all immigrant communities to some extent. The question of what to adopt from the cultural norms and values of the new home and what to retain from the immigrants' country of origin has, in no small part, fed into the evolution of conceptions around 'British Islam', in a way that in many respects has not been dissimilar to the experiences of other immigrant groups.[2]

An array of approaches and solutions to these questions has been evident from the diverse range of mosques, local and regional associations and then representative and advocacy bodies, the establishment of which began in earnest from the 1960s onwards, demonstrating how the notion of British Islam (just as the notion of 'Britishness' itself) is both broad and variable in its meanings and connotations.[3] This is not least because non-religious factors that feed into identity and self-perception have been and continue to be so varied. There have been several sketches of the range of Islamic groupings and socio-political trends in the UK (and, more generally, Europe).[4] Varying from the religiously ultra-conservative to the more liberal, and encompassing an innumerable range of sects and theological groups, political radicalism, extremism, passivity, and quietism, British Muslim self-identity has notoriously found it difficult to divorce itself from vestiges of overseas, 'back home' influences. This situation is only complicated by the fact that Islamic cultures and beliefs are understood and practiced in a multitude of different ways across the globe.

In analysing these influences, many will point to the 'South Asian factor', which I have alluded to in the previous chapter. However, there are also more 'generic' factors that have influenced a wider range of British Muslim communities – for instance, the fact that many have their origins in post-colonial nations in Africa and Asia where democratic government and civil society politics are present only in part, if at all, and very recently so at that. The replication of political trends that have emerged over recent decades in countries of origin has been another feature of this situation, whereby Islamist, tribal and theological shades of community organisation have all played a part in shaping opinion and preferences on the 'British Muslim street'. Philip Lewis illustrates this point well with his observation of a group of councillors in Birmingham who in 2001 were 'voted in on the back of a discrete Kashmiri political party'.[5] This was the People's Justice Party, which was originally formed to campaign for the release of political prisoners in Kashmir, but later took on local issues, appealing directly to the sizeable Kashmiri population in the city.

This debate and discovery associated with Britishness and British Islam is ongoing. Later chapters will hone in on chosen aspects of its evolution in much more detail, but for now it is necessary for there to be an appreciation of the complexity and intricacy that the matter has continued to involve over time, and how this has played out in the formative moments of an 'officially recognised' identity politics for British Muslims.

MUSLIMS IN 'PRE-MULTICULTURAL' BRITAIN

Although the most numerically significant waves of immigration that have gone on to form the UK's Muslim communities occurred during the mid-twentieth century's chain migration period of South Asians, these were by no means the first Muslim communities to settle and to publicly organise and identify themselves by their religious affiliation. Any history of Muslim presence in the British Isles will trace it back to at least 1,000 years prior to this, so it is worth looking first at some earlier examples of British Muslim identity politics.

Apart from *lascars* (maritime workers recruited on East India Company ships from the seventeenth century onwards), servants and members of Anglicising Indian elites settling in various parts of London, the UK's South Asian Muslim communities were also preceded during the nineteenth century by large numbers of Yemeni and Somali sailors who settled in areas such as South Shields in northern England and Cardiff in Wales.[6] These settlers differed from the post-World War II waves of immigrants in that many did not bring their wives and families over from their countries of origin. However, a sizeable proportion did marry or enter into relationships with locals,[7] and in this way families and communities came about. These new families and their children, who were of mixed race and culture, continued to experience difficulties in matters of social integration, acceptance and equality of treatment right through to the interwar period. This was partially due to factors of lesser economic and social class status, as well as outright racism and prejudice.[8] Efforts were made to organise communities together for cultural purposes, including cultural and religious activities for children. Where difficulties and discrimination were encountered in working conditions and other aspects of social life, efforts were made to organise and represent these communities, putting forward relevant complaints and demands.[9]

Mention must also be made of the Liverpool Muslim Institute and its founder, Abdullah (William) Quilliam. Founded in the late nineteenth century, Quilliam and his Institute engaged in numerous social and philanthropic works, including the establishment of schools, an orphanage, congregational religious services, and publishing a journal, *The Crescent*.[10] Quilliam's story is particularly interesting as his legacy has enjoyed longevity and a recent surge in interest.[11] Although some efforts have been made to portray Quilliam and his community of British Muslims as a historical model for an active yet quintessentially 'native' Islam, all evidence points to him and many of his contemporaries not only being highly politicised and overtly self-conscious about their identities as British Muslims, but also rather upfront about their not-so-'British' political views and affiliations.[12] Quilliam even fulfilled something of an ambassadorial role in his relations with the Ottoman Sultan as well as with dignitaries in various other Muslim lands, earning from the former the accolade of '*Shaykh ul Islam* of the British Isles'.

Other personalities included Lord Rowland Headley, who served as president of the British Muslim Society and who travelled for Hajj with an Egyptian delegation,[13] yet (perhaps understandably given his position in politics) was not as strident as Quilliam in his criticism of the Empire's overseas policies. Nonetheless, he did make representations to the government on behalf of British Muslims. In 1916 he petitioned Austin Chamberlain, the Secretary of State for India, requesting that a mosque be built in London 'at the country's expense … in memory of the Muslim soldiers who have died fighting for the Empire',[14] and later travelled to various Muslim countries seeking contributions and support towards the London Mosque Fund.

Abdullah Yusuf Ali, a lawyer in the Indian Civil Service (better known for his widely published English translation of the Qur'an) exemplifies a British Muslim whose political stance was one of almost unquestioning loyalty to the government and crown. A British subject (not a citizen), Yusuf Ali married and settled in England and maintained close ties with the establishment through correspondence and personal relationships with key figures. During World War I, his enthusiasm for assisting the war effort, and answering 'the call of the Empire',[15] was warmly and eagerly expressed. Indeed, his dedication was rewarded when he was later chosen on several occasions to join international government delegations and to represent the government (for instance, in a 1918 mission to Scandinavia and at the post-World War I Paris Peace Conference in 1919). Here and in several speeches and writings, Yusuf Ali expressed a reverential, and at times even jingoistic admiration and loyalty to the British Empire,[16] a stance that was unpalatable to many of his contemporaries, given misgivings among Muslims in Britain about supporting the war effort against the Ottoman Empire.[17]

During the interwar period, there were notable moments of significant political mobilisation among Muslim communities in other parts of the UK. Arab Muslim seamen in South Shields organised to protest against rife discrimination and vilification both from among co-workers, and the communities in which they lived. When the Muslim seamen regularly demanded representation within the National Union of Seamen, they were faced with refusal and the union indulged in further attacks using popular derogatory stereotypes to further victimise them.[18] Ali Said was one key figure who was vocal in making the case for the Arabs' 'right to employment on equal terms with white sailors'.[19] Facing similar challenges, Arab and Somali seamen in Cardiff also organised to campaign against racist discrimination and to demand equal treatment. Some Muslim seamen collaborated with other 'black' seamen, joining the Cardiff Coloured Seamen's Committee, and later the South Wales

Association for the Welfare of Coloured People. Others made representations from within Muslim or Somali groups such as the Islamia Allawia Friendly Society, holding public meetings and running poster campaigns.[20]

The above examples illustrate together how the existence of a self-ascribed, politically and socially active British Muslim identity dates back to the nineteenth and early twentieth centuries, and that the nature and form of their politics was remarkably varied, following no single pattern and reflecting the diversity of each of their other origins, affiliations and relationships both in Britain and abroad.

IDENTITY POLITICS, RACE RELATIONS POLICY AND EQUALITY IN THE UK

Politics of religious identity

It seems appropriate here to reiterate my understanding and usage of the term 'identity politics'.[21] It refers to the use of identity as a primary or defining characteristic for individuals or groups in the sphere of politics. It sees identity as a factor that is separate from self-interest when it comes to political negotiations[22] in its nature as an integral, or 'constitutive', aspect of a person's being.[23] Identity can also be considered as something worthy of special respect or recognition, either because it is an unchosen aspect of someone's existence (such as gender or race), or because it relates to conscientious decisions (such as religion) which are widely thought to deserve special respect due to the gravity and importance that they command. The obvious difference between these two descriptions is that, in the case of race and gender, disadvantage and discrimination experienced on account of these unchosen characteristics is, in the most part, more readily apparent and easier to prove. As for religion, there are both practical and theoretical obstacles that arise in the articulation of a politics of identity. Practically speaking, there is far greater room for debate as to where to set definitions and boundary lines. There are also a number of theoretical hurdles. Noteworthy among these are: firstly, the apparent paradox between a 'religious politics of identity' and the age-old liberal principle that conviction and belief should be firmly matters of choice, beyond official control or restriction,[24] be it by a state, or by group or community hierarchies that have often been observed to flourish and benefit from the cultivation of such politics.[25] Secondly, there is a subsequent question: granted that freedom of belief is to be considered as 'special', can the wider political community be required to assist a religious citizen in bearing any consequences of their belief – ones which prove particularly cumbersome against a backdrop of contrasting or opposing socio-political norms?[26]

Supporters of identity politics vary in the role that they see for it, ranging from those who envisage it to be of temporary necessity, until sufficient headway is made in rectifying present injustices, to those who look to an 'ideal of diversity',[27] where political recognition for identity is available.

Race relations policy in the 1960s and 1970s

The practical problem at the heart of the question of equality is that of how to facilitate a pluralist polity where the gradual establishment of minority groups of immigrant extraction has prompted a fresh look at existing political set-ups and raised questions as to how well they may or may not serve the cause of equality in this context. In the UK, it was this sort of concern that provided the decisive impetus to the development of a race relations strategy among Labour politicians during the late 1960s.[28] With the increasingly permanent settlement of the UK's African-Caribbean and South Asian communities, both regions formerly linked to the British Empire and now part of the Commonwealth,[29] the sentiment that policy needed to consider the implications of how these new communities and their members were to be best catered for by the state in view of the specific challenges of discrimination and inequality that they faced became more wide-spread and accepted.

It was in this spirit that the first race relations legislation was passed in 1965, in the wake of notable incidents of racial strife and heated public debate on matters of immigration and race relations. Central to the emerging race relations strategy during this 'liberal hour' of British politics was the increasingly apparent fact that contemporary legal and social norms did not make illegitimate the arbitrary differential treatment or discrimination against certain members of society on the basis of their race or ethnicity. As a result, the direction of policy development was deeply concerned with managing in tandem the two related challenges of immigration and of race relations. Both those on the left and on the right of British politics were increasingly aware of the need to rectify features of unfair differential treatment in each of these two areas.

As for immigration, there was by this point a clear sense that during the 1950s and 1960s there had passed unchallenged discrimination with respect to members of the 'New Commonwealth'. One illustration of this type of attitude was the visible use of the 'pressure to emigrate' argument in public (immigration) institutions, differentiating between white and non-white immigrants and suggesting that the latter were 'more likely' to utilise illegitimate methods of gaining entry into the UK on the basis of the greater political and economic incentives that they had to leave their home countries;[30] an argument which with time was acknowledged by both the political right and left to be indefensible. On the other hand, it was becoming much more widely felt that tangible measures needed to visibly be taken in order to minimise any possibility for social conflict or disturbances to public order. The development of a race relations strategy was to keep in check any potential threat of such disturbances to public order, with its goal of facilitating the integration of the newly arrived immigrant communities. An important factor for the achievement of these goals was to place some limit on immigration numbers, so as to allow already arrived new migrants the space to settle and establish some 'demographic stability', and to allow the majority the space and time to adjust. In this way, it was argued that conditions for more lasting integration of immigrants would be better facilitated.[31]

That instances of discrimination such as those mentioned above could (and did) pass unchallenged by the law was considered problematic, and is indeed problematic by the standards of the perspectives on equality discussed in Chapter 2. The professed aims and objectives of the race relations strategies that successive governments pursued naturally varied and fluctuated in their emphases, just as they were coloured by the perspectives of different key players and the prevalent tone, discourse and pressing issues of politics. Nonetheless, we can with some accuracy extract a sense for the main ideals that policy-makers argued they were working towards. Key to these ideals was the goal of *cohesion* in community relations,[32] and that of the *integration* of newly arrived minorities into the fabric and machinery of British politics and society.[33] In the articulation and understanding with which both of these goals were presented, the achievement of equality for individuals from the minority groups in question with those who were part of majorities in society was held as central, and legislation sought to lay down specific expectations and legal norms in this regard.[34]

It has been argued that much of this new political attitude to racism and discrimination was informed on one hand by successive Labour governments' concerns with the direction that the immigration debate was taking and their anxiety to be seen to be 'balancing' apprehensions on immigration that called for limits on it, with efforts to tackle racial discrimination.[35] Race relations were the subject of intense political and public attention during this period, as racism, biological or cultural, at various levels in British society in the 1950s and 1960s engendered resistance to it by those groups at the receiving end. Out of these antagonistic interactions emerged a certain kind of ethnic politics of identity. The outbreak of race riots in the Notting Hill area of London in 1958 only intensified racial tensions in the eyes of many.[36] By the 1970s, the Asian Youth Movements (AYMs) were in their heyday, and the radical politics they espoused in response to the daily experiences of institutional racism and street violence from the likes of the National Front faced by second generation British Asians grabbed national attention,[37] giving politicians no choice other than to make efforts to deal with some of the grievances that fuelled them.

The establishment of race relations legislation was one way of doing this, and the laws that were passed outlawed discrimination that had been occurring in areas of public life including education, employment, housing and public services, as well as covering incitement to racial hatred.[38] Such measures were not introduced all at once and there were several revisions to and developments of the initial Race Relations Act (1965), perhaps the most notable being the

1976 Race Relations Act, which established the Commission for Racial Equality (CRE). In the discussion that preceded the 1976 Act, the government made clear that its aims were achieving equality of opportunity and integration for the first generation ethnic minority immigrants to the UK as well as for their children, who as the second and third generations, it acknowledged, were facing challenges of their own, despite their having been born, brought up and educated in the UK.[39]

With this formalisation of race relations strategy through statute and the establishment of specialist institutions, UK equalities policy entered a new era. Whereas previously issues around race were largely only discussed in connection with immigration (and often negatively, in relation to concerns around immigration), this new era saw race relations and the tackling of discrimination emerge as a permanent and pressing domestic issue. This development was paralleled by a growth in the number and prominence of civil society and campaign groups with race at the heart of their agendas. While many of these groups developed organically out of genuinely held experiences of prejudice and discrimination that existed at a grass roots level in their respective communities, it can also be observed that they could not but have been influenced and encouraged, at least in the way that they were framed, by the pursuance of a race relations strategy in government circles.

Thus began the development of race identity politics in government-community relations. It was recognised by actors on both sides that, up until this point, little had been done to incorporate the newly settled communities of the UK into the nation's political structures and public life, and many people attributed the realities of discrimination and inequality among citizens to this absence.[40] By this argument, the equality of citizens from minority groups remained only a distant aspiration so long as they could still legally suffer on one hand from the effects of prejudice and discrimination in areas of public life (such as allocation and treatment in employment and housing) and, on the other, were structurally disadvantaged when it came to engagement with political institutions and articulating their viewpoints and concerns on a par with other citizens who 'fitted' much more easily into the majority background culture and norms. The unacceptability of the first of these is hardly a matter of much disagreement among theorists – this sort of discrimination is unjustifiable by any sound conception of equality. As for the second, the arguments of recognition theorists would strongly advocate that measures should be taken to equalise conditions and to enable minorities in their civic participation by means of their representation or wider 'presence'. In this light, the proactive efforts of government to invest energy and resources into the development of race relations and integration policy was seen as commendable – since it signified a deliberate step towards recognising and thus assisting otherwise unjustifiably disadvantaged sections of society in attaining parity with a majority who are, by default, in a more advantaged position when it comes to articulating their concerns and engaging with the state and its related institutions.[41]

A changed political agenda for equality

Race identity politics represented a key milestone on the path towards equality for newly arrived minorities in the UK. The placing of race relations firmly on the political agenda had the trickle-down effect of setting standards and influencing a 'culture change' in national government across the board as well as local government in a way that meant that racial discrimination could no longer be overlooked, and that concerted efforts were made to assess the exclusion of minority communities (either in presence or in perspective) from the political arena, since this was deemed to be a contributory factor to inequality, or at least a reason for the belated action from authorities to tackle it. It was an evolving field, and policy developed over time in its scope and the extent to which it protected minorities from discrimination. In the 1960s, the initiation of a race relations strategy was considered a milestone in itself. Four decades later, the Race Relations Amendment Act of 2000, which followed the 1999 Macpherson Report,[42] was hailed as a landmark step forward, significantly in its singling out of 'institutional racism' as a major obstacle to the realisation of equality for minorities. This was defined as the collective failure of an organisation to provide an appropriate and professional service to people because of their colour, culture or ethnic origin. It can be seen or detected in processes, attitudes and behaviour which amount to discrimination through unwitting prejudice, ignorance, thoughtlessness and racial stereotyping.[43]

The significance of this definition and its application to the Metropolitan Police in the wake of the report cannot be overstated. For the first time, a major state institution was taken to task for discriminating against minorities, and made to bear collective responsibility, thus preventing shortcomings from being blamed on a few 'bad apples'. This acknowledgement is credited with precipitating a cultural shift within the police service,[44] as well as providing strong grounds for accountability and criticism in the future. To what extent this cultural shift has actually taken place remains questionable given the more recent media disclosures regarding the efforts of Metropolitan Police officers at concealment of information regarding their 'spying' on Stephen Lawrence's family and friends.[45]

The route of multiculturalism that Britain followed was one which differed from the approach of some of its neighbours on the continent. France during this time (and enduringly) placed emphasis on the integration of minorities into a more rigid conception of a national culture. In the UK, the race relations agenda had as its goal a 'multicultural nationalism'.[46] This is to say, a vision of a nation where a common understanding of civic rights and responsibilities and an idea of a shared future would keep the nation together.

Once the race relations agenda had become an established part of the political arena, it set a precedent, almost as a model for community–government/establishment relations – one against which all future endeavours in addressing equality for minority communities would frame their claims. Once certain standards of protection from discrimination and equal treatment became established for racial/ethnic minorities, future claims for equality for religious minority groups (namely Muslims) were able to ground their arguments not just in the 'difference/recognition' philosophical justifications that have been discussed, but also more practically in the argument for parity of treatment with other minorities, *within* this model of equalities strategy that was being developed.

MUSLIMS AND IDENTITY POLITICS – FROM SUBSISTENCE TO THE LONGER VIEW

The first consistent and sizeable waves of immigration to Britain from Muslim-majority countries began in the postwar period, during the 1950s and 1960s, and included groups of young, male, manual labourers from the Yemen and the Indian subcontinent who, after initially coming over to work, settled in the UK as economic migrants. In time, there grew a trend of chain migration as these first migrants were joined by their families and began to establish themselves more permanently. For these early communities, the preoccupation was to secure the basic necessities of life, such as a steady income and a roof over their heads. Settling in industrial towns or the inner-city areas of larger cities, many first-generation immigrants maintained links with their countries of origin, through family members that had remained to whom they might pay visits or send remittances. But also through the fairly concentrated settlement patterns that they had happened to follow upon immigration, whereby whole sections of communities from 'back home' settled in close proximity to one another, sometimes in near-replication of their original neighbourhoods.

At this stage, interaction for these early communities[47] with the public sphere was limited in a large part to the relevant authorities and institutions providing for the needs of work and very basic housing.[48] Permanence of settlement did not feature strongly in the initial aspirations of these first migrants. Concurrently, on the part of the 'host' authorities and the state, there is little to suggest much expectation that these new immigrants would eventually settle permanently, or, if they did, that much would be needed in the way of discussion regarding whether any strategy of integration might be required, what shape it should take and how it might be pursued. The underlying assumption was that their stay in the UK would be a temporary one. This was often expressed explicitly, and certainly implicitly, in the notable sparseness of any policy attempts to address the needs of these growing Muslim communities,[49] or any serious efforts to study how things might progress into the long term. Indeed, there are indications that in contrast to other large European states which were also in receipt of Muslim immigrant workers during this period,[50] no British efforts were made to encourage it. On the contrary, there were expressions of hostility and unease in Whitehall, from both Labour and Conservative administrations regarding this latest wave of non-white immigration.[51]

This is not to say that political interaction and engagement on the part of these emerging communities were entirely absent. A number of concerted campaigns are recorded as having taken place, which sought to highlight discrimination and unfair disadvantage that existed in areas such as employment and housing conditions, even from as far back as the early twentieth century.[52] In addition to this, there were also a wide range of Muslim personalities who achieved considerable and often distinguished successes in public life and public service as well as in establishing business and professional ventures, quite often attaining consultative status and maintaining good relationships with key sections of government and the establishment. However, noteworthy as these advances were, they should nonetheless be differentiated from the type of identity politics that are the concern of the discussion at hand. The main difference being that they were conducted largely on a more localised, or micro-political level,[53] whereas Muslim community organisation in the later twentieth century featured a growth in the focus on macro-politics.

Indeed, by the mid-late twentieth century, macro-politics became of increasing importance. The inevitable questions of longer-term self-preservation arose, and these went hand-in-hand with instinctive concerns over how to secure interests that appeared not to be recognised by a state which was only belatedly coming to appreciate the permanence of its Muslim population. As we have seen, earlier efforts by the state to accommodate permanent settlement of new communities, through race relations legislation or through political inclusion initiatives, were framed primarily in ethnic terms. These did not preclude the palpable feeling among a growing number of

Muslims that an Islamic identity of some kind was worth cultivating and preserving as a positive value and a key component of identity and lifestyle. There was often some overlap between culture and religion, but the increasing attention given towards preserving religious identity and heritage did feature to some noticeable degree even at the earliest stages of settlement, with importance being attached to the development of makeshift mosques and prayer rooms as well as arrangements for the *halal* slaughter of meat as possibly the two most noticeable of Muslim communal organising efforts during this time.[54] During the later decades, as priorities began to shift, one key area where micro-level Muslim identity politics was initially most conspicuously played out on the ground was that of education.

Education and local Muslim identity politics: two Bradford case-studies

So the entry of these Muslim communities (as 'Muslims') into the political 'public sphere' was in effect a matter of circumstance rather than any intricately planned and executed strategy. One important factor in propelling this development forward was the emergence of the second generation, who in their own right markedly modified the scale, type and urgency of the primary concerns that their parents had held as newcomers to the UK. Children went to school and thus interacted with the 'mainstream' in ways that their parents may not have done. Other spheres of interaction that were necessarily entered into with the arrival and growth of families included the healthcare system and other public services. This demographic development coupled with the belated realisation and acceptance by many that they were now to be permanent residents of the UK led to a shift in the self-perception and, in turn, the aspirations of these communities. Whereas the first wave of worker-immigrants might have been content with the basic essentials of working and living, these new families now had changed priorities and sought to consolidate communities and consider their long-term survival in their new home.

This was evidenced by the prevalence of education and education-related issues as the centre of Muslim political activism.

The first coordinated efforts that were organised in this respect began during the 1960s. The Muslim Educational Trust (MET) was set up in 1966, and based in London to represent and cater for Muslim needs in national educational matters and curricula, as well as in areas of schooling where norms, practices and expectations were considered to pose difficulties or additional hurdles for observant Muslims. This ranged from providing guidance to parents on their rights in matters where there was some cultural apprehension,[55] to the production of textbooks and school resources on Islam and Muslims that remain in use to this day.[56] Increasingly emotive areas of contention relating to the education and school system included collective religious worship, physical and religious education, the provision of *halal* food, school uniform regulations and, of course, faith schools for Muslims. That these issues attracted sufficient attention and led to advocacy bodies being determined to coordinate and develop a longer-term vision is evidence of the progressively changing mindset and aspirations within Britain's Muslim communities.

Two examples can be used to illustrate that this heightened level of commitment to educational issues signified a shift in vision and priorities. The first is that of the Bradford Muslim Parents Association (BMPA), which, along with the MET, in 1974 fronted the campaign against the closure of Bradford's last remaining girls-only secondary school.[57] This campaign was prominently identified in the press with the case of an Abdullah Patel, who withdrew his teenage daughter from full-time education at the co-educational school that she was allocated to, in protest, and out of religious conviction that 'When a Muslim girl reaches puberty, she is not allowed to mix with males other than close relatives'. Both the understanding of the cause in question and the style of discourse that was used by the BMPA to articulate their position were essentially framed by an idea of an 'Islamic' culture and identity – one which, in this context, it was imperative to protect and nurture as far as possible in the younger generation. Moreover, the very idea of a 'Muslim community', although by no means new,[58] was being used to mobilise a fresh and enthusiastic new constituency that was increasingly aware of the potency of manpower that it had the potential to tap into. This notion was to prove both necessary and instrumental in shoring up legitimacy for both the existence of Muslim representative and lobby bodies, and for the claims that they argued for.

Later on, in 1984, the Honeyford Affair also sparked off heated campaigning and activism as an expression of strongly felt views on education and schools from Muslim parents. This widely reported affair involved Ray Honeyford, the head teacher of Drummond Middle School in Bradford, a school attended overwhelmingly by Muslim pupils. His writings on race and education, most prominently those in the right-wing *Salisbury Review*, took a highly critical position on what he perceived as regressive accommodations that were being made in Bradford schools towards large Asian Muslim populations, including the provision of *halal* meat in school meals, religious instruction by Muslim leaders, as well as demands from the BMPA for single-sex schools and the conversion of five state schools into Muslim voluntary-aided schools.[59]

Honeyford's writings provoked heated protest and local unrest among parents and the community, in response to his criticism of unfair 'accommodations' that were being made for Muslim and Asian children in schools and more generally of what he clearly saw as backward and intrinsically inferior immigrant cultures.[60] With Honeyford seen to be personifying opposition to the very concerns that many Muslims had for their children in the education system, the level of organised and vocal objection to his continued position as headmaster – through political campaigns in school and local government, boycotts, picketing and the media – was telling of a confident solidarity in the community that had found cause in defending and nurturing what were understood to be Islamic aspects of identity that were felt to be under threat, either through external hostility (as with Honeyford) or through their own previous lack of adequate attention to its preservation. Significantly, one of the leading opposition groups to Honeyford was the Bradford Council of Mosques, which claimed wide representation of the city's Muslim population and commanded a certain 'pressure group' authority, and the campaign was also supported by the (Muslim) Lord Mayor of Bradford, Muhammad Ajeeb. The campaign grew quickly, attracting some support from other Asian and ethnic minorities, but also drawing some opposition, to the extent that it soon dominated much of Bradford local politics and gained significant coverage in the national mainstream media, including a BBC Panorama documentary. Honeyford's critics accused him of 'cultural chauvinism', and mobilised parent governors at the school, organised petitions, and withdrew their children. Honeyford, on the other hand, protested that his free speech was being curtailed and strongly resisted calls to resign.[61] By the close of 1985, Honeyford had been suspended, with the whole episode turning him into something of a martyr for free speech in the eyes of his supporters,[62] and while it is not clear that the Muslim campaigners considered the Honeyford Affair in quite the same light, the controversy was definitely a major demonstration of the organising power that Muslim identity politics could have, and in this sense it could be considered to have been a pre-cursor to the Rushdie Affair.

With the state also waking up to the new multicultural realities in the country's population, a revision of aspects of the education system was ushered in via the Swann Report of 1985. Boldly entitled 'Education for All', it looked (among other things) into the various challenges relating to religious, cultural and linguistic diversity in schools, and made recommendations as to which avenues would be most appropriate for schools and government to pursue. Among the increasingly customary 'Muslim community responses' that were put forward to the report's findings by bodies such as the Muslim Educational Trust and the Union of Muslim Organisations, there was a clear sense that the report had hardly gone far enough. There was consternation regarding a lack of uptake on requests for Islamic religious instruction for Muslim pupils and 'official' adjustments to uniform.[63] This is not to mention the growing momentum in calls for the establishment of government-funded Muslim faith schools – the earliest of which seems to have come in 1975, in Bradford.[64] However, there was progress in that the report itself was commissioned, and that it seriously considered these issues, leaving (at least overtly) flexible recommendations for community cooperation and dialogue with schools and for community use of school buildings out of school hours for cultural or religious supplementary education. This was a sure sign that the landscape was beginning to change and that Muslim community groups were making some, even if minimal, headway as recognised interlocutors and stakeholders in the formulation of policy.

Parallel to developments in local campaigning for 'Muslim' issues, attempts were also being made to establish unity organisations with a national focus that sought to bring together Muslims from across the UK, and to represent them. At the same time, Islamic movements with their origins in the Muslim world began to build a visible UK presence. In seeking to cater to their members who had by now settled with their families in the UK, they were significantly concerned with the notion of preserving and promoting Muslim identity, as they understood it. In the remainder of this section, I look at these two developments in further detail.

In search of unity in the 1960s and 1970s

Formally established in 1963, the Federation of Student Islamic Societies in the UK and Ireland (FOSIS) lays claim to being the oldest continuously established British Muslim community organisation. Although its focus was on unity of student bodies, in its earlier years FOSIS also fulfilled the role of voicing community concerns and aspirations in a range of forums. The demographics of Muslim students in Britain during the 1960s and 1970s contrasted with the present day in that a far greater proportion of them were foreign students.[65] Some of these made their stay in the UK temporary, whilst others eventually chose to settle with their families. There was also the notable difference of an older age profile, since many were postgraduate students who had already completed preliminary degrees. These characteristics had an impact on the key priorities and concerns of the organisation. Finally, the fact that FOSIS was the main and only national Muslim community organisation in Britain during this early period meant that inevitably there were non-student individuals who got involved, if only for the lack of other available avenues towards community service and activism.

The early FOSIS grappled with issues such as the preservation of Islamic culture in a 'hostile' and 'permissive' environment.[66] A survey of speeches from the organisation's annual conferences as well as articles from its magazine, *The Muslim*, offers an insight into some of the issues with which FOSIS membership were preoccupied. Among the most popular themes was that of an 'Islamic movement', which, although rarely defined, was understood to imply international efforts to establish Islamic governments in the Muslim world, or at the least to oppose the various post-colonial dictatorial regimes in the region which were largely seen as being puppets of 'the West'. Additionally, the Islamic education and upbringing of children[67] and the role of women were occasionally discussed in its publications, with attitudes tellingly in favour of the more 'traditional' roles for men and women.[68]

Thus, priorities that were advocated in speeches and articles included the Islamic education of children and the preservation of culture and religious values. There were also examples of political activism and efforts at representing the community's demands at times when it was felt that it had been slighted. In 1970, FOSIS along with others organised a protest march to Trafalgar Square, objecting to an offensive portrayal of the Prophet Muhammad in an article in *The Times* newspaper.[69]

FOSIS maintained working links with a range of community initiatives that were on the increase during this period. These included the Muslim Students Society, the UK Islamic Mission and the London Islamic Circle, amongst others. Additionally, FOSIS engaged in criticism of what it perceived to be corruption and indolence on the part of out of touch community leaders – a key example being the London Central Mosque. The Mosque was a regular target in the Federation's publications, and its director and trustees were chastised for being aloof towards the community's needs and aspirations. Calls were regularly made for the replacement of its foreign-appointed staff with people who were actively involved in the community's day-to-day life, who would be able to run the mosque's affairs with more faithful reference to the community's needs and aspirations.

Perhaps the earliest effort at creating a comprehensive nationwide platform for unity and representation, the UMO was originally set up in 1970 by Dr Syed Aziz Pasha, a lawyer of Indian origins. This was the first organisation of its kind in bringing together Muslim bodies from a range of focuses and geographical bases.[70] It appears to have been inspired by, or at least had some very initial involvement from, diplomatic personalities, specifically the Egyptian government and its diplomatic representatives in the UK, who were reportedly very keen to get some sort of unifying project off the ground.[71] However, it was not long before Dr Pasha himself firmly took the reins of the organisation, and he was to dominate it for the next four decades.

As an idea, it appears to have been fairly advanced thinking for its time. Indeed, it has been described as 'premature' by some, a nod to the limited enthusiasm that the organisation received from *within* the Muslim community.[72] The UMO, and specifically Dr Pasha, tirelessly pushed for a 'Muslim Bill of Rights' throughout the 1970s and 1980s, at a time when many other British Muslim organisations were preoccupied by foreign Islamist causes or at least substantially influenced by personalities from abroad.

However, despite its comparative foresight, sources suggest that the UMO made very limited headway – even at two-and-a-half decades old, it seemed to have made little progress in bringing together any significant range of community efforts. Its main campaign causes were very slow to progress during this time period, indicating that its achievements were scarce. For example, the organisation's Silver Jubilee publication showcases the highlights of its first 25 years. The section on 'national issues' includes a campaign agenda with priority issues on which the UMO sought to lobby government and the main political parties. A 1979 letter sent to the leaders of all main parties outlines this agenda in the run-up to the general election – a similar letter was circulated before the 1983 election with practically identical wording and contents to the 1979 letter – giving the impression that achievements during the intervening period had been too few to mention.[73]

By the 1990s, the UMO had demonstrated consistency and commitment through its regular community activities, which included conferences, youth excursions, celebrations of *eid* and *milad ul nabi* (the Prophet Muhammad's birthday), all of which took place annually. On the political engagement front its work also continued, with the most persistent campaign issue being a call for the application of Muslim family law as an option for British Muslims, as well as provisions for exemptions in matters of religious practice or sensitivity at school and the workplace.[74] Such representations were regularly rejected by the government officials and political figures to whom they were addressed, often on the grounds that they were unreasonable demands and a call for some sort of exceptional or separate treatment for Muslims.[75]

Thus the UMO's potential to make progress in the political arena was marred by the limited scope of its appeal and outreach both within the various Muslim communities and towards government itself. Heavily dominated by the personality of Dr Pasha, there was little opportunity for the engagement of others beyond a small circle of individuals. Therefore, the organisation's priorities and strategy were rarely revised, and often repetitive. Consequently, it became gradually clear that government officials and civil servants were seeking to build relations with a more contemporary, dynamic representative body that was more attuned to the grass roots.

ORGANISING TO PRESERVE AND PROMOTE IDENTITY

In addition to the above-mentioned locally based campaigns, and early initiatives to unite and represent Muslims on an official level, there was also an increasing number of organisations established at grass-roots level, for whom Muslim identity was a central focus. These were without exception organisations that were heavily influenced, if not directly linked with, Islamic political movements abroad, specifically in South Asia, and also in the Middle East. While they were not set up to *formally* represent Muslims as such, in the same way that the UMO or even FOSIS did, they did share a common preoccupation with Muslim identity, and with preserving it (especially among the younger generations), as well as promoting it (in the form of *da'wa*, the evangelical call to Islam). In doing so, several of these groups did occasionally venture into the field of political representation, even though this was not their primary or main purpose. When British Muslim 'umbrella' organisations developed in the late 1980s and the late 1990s respectively (see Chapter 4), a great many of these Muslim community organisations threw their weight behind them, recognising the benefits of collective representation and a unified voice to the furtherance of claims-making and engagement with the government. Moreover, many individuals from these various organisations later graduated to hold leading roles in the MCB, having been primed through their involvement with several of these community organisations to then take on positions of communal leadership and representation.

Transnational Islamist movements, their UK branches and offshoots

A number of movements had been established in the post-colonial Muslim world to address what was felt to be a decline in the proper understanding and practice of faith.[76] There were variations between them, but what they shared in common was an understanding that the faith of Islam and Muslim identity deserved, indeed demanded, a far greater centrality to society and everyday life than they were being afforded. For purposes of clarity and space, I group them into three very broad categories: those which had minimal political engagement (puritanical), those which sought to be actively engaged in the existing political system (reformist), and finally those wanting to set up a separate or alternative political system (radical). Sadek Hamid has conducted a useful illustration (and more elaborate mapping) of the various Muslim organisations in Britain, applying to them a typology set by Tariq Ramadan to reflect the spectrum of tendencies within contemporary Islamic activism.[77] Following Ramadan, he places contemporary Muslim organisations under six categories: *salafi* literalism, scholastic traditionalism, political *salafi* literalism, *salafi* reformism, Sufism and liberal rational reformism. While Hamid's analysis is of the contemporary landscape of British Muslim organisations, many of the groups he assesses were established during the period under discussion (1960s–1980s), hence it is useful to use his application as a starting point. I reproduce an adaptation of his visual representation of it here, for ease of reference. Hamid's analysis[78] can be roughly correlated to my three broad categories of political engagement, and I demonstrate this in Figures 1 and 2.[79] However, it is important to point out that these classifications are not discrete, and that within these broad categories, there were cases of overlap, for instance, where certain puritanical organisations adopted radical methods or terminologies, as well as more intricate distinctions and differences within the broad categories.

Puritanical – minimal political engagement

Those which I class as puritanical felt that for many Muslims the understanding of piety had lapsed into a 'blind' adherence to rituals and cultural practices from which the faith of Islam needed to be 'purified'. These included the Wahhabi movement of Saudi Arabia, which was at the forefront of modern Salafism. Salafism calls for a return to the two primary sources of Islam, the Qur'an and the Sunnah, and claims to follow *al salaf al salih*, the 'pious predecessors', the earliest three generations of Muslims, whom they consider to have practiced an Islam that was as yet uncorrupted by cultural influences, in particular what was viewed as innovation and excess in the area of spirituality. In the UK, the pre-eminent *salafi* organisation was JIMAS (*Jam'iyat Ihya Minhaj Sunnah wal jama'a*), which translates to The Society for the Revival of the Prophetic Way. It was founded and led by Manwar Ali in 1984 (throughout the 1980s and 1990s he was more commonly known by his *kunya*, Abu Muntasir) and for the best part of a decade could claim to be the hub of Salafism in the UK.[80] Taking off from foundations which had been laid by the Ahle Hadith movement,[81] JIMAS attracted and brought together the younger generations of British Muslims who were drawn to the same theological positions. Salafism was defined by a 'back-to-basics' approach to religious practice and an ideal of Islam that was unadulterated by 'innovation' such as the practice of following a *madhab* (Islamic jurisprudential school of thought),[82] as well as a preference for stricter understandings of Islamic practice. For example, some Salafis continued to consider music, various art forms and even photography or filming to be forbidden in Islam. But JIMAS were keen to make their discourse more relevant to the UK, for instance by adopting the English language in their meetings rather than Urdu, which had been preferred by their elders.[83] JIMAS attracted many of the British Muslims who had studied at the Islamic University in Medina, and through this, firmly established a direct channel from the UK to Saudi state-sponsored theology in the form of heavily subsidised publications, religious preachers, and ultimately funding for mosques.[84] This subsidisation of institutions, publications and preachers helped the influence of JIMAS and *salafi* thought to reach far wider audiences than their limited numbers would otherwise have allowed.[85]

From 1995, schisms began to emerge within JIMAS, reflecting ongoing factionalism among Salafis in the Gulf region, and this led to the formation of breakaway groups.[86] The most prominent of these was the Organisation of Ahl asSunnah Islamic Societies (OASIS), led by the Birmingham based Abu Khadeejah (Abdul Wahid).[87] OASIS took to siding with the official line of Saudi government scholars — loath to criticise corrupt regimes in the Muslim world, it promoted instead political quietism in the name of 'loyalty' to the Muslim ruler. They argued that there was a more pressing need to correct 'deviant' beliefs and practices among Muslims that were rooted in culture, rather than to call for political reform. This led to their being dubbed rather dismissively 'Saudi Salafis' or 'Super Salafis' by their opponents.[88] Notwithstanding this criticism, 'Saudi Salafis' have also been credited with running important local community projects that have challenged the radicalisation narrative of Al Qaeda and drawn vulnerable youth away from it.[89] This is a feature that is shared with some Islamist groups,[90] and shows that while general theological and political trends can be delineated within British Muslim communities, they are not discrete and, just as there can be overlaps among them, there can also be political contestations within them.

Another trend that also placed emphasis on puritanism as well as scholarship was the *Deobandi* tradition. With its origins in Indian religious seminaries, it came to be represented among Gujarati Indian communities in the UK by the *Tablighi Jamaat* (TJ) movement.[91]

The *Deobandis* eschewed what they considered to be excessive and innovative devotional practices favoured by the *Barelwi* tradition, a South Asian form of popular Sufism which placed great emphasis on the performance of traditional customs and rituals as well as the reverence for saints. It was a religious missionary movement, which invested a great deal of resources into developing religious training through schools and seminaries (*Darul Ulooms*), which have gone on to graduate probably the most consistent stream of British-trained imams and religious leaders. Among the more prominent of these have been Shaykh Abu Yusuf Riyadh ul Haq, one-time Imam of Birmingham Central Mosque and currently director of Al-Kawthar Academy in the same city; Mufti Muhammad ibn Adam al-Kawthari, who runs Daruliftaa (the Institute of Islamic Jurisprudence) in Leicester, as well as Shaykh Ibrahim Mogra, a Leicester imam, veteran interfaith activist and previous Assistant Secretary General of the MCB.

Reformist – active engagement in existing political structures

The reformist strand owes its origins and inspiration overwhelmingly to *Jamaat-e-Islami* (JI), a major reformist Islamist movement in the Indian subcontinent.[92] JI followers were critical of weak political stances taken by 'puppet' leaders who had been installed or propped up by the Western colonial powers, and thus called for Islamically inspired political reform. They also engaged in Islamically inspired social welfare schemes with the aim of encouraging people to see religion as a key aspect of their identity which could give meaning and solutions to everyday challenges and issues. Members of the JI who had settled in Britain initially set up the United Kingdom Islamic Mission (UKIM) in 1962, to provide a base and an outlet for individuals associated with the JI to continue with their activism in the UK. Thus, the structure of the UKIM broadly reflected that of the JI, and concepts and key texts were the same as those which were used by the JI, prominently featuring the works of Sayyid Abul A'la Mawdudi, the JI's founder. In fact, in the early years, the UKIM was widely referred to informally as 'the *Jamaat*'. Over time, the UKIM set up mosques and Islamic centres across the UK. These provided a range of services, including supplementary Islamic education for children through an extensive *madrassa* system, regular Islamic teaching for men and women and charitable work.[93] To this day, the UKIM still boasts a wide network of well-established mosques, including several in London and all the major UK cities.

By the late 1970s, encouraged by the settling of a new wave of Bangladeshi exiles in the wake of the 1971 War of Independence – and in a bid to counter the emergence of nationalist and secular Bangladeshi-identity groups in the East End of London[94] – the Bangladeshis within the UKIM formed their own group. *Dawatul Islam* (The Call of Islam) had its own youth organisation, the Young Muslim Organisation (YMO), and, for a period, took on the role of running the East London Mosque, especially after the opening of the Mosque's new purpose-built premises in 1985.[95] Divisions among the Mosque's trustees eventually led to those who were affiliated with *Dawatul Islam* leaving the Mosque, and many of the remaining trustees forming a new organisation, Islamic Forum Europe (IFE).[96] All of these groups functioned within, and primarily served, the Bangladeshi community, with their inspiration, focus and personalities still very much grounded in the JI framework.

In 1973, leading figures of the JI set up the Islamic Foundation in Leicester. This was a research body and publishing house that has been credited with successfully bringing the works of major reformist ideologues of the JI as well as of the Muslim Brotherhood to a worldwide English-speaking audience.[97] Additionally, it spearheaded the first contemporary, colourful and accessible collection of children's books on Islam and Muslim tradition in the English language.

A further development to the growing list of JI-inspired reformist groups was the establishment in 1984 of the Young Muslims UK (YMUK), the brainchild of Khurram Murad, a previous leader of the JI's student wing and then a deputy-leader of the JI itself. YMUK was constitutionally linked to the UKIM at its inception, intended to cater for the younger generation of British Muslims, and was pioneering in its commitment to the use of English as its language of operation. It also benefited from a cohort of highly competent and motivated youth leaders who were personally trained by Murad to deliver activities that were dynamic, in-touch with everyday social and political issues and conversant with Islamic beliefs and teachings, of which they were unashamedly proud.[98] However, its affiliation to the UKIM was short-lived as by the late 1980s YMUK eventually asserted its independence, and it was not until 1994 that it became attached to another 'parent' organisation, as I go on to discuss.

Also within the reformist trend were organisations established by members and sympathisers of the Muslim Brotherhood (MB). The Muslim Students Society (MSS) was set up in the 1960s and catered for a growing number of Arab and Arabic-speaking students in the UK. Many of these had prior involvement with the Muslim Brotherhood back in their home countries, and the MSS was a facility both to keep them in touch with the MB networks, to cater for their spiritual and religious development, as well as providing a social and community support mechanism.[99] As I have mentioned earlier, when FOSIS was set up in 1963, the MSS affiliated with it. Another notable establishment of the MB was the Muslim Welfare House. This was set up in 1970 as a support and community facility for Arab students who had come to the UK, and for many years its building in Finsbury Park in London acted as a base for MB members, hosting visiting personalities from abroad. Its role has since changed and developed considerably, now serving as a community and service centre for its immediate area.

Radical – seeking an alternative political system

The final category, the radicals, aspired to overturning what were deemed to be 'un-Islamic' governments and establishing a *Khilafa* – a nostalgic vision of the system of government instituted by the Prophet Muhammad and his successors (the *khulafaa'*). *Hizb-ut-Tahrir* ('The Party of Liberation', HT) was the main purveyor of this thinking in the UK. The movement itself was founded by the Palestinian Taqiuddin Nabhani in 1953, as he broke away from the Muslim Brotherhood. It adheres to a rather polarised worldview that calls for the establishment of an Islamic state (or *khilafa*) in the mould of the imagined heritage of the Ottoman Caliphate that fell in the early twentieth century. HT was brought to Britain in the 1980s by exiled members of the group who arrived from the Middle East, initially working with foreign students in the hope that they could then take their message with them on their return to their home countries.[100]

By the 1990s, HT had begun to organise openly within British Muslim communities. It functioned as a vocal mouthpiece criticising governments and leaders of Arab and Muslim countries, in particular accusing them of corruption and straying from the imperative to establish and rule by the *khilafa*. HT in Britain agitated for the return of this *khilafa*, and anticipated that its establishment would bring an end to all forms of Muslim suffering and oppression. In the 1990s this was frequently pursued using daring and provocative language and techniques. Actual acts of violence have never been claimed or endorsed by the group, however it has been argued that HT was guilty of 'cultivating the right conditions' for violence[101] – although this analysis is only directly linked with a single incident, namely the murder of a Nigerian Christian student in 1995, in which it has been claimed that drug dealing, gang violence and rivalry also played a key part.[102] There is stronger evidence to suggest that HT splinter groups such as *Al Muhajiroun* (est. 1996) and its later offshoots such as *Al Ghurabaa*, The Saviour Sect and Muslims Against Crusades have been responsible for encouraging violent crime.[103]

By the 1980s, the various groupings that constituted these three broad strands had played a significant role in energising a sense of Muslim consciousness,[104] increasingly among the younger generations. These strands and their respective organisations may have been established to provide familiar havens for activists among first-generation immigrants, but by the 1990s their differences began to be played out as rivalries, as each trend sought to attract as many recruits from the second and third generations as possible. This rivalry was especially noticeable on university and college campuses,[105] where the dynamics within and between many of these groups have been likened to those of football fans.[106] While this period might be accurately characterised as a time of tribalistic 'struggle for hegemony in the field of Islamic activism' between these groups,[107] it demonstrated that young British Muslims were taking greater ownership of their religious identity, and while parent organisations from abroad were still revered, young Muslims were beginning to also assert their own views and preferences.[108]

As a final note, and perhaps as a premonition of these movements evolving and increasingly adapting in their own ways to the UK, it is worth highlighting a few developments within some of these trends during the 1990s. The Islamic Society of Britain (ISB) was established in 1990 as a joint endeavour by individuals from JI and MB heritage with the aim of catering to the growing numbers of second- and third-generation British Muslims, as well as converts, to whom an 'indigenous' Islamic movement would most appeal. It grew to attract many graduates of youth groups within the reformist strand, particularly of YMUK, which in 1994 took the step of merging with the ISB and thus becoming its official youth wing. The early ISB was distinguished by a discourse that was clearly and comfortably 'at home' in Britain, which back in 1990 was in sharp contrast to various other movements that were regularly preoccupied with agitating for international change abroad, or simply for 'Muslim rights' at home.[109] This is exemplified by its Islam Awareness Week project which was initiated in 1994 as an annual nationwide campaign 'to raise awareness and remove misconceptions surrounding Britain's second largest faith group'.[110] In 1997, the Muslim Association of Britain (MAB) was set up as a hub bringing together various MB members and groupings that existed around the country, again with a focus on Britain as home, but also with a proud connection to the international MB, something which, especially after 2005, it has subsequently taken steps to play down.

Within the radical strand, *Al-Muhajiroun* was set up in 1996 by Omar Bakri Mohammed as a splinter of HT. Mohammed had been expelled from his leadership of HT in Britain in the same year, allegedly for displeasing the movement's central leadership in the Middle East with his outrageous and confrontational tactics, which 'it was felt distracted focus from the party message'.[111] Following the departure of Mohammed and his followers, HT in Britain underwent a 'stage of re-groupment', with *Al-Muhajiroun* continuing to occupy the more extreme and confrontational end of the spectrum, and HT itself re-emerged projecting a more serious image of itself as an organisation with its concerns grounded in mainstream domestic issues as well as international affairs, especially with respect to Britain's role in them.[112]

All of these examples together serve to illustrate how the various groups that owed their provenance to transnational Islamic movements abroad were already in flux by the 1990s, and that they were, albeit in different ways, beginning to engage with the realities of a permanent and indigenous presence of Muslim communities in the UK. In the following chapter, I move on to look at the early initiatives to unite and eventually to represent different Muslim organisations around the UK – firstly for better co-ordination, but soon after also for the purposes of more effective claims-making.

The period between the 1960s and 1980s was characterised by a drive towards identity preservation in various quarters of Britain's Muslim communities. This was manifested on a local level through a broadening of community interests from more functional issues such as the establishment of mosques, prayer congregations and the provision of *halal* meat, to concerns around the preservation and promotion of religious identity among the younger generation. This preoccupation clashed with more right-wing, conservative and arguably racist perspectives; and one key location where these concerns were played out was in the arena of schooling and education. The experience of Black community organising to confront racism and to call for the recognition and rectification of racial inequalities and discrimination provided inspiration and a reference point for increasingly identity-conscious Muslims. From a policy perspective, it also served as a useful precedent, whose institutions could be utilised by emergent Muslim community organisations.

A diverse range of UK-wide groups emerged from the 1960s onwards, with the aim of organising and, occasionally, representing Britain's Muslim communities. These were each dominated by different political and theological trends, and their strengths and weaknesses have been reflected in the varying extent of their ultimate effectiveness. Some have survived while others have been short-lived. The UMO in particular was a pioneer in the field of communal representation to both the government and to the wider public, however its progress and development was hindered by an inability to broaden its reach to become more inclusive of the extensive theological, ethnic and geographical spread across Britain's Muslim communities. This shortcoming was compounded by its failure to develop an open, modern and transparent structure, which would in turn have invited broader participation and input.

FOSIS has lived on and developed apace, but became increasingly focused on the needs of a fast-expanding domestic Muslim student population, while other community organisations took on the role of centralised representation. However, FOSIS was to prove a crucial starting point for many British Muslim activists and community leaders. Additionally, it regularly provided support for and input into future unity and representation initiatives. Similarly, the wide range of Muslim community organisations that developed in the period from 1960 through to the 1980s played an important role in engraining a sense of Muslim-consciousness, which proved foundational for the formalised identity politics that came about in the next decade. They also gave ample opportunity for community leaders to emerge and develop, particularly on a local level, through the building of campaigns and alliances. This too was to prove useful in the coming phase of formalised identity politics. But as the following chapter shows, an important difference was that these local campaigns generally related to single issues of concern to a local community, whereas the centralised formal identity politics of the later 1980s onwards sought to build a national consensus and a unified voice representing a whole range of Muslim communities from across the country.

CHAPTER 4

The Formalisation of Muslim Identity Politics: Responses to Hate Speech, Discrimination and the Equality Gap (1980s–2001)

This chapter explores the 1980s and 1990s, decisive and formative years when the now familiar basic structures and channels of communication of modern British Muslim identity politics developed. In the context of the inability or unsuitability of FOSIS and the UMO in representing Britain's Muslim communities, and while Muslim identity organisations with links to international Islamist movements were gaining increasing publicity and media exposure, there emerged numerous attempts at unity and representation during the 1980s. These include local and regional campaigns that articulated growing tensions between aspects of aspiration and self-identity of groups among British Muslims and wider society, specifically relating to social and cultural issues of mutual concern. Most notable among these were the numerous community advocacy and representation initiatives that emerged in the wake of the Rushdie Affair. It was at this moment when Muslim activists began to consistently present claims that could be articulated as what I term an Equality Gap.

By the mid-1990s, the MCB emerged as the pre-eminent representative body, and remained so through to 2001. After considering the period preceding the MCB's official launch in 1997 followed by a more detailed account of its establishment, this chapter assesses how the MCB came to occupy a position of primacy, the key issues that framed its relationship with government and mainstream politics, and how and why this relationship developed during the time period under discussion.

The MCB was heavily influenced by an aspiration to learn from, and to emulate the greater experience and superior political leverage that was enjoyed by institutions at the helm of British Jewish identity politics, primarily the BOD, and, in specific contexts, the position of Chief Rabbi. British Muslim community leaders expressed clear ambitions to achieve this, and this was also encouraged by successive governments, since it made the practicalities of its relations with religious minority communities more manageable.

A straightforward emulation of the 'Jewish model' was not easy, and highlighting differences and similarities between the British Muslim community's experiences of political engagement and those of the British Jewish community helps to illustrate this. Ultimately, Britain's Muslims benefited greatly from the Jewish community's antecedent successes in terms of acquiring 'staple' legal exemptions and recognition necessary for religious observance, and the MCB benefited from the BOD's model of communal representation and lobbying. However, the MCB found that it had to make its own way in some areas due to the contrasting features and circumstances of the two communities.

I then look closely at the key argument at the centre of contemporary Muslim identity politics – the argument that ultimately represents a major justification for the continued existence of Muslim identity politics. I refer to it as the Equality Gap, since it essentially hinges on the notion that the structure and mechanisms for equality and recognition in the British legal and political systems suffer from a gap with respect to the treatment of Muslim minorities on a par with other minorities. I will examine the basis for the argument that this Equality Gap exists, in light of the Rushdie Affair, this being the crisis under which it first began to be articulated. I conclude by looking at how it has continued to be expressed, the contexts in which it has been called upon in politics, and by observing how the gap has had continued implications for the nature and style of Muslim identity politics since the late 1980s.

MUSLIMS AND RACE RELATIONS POLICY – THE EQUALITY GAP

Although best known for the fiery mass protests that it ignited, the publication in 1988 of Salman Rushdie's *The Satanic Verses* proved an instrumental moment in the eventual development of formal and centralised British Muslim identity politics, as well as an important milestone in coherent claims-making to the government. This was because it brought together a potent combination of factors – the outrage of so many British Muslims at the offending novel, the interest of foreign nations, the highly sensitive nature of the very subject of freedom of expression in public and political consciousness; all forced Muslim community organisations to seek a united platform from which to make their representations.

In many respects, this experience of community self-expression, engagement and representation did not differ very much from that of other ethnic-minority immigrant communities to the UK from the Commonwealth. But while a race relations agenda was evolving in the sphere of policy, ultimately circumstances were more influential than strategy in propelling Muslims into the mainstream political sphere and triggering the growth of collective identity politics based around religion. Several chronological accounts have been drawn that trace this development,[1] varying in the emphasis and importance that they place on different aspects. However, it is virtually unanimously agreed that the single most formative event in the political development of the UK's Muslim communities during the late twentieth century was the Rushdie Affair and its aftermath. The publication of *The Satanic Verses* triggered off predictable uproar among Muslims in the UK who, among other emotions, felt outrage and deep hurt at what they understood to be a gratuitous and insulting attack on the Prophet Muhammad and other deeply revered personalities, as well as on the Qur'an – the sacred scripture of Islam.

Responses varied, but two particular products of this affair are of relevance to the discussion at hand. The first is that it brought about urgent momentum for unity and representation through the creation of civic organisations as channels for the articulation of a 'Muslim viewpoint' or response to what was felt in many ways to be an attack. The organised response by community groups and spokespeople took very seriously the precedent that had been laid for it in terms of the growing number of representations to government and the press by race relations bodies that had been made in recent decades. This development of a conscious Muslim identity politics, one that articulated a sense of grievance at not being given equal treatment by the law, and not being treated on a par with other minorities,[2] was both unprecedented and was to have an impact that long outlived the Rushdie Affair.[3] Secondly, and partly as a consequence of the first product, was the equally unprecedented scale of scrutiny and debate to which the UK's Muslim communities were subjected in the public domain, including academia, political commentary, public discourse, the media, the arts and eventually even in diplomatic relations. Both of these proved instrumental in shaping a new landscape against which Muslims came to view themselves and be viewed, and a new approach that was adopted in the formulation and articulation of claims and rights to the state.[4] The new sense of urgency that many Muslims felt both in response to the publication of *The Satanic Verses* and in frustration at the polarisation and dissonance of positions that their protests were met with by those around them, created a space for the development of community organisations, leaderships and other efforts of representation and interlocution on a new level.

THE RUSHDIE AFFAIR AND EQUALITY

Two main demands were made on the grounds of equality, both of which relied primarily on expectations of a principle of *equal treatment*. The first interrogated the rationale behind the inherent privilege that was enjoyed by the Church of England, as the established church of the UK, in the protection that it had as a religion from blasphemy under the law. Under this arrangement, it was (and remained so until 2008) possible to prosecute against forms of expression or publication that were ruled to 'contain any contemptuous, reviling, scurrilous, or ludicrous matter relating to God, Jesus Christ or the Bible, or the formulas of the Church of England as by law established'.[5] This arrangement was objected to as a form of discrimination that, by some interpretations, was symptomatic of a biased background political culture that placed Muslims (as non-members of the Church of England!) at a fundamental disadvantage. The existence of a blasphemy law protecting the Church of England made the language that was employed at the time in defence of 'freedom of speech and artistic expression' appear acutely unfair and discriminatory. Some Muslims wondered whether they could ever be accepted as equal citizens without giving up essential aspects of their beliefs and identities. Thus, many of the earlier representations that were made in the wake of the Rushdie Affair focused on calling for an extension of the blasphemy laws to cover all religions and denominations.[6] In the words of UKACIA's correspondence with John Patten: 'The crisis over *The Satanic Verses* refuses to go away ... (because) our legal framework does not envisage a situation in which an offence of sacrilege could be committed against religions other than the Anglican faith'.[7]

The second demand focused more directly on the growing race relations agenda itself, as an object of reform. It was argued that, although welcome, in concentrating solely on ethnicity as a factor of difference, the anti-discrimination legislation that had been passed thus far lacked nuance and the necessary recognition of minority groups that were not identified primarily by ethnic terms. This, in itself, was one objection. However, it was complicated by the fact that as time wore on and the legislation was utilised in discrimination cases, it emerged that members of *some* religious groups could legitimately be protected from discrimination and hate speech by the very same race relations laws that excluded members of other faiths. The rationale behind this was that the religions concerned (Judaism and Sikhism) were identifiably linked with particular ethnic groups (Jews and Punjabis), and that racially motivated discrimination or hate speech against them was in effect impossible to separate from similar forms of hostility that were religiously motivated. Legal precedent had determined that the Jewish and Sikh faiths were 'mono-ethnic',[8] thus facilitating the prosecution of an attack against a Jew or a Sikh by appealing to the existing Race Relations Act. The most obvious religious 'minority' exclusion to this anomaly were Muslims, since even though it was possible to classify certain ethnic groups as being overwhelmingly Muslim (for instance, Pakistanis or Bangladeshis), it would be impossible to group Muslims themselves into any ethnic category since adherence to Islam itself does not follow any ethnic pattern.[9] This legal loophole was indicative of an inherent disadvantage that Muslims faced when seeking redress against discrimination or looking to combat hate speech that could take advantage of it.[10]

This second position encompassed two main strands. The more 'basic' of these was the charge that if the anti-race discrimination laws protected in their scope both Jews and Sikhs, then, for the sake of fair and equal treatment, they needed to be extended to include Muslims as well. The other charge was that Muslims were facing a specific type of prejudice and discrimination that called for their inclusion in equalities legislation as a way of securing legal parity. This was to say that Muslims suffered disadvantage and discrimination because they were perceived and treated in a manner that was racist in its motivation and nature, and that this in turn meant that the experiences of discrimination that were felt by Muslims could not, straightforwardly at least, be approximated to experiences of racism that were founded on ethnic differences. Therefore it would be inaccurate to consider Muslims (from an equality and justice perspective) simply as members of their respective ethnic minority groups that suffer from socio-economic and other forms of disadvantage and discrimination. To do so would be to view them through the lens of the 'mode of oppression' rather than through the fairer and more accurate 'mode of being'.[11] This mode of being was not articulated only, or even mainly, through ethnic terms, and thus was reason enough to treat Muslims as though they were a race or, to use Tariq Modood's phrase, an ethno-religious group.[12] Modood points out in reference to '1980s antiracism in Britain', that 'most Muslims – suffering all the problems that antiracists identify – hardly ever think of themselves in terms of their colour'. Because of this, and because of the 'racialised' way in which they were sometimes prejudicially viewed, 'ethno-religious' as a category made more sense. For him, the understanding of race that had thus far informed race equality legislation was impoverished insofar as its definition of race excluded Muslims.[13] In addition, his findings as well as research carried out for the Cabinet Office indicate that religion can and does constitute a factor in the actual degree and nature of disadvantage and social exclusion that communities face.[14]

In short then, there have historically been two 'gaps' in the law that the experience of Muslim identity politics has identified and argued against:

(a) Speech: Whether it is the Church of England being given 'special treatment' through the continued existence of blasphemy laws,[15] or the arguable shortcomings of current legislation in proscribing incitement to religious hatred.
(b) Actions: The inadequacy of race relations policy (and specifically anti-discrimination legislation) in appreciating the complexity of the British Muslim experience of discrimination as an 'ethno-religious' group, and therefore the need for it to be revised. The gap here being illustrated by the inclusion of Jews and Sikhs (but not followers of other religions) under anti-race discrimination legislation.

The first of these gaps is more straightforwardly provable than the second, and has endured as a focal point for Muslim representative and lobby groups until this day. It informed the representations against *The Satanic Verses*, and since then it was also, famously and controversially, the direct impetus behind the strong support from a very broad spectrum of Muslim groups for the introduction of a 'religious hatred' offence.[16] The offence that was eventually introduced in 2005 was not, as many had hoped, as stringent and wide-ranging as the comparable sections of race relations legislation. However, even as symbolic recognition of Muslims as an identifiable group that needed to be catered for in integration policy, it received a measured welcome as a step in the right direction.[17] It is worth noting here the development with time of a shift from the emphasis placed by Muslim groups on the extension of the blasphemy law as a way to achieving equality to a more focused and more human rights-grounded demand for protection from hate/Islamophobic speech.[18]

As for the second gap, it motivated the terms of the successful campaign for the recognition of religion as an identity-category in official matters through the inclusion of a 'religion question' in the 2001 National Census. Without the collection of such data, it was argued, there would never be any accurate and comprehensive aggregation of population numbers and demographics for the UK's Muslims; and without this, it would never be accurately known how many Muslims actually *were* experiencing discrimination. It was only once such statistics were obtained that the more formidable task of assessing how much of this discrimination was based on their 'Muslimness', and how much was founded on other aspects of identity. Those involved in the campaign contended that it 'represented a long-standing dissatisfaction with the focus on race and ethnicity alone as a statistical marker for planning and resource allocation in the public sector' and that 'without it, British Muslims would remain statistically invisible'.[19] Interestingly, and in support of the earlier arguments that I have made, the rationale behind this campaign also followed closely the push for an 'ethnicity' question that had taken place ten years prior and had achieved success in time for the 1991 census.

While each of these examples represents differing goals, they both provide useful illustrations of how the case for addressing the Equality Gap is gaining increasing currency. With the benefit of time and experience (their own and that of race identity politics), the articulation of the gap by Muslim civic organisations and lobby groups is becoming clearer and stronger. It is also becoming more evident to policy-makers that without addressing the gap, equality as recognition – in the tradition that has been set by the British race relations policy agenda – can hardly be claimed to have been fully achieved. From a philosophical perspective, the understanding of recognition that I outlined in the first section requires that the gap be closed, if we are to move beyond addressing (simply) the socio-economic disadvantages that many immigrant and post-immigrant communities face, and aim for an arrangement not only where we are aware that there will be specific challenges and disadvantages faced by each community, but to also find ways for the legal and political system to respond to those disadvantages that are unjustifiable or have disproportionate impact. From a practical perspective, straightforward equality of treatment under the law also means that a reassessment of present anomalies (such as the ambiguity around the inclusion of Jews and Sikhs in race relation legislation, and the legal disadvantage under which this leaves Muslims and members of other minority faiths) is also called for.

INITIAL LARGE-SCALE REPRESENTATION ON A NATIONAL LEVEL

By the mid-1990s, the almost two-decade-long succession of Conservative administrations was drawing to a weary close, and there was a perceptible air of enthusiasm, both broadly speaking in politics and more specifically among Muslim advocacy bodies. A number of factors catalysed or at least encouraged this enthusiasm. In terms of the intra-community situation, there had been growing realisation from many quarters that some form of coordinated voice would most effectively serve the shared aspirations of political voice and recognition that were now being so vigorously called for in the wake of the Rushdie Affair. The arrival of these new unity initiatives effectively illustrates how the UMO was becoming overshadowed and overtaken in its ambition to remain as the main representative and advocate for British Muslims. The Muslim Parliament and the UK Action Committee on Islamic Affairs were two of the most notable efforts in this regard.

The Muslim Parliament
Launched in 1992, the Muslim Parliament of Great Britain was founded on the premise that 'all political parties and the mass media in Britain are now engaged in a relentless campaign to reduce Muslim citizens of this country to the status of a disparaged and oppressed minority', and that as such, 'greater cohesion and dynamism' was needed among mosques and institutions in order to implement a 'strategy for survival'.[20] Dominated by ex-*Guardian* journalist Kalim

Siddiqui, and funded by the Islamic Republic of Iran, the Muslim Parliament (MP) was heavy on ideology and rhetoric yet apparently quite sparse in terms of concrete action. In many ways an overambitious and staunchly confrontational endeavour, it devoted its efforts to the planning of a comprehensively self-sufficient and parallel infrastructure for the Muslim community, encompassing a parliament (basically a council), a central community fund (*Baitul Mal*), educational institutions including schools and a university, a research body (The Muslim Institute), as well as youth and women's organisations.

Although the MP did not ever officially cease to exist, it can be considered to have been short-lived for a number of reasons. Firstly, as with most projects that revolve around single personalities, it was dealt a heavy blow with the demise of its leader, Kalim Siddiqui, in 1996. This left the crucial role of a central, unifying figure in the organisation unfulfilled, allowing for in-fighting and divisions to emerge amongst the MP's ranks. Eventually this took the form of a split – with Kalim Siddiqui's son, Iqbal, leading the newly created splinter – the Institute of Contemporary Islamic Thought (ICIT), and Muhammad Ghayasuddin Siddiqui (no relation) assuming the role of the MP's leader, a position that he still occupies today. Neither branch has ever really been successful in achieving either support or influence beyond their immediate sphere of contact, and neither has since proved capable of enjoying the degree of influence or recognition that they have aspired to.

While Ghayasuddin Siddiqui has continued to perform an occasional role of spokesman through the MP mouthpiece on eclectic issues, this has been of a rather limited reach, and often as a 'lone voice' in relation to the rest of the community.[21] On the other hand, Iqbal Siddiqui's ICIT is practically obscure to the public eye. Its website does not appear to have been updated since 2000, and its principal preoccupation has been to present a history of the MP and Muslim Institute under Kalim Siddiqui as well as to promote his ideas through providing access to a collection of his articles and papers.[22] Its magazine, *Crescent International*, does however continue to be published online, although it primarily deals with international political affairs rather than issues more directly concerning British

Muslims.[23] Other than these functions, the ICIT is, to all intents and purposes, non-existent.

UKACIA

In a related vein yet with much more direct ambitions, the UK Action Committee on Islamic Affairs (founded in 1989) had built up substantial momentum among local and regional groups,[24] and by 1993 had already accrued enough rapport with government to be able to submit its report entitled 'Muslims and the Law in Multifaith Britain: the need for reform', as a contribution to the CRE's consultation for the second review of the 1976 Race Relations Act.[25] This collection forthrightly advocated that the persistence of several issues of inequality in British politics and public life was in urgent need of redress by government. Supported by articles from academics in law and politics, it drew arguments from the perspective that British Muslims constituted a group requiring advocacy and representation in law and politics on a similar level with ethnic minorities. These arguments were largely grounded in terms of the Equality Gap – that the need for recognition and greater representation was not simply because their shared religion was considered to sufficient to qualify them as a distinct group, but more because the status quo in law and politics left British Muslims a conspicuously vulnerable minority.

UKACIA set out to avoid the challenges that had earlier faced the UMO and the MP by calling together a considerably more diverse group of community representatives, including various regions in the UK as well as a range of religious and political persuasions and cultural backgrounds. Moreover, it made resourceful use of established institutions, such as the London Central Mosque in Regents Park (where it became based), and by making appeals for support to the UK ambassadors of several Muslim countries. The Director of the London Central Mosque, Dr. Ali Al-Ghamdi, served as chairman of UKACIA's steering committee and later became Co-convenor of the organisation along with Iqbal Sacranie.[26] The combination of these factors appears to have contributed towards earning it considerable standing and recognition in its relationship with the government. So by the mid-1990s it held a central position as interlocutor for 'religious' concerns of Muslims, as distinct to concerns rooted or understood through the lens of race or ethnicity.

Nonetheless, UKACIA did have significant limitations. Key among these was that it was in essence a collective that was founded on the notion of protest, this being both a reactive and a primarily defensive organising tactic. With the Rushdie Affair and offensive representations of Islam and Muslims in literature and the media as its main preoccupation, it became somewhat defined by its call for a widening of the blasphemy laws. As such, it did not appear to offer British society any tangible positive contributions, and this may have detracted from the seriousness with which its demands were received. Moreover, while it did enjoy some levels of prominent support in the community, there was no real consensus that it was to be *the* official representative or umbrella body for Muslim groups in the UK. Its diverse constituent groups meant that sufficient assent to an official status for UKACIA was all the more important, and that, following on from this, regulated and standardised structures and mechanisms were also necessary in order to ensure viability and survival as an established organisation into the long-term. In addition, a certain level of reliance upon overseas support and funding may have played a part in creating perceptions of UKACIA as being somewhat agenda-driven.[27]

Both the Muslim Parliament and UKACIA displayed a keenness to push forward with presenting a case for equal treatment for Muslims, albeit using different styles. Whilst the Muslim Parliament adopted a more confrontational tone, its level of influence both in terms of community backing and durability was relatively limited in comparison to that of UKACIA. On the other hand, UKACIA was rather more broad-based, whilst at the same time officially preferring 'to channel Muslim protest through economic, legal and diplomatic pressure'.[28]

Although this new level of dialogue was originally ignited by anger at the realisation that they had no recourse to the law against what was considered grave blasphemy, it signified an important step up for British Muslims into a national level of advocacy that was both more focused and more coordinated than any preceding experience. What is more, it gave scope to the development of more coherent arguments regarding both the sense of hurt that was felt by Muslims on issues such as blasphemy, and in the areas of legal rights and claims-making.

THE FORMALISATION OF UNITY AND COMPETITION FOR REPRESENTATION

The need for coordination and unity in political advocacy had become most apparent back in 1988 when the first reactions to the Rushdie Affair were being formulated. It was at this point, more than at any preceding juncture, that Muslim community leaders became desperate to make their case heard with a united voice. Sources from this period are telling of a sense of being misunderstood, and a frustration at the sheer level of opposition that they were being faced with.[29] One example is worth quoting at length. M.H. Faruqi argues that Muslim protesters against *The Satanic Verses*:

> (b)elieved that they were raising the most ordinary point about decency and dignity. They were not concerned about the faults or merits of the 'novel' ... or its 'theological' or 'scholarly' criticism. They had no wish or intention to challenge anyone's freedom of expression or to impose their 'mediaeval' or 'censorious' values over the 'civilised' world.

> What they (wanted) was not even exclusively Islamic, it was the universal value ... that it is not civilised to abuse and insult whatever the context or form of expression. They did not assume any malice on the part of the publishers.[30]

Furthermore:

> There was never an attempt to understand Muslim feelings of deep hurt caused by the book, yet they were condemned *ex parte* as vandals and enemies of freedom! ... The climax of incomprehension came when the Home Secretary armed with such sensational appreciation of the situation travelled to Birmingham to lecture the community to abide by laws of the country or else – to get out ... (Yet) Their expression within the laws and etiquette of their country of citizenship was in fact an act of integration but surprisingly they (sic) are construed as refusal or unwillingness to integrate.[31]

This sort of sentiment convinced Muslim community leaders of the imperative need for unity in order to maximise their effectiveness and to achieve their common goal.

Extant unity initiatives were limited in scope and out of touch with their self-ascribed community constituents. As we have seen, the UMO provides a notable example in this regard. Its aspiration to be an umbrella body bringing together local and regional organisational efforts to facilitate a united voice had more success on paper than in practice. The Muslim Parliament, although outspoken and vociferous in its tone, was hindered by its lack of broad-based support and probably also by its closeness to the Iranian regime from which it received funding.[32] In addition, both the UMO and the Muslim Parliament appear to have had little presence outside of London, and thus could hardly have any influence in areas beyond the capital city. The UKACIA was also hindered by its apparent close association with the Saudi regime. Indeed, it has been suggested that the support of the Saudi and the Iranian governments for the UKACIA and the Muslim Parliament respectively was part of the wider rivalry that the two regimes were engaged in, as they vied with one another over who could claim the greater influence within the 'Muslim world'.[33]

What was left, therefore, by the early 1990s, was a situation in which there were a number of different bodies each claiming to possess mandates for representation and a more authentic or legitimate connection with the UK's Muslim communities. However, each body was subject in its own way to significant limitations. These limitations were most clearly played out in the form of a sort of rivalry or competition that took place between them for exposure and attention. A clear example of this rivalry is evident in the drifting apart of the ICIT and the MP, and the manner of their subsequent references to one another.[34] Each tried to portray the other in a negative light as a way of affirming its own exclusivity and legitimacy. In the meantime, work undertaken by the UMO's National Muslim Education Council and the Muslim Educational Trust (MET), while pursuing very similar aims, was not linked or co-ordinated in any visible way.[35] Similarly, there was overlap between work of the UKACIA on political engagement and media monitoring and that of the UMO, and specifically the latter's Vigilance Committee, which also kept a watchful eye on press and public bodies for any 'offensive' or 'anti-Islamic' discourse.[36]

Efforts to rectify these regular obstacles to effectiveness were commenced a few years later – driven in a large part by individuals who had been involved with UKACIA. Preparatory meetings of a National Interim Council for Muslim Unity (NICMU) took place between 1994 and 1996, identifying widespread consultation as their main objective. Having already accepted the need for organised unity for advocacy and representation, the 50-or-so community networks behind NICMU visited and corresponded with Muslims across the UK as a way of gauging support for the project, and receiving consultations on the form and structures that it would adopt.[37] These exercises paved the way for the establishment of the MCB, which set out to assume the role of a credible and effective interlocutor between Muslims and government – one which was genuinely and independently rooted in the UK and which was able to occupy a position which both parties were keen to see filled. By extension, this role gave the MCB the requisite capacity and exposure to occupy the prominent position of 'authoritative spokesman' on Muslim affairs in the media.

As much as it could be criticised for other limitations, the early MCB did have the unprecedented asset of being the first Muslim body of its kind with a significant and authentic mandate and legitimacy to undertake leadership and representation. In its first year of existence, it attracted affiliations from 250 organisations from around the UK, a number that has continued to increase consistently. Its legitimacy was also bolstered by its institution of transparent (if overcomplicated) procedures for membership, voting and decision making that were eventually formalised in its constitution and which made up the substance of its official launch in 1997. As such, the MCB quickly became the *de facto* port of call for government and official bodies when seeking dialogue or negotiation with Muslim community representatives. Further, this arrangement added important credibility to any pro-active lobbying that the MCB or individuals backed by the MCB decided to undertake.

NEW LABOUR AND MUSLIM REPRESENTATION

Apart from the formal establishment of the MCB, 1997 was politically important for many other reasons, most of which are related to the Labour general election victory of that year. Many of the manufacturing-class immigrant communities that had grown from the 1960s and 1970s had traditionally been Labour supporters. For them, the prospect of a Labour government represented a new hope, upon which many an expectation was pinned. It was anticipated that what had been variously characterised by so many Muslim commentators as the cold, post-colonialist or just plain anti-Muslim track record of the Conservative governments of Margaret Thatcher and her successor, John Major,[38] could only be improved upon by the comparatively upbeat and keen manner that was shown by New Labour to address the main issues of concern put forward by Muslim advocacy groups.[39] What is more, the broader promise of a more approachable style of government under Labour was a source of encouragement for Muslims that they would be given the space and resources to voice their issues, and that government was prepared to genuinely listen to them *as Muslims*.

What did Muslim 'identity politics' mean?

Before examining how a British Muslim identity politics was formally institutionalised, it is worth establishing what practical meanings the term itself carries. I argue that it was about recognition, rights and the capacity to lobby, by Muslims *qua* Muslim. The first aspect relates to *recognition*. As we have seen, the need for recognition is quite often the first motivator for the expression of identity in politics by a minority or marginalised group. The initial way in which this need was expressed took the form of self-identification. This includes the titles by which community organisations choose to refer to themselves and to their leaders, all of which indicate the strong primacy of the Muslim aspect of their identities, before any other.

Following on from this, the nature of the claims made to the state by Muslim advocacy bodies indicates the desire for recognition as Muslims, in the sense that they were both framed and premised on the idea of a communal Muslim identity that required both *acknowledgement* and *rights* in order for equality to be delivered. In other words, that the Muslim community required access to both official acknowledgement and to certain rights (be they exemptions from legal restrictions, or rights that were already accorded to the mainstream, but where a loophole currently excluded them), in order to have true access to equality on a par with other citizens.

This main aim of identity politics naturally leads to the final aspect, which is the space and capacity to *lobby*. All of the Muslim representative organisations that I discuss here have lobbying as the most central of their functions. While they could never have been denied the right to make political representations or seek to apply influence or pressure on matters of concern to them, what British Muslim organisations have sought to achieve has been the establishment and formalisation of a direct, centralised channel of communication towards government, decision-making bodies and the media. This direct channel, it was hoped, would hold the same position as the one enjoyed by the BOD.[40] Although the BOD, and the Chief Rabbi, have not been without their own share of critics, they have each established over time widely recognised roles as spokespersons for British Jewry on both domestic and international politics as well as issues specifically relating to the state of Israel.

This same aspiration to emulate what was seen as Jewish success in achieving effective ecclesiastical leadership is also illustrated by attempts in October 2010 to create a 'Grand Mufti' for the UK, claiming credence from Egypt's Al-Azhar University, and envisaged as some sort of counterpart to the Chief Rabbi and the Archbishop of Canterbury.[41] However, the enterprise failed to take off and was disowned by several quarters as inauthentic, 'divisive' and 'regrettable'.[42]

At this point, it is worth casting a glance at the establishment of Jewish identity politics in Britain – British Jews being another religious minority group with largely migrant origins. A survey of the development of communal organisation among British Jews can aid our understanding of how the Jewish experience provided inspiration and an exemplar for the institutionalisation of a formally recognised Muslim identity politics, through the MCB, to aspire to.

JEWISH COMMUNITY ORGANISATION IN THE UK – A SURVEY

The political engagement of both Jewish and Muslim immigrant communities was affected by cultural prejudices, migratory conditions, international connections and migratory mindsets. While there were common factors experienced by both communities, they interacted with them in different ways. Ultimately, a combination of migratory conditions and subsequent political choices greatly facilitated the BOD's establishment and acceptance into the UK's political landscape. While the MCB and its predecessors tried to forge a similar path, their success was limited by their interactions with their own migratory conditions and, crucially, a much slower coming to terms with permanent settlement in the UK on the part of immigrant Muslim communities.

British Jewish community organisation: a brief history of early achievements

British Jewish community organisations have a far longer history than their Muslim counterparts. British Jews have long been engaged in the politics of identity, since the circumstances of their arrival, as exiles and refugees, meant that the intention to settle permanently was clear from the outset. Consequently, both institution-building and political engagement have been more focused. The BOD, which has long enjoyed a quasi-official status as the official public representative of Anglo-Jewry, traces its origins back to 1760, when the first coordinating meetings took place between delegates appointed from each of the *Ashkenazi* and *Sephardi* congregations in the UK.[43] Of course it will be impossible to do justice here to its history of over two-and-a-half centuries. However, what I will do is to point out a few major milestones and show how they have been relevant in shaping the developing role of the BOD, and of Jewish representative politics more broadly.

In this first instance, the BOD's purpose was to arrange for the two congregations' joint communication to 'testify their homage' to King George III on the occasion of his accession to the throne. There followed a formal agreement that those delegates would 'thereafter ... deal with the most urgent matters which present themselves in connection with our nation'.[44] However, the BOD (or the London Committee of Jewish Deputies, as it was initially known) met sparsely and irregularly during the early decades. Its first major spurt of development is generally associated with the presidency of Sir Moses Montefiore in stints between 1835 and 1874. Montefiore has been widely credited with laying down firm institutional foundations for the BOD, formalising its constitution and structure, earning official recognition from the government, and giving it an overall sense of permanency.[45]

The BOD consisted of lay representatives, who were delegates from the various member congregations. Although technically open to congregations from across Britain, it was nonetheless dominated by those in and around London.[46] As time passed, its remit broadened to cover not only official community representations to government, but also the role of regulation and authorisation of institutions and religious rites within the community, a role that often required cooperation with the two 'ecclesiastical authorities', the Chief Rabbi of the United Synagogue as well as the *Haham* of the *Sephardi* congregations. In theory these two posts were parallel ecclesiastical authorities, representing the *Ashkenazi* and the *Sephardi* congregations respectively, but in practice the Chief Rabbi has come to be the more dominant, due in part to the superior numbers of the congregations over which he claims authority, as well as a more extensive demographic spread, and more effective communal infrastructure.[47] So while its initial role was one of providing a platform for British Jewry to express their loyalty to the Crown, the progressive institutionalisation of the BOD and its development has led to its current status as the quasi-official representative body of Britain's Jewish communities, participating in national events and negotiating on behalf of British Jews on matters of concern. The extent to which it has been successful is debatable, and it has not been without its critics from among British Jews themselves. However, the BOD's continued existence has been an important symbol of Jewish identity politics and provided a focal point both for the political establishment and other minority communities (such as Muslims) who looked to emulate it.

Overcoming legal hurdles

Ever since formal emancipation was inaugurated by the 1830 Jewish Relief Act, there has been a succession of legal developments removing official barriers that had previously restricted the civil and political rights of non-Anglicans. Many of these laws were passed specifically with Jews in mind, and so procedures specific to the Jewish communities were sometimes incorporated. These specific procedures helped to tacitly establish the BOD as the official custodian of Jewish civic and political affairs. They also established legal rights and exemptions that were later crucial for the integration of future religious minorities, in particular Muslims.

For instance, the Marriage Registration Act of 1836 recognised the London Committee of Jewish Deputies, as it was then known, as the sole body that was permitted to certify Jewish places of worship for the purposes of marriage registration. As the first legal acknowledgement of the Committee, this implicitly conferred upon the BOD a status of authority and legitimacy within the Jewish community, and recognised it as a representative body. The Act also bestowed legitimacy on the Chief Rabbi, albeit by proxy, due to the BOD's effective deference to the Chief Rabbi as its ecclesiastical authority. The 1846 Religious Disabilities Act gave legal recognition to Jewish schools, places of worship and educational and charitable funds, thus putting their legal status on a par with counterpart nonconformist Christian institutions.[48] By 1858, and after much wrangling between both Houses of Parliament, provisions were made in the Oath Act for Jewish MPs who had been elected to take up their seats in parliament by omitting reference to 'Christian faith', and subsequently, that year Lionel de Rothschild became the first Jewish MP to take up his seat in parliament.[49]

Similarly, the success of Britain's Jews in securing official recognition and the relevant legal exemptions for specific aspects of religious practice also paved the way for Muslims. The Slaughter of Poultry Act 1967 and the Slaughterhouses Act 1974 both provide for exemptions on religious grounds for the practice of *Shechita* (Jewish ritual slaughter) from the otherwise-blanket requirement to stun animals before slaughter. The development of *Beth Din*, Jewish arbitrational courts to resolve civil disputes outside of English courts, preceded the later establishment of Islamic Shari'a Councils to fulfil similar functions. Interestingly, an indication of a changed context to identity politics is that although *Beth Din* have been functioning for centuries, they have never generated the kind of controversy, criticism and opposition from wider society that Shari'a Councils have, in particular, the vitriolic media reactions to the reflections on the incorporation of certain aspects of *shari'a* by the former Archbishop of Canterbury, Rowan Williams, in 2008.[50]

All in all, the lifting of various restrictions relating to education, civic participation and public office meant that Britain's Jews were unwittingly blazing a trail – tackling the hurdles that they faced to equal citizenship meant that later on Britain's Muslim communities would not have to face them either.

INSTITUTIONALISATION OF MUSLIM IDENTITY POLITICS IN BRITAIN – UNIQUE CHALLENGES

To return to British Muslims, the institutionalisation of the MCB took place in a wholly different era and context to that of the BOD. Whereas the latter had the benefit of the contemporaneous Board of Dissenting Deputies (est. 1732) to look to for inspiration, the MCB was on its own. This was coupled with several unique challenges that Muslim communities faced when it came to successfully establishing and maintaining political engagement, as compared with Britain's Jewish communities. I place these under four headings: cultural prejudice, international connections, background and migratory conditions and migratory mindsets. In discussing these challenges alongside the experiences of British Jews, we can understand how they contributed towards a unique set of circumstances within which Muslims in Britain were to forge their path towards formal political engagement.

Cultural prejudice
For both Islam and Judaism, there is a history stretching as far back as medieval times of fear, prejudice and demonisation in popular English culture that has regularly been reflected in official channels

through policy or discourse. Jews have long borne the brunt of historical 'Christian theological contempt for Judaism',[51] which painted a picture of them as being in league with the devil or the Antichrist, as blasphemers and enemies of Christians and Christianity. Added to this there were popular stereotypes that utilised and exaggerated derided 'features' of the Jews – Shylock the rich and stingy moneylender in Shakespeare's *The Merchant of Venice*, and Fagin, leader of a gang of child pickpockets in Charles Dickens' *Oliver Twist* are both examples of characters which provide ample material on the nature of negative Jewish stereotyping in English culture.[52]

Yet although there were significant historical differences and divergences between Judaism and Christianity, there was nonetheless perceived to be more common ground between the Jewish communities and the background political culture of the Britain in which they had settled than there was between British culture and the UK's immigrant Muslim communities. A shared Judaeo-Christian religious heritage meant that while some cultural and ritualistic aspects of Jewish religious identity may well have seemed foreign, they were comparatively more fathomable to the average person than cultural and religious practices of the Muslim immigrant communities that were to later arrive on Britain's shores. Since Judaism historically precedes Christianity, there is an overlap of shared biblical heritage from which a sense of familiarity can be extracted. As much as there has been historic prejudice and hostility towards Jews, the Old Testament remained a text that Christians recognised and referred to and, importantly, were much more likely to have come across than the Qur'an. Islam, being the newest of the three faiths, arrived in substantial numbers in modern Britain in the form of the spiritually infused, folklore-influenced faith, as practiced by Muslim immigrants from rural South-Asia.[53] When political organising picked up and the first Muslim advocacy organisations were established, they were often headed by individuals associated with Islamic political movements 'back home' in their countries of origin.[54] British Jews, on the other hand, were for a long time very wary about 'importing' ideas or techniques from political movements abroad. This is demonstrated by the vehement opposition that

Theodor Herzl received when he first mooted his ideas about a Jewish state in the *Jewish Chronicle* in 1896.[55]

International connections

Both Jewish and Muslim immigrant communities arrived in the UK with links and affinities to counterpart communities, whether 'back home' in the countries from which they emigrated, or more generally wherever Jews and Muslims reside. For Muslims, there is often a sense of affinity to the *ummah* or the 'Muslim world', and for many Jews there has often been a similar sense of loyalty or attachment to the wider diaspora as well as the state of Israel, both as an aspiration in the early twentieth century, and after its eventual establishment in 1948. Yet it seems fair to say that the two communities interacted with these connections differently.

In their formative stages, Muslim community organisations were far more prone to overseas influence and even control. This is exemplified by the influence of transnational movements on Muslim identity organisations; additionally, the UMO was initially linked to the Egyptian government's aspirations for an international network of pan-Arab/Muslim organisations, and the UKACIA and Muslim Parliament were financially linked to Saudi Arabia and Iran respectively. Additionally, the MCB has been dominated ever since its establishment by individuals who bear (at least historical) links with the *Jamaat-e-Islami* and similar Islamist organisations from the Muslim world. Although there has recently been a palpable distancing between Muslim organisations and Muslim political causes abroad, particularly since 7/7, this development has come effectively in reverse order to the Jewish community's experience. As David Cesarani has argued, support for Zionism and the idea of an Israeli state seems to have picked up in official channels among British Jews, and specifically the BOD, only *after* the Holocaust.[56] Prior to this, Zionism had received a poor reception for fear that it carried an implication that Jews 'could not assimilate into Europe'. In fact, the BOD actively opposed 'Zionist aspirations' during World War I, and through to the interwar period,[57] and its vocal backing of Israel, now so confident that it has often been divisive, only really began to gain momentum in the latter half of the twentieth century, when it was over one-and-a-half centuries old.

Background and migratory conditions

Unlike Britain's postwar South Asian Muslim immigrants, Jewish immigrants in the UK were 'twice-minorities'. They hailed largely from Eastern Europe, where they had already lived as minorities, and where they had often faced far more acute persecution and discrimination than they would ever encounter in the UK. Indeed, for many the UK was positively a safe haven where they could escape from a history of pogroms and the day-to-day experiences of anti-Semitism, as well as (much later) the Holocaust.[58]

For these Jewish immigrants, there was a clear intention to settle in the UK from the start, and this is exemplified by the early but cautious and measured forays into politics as well as ready expressions of loyalty to crown and country. An important example of this is the keenness of 'acculturated, middle-class Jews' to volunteer in World War I as a demonstration of their loyalty.[59] The establishment of schools, community arbitration courts (*Beth Din*) and synagogues among other aspects of community infrastructure all took the shape of a community aspiring to permanence and indigenousness.

The wave of Muslim arrivals of the 1950s and 1960s was the product of completely different circumstances.[60] These were mostly young, male labourers who arrived without their families, seeking to earn some money by filling a gap in the labour market of postwar Britain. In the main, they did not arrive with the resolve to settle, hence their willingness to put up with squalid living conditions and their belated interest in family-oriented community projects.[61] This initial assumption that migration to the UK was primarily a temporary, economic measure meant that long-term planning did not feature so heavily in the life of Britain's immigrant Muslim communities.[62] The 'myth of return' endured, leading to lack of commitment to their newly established 'homes'. Community institutions were built in a more gradual, piecemeal fashion. Even economic investment was often channelled directly to supporting family members 'back home' – a direct contrast to the long tradition of philanthropy amongst wealthy

Jews, many of whom funded schools, synagogues and a range of other community establishments.[63]

Migratory mindsets

From its inception, the BOD self-consciously sought to present itself to the establishment in a similar light to representatives of Christian nonconformists of the day.[64] The very name, 'London Committee of Jewish Deputies', bore obvious parallels to the pre-existing London Board of Dissenting Deputies and, according to Michael Clark, was 'a clear statement of the place Anglo-Jewry believed it inhabited in Britain's religiously plural society'.[65] This approach indicates an aspiration from the outset for the BOD to pursue an 'integrationist' path. By this I mean one where it hoped the Jewish community would fit in to the existing British socio-political landscape, rather than mark itself out as separate by functioning outside the political set-up of the day. That the very establishment of the BOD was triggered by a desire to present a united expression of allegiance to the Crown is once again telling of the overarching desire to integrate and 'fit in'. In contrast to this, the beginnings of representative groups within Britain's Muslim community are found to have been moments of crisis and perceived attack, most famously exemplified by the Rushdie Affair, which triggered the formation of the UKACIA and the Muslim Parliament.[66]

This same aspiration to integrate and 'fit in' is aptly illustrated by contrasting the apparent motivations behind the establishment of Jewish and Muslim community schools. Michael Clark notes how early Jewish communal education was 'not designed to inculcate religion.' Rather, 'The separate Jewish schooling network was maintained in this era primarily for the purposes of disciplining, occupying and "improving" the Jewish poor'.[67] The Jews Free School (JFS) in London clearly saw social mobility for the community's poor as its main target, while the children of middle- and upper-class families were sent to mainstream schools, where they were expected to 'mingle' with their Christian peers.[68] In a similar vein, teachers at the JFS forced school-children to change Yiddish-sounding names – evidently part of wider efforts towards acculturation and integration of the Jewish poor.[69]

So the focus was on building academic achievement and 'culturing' for the sake of social mobility and integration. There was of course some religious ethos in Jewish day schools, but more intensive, traditional-style religious instruction was generally the preserve of *Hadarim*, small after-school enterprises providing religious teaching in immigrant districts. These were also frowned upon as a barrier to integration.[70]

Muslim community schools on the other hand were clearly established specifically to safeguard the Islamic education and identity of Muslim children. The aim does not seem to have always been specifically to establish *separate* education *per se*;[71] it was more the difficulty that Muslim parents had in securing their desired adjustments to the state education system that propelled them towards setting up a Muslim school sector. These included, variously: segregation of the sexes, especially girls; exemptions from music, art, physical education, religious education lessons and religious assemblies; arrangements for prayer rooms or Friday congregational prayers; adjustments to uniforms to incorporate Islamic notions of 'modesty'; the provision of *halal* meat in school meals.[72] Muslim schools were regarded as a comprehensive solution to these various challenges, preventing the dilution of culture and providing a safe space for Muslim children to learn about their faith alongside their wider education, without having to necessarily make 'compromises' to their beliefs and culture that were demanded by participation in the mainstream sector.[73]

The MCB and its genesis

There is an old clichéd story that is told of how the MCB was set up or at least crucially supported and decisively moulded by the interests of New Labour, and that its first decade of existence was delimited by a relationship of understanding with successive government personalities and sections of the civil service.[74] By this account, the nature of the most successful British Muslim representative umbrella body to date would almost be that of a quango (quasi-non-governmental organisation), one that, although not formally instituted at the behest and direction of government, was nonetheless indebted to the Labour government for its impact and success, and thus for its continued existence over the course of its early history.

In fact, evidence shows that unity initiatives among Muslims date significantly further back than 1997. Back in 1994, representations to the Conservative government were deemed not to merit serious consideration since they came across as insufficiently coordinated and lacking in a clear voice. This sentiment was perhaps most directly expressed by the then home secretary, Michael Howard, who suggested to Muslim leaders that their various representations surrounding the common issue of religious discrimination would be more attentively received if they were to present their political case under a single, authoritative body.[75] The idea was that this arrangement would provide the requisite coordination in voice and action for coherent government-community negotiation to develop. Since there was greater potential for misunderstanding to occur during this stage,[76] the need for a coordinated voice and coherent organisation is understandable.

As I have described, the MCB was not the first attempt by Muslims to organise themselves under a unified banner for purposes of representation and advocacy. Indeed, many key figures among the MCB's founding 'old guard' are veterans of preceding initiatives in communal representation. Iqbal Sacranie served previously as the convenor of UKACIA, while Muhammad Abdul Bari, his successor as MCB Secretary-General, was a previous president of the Islamic Forum Europe, a federal organisation linking various community initiatives in London, around Manchester and beyond, as well as a long-serving key figure at the East London Mosque.[77] Since its inception, the majority of the MCB's office bearers have tended to be drawn from a common 'pool' of prominent individuals, many of whom found their first calling in the field of national politics in the wake of the Rushdie Affair,[78] and a majority of whom also have backgrounds in the 'reformist' strand of community activism.[79] However, unlike its predecessors such as the UKACIA, the UMO and the MP, the MCB garnered from the outset a high level of endorsement from government and the establishment that proved pivotal in cementing its position as the primary point of contact or liaison whenever the need arose. This advantage paid substantial dividends in the form of credibility and networking, both of which have been crucial in maintaining the rate of success that the MCB has had in effective lobbying and having the establishment and the media's 'ear'.

The view from mainstream politics during this time was also conducive to the MCB's growth and stability, as the building of the New Labour project under Tony Blair's leadership represented the prospect of a substantially fresh style of politics – one which took an altogether different tone to emphasise new priorities and concerns. This was not least due to Labour's acute appreciation that if it was to survive, and even hope to thrive into the long term, it needed to appeal and relate to a much broader constituency than that to which the party had ever done before. As such, the level at which senior Labour figures engaged with Muslim representatives was both more frequent and more promising in its approach.

NEW LABOUR AND THE MCB – EARLY ACHIEVEMENTS

Directly after the General Election of 1997, there were hints that a Labour government would be favourable towards the conferment of government funding on Muslim schools, and that there was sympathy with the case for anti-religious discrimination legislation, the possibilities for which would at least be seriously considered.[80] This build-up served to raise the bar of expectations as to what Muslim representatives hoped could be delivered under Labour. On its own initiative, Labour endorsed Mohammad Sarwar as the first Muslim to run for a safe parliamentary seat, in the 1997 elections. Sarwar won the election and thus became the first Muslim MP in the UK, representing Glasgow Govan. This milestone was shortly followed in 1998 by the appointment to the House of Lords of two Muslim peers, also from the Labour party – Nazir Ahmed of Rotherham and Pola Uddin of Bethnal Green – making them the first Muslim peers in postwar Britain.[81] As such, the late 1990s was a time when both government and community representatives felt that there was much to be gained from forging greater mutual understanding and a fresh, more flexible approach towards calls for recognition.

Muslim activists on the matter of education and schools were heartened that the prospect for state funded Muslim schools was drawing closer,[82] and consequently campaigning was stepped up by the Association of Muslim Schools and in particular the Islamia School in north-west London, which had submitted its first application for state funding in 1984. Sure enough, by January 1998, only eight months after Labour came to power, both the Islamia School and Al-Furqan School in Birmingham were granted government funding. This decision signified a policy change from the consistent refusal with which funding requests had previously been met by successive Conservative governments. Labour's active engagement with the MCB on the census' religion question consultations, and on the issue of religious discrimination legislation, were both also seen as promising signs of a future of greatly enhanced cooperation and understanding between Muslim groups and the government.

There were other gestures that provided both symbolic and practical encouragement to British Muslims. In 1999, the post of Muslim Advisor to the Prison Service was created. The role included coordination of the work of dozens of imams who were already providing (often voluntary) religious support services for Muslim inmates within the UK's prison system, as well as the provision of official advice and guidance on all matters relating to Islam and Muslims, including dietary needs, religious obligations and religious holidays.[83] This development had come about after several years of consultation and representations to the government from the Iqra Trust and the Islamic Cultural Centre (the London Central Mosque), both of whom had been engaged in support and educational work within prisons for some time.

The same year also saw the launch of the first government-backed British Hajj Delegation. This was a scheme whereby the Foreign and Commonwealth Office funded and organised the stay of a British medical team of volunteers to provide on-hand medical assistance to British pilgrims to Mecca and Medina during the Hajj season, should they require it. Additionally, there was a consular aspect, which ensured that basic consular assistance and advice was on hand. The scheme was enthusiastically received not only for the genuine services and reassurance that it provided for pilgrims and their families, but it was also appreciated as part of a friendly approach from the government in taking the recognition of the specific needs of British Muslims beyond lip-service, by providing actual resources into improving an area where there was specific need.

On the matter of religious discrimination, and quite in line with the prevailing political mood of the time, the year 1997 also saw the release of the Runnymede Trust's report on Islamophobia.[84] This represented the moment when the term 'Islamophobia' first began to be used in public discourse, in itself a sign of much wider recognition for the Equality Gap, its existence and its problems. Defining the term as 'unfounded hostility towards Muslims, the dread and hatred of Islam – and, therefore, to fear or dislike all or most Muslims',[85] it is credited with having opened the way towards an unprecedented level of official attention in addressing the problems of Islamophobia and anti-Muslim discrimination.[86] Whereas preceding Conservative governments had simply refused to acknowledge issues of anti-Muslim discrimination as warranting official attention, the ready reception of the Runnymede report in 1997 was again indicative of Labour's preparedness to forge a new approach towards Muslim identity politics.

Yet it proved not enough for the Labour government to simply be prepared to acknowledge Islamophobia as a real and pressing social ill. The MCB's principal aim was a concrete legal development that would protect Muslim citizens from discrimination or harassment on the basis of religion. While amendments to the Crime and Disorder Act in 1998 created separate offences for crimes that were 'racially or religiously aggravated',[87] thereby providing for the prosecution of any religiously aggravated crime that could be shown to be even partially racially motivated, these were still considered to be inadequate by the MCB:

> Even the last minute amendments to the Crime and Disorder Act do not apply to me or those like me. I cannot summon indirect reference to my race – and find protection there. Indeed why would I want to? I feel sorry for those who are forced to surreptitiously use the clever language of the law to find protection.[88]

While the Labour government did show initial indifference towards supporting this specific cause of legislative reform, campaigning continued apace until finally in 2006 the Racial and Religious Hatred Act was introduced.[89] Although this did take several years, the MCB had assiduously sustained the debate and maintained dialogue with the government throughout this period.

Overall, the period between 1997 and 2001 was a time when relations between the newly formed MCB and the newly elected Labour government were marked by a mutual desire for progress in terms of recognition and understanding of the needs of British Muslims, and generally for better relations for the future.

The period between the 1980s and 2001 contained the most formative and defining years for contemporary Muslim identity politics. Preoccupation with and organising around identity preservation continued during the 1980s, and the Rushdie Affair towards the end of the decade prompted urgent steps towards the co-ordination and formalisation of communal representation efforts across the UK. This opened up the way for more effective calls for recognition as a community and a much more coherent articulation of claims to the government and the wider establishment that, it was hoped, would bring about greater civic equality for British Muslims. I have summarised these claims in the context of what I have termed the Equality Gap, and various aspects of this gap have continued to form a justificatory basis for the ongoing functioning of Muslim community and representative groups. The persistence of Muslim community activists in raising the Equality Gap as an issue over the decades is indicative of the reality of the challenges and obstacles that are posed by its continued existence. The Rushdie Affair and its aftermath represented a learning curve for both government and the Muslim communities' new-found representatives. Over time, arguments and approaches have been revised and fine-tuned, whilst some have been discarded altogether in favour of new ones. The most enduring grievance that has been voiced in the context of several claims and requests put forward to government has been that of the Equality Gap. Thus, I will proceed to look at Muslim identity politics with an understanding of the central justification that the Equality Gap embodies, with a special focus on the role and experience of civil liberties in their development.

In the wake of the Rushdie Affair, there had emerged a number of structures aspiring to voice the concerns of British Muslims and to secure their rights. Some, such as the MP, took a more confrontational approach, others such as UKACIA preferred to pursue dialogue and diplomacy by campaigning and making representations to the government. But by the late 1990s, a combination of years of consultative groundwork and active encouragement from the government had placed the newly formed MCB at the helm of British Muslim identity politics.

The MCB has been the most long-lived of these and the most successful to date, not least because of the substantial endorsement that was afforded to its establishment by the government, and also because of its efforts to secure legitimacy through bringing on board affiliates from across the country and from a range of different sections within British Muslim religious and cultural spectra. By the closing years of the twentieth century, the establishment of the MCB and its early development can be considered as something of a formalisation of British Muslim identity politics, in the same way that Jewish identity politics had been formalised over the years through the functioning of the BOD. Indeed, a survey of the development of identity politics and community representation among both British Jews and British Muslims reveals interesting points of comparison as well as contrasts.

Different migratory conditions have meant that each community approached its settlement in the UK differently. Long-term community planning played a greater role in the establishment of Jewish pan-community representation, whereas for Muslims this came about more as a reaction to external circumstances. Ultimately, the formalisation of Muslim identity politics came about as a result of a sort of trial-and-error process, as consecutive efforts – from the 1960s through to the mid-1990s – to unite British Muslims and represent them politically encountered hurdles, and fresh efforts took their place.

Yet despite these unique challenges, by the turn of the century, Muslim identity politics had resulted in a number of tangible achievements. A favourable political climate had afforded the MCB the type of official recognition that had long been craved by Muslim communal leaders, and with this came the achievement of considerable milestones in narrowing aspects of the Equality Gap – the first state funding for Muslim schools, a commitment from government to tackle religious hatred in the law, the success of the MCB-led campaign to include a religion question in the national census, as well as greater political representation, and formal state recognition and provision for the specific needs of British Muslims in various areas. In the next chapter, I show how the terrorist attacks of 11 September 2001 prompted a turning point in this quasi-official status that Muslim identity politics, primarily through the MCB, had recently acquired.

CHAPTER 5

Identity Politics in the Aftermath of 9/11 (September 2001–July 2005)

The period between September 2001 and July 2005 was characterised by a sharp increase in the level of Muslim political agency and the intensity of community organising. Much of this increase came about as a direct response to the rapid alterations that were taking place in the global and national arenas in reaction to the US terrorist attacks of 9/11. The introduction of heightened security measures and the discourse and thinking behind the resulting 'war on terror' provoked concerns in many quarters about silencing, restricting or channelling of expression and dissent as effects of:

- Restrictions and proscriptions imposed by anti-terror laws, and
- Disenchantment with perceptions of attitudes and motives in government foreign and domestic policies.

These presented Muslim representatives and the government with fresh challenges that resulted in a defining moment in their relationship, leading to a somewhat cool and more cautious attitude between them. At the same time, there was a reactive drive among Muslims to state clearly their positions on matters on which they felt they were being misunderstood and seriously misjudged, including the denouncement of terrorism and violence, issues of loyalty and

citizenship, and the notion of separate cultures and the irreconcilability of Islam with Western democracy – often characterised as a
'clash of civilisations'. The latter concept, as I show later on in this
chapter, became increasingly utilised as a tool by the far-right and
others to justify an emergent 'clean-faced', respectable form of
Islamophobia.

This period also saw a growth in Muslim involvement within broad-
based social and political coalitions such as the anti-war movement, as
well as the emergence and development of various new and more
creative modes of Muslim self-expression to join pre-existing ones.
It also witnessed a refreshed, more nuanced approach to reasoning that
was used by Muslims to argue for their causes in the public-political
domain, in particular the enduring issue of a legal response to religious
discrimination and incitement to religious hatred.

In this chapter, I first outline notable aspects of British Muslim
political consciousness in the few years prior to the attacks of 9/11,
thus drawing out exactly how this juncture represents a turning point
and the role that freedom of expression and civil liberties played in
these changes. I look at the reactions to 9/11 across government and
Muslim advocacy groups and then discuss the changes that took
place during the four years between 9/11 and the summer of 2005
under four main headings: new security legislation and the language
of securitisation, relations between the government and the MCB,
far-right Islamophobia, and innovation in self-expression among
young British Muslims. I then analyse what the various developments
under each of these four themes meant for Muslim groups, in
particular the MCB, and also what they meant for the government's
relations with them as well as British Muslim political consciousness
in general, including a consideration of the policy developments
related to each of these respective themes.

BRITISH ISLAM AT THE TURN OF THE MILLENNIUM

In the years running up to the new millennium, British Muslim
public and political life was developing to become both outgoing and
highly confident. The intense efforts at institution building that took
place during the 1990s paid off by creating a generation of young,

politically conscious and religiously committed British Muslims who viewed their Islamic identity and its primacy in their lives not only as something to protect and preserve, but also to positively promote.

As I have discussed in the previous chapter, religio-political activism in the wake of the Rushdie Affair had attracted the interest and subsequently consolidated the influence of Islamic movements from around the Muslim world on the Muslim communities of the UK. One impact of this was that young British Muslims found that they now had easier access to a whole range of different political interests and perspectives – each was keen to widen its sphere of influence as far as possible. The fact that their 'Muslim identity' could be represented in such a variety of ways was something of a collective discovery for them. Youth and student groups, spurred on by this growing 'Muslim-consciousness', vied with one another to win a following amongst the second and third generations, who had grown up without the kinds of psychological and practical struggles that their parents had faced. Whereas the newly arrived first generation had been preoccupied with laying down foundations for their families' basic needs, their children enjoyed a far greater degree of confidence and the capability to assert what was distinctive about their own identities rather than trying hard to blend in with wider society.

The new 'primarily Muslim' religious identity that had been fostered by the events of the Rushdie Affair was carried with pride by many of the community's young people. Visible manifestations of this included a steady increase in those who preferred to wear traditional religious or cultural dress. While such a development is clearly difficult to measure since no statistics directly measuring such a fluid aspect of individual choice as clothing can be obtained, anecdotal evidence sourced from articles and accounts written about this period are useful in giving an idea of how much the 1990s were a period of religious discovery and self-assertion for young British Muslims.[1] And while the socio-economic status of many Muslim communities remained relatively low, significant numbers of young Muslims had nonetheless enjoyed access to good education, often better than that of their parents. Their entry into universities and the professions injected greater levels of confidence within their communities, not to mention diversity of opinion, aptitude and expertise.

Strides had been made in political representation, too, and the number of Muslims entering local politics was on the increase. While the statistics for Muslims in local politics can only be approximated from more general statistics on race and ethnicity in the field, they are definitely indicative of a steady, if limited, rise during this period,[2] although as Hussain notes, this was largely due to individual endeavours rather than group participation or mass-organising. Indeed, where there were attempts at group participation in politics, such as the Islamic Party of Britain[3] and the MP, results were poor and projects were short-lived.

In terms of self-image, and how Muslim communities saw themselves reflected in the mainstream, it was not uncommon to find a deep suspicion and mistrust of the portrayal of Islam and Muslims in the media ingrained in the collective psyche of many in the Muslim community. A large part of this can be put down to memories of the Rushdie Affair, which were still fresh,[4] but it also goes back much further into the past.[5] Both print and broadcast media were frequently portrayed as a form of enemy, who had ulterior vested interests in projecting a negative image of the Muslim community to their wider audiences. Such an understanding fed neatly into a polarised postcolonial perspective of 'The West versus Islam', which featured Islam and Muslims as downtrodden and mistreated by an exploitative and godless (or at least anti-Islamic) 'West'.

Britain was by this stage sheltering a whole host of different political refugees from the Muslim world, who were attracting followers from among the country's own Muslim population. For better or for worse, the UK's perceived leniency when it came to allowances for political asylum seekers made it a popular destination for those Islamic political activists who were in exile or on the run from oppressive regimes in their home countries. Many exiled dissidents would cite the UK's scope for freedom of expression as well as its historic reputation for sheltering 'foreign dissidents, from Karl Marx to Victor Hugo'.[6] The UK's position as a 'destination of choice' was no doubt enhanced by its geography. In terms of distance, it was not too far to travel from their home countries in the Muslim world (as compared with North America, for instance); the UK also had the benefit of easier access to mainland Europe, as well as the fact that the English language itself is widely spoken as a second language. In addition, Britain's imperial past may well have fed into a sense of entitlement among political agitators seeking asylum, insofar as their utilising the UK as a haven amounted to 'taking back' from a former empire that had previously exploited and dominated their homelands.

The influence of international political dissidents was not limited to those who were resident in the UK – leading personalities from a spectrum of Islamist movements operating abroad were regularly hosted to speak at events in the UK. Such gatherings were used not only to spread their ideas and drum up support in the UK, but also to fundraise for these political movements.[7] Hailing from countries such as Algeria, Bangladesh, Egypt, the Sudan, Pakistan and Syria, the UK provided opportunities for speeches and fundraising activities that were rather more difficult for these movements to arrange within those home countries that were the objects of their struggles.

International events such as the first Gulf War and later the conflict in former Yugoslavia and genocide in Bosnia, all served to rally together a sense of communal or, as Modood puts it, 'associational' identity.[8] Such events also prompted difficult questions about loyalty for British Muslims, many of whom opposed their government's support for the war against Iraq and had natural ties and sympathies with the wider *ummah* abroad. This dilemma was only exacerbated by the perspective amongst some that the conflict in the Gulf was one between the 'imperialist' Western Allies and the 'anti-imperialist' Saddam Hussein. Long-standing grievances about US and British support for Israel were also invoked by radical groups such as HT to further support this characterisation. Furthermore, Saudi Arabian official 'collusion' with the Western powers was vigorously denounced as traitorous, and evidence that, as per HT's worldview, regimes in the Muslim world needed to be toppled and replaced by a virtuous *Khilafa*.[9] As for the war in Bosnia, the close proximity of the conflict and the 'European-ness' of Bosnian Muslims, coupled with the perceived reluctance of Western nations to sanction military intervention, simply reinforced the dilemma around loyalty and identity. As McRoy notes:

> The Bosnian crisis shocked the community, partly because Bosnian Muslims held the very identity that government ministers were understood to be suggesting for British Muslims, yet this did not prevent their being slaughtered. This discredited government statements at the time of the Rushdie crisis yet further ... Their perception was that Muslims were unwanted in Europe, and that this prejudice had led to the massacre of their brethren elsewhere on the continent ... Muslim voices expressed concern that they could be the next victims of European Islamophobia.[10]

These international events contributed towards a reinforced sense of pride and association with the *ummah* on one hand, and a sense of distrust of or, at least, a sense of grievance towards 'the West' on the other. Among the manifestations of this attitude were conspiracy theories around Zionist-US plots to control or bring down the Muslim world. By the mid-1990s, these factors combined had all contributed to a general heightened awareness of the *ummah* among British Muslims. Right-wing commentators would have us believe that there was some kind of loyalty trade-off, whereby young Muslims who had been deeply affected by injustices abroad began to feel greater allegiances towards the *ummah* at the expense of the UK. Yet sources from the time convey less of a hostile sentiment towards British civic life or disengagement from it, than they do a feeling that double-standards were being employed towards Muslims when it came to foreign policy.[11]

Somewhat linked to this was the display by many Muslim organisations in their discourse and activities of a confident (perhaps overconfident) and uninhibited sense of openness that was raw, fresh and even acutely naïve in its choice of language and emphasis. Among the mainstream groups there was sometimes a sense of pride in harbouring the desire to bring Islamic rule to the UK. In the main, it was hoped to achieve such ambitions through peaceful *da'wa* (the evangelical call to Islam), however, there was some talk among the most extreme of more violent means, although how seriously such talk was intended is a matter of debate, which I will come to shortly.

More moderate thinkers within this strain spoke of a Britain that was 'in search of a vision and a direction' and to which its Muslim citizens bore the responsibility of offering guidance.[12] On this basis, they emphasised the importance of civic participation. However, this was often accompanied with the qualification that responsible citizenship would further the cause of *da'wa*, and that community service was a means through which Islamically inspired social values could be disseminated through to wider society. By highlighting this aspect, I am not suggesting that this attitude towards social participation was inherently disingenuous or insidious; however, it is telling that these sorts of justifications were so readily used. As I shall go on to demonstrate, the experience of building broad political partnerships post-9/11 catalysed a change in approaches to civic participation, such that it became more open, more pragmatic and less conditional upon religiously grounded caveats and justifications.

On the more extreme end of the scale, the British arm of HT, an Islamic political party with its roots in the Middle East, provides one window into perspectives among radical Muslims during this period.[13] During the 1990s its activities regularly grabbed headlines for their dramatic and confrontational nature.[14] HT provoked anxiety and outrage in equal measures as it called for the 'supremacy' of Islam and preached separatism to its followers, in addition to indulging regularly in anti-Semitism and clashes with gay and Jewish groups on university campuses.[15] Probably its most highly publicised activity during this period was an international '*Khilafa* Conference' that was organised in August 1994 at the Wembley Arena in London. The event courted plenty of controversy before it even happened. Bright, luminous publicity stickers were posted in high streets and public places, boasting of: '*Khilafa* – coming soon, to a country near you'.[16] Invited speakers included individuals who were linked with the organisation from various Arab and Muslim countries. The conference organisers spoke of bold ambitions to 'fly the flag of Islam above Number 10 Downing Street', and there was even a call for the assassination of Prime Minister John Major from the leader of HT.[17] However, although organisers anticipated 8–10,000 attendees and an enthusiastic reception (*Guardian* and *Independent*, 4 August 1994), the conference did not meet these expectations, with a much more modest audience turning up and barely any tangible impact beyond the few alarmist newspaper headlines that were generated.[18] While the comparison of HT-type views with those of the 'moderate mainstream' is stark, in many instances they both rely to some degree on the notion of Islamic religious and cultural primacy, juxtaposing it with some notion of Western decadence.

Another example is a case among groups with more *salafi* (literalist) and *jihadi* leanings.[19] Jonathan Birt sheds light on a mood of isolationism in which self-identification was constituted in opposition not only to 'the West', but also to their own communities, both locally and as an *ummah*. All of these were seen to be misguided in various ways, whether through godlessness, or through 'associating with' or 'following' the godless West. Central to this way of thinking was the notion of '*al wala wal bara*', a concept with roots in early Islamic thought which roughly translates as 'loyalty and disassociation'. Many *salafis* and *jihadis* would use this as a mantra to justify an exclusivist and self-righteous world view whereby their own remaining on the 'straight and narrow' was inextricably linked with a vehement denouncement of those around them for their misguidance, whether wilful or erroneous. So at a meeting of a typical *jihadi* study group, Birt reports a mentor urging attendees to 'cut your ties from the people of *shirk* (polytheism), because you can't cut your ties from *shirk* except that you cut your ties from the people of *shirk*'.[20] He then goes on to elaborate on the grave differences between 'believers' and *kuffar* (unbelievers), including the direct link, as he sees it, between faith and an obligation of *jihad*, in addition to emphasising the 'need' for true Muslims to migrate to the Muslim world, to *dar al Islam* and away from *dar al kufr*,[21] since doing so was an appropriate and necessary demonstration of their loyalty to the faith and their disassociation from disbelief and decadence.

The language and approach that was used by these types of groups is chilling and would certainly raise alarm bells in today's securitised post-9/11 Britain. Talk of an obligation of *jihad* and of disassociation from non-believers would hardly be permitted to take place openly in mosques, nor would such conversations happen in open gatherings that members of the public could freely join. When considered with the benefit of hindsight acquired over the past decade, this sort of approach may well give the impression of an aggressive or threatening desire to violently dominate Britain and impose Islamic ideals on culture, politics and society in general. However, it is important to resist forming an instant teleological judgement of these groups, and to consider the period and context in question. As Birt (and others)[22] point out, the mainstream of the Muslim community rarely took such groups seriously and preferred instead to ignore or sideline them. For many, Muslims and non-Muslims, these types of characters were nothing more than 'affable fools',[23] rather than an urgent threat. At the same time, these groups in actuality had very little to hide – in essence many of them were talk-shops, gathering together disgruntled Muslim youth who faced common grievances or who were dealing with similar challenges in life. Often these included day-to-day issues such as difficulties in education or finding work, providing for their families or simply 'fitting in' with their peers. Overlapping with or running alongside these were the challenges of practising their faith, reconciling their Britishness with their cultures of heritage and dealing with experiences (whether real or perceived) of discrimination and injustice, such as Islamophobia or cases of unequal legal treatment, as well as frustration at aspects of British foreign policy that were interpreted as being anti-Islamic.

The British Muslim 'scene' by the turn of the twenty-first century was one of increasing diversity, confidence and growing sophistication in the nature and style of its political participation. However, many within the Muslim communities retained a strong element of naïveté regarding the true nature and meaning of citizenship and civic participation.

MUSLIMS, CIVIL LIBERTIES AND SECURITISATION IN POST-9/11 BRITAIN

The date 11 September 2001 has come to be seen as a historic watershed moment in so many different respects the world over, but extremely acutely so for the Muslim communities of Western countries. British Muslims are a case in point, and the 'before' and 'after' comparisons that can be made are innumerable. From the very outset, a deep sensitivity was attached to the attacks that took place in the US, both as a reaction to their very happening, and in response to the implicit or explicit association that was widely made between them and the Muslim faith. I consider how this turning point came about in each of three areas: government, Muslim representative organisations and among Muslims at the 'grassroots' level. I will then discuss the impact of the changes in discourse and communication that were precipitated by the events of 9/11 under four main categories: security, Islamophobia, government-community relations and innovation in self-expression.

For the government, the most immediate and pressing concern was naturally that of national security. The attacks were of such a large and unprecedented magnitude and the potential threat to British national security consered so pressing, that an immediate response was called for. At the same time, the fact that *Muslim* terror networks were implicated meant that government had to deal with the impact of the attacks on community relations and, most specifically, to minimise the impacts of the backlash against Britain's Muslims through the racism, discrimination or 'revenge attacks' that took place across the country,[24] to reassure Britain's Muslims by emphasising unity, shared values and especially a shared abhorrence of terrorism, violence and victimisation.[25]

From the security perspective, steps were taken to revise existing anti-terror legislation in order to have it reflect the new threats that the post-9/11 era would pose. This primarily included an extension to the recently introduced Terrorism Act of 2000 (TA 2000), which had superseded pre-existing anti-terror laws, and broadened their scope by addressing terrorism beyond activities that were associated specifically with the Northern Ireland conflict. The TA 2000's defining features were its identification of a list of international terror organisations – association with or support of which was to be banned. In addition, it made provision for the first time for police to be allowed to detain terrorist suspects for questioning, for up to seven days. This act itself had not been passed without intense debate and scrutiny, and indeed was watered down on its way to the statute books as part of this process.

The 2001 Anti-terrorism Crime and Security Act sought to complete the 2000 legislation by making provisions for foreign terrorist suspects to be detained indefinitely pending deportation, even where deportation is ruled prohibited (for instance due to a real risk of torture at the destination country). It also introduced new regulations pertaining to the security and detention of aircraft where there is suspicion of an act of violence against a person on board, allowed police to obtain fingerprints and other identifying features to ascertain an individual's identity by force, and gave powers to the Home Secretary for the regulation of internet and telephone communication companies' retention of data for the purpose of national security.[26]

In addition to these legislative measures, Tony Blair's Labour government advanced decisive policies at home and abroad to ensure that it was seen to be in control in dealing with the new terror threat. These included a more hard-line approach in matters of immigration, for instance through the introduction of compulsory citizenship tests. This attitude was also played out in a new phase of foreign policy, one which placed much emphasis on Great Britain's 'special relationship' with the USA and the shared interest in combating international terrorism, through increased security measures as well as going to war in Afghanistan.

GOVERNMENT-MCB RELATIONS

On the home front, the government took steps to indicate its commitment to containing and minimising the terrorist threat, and, significantly, ensuring stability and cohesion within and among the country's communities, in particular with regard to Britain's Muslims. On 12 September, the day following the attacks, Tony Blair made specific mention of the 'British Muslim Council' (sic) in his address to the nation from Downing Street, praising their 'strong statement of condemnation' and going on to assert that 'the vast majority of Muslims are decent, upright people who share our horror at what happened.'[27] On 14 September, at an emergency session for which the House of Commons had been recalled, he addressed 'our Arab and Muslim friends' and referred to the attacks as 'barbarism that is totally foreign to the true spirit and teachings of Islam'.[28] On 27 September, Blair held a meeting with MCB representatives at which they stood together for the press, presenting the powerful image of a united front.[29] Blair declared that racism and revenge-type attacks on Muslims 'have no proper place in our country', and remarked upon the shared heritage between Islam and Christianity, in an effort to inject positivity into a mood that was weighed down by feelings of anger, suspicion and vulnerability.

Together, these remarks represent an affirmative drive on the government's part to speak to Muslims in the UK, and also internationally. This drive was a first in terms of its scale and its pro-activeness and was indicative of a conciliatory desire to open up dialogue and build partnership and trust. From the perspective of securing community cohesion and diffusing the very real atmosphere of unease and apprehension that was stoked by sensationalist media coverage of 'Islamic terrorism',[30] this kind of language and gesture from the government was absolutely needed. However, when considered alongside the evermore stringent and heavy handed legal strand of the Government's post-9/11 response, it is difficult not to suspect that the associated motives must have contained some element of instrumentalism. Perhaps it was thought that the ongoing introduction of restrictive and highly controversial anti-terror laws coupled with the pursuit of a foreign policy approach that attracted widespread opposition could be sweetened with efforts to reassure British Muslims and underline their (at least nominal) inclusion in the evolving national conversation on security, citizenship and cohesion.

As for Muslim organisations, there was a near-unanimous immediate reaction of swift and unequivocal condemnation.[31] Press releases and a dense, consistent flow of media writings and appearances were the hallmark efforts of all Muslim advocacy groups and representatives, whatever their size, constituency or location. The MCB was most prominent in this respect – with daily media appearances, it quickly built up a public profile as the official Muslim interlocutor on matters relating to the US terror attacks in particular, as well as more generally on questions pertaining to Islam and

Muslims themselves. The attacks had sparked a remarkable level of public interest in Islam that was motivated by curiosity and a desire to better understand just as often as it was driven by hostility and paranoia.

With proficient and media-friendly spokespeople, this was a role that the MCB readily assumed. The benefit of this was that there was always somebody to 'speak' for the Muslim community. The established and organised channel of communication that both Muslim activists and the government had so long desired seemed to have finally found its calling and come into its own, albeit under extraordinarily highly pressurised circumstances! On a community level, the MCB worked consistently to encourage and promote initiatives by its affiliates to develop 'positive' responses to the 9/11 attacks. For example, the annual Islam Awareness Week in November 2001 had as its theme 'Islam for Peace and Justice' and held events across the country with the aim of dispelling the abundant tabloid myths of an inherently violent Islam as well as tackling questions on the nature of a just and commensurate response to the attacks.[32]

There were drawbacks to the MCB's newfound role as the voice of Britain's Muslim communities. The intensity of the spotlight on the MCB meant that it was open to greater scrutiny and more readily held to blame for flaws and shortcomings that may otherwise have passed unnoticed. The tenuousness of this situation was played out in the two years after 9/11 as securitisation and foreign policy concerns became heavily influential factors in government relations with the Muslim community.

The MCB's concerted efforts at speaking in condemnation of the terrorist attacks could not easily be followed by a reticent silence against the backdrop of government foreign policy that was preoccupied with preparations to enter war in Afghanistan, and later in Iraq. As such, there were delicate decisions to make relating to its stance on post-9/11 foreign policy – the MCB could not command credibility by diplomatically 'sitting on the fence', yet at the same time, just one 'wrong foot' could damage the organisation's hard-earned position as quasi-official gatekeeper to British Islam.

After some deliberation, the MCB eventually found itself faced with 'an important trade off' to make.[33] Initial hesitation to vocally oppose the War on Terror was met with growing disquiet amongst its affiliates, and the Muslim community in general.[34] As Birt points out, this coincided with repeated attempts from the Blair government to keep the MCB 'on side', or, at the very least, to keep it passive about the invasion of Afghanistan. The situation was difficult, to say the least. Here was the first time that a British Muslim representative body had simultaneously earned real credence among communities *and* was given respectability in establishment circles; yet here it was being expected to toe the government line on an issue that its constituents were overwhelmingly and strongly opposed to. Diplomacy, political bartering and even threats were all employed to win the MCB over,[35] yet in the end it proved inconceivable for the MCB *not* to oppose the war. With the vast majority of Britain's Muslim communities actively opposing military action, anything short of this from the MCB would effectively have been political suicide.

When the Council *did* make a decision to come out clearly against the war, it precipitated a moment when the government, the MCB itself and Muslim community groups all came to important realisations. For the government, that it was important not to 'put all its eggs in one basket' again, by relying solely on the MCB as the official representative of the Muslim community and its channel of communication with it.[36] The MCB realised that it could not assume that either government support or that of its constituency (primarily its affiliate groups, but also British Muslim communities in general) was automatically theirs by right. Politics was politics at the end of the day, and support, respect and credibility had to be earned and sustained, as with any other advocacy or lobbying arrangement. For Muslim grass-roots organisations, this experience opened up doors to new ways of making their voice heard. Uneasy with the slow pace with which the MCB's position developed, a number of community groups generated their own responses in opposition to the War on Terror. Most significantly, these included partnerships with the left-wing Socialist Workers Party to create the Stop the War Coalition (StWC). The MAB (an MCB affiliate) took a lead role in this, as did a

number of other local and regional groups.[37] Activities largely
consisted of organising mass protest marches and demonstrations as
well as petitions and campaigns to build up public awareness of and,
ultimately, opposition to what was seen as Britain's gravely mistaken
foray into unjustified international pursuits led by self-serving
ambitions, and those of a 'neoconservative' US administration.

ISLAMOPHOBIA OF THE RISING FAR-RIGHT, AND RELIGIOUS HATRED LEGISLATION

Another noteworthy change that came about during this period was a
rather bold resurgence of the Islamophobic far-right. Racist groups
were able to play on genuine fears and paranoia in the wake of the
9/11 events and build up hostility that was directed squarely at Islam
and Muslims in the UK. The British National Party exploited legal
loopholes (the Equality Gap) and launched a 'Campaign Against
Islam',[38] focusing its efforts particularly in areas of the country which
housed large Muslim communities. On the back of recent race riots
that had taken place in the Northern towns of Burnley and Oldham
during the summer of 2001, coupled with the fallout from the 9/11
attacks, these campaigns made use of a number of widespread
stereotypes regarding, among others, violence, intolerance and the
subjugation of women, and sought to warn the public of the perils of
the impending 'Islamification' of Britain, and the need to stop it in its
tracks.

Chris Allen has demonstrated how the arguments employed in
the party's literature and campaign material were built on
remarkably shaky and highly skewed foundations.[39] Indeed,
judging by the sheer absurdity of the numerous implausible
accusations that were made, it seems that the BNP was intent on
transferring the blame for each and every social ill or irritation that
the 'indigenous Anglo-Saxon white working classes'[40] suffered from
onto the shoulders of Britain's Muslims. In addition to the 'usual'
charges of 'stealing' the 'native' population's jobs, housing and
public services, the BNP promoted the notion that the religion
and culture of Muslims were intrinsically and irrevocably sinister
and incompatible with British life. Nick Griffin, speaking to a

gathering in Keighley, Yorkshire, claimed that the Qur'an instructs Muslim men to rape white women and children:

> ... and you will find verse after verse after verse which says that you can take any women you want as long as they're not Muslim women – any woman that your right arm can own. That's the sword arm, it's the fighting arm, it's the arm you hit a white lad with a baseball bat with ... Any woman that they can take by force or guile is theirs. If they get a non-Muslim girl and they get her pregnant then her community doesn't want her and the child generally grows up to be a Muslim. And that's the way that this wicked vicious faith has expanded from a handful of cranky lunatics about thirteen hundred years ago, till it's now sweeping country after country before it all over the world ... [41]

He went on to insist that 'You have got to stand up and do something for the British National Party because otherwise they [Muslims] will do for someone in your family, that is the truth.'[42] Further, campaign leaflets distributed by the BNP during this period depicted Islam as an acronym, ISLAM = Intolerance, Slaughter, Looting, Arson, Molestation of Women, which reinforced the message that the faith itself was centrally linked to despicable social ills and criminality.[43]

Although politicians and public figures of every shade did denounce and distance themselves from this bold new trend in the far-right political agenda,[44] much of it remained technically legal, and this reality highlighted anew the old problem of how to deal with prejudice and discrimination when it was targeted at groups that were identified by their religion, or where, as Kay Goodall describes it, 'religion is used as a surrogate for racism'.[45]

While the BNP's anti-Islam campaign was ongoing, activity was stepped up during election time (council elections in 2002, European, London Mayoral and council elections in 2004, and the General Election in 2005), targeting areas with large Muslim populations and where segregation was a problem. The language that was used exploited a gap in anti-discrimination legislation which at that point did not yet outlaw incitement to hatred on the basis of religion. Publicity material – both printed and online – was careful to criticise Islam and Muslims as a religion and culture rather than in a racial way.[46] It also defined the party as defending Britain's 'heritage', its 'Christian values', and guarding against their dilution, partly through immigration and partly through its incorporation of immigrants (in particular Muslims) into society through access to resources. Another tactic employed by the BNP was to showcase its 'ethnic' membership in a bid to shake off its racist image, while simultaneously attacking Islam and Muslims. This included featuring a turban-wearing Sikh man in its 2004 election broadcast and fielding Jewish and mixed-race candidates.[47]

On the policy side, this new wave of open Islamophobia generated renewed debates on whether the Equality Gap's continued existence could be justified. It also prompted discussions on the arguably fine line between calls for the criminalisation of incitement to religious hatred, and instituting what could be construed as a new form of blasphemy law whereby criticism of any religion or its texts could be penalised, and free speech restricted as a result.[48] Lobbying from the MCB[49] and other Muslim bodies[50] was bolstered by recommendations that had been made throughout this period from organisations such as the Runnymede Trust's Commission on British Muslims and Islamophobia, which published in 2004 a report reviewing and discussing progress and developments since its previous (1997) ground-breaking report on Islamophobia.[51] The 2004 report was extensive in its coverage and comprehensive in its analysis, making specific recommendations for adoption by a whole range of government departments as a way of tackling Islamophobia. Importantly, it made detailed recommendations regarding the need to 'make discrimination on religious grounds unlawful', noting that while EU laws had brought this about in the area of employment, 'the government's continuing failure to deal robustly (on all levels) with this matter remains a matter of great concern'.[52]

The government made several attempts to pass a law during this period dealing with religious hatred, but these were regularly opposed and voted out by the House of Lords. Nonetheless, a Select Committee was set up to look into the matter, and by the 2005 General Election the government made a firm manifesto commitment that it would:

> give people of all faiths the same protection against incitement to hatred on the basis of their religion. We will legislate to outlaw it and

will continue the dialogue we have started with faith groups from all
backgrounds about how best to balance protection, tolerance and
free speech.[53]

A law was eventually passed in 2006, and although this falls just
outside of the time-frame under consideration in this chapter, I shall
discuss it briefly, since its enactment can be attributed in a large part
to the post-9/11 discussions that took place on the matter.

The Act weathered significant resistance and controversy from
diverse quarters. Outside of parliament, a host of actors, comedians,
writers and artists opposed the law, seeing it as a threat to freedom of
expression and artistic freedoms, including the space to be able to
laugh at religion, religious dogma and establishment. The civil
liberties body, Liberty, while acknowledging the need to protect
minority groups, argued that freedom of speech was a value far
worthier of preservation. Moreover, it argued (along with the
Discrimination Law Association, and many others) that the
legislation, as proposed by the government, was not much more
than an effort to 'placate' Muslim communities, in particular the
MCB, who were aggrieved by foreign policy and relentless draconian
anti-terrorism measures at home.[54] Within parliament there was a
large voting rebellion by Labour backbenchers and strong opposition
from the Conservatives, Liberal Democrats and many in the House of
Lords. As a consequence, the final piece of legislation was passed with
two amendments introduced by the Lords. These changes stipulated
that the law should only criminalise 'A person who uses threatening
words or behaviour, or displays any written material which is
threatening ... if he intends thereby to stir up religious hatred',[55] thus
limiting its application so that it could not cover words that were
'merely' abusive or insulting; in addition to making it a requirement
for there to be an actual intention to stir up hatred, rather than
simply a possibility.

It was this last requirement of intent that proved a disappointment
to supporters of the law. With the requirement of intent clearly
stipulated, it meant that in cases where defendants denied intent,
prosecutors would be faced with the almost impossible task of
proving it. This, as Goodall points out, renders the new legislation

'almost unenforceable', since while 'extremist clerics who confess their intentions may be caught ... racist activists will have little trouble adapting their rhetoric'[56] to avoid falling foul of the intent clause. The MCB expressed its dismay at this development, arguing that it had now created 'a hierarchy of rights among British citizens'.[57]

The government's clear resolve by 2005 to pass a law on religious hatred, despite the fierce controversy that it drew, represents how much had changed during this period in its policy relations with the Muslim community. Back in 1997, Home Secretary Jack Straw had been unwilling to consider any such legislation,[58] yet by 2005 his party was on its third attempt to pass religious hatred legislation and was prepared to suffer extensive criticism and one of its most humiliating Commons defeats in order to have it enacted. When considered in context, this new commitment must have been prompted by factors that were not present in 1997, and, as was suggested at the time by the government's critics in parliament, a desire to appease otherwise disgruntled Muslim communities seems a convincing explanation.[59] Nonetheless, it also represents progress in the maturing government-community political conversation, as the lobbying by the MCB and Muslim pressure groups was lodged squarely in the language of equalities legislation,[60] and all but discarded entirely the argument based on blasphemy that was so often rehearsed during and after the Rushdie Affair. As such, the MCB was able to confidently present its case alongside other interest-groups, as their support for the law shared common foundations. For example, in January 2005 it held a meeting at the House of Commons jointly with the CRE, the British Humanist Association and Justice on 'The Need to Protect Faith Communities from Incitement to Hatred'.[61]

In addition to the developments in the area of religious discrimination, another reaction to the rise of the 'respectable' far-right was in the field of immigration and the integration of immigrants and minority groups. As I have mentioned, the main parties were regularly at pains to denounce and isolate the BNP. However, the BNP's very act of raising such issues, coupled with the constant (often media-fuelled)[62] public concerns around security, meant that the main political players were forced to tackle them in their own political agendas, if only as a matter of political expediency, to retain voters who were being attracted to the BNP, and to allay public fears regarding immigration and security.[63] What this meant was that while there was a politics of reconciliation towards minorities in matters relating to tackling discrimination and racism, there was a concurrent rise in 'tough talk' on immigration – especially so when it came to immigrants from outside the European Economic Community. In real terms, this trend impacted on Muslim communities more strongly than other minority communities. Legislation tightening the conditions required for immigrants to obtain citizenship called for applicants to learn to speak English to a minimum standard and to pass a test on 'Life in the UK'. Other legislation made seeking asylum a far more rigorous process, making detention and deportation very real outcomes of asylum-seeking attempts for those who could not provide watertight evidence to support their cases.

PROACTIVE SELF-EXPRESSION – THROUGH POLITICS, CIVIL SOCIETY AND CREATIVITY

A final development worth noting is the gathering momentum in the field of diverse and creative forms of expression within Britain's Muslim communities during this period. I have already discussed the significant political leap that was taken by several Muslim groups by entering into partnerships with left-wing organisations to voice their opposition to the war. It is arguable that this move was made more out of circumstance than any preference, since it came about only after the MCB failed to move swiftly and decisively in leading a Muslim opposition to the war. Nonetheless, pragmatic though it was, it was a deal which was entered into wholeheartedly, and this move in itself represented a capacity among British Muslims to explore new avenues for self-expression and making themselves heard.[64] Earlier I observed how the British Islam of the 1990s was somewhat constrained by an underdeveloped sense of citizenship and a rather overblown sense of self-mission. By the early 2000s, this mindset was changing at a steadily growing pace.

The MAB positioned itself as a key partner in the British anti-war movement, playing a central role in organising for the epic demonstration of March 2003 that took place on the eve of the invasion of Iraq. Its alliance with the left was not without criticism (both from more extreme Muslim groups such as HT, and the liberal, pro-war left).[65] However, the support it enjoyed was widespread, and the partnership provided invaluable learning experiences and networking opportunities for Muslim anti-war activists and groups. This intensive participation in mainstream political movements paved the way for Muslim anti-war personalities standing as candidates for the recently formed Respect Party during the 2004 European, council and London mayoral elections. These included Anas Altikriti, himself a former President of the MAB, and Salma Yaqoob, who cut her political teeth as a founder and leader of the StWC in Birmingham in 2001, as well as Yvonne Ridley, a former *Sunday Express* reporter who had been held captive by the Taliban and subsequently converted to Islam. The experience of working with the Left served to broaden the political experience of many within the Muslim community, in addition to accelerating the pace at which their level of mainstream political engagement intensified.

The burgeoning of Muslim self-expression was not limited to politics and foreign affairs. This period also witnessed a growth in Muslim press and media. Q *News*, originally founded in the early 1990s as a Muslim community newspaper with local preoccupations and a limited circulation, had recently reinvented itself as a glossy magazine. Post-9/11 Britain was an optimal environment within which it could flourish – and it did, with impressive (albeit irregular) issues covering wide-ranging, topical and controversial topics. *The Muslim Paper, The Muslim Weekly* and the *London Muslim* were altogether new newspaper initiatives born during this period, each devoting large sections of their publications to politics and Muslim identity issues, yet also making space for art, culture, sport and finance. 2003 saw the launch of *emel*, a Muslim lifestyle magazine which sought to provide an upbeat yet honest perspective on British Islam by providing 'a window into the Muslim community away from the clichés'.[66] In the area of new media, websites and blogs grew at a phenomenal rate, being used especially by younger Muslims to express themselves and make connections and networks in ways that weren't possible before. Some are worth particular mention due to their longevity and continuous development since this period, proving their utility of purpose and relevance. These include www.salaam.co.uk, which was devoted to documenting wide-ranging information and data on British Muslim history as well as providing magazine-type features and directories of services, mosques and jobs; and www.deenport.com, a multi-faceted internet portal bringing together discussion forums, blogs, articles and artwork. Both of these sites were first set up in 2003 and have served as a point of expression, conversation and information on British Muslim communities for the individuals who run them as well as their users.

On the more creative side, this period also witnessed a bolder proliferation and experimentation with traditional *nasheeds*. A notable example is the release in 2003 of the British artist Sami Yusuf's first album. Yusuf's songs blended authentic English with authentic Arabic, eastern music with western, and, importantly, shifted away from the direct religious preaching-style that had traditionally been the norm. Instead, he offered a blend of spirituality and social justice themes, a style which proved accessible and appealing to a very wide audience. The idea of a young, indigenous British Muslim identity that was comfortable with its heritage and history as well as confident about its future was also something that Yusuf was keen to promote. To quote him:

> I feel as though (my fans) see me as representing them, not Osama Bin Laden ... A lot of young guys are going through an identity crisis and I think that's where people like me come in and say you can be British, you can be Muslim, you can be hip, you can be having fun – it's not either or.[67]

Yusuf's work has been credited not only with triggering a 'revolution in Islamic pop', demonstrated by the veritable explosion in the *nasheed* and 'Islamic entertainment' genre that has take place over the past 15 years, but also with playing an immensely positive international ambassadorial role for Britain. For instance, he has been invited on more than one occasion by the British Council and the Foreign Office to feature at their events.[68]

Other initiatives included *Living Islam*, a large four-day summer country residential event for Muslim families which was first organised by the Islamic Society of Britain in 2003, incorporating arts, culture, speeches and debates as well as children's activities and entertainment. In July 2005, a weekend Islam Expo was organised by many of the personalities who had spearheaded the MAB-StWC alliance. Showcasing Islamic contributions to art, culture, science and civilisation, politics was nonetheless central to this event's programme, which boasted participation from political figures across the spectrum, but in particular, the patronage of the then London Mayor, Ken Livingstone. Interesting parallels have been drawn between this event and the European Social Forum that was held prior to it, in London, in 2004. Both used Alexandra Palace in North London as their venue, and both events followed very similar formats, suggesting a direct link between the Muslim-Left alliance and the nature and direction in which aspects of Muslim civic engagement had developed. Finally, in the field of media and research, Anas Altikriti, veteran anti-war leader and Respect Party candidate, established the Cordoba Foundation, a research and public relations organisation with the aim of promoting dialogue and peaceful coexistence between cultures through research, facilitation and advisory roles.[69]

All of these developments paint the picture of a sharper, more complex landscape in British Muslim identity politics by 2005, owing a great deal of its evolution to factors related to the events of 9/11 and reactions to it. Indeed, if the impact of 9/11 gifted British Islam(s) with anything, then perhaps it could be said that this was it: a deepened sense of humility, bringing with it a more accurate understanding of their exact place in the wider scheme of things. The magnitude and suddenness of the 9/11 attacks and the overwhelming nature of the world's reactions to it meant that Muslims really had to 'think on their feet', to be able to deal with the immediate shock, question their feelings and identity, affirm it, defend it and make their views on the War on Terror known, all practically simultaneously.

This four-year period was one of momentous change and development for British Muslim identity politics. 9/11 threw open a large public window onto British Muslim communities, creating an atmosphere of pressure, urgency and self-defence. Faced with pressing security concerns, the government strove to address them, but found it difficult to maintain a balance between fulfilling its foreign policy commitments and winning the loyalty of a Muslim community which sought political even-handedness both at home and abroad. Community organisation and representation definitively came of age in the crucible of post-9/11 politics, pushing for age-old Muslim issues such as the criminalisation of religious hatred in a more contextual, mature and inclusive manner. Islamophobia and its manipulation by the rising far-right prompted serious government attention to this matter, as well as to the restriction of immigration and a more stringent approach to the integration of minority communities and newcomers to the country. Finally, a host of factors, in particular the decision to enthusiastically participate in mainstream political activity alongside other interest groups, sparked real development, change and diversification within the British Muslim political landscape, which, when compared with that of the 1990s, shows just how far British Muslim politics travelled over this period.

CHAPTER 6

Identity Politics and Terrorism at Home (7 July 2005–June 2010)

This chapter will consider how the terror attacks that took place in London on 7 July 2005 heralded a second major turning point in the development of British Muslim identity politics, from the perspective of freedom of expression specifically and civil liberties more generally. The acute and urgent nature of the 7/7 attacks, being in the UK's capital city and carried out by British citizens, instigated sharper reactions from each of the parties under discussion.

In terms of legal developments initiated by the government, a twin-track approach to anti-terrorism was pursued. The 'hard' approach involved the introduction of tighter anti-terrorism legislation, and the 'soft' approach was represented by the Contest scheme, and especially its Prevent strand, which focused on the task of combating radicalisation by 'winning hearts and minds' from what became known as 'violent extremism'. Utilising selected case studies, I show that the government's keen pursuit of a 'hard' legal path proved detrimental to developing Muslim identity politics and failed to achieve its desired outcomes. 'Softer' tactics that were pursued by the government during this period primarily included various aspects of the Prevent strategy and affiliated outreach and engagement initiatives, as well as attempts to gather and 'map' information about groups and individuals within Muslim communities. These developments had inevitable implications on the Equality Gap.

The MCB, as the pre-eminent Muslim advocacy and representative group at the start of this period, came under increasingly intense public scrutiny and criticism. I explore how and under what pressures the MCB eventually took the step of acknowledging and attempting to deal with the realities of the 'violent extremist' influence within Muslim communities, and how these developments panned out in the language and attitudes through which the MCB chose to express itself, both in its relations with the government and with other Muslim groups. The MCB was distinguished by its readiness to adopt a more independent and occasionally critical line towards the government whilst at the same time developing greater self-confidence and humility in recognising its own limitations. Faced with increasing 'competition' in the form of a growing number of Muslim groups clamouring for representative 'status', the MCB took steps, albeit reluctantly, towards acknowledging the contributions of other players in this field by gradually letting go of its previously characteristic insistence on exclusivity when it came to negotiations with the government and the public representation of British Muslims.

Finally, I look at the emergence of a broad multitude of Muslim voices and organisations from 2005 onwards, each seeking to speak for Muslims, and argue for various 'Muslim causes' (loosely defined). Tensions and disagreements between the government and the MCB created a suitable environment for Muslim identity politics to thrive and diversify, and for these various voices to come to the fore. Yet many of these newer initiatives were sponsored financially or ideologically by parties that harboured interests in the direction of the public debate on British Muslims and security issues, a feature which has had a bearing on the stances that these groups have chosen to adopt at various junctures.

This second turning point heralds the end of Muslim identity politics as we have come to know it. The challenges of post-7/7 Britain have led to a far more fluid relationship between government and Muslim communities. This has not decreased the importance of communication and co-operation between the two, but it has meant that the scenario is much less clearly defined than it was between 2001 and 2005, during the days of the Labour government's acquiescence to the MCB's pre-eminence.

In Chapter 5, we saw how the period between September 2001 and 2005 was overwhelmingly defined by the 9/11 attacks and the ensuing fallout. They, along with the government's response in the area of security, framed the priorities for Muslim identity politics during this period and the course that it was to chart. Despite the intense pressures that this period placed on Muslims, it proved to be a time of significant strides in the maturing of Britain's Muslim communities. Met with new and unexpected challenges, the British-born Muslim generations showed confidence and effectiveness in their political engagement, developing and enhancing the arguments that they deployed for recognition on various fronts. There were signs of a more assured sense of self within Britain's Muslim communities, as partnerships were forged with others on the basis of shared interests and through embracing far more creative and diverse modes and subjects of self-expression. The recently established MCB managed to hold onto good relations with the state whilst opposing aspects of its foreign policy, thus cementing its position as primary interlocutor for Muslims within the British establishment. And while a resurgence of the far-right posed new challenges, strides (albeit limited ones) were also made in narrowing the Equality Gap through legislation. But the events of July 2005 were to stimulate another turning point, when terrorism struck the British capital as four co-ordinated explosions took place on London's transport system, killing 52 people.

7 JULY 2005: TERRORISM ON HOME SOIL

Thursday 7 July 2005 has come to represent a moment in history when striking changes took place in the UK both in the shorter and the longer term. The former is best illustrated by contrasting the public mood in London on 7 July with that on the preceding day. Wednesday 6 July had witnessed great expressions of jubilation and pride in the capital as news of its successful bid to host the 2012 Olympic Games was celebrated in Trafalgar Square, and indeed across the country. The capital's cultural diversity and international connections were presented as sources of strength – assets that had helped to win the bid for London and that would make the 2012

Games all the more successful and welcoming to athletes as well as spectators. The fact that London had beaten Paris in the final lap of the race to host the 2012 Olympics was hailed by many as a testament to the strength and durability of the British capital's confident approach to diversity and multiculturalism over the French establishment's preference for *laïcité* and reputed disdain towards multicultural pride.

Multiculturalism in both countries (as, indeed, across Europe), had been drawn into question by the recent experiences of serious urban unrest involving young people from minority ethnic backgrounds. England's northern towns of Bradford, Oldham and Burnley experienced severe race riots in 2001, memories of which were still fresh, and simmering socio-economic problems in Paris's *banlieues* eventually erupted later on in 2005 in the form of heavy rioting involving youths of North African immigrant parentage. Both of these occurrences shone a light upon the dramatic clash between the far-right's aspirations to assimilate ethnic and religious minorities, or exclude them, and the realities of multicultural urban life. Additionally, they highlighted the urgency of problems around social deprivation, equality of opportunity, and discrimination as well as the need for greater social cohesion in areas that were inhabited by large immigrant communities (in both these cases, Muslim immigrant communities).[1]

Yet despite this troubled background to multiculturalism, the city of London, and crucially its Mayor, Ken Livingstone, was able to present an image of multiculturalism not only being accepted as a reality, but positively celebrated as a source of vibrancy and strength.[2] However, if the celebration of a successful Olympic bid on 6 July symbolised a peak in optimism about London's multiculturalism and sense of unity, the shock and horror of the attacks the following morning ushered in something of a rude awakening, prompting deep, raw and searching questions about the nature, depth and durability of the nation's civic unity.[3] The 7/7 attacks also served to inject a renewed sense of urgent seriousness to a national vigilance towards security, and proponents of a 'Londonistan' thesis, that the UK had for too long turned a blind eye towards extremist ideas on its very doorstep, or at least allowed them to go unchecked in the name of multiculturalism, argued that an ideological battle was absolutely essential to defend 'our values', at home as well as abroad.[4] As to the longer-term impact of the attacks – this became evident in the changing approach of government in the areas of anti-terror legislation, relations with the Muslim community and with Muslim community organisations, and the direction in which public discourses on radicalisation, identity and national security developed.

THE PERPETRATORS, AND RADICALISATION AMONG YOUNG BRITISH MUSLIMS

On the face of it, the lives of the four perpetrators seemed unremarkable. There do not appear to have been any obvious major dramatic incidents that specifically or personally marked them out from their peers. Indeed, there were outward indications that they were 'the very epitome of assimilation into British society',[5] and their day-to-day lives did not display any significant indications of internal cultural or religious conflict or any antipathy towards Britain. Friends and acquaintances of Mohammed Siddique Khan related that he

> was called 'Sid' at school, had more white friends than Asian ones ... He was not interested in religion. He ignored debates about the plight of Muslims abroad ... [and] apart from the colour of his skin, he was just an English lad.[6]

Thus, conclusions have varied widely – at one end of the analytical spectrum is the view that these bombers were second-generation children of immigrants and thus enjoyed greater privileges to those that their parents had had access to – including education, opportunity, leisure and all the amenities associated with modern Western lifestyles. In this narrative, it is often deduced that their main motivation was ideological and this is often used to support the 'clash of civilisations' thesis and more generally what has become known as the 'neoconservative' world-view.[7]

At the other end, attention is drawn to the fact that while these were of course Westernised young men in so many senses of the word, they nonetheless experienced social exclusion and alienation on a number of levels. None of the 7/7 bombers were educated to a professional level. Most did not proceed beyond the minimum level of schooling, and of the few who did, the most successful was 'ringleader' Mohammed Siddique Khan, who worked as a classroom teaching assistant. Moreover, even if they did not *directly* experience social exclusion, they certainly were witnesses to it. Each of them hailed from towns in North Yorkshire where racial segregation was a problem and where Muslim communities received consistently low scores in all socio-economic indicators. They had all attended the Hamara Youth Centre in Beeston, where Mohammed Siddique Khan was a youth worker, and they undoubtedly must have come into regular contact with young people who may have faced difficulties in life such as poverty and racism.

At the same time, retrospective evidence shows that all of them seem to have been disaffected or frustrated in some way by what they saw as injustice, whether abroad, against fellow Muslims in the shape of the war on terror, or at home in the form of Islamophobia (be it through real, direct experiences or internalised).[8] What this points to is that the bombers were in dire need of an outlet through which they could vent their internal feelings of anger and frustration. In the absence of any positive channels, the appeal of terrorism was perhaps that it was a concrete action that they could take, which they believed would go some way to rectifying the wrongs which so troubled them, coupled with the inestimable, otherworldly 'promise' of reward that they stood to gain from.

Moreover, as much as they may seem to have been integrated in terms of appearance, language and lifestyle, the bombers evidently felt sufficiently detached from British society not only to have been capable of carrying out the attacks themselves,[9] but to have (as did Mohammed Siddique Khan) addressed society as a separate/foreign entity: '*Your* democratically elected governments continuously perpetuate atrocities against *my* people'.[10]

This rather normal and perhaps familiar nature of the 7/7 bombers and their daily lives emphasised further that there was a real problem of radicalisation among sections of Britain's Muslim youth, and that addressing this problem was a matter of urgency. The government recognised this urgency, but chose to view potential solutions overwhelmingly from the perspective of national security, a perspective which risks overlooking social, political and economic root causes of discontent that have regularly been cited as the main push factors towards radicalisation.[11] Hence it decided to embark with vigour on a range of different schemes to combat radicalisation, with security at the top of the agenda. It utilised a two-pronged approach – firstly using 'hard power' through the introduction of new anti-terrorism legislation, and secondly, using 'soft power' through community centred initiatives aimed at using ideas to win over the loyalty of young British Muslims and defeat violent extremism, in a battle of ideas.

The British government straightaway adopted a forceful and direct tone in the language that was used to respond to 7/7. Tony Blair spoke on 5 August 2005, less than a month after the bombings, declaring that 'the rules of the game have changed',[12] and signalling firmly that a far more hard-line approach would be adopted towards the expression of radical and extremist ideas, specifically those that were deemed to 'glorify terrorism'. The implication of this approach was a recognition that the root causes and processes by which young Britons were radicalised needed to be understood, analysed and stopped.

This in itself was a step forward from the approach of the preceding five years. While in the wake of 9/11 the government had concentrated its security efforts largely on Britons who were thought to be actively supporting terrorism abroad, the post-7/7 approach was characterised by a determination to root out the very catalysts that set young people on the path of extremism.

The 'harder' concrete legal changes that were introduced as a result of 7/7 include aspects of the Terrorism Act 2006, specifically those concerned with classifying forms of expression and speech as illegal, such as the outlawing of the 'encouragement' and the 'glorification' of terrorism. The government also invested a great deal of resources into 'softer', community-based approaches to countering extremism, including the Preventing Violent Extremism (PVE) working groups that were set up immediately after the attacks, as well as the CONTEST scheme itself – and specifically Prevent, its most prominent strand – that lasted throughout the remainder of the Labour administration, and beyond.

LEGAL CHANGES AND THE TERRORISM ACT 2006: THE 'HARD' APPROACH

A new terrorism bill was swiftly put together and passed in February as the Terrorism Act 2006. It sought to emphatically bring home Blair's earlier assertion that the government would be tougher and more decisive than it had previously been in all matters relating to terrorism, and what was henceforth to be consistently referred to as 'violent extremism'. The hallmark of this new legislation was its direct and deliberate entry into the realm of speech acts, sometimes referred to collectively as 'encouragement offences'. These constituted clauses which made provisions to prosecute those who encouraged or glorified terrorist activity, as well as to allow for the proscription of organisations that glorified terrorism. Additionally, it introduced a penalty for the 'dissemination of terrorist publications' and for the 'training for' or 'attendance at a place used for terrorist training',[13] designed to address bookshops stocking 'extremist' material, and terrorist training camps, respectively.

A major source of disquiet was that the descriptions included in these clauses were broadly defined and left a great deal open to subjective interpretation by the courts and the Home Secretary, thus potentially leaving the door open to huge miscarriages of justice.[14] Human rights advocates argued that such legal developments, while perhaps well-intentioned, were not the most effective way of tackling radical views and preventing terrorism, since they limited opportunities for vulnerable young people (those who were most at risk of being 'lured' towards violent extremism) to discuss or explore issues and grievances that were troubling them in a safe and responsible environment. Indeed, Article 19, the campaign group for freedom of expression, argued that the new offence of 'encouragement of terrorism' would 'discourage the peaceful expression of controversial opinion',[15] a view that was backed by the UN Human Rights Committee as well as a number of other researchers, and legal and community practitioners.[16]

Muslim community groups also expressed concerns that the outlawing of radical speech would have a chilling effect. Rather than rooting out extremist voices and curbing the spread of their influence, it would instead simply lead them to operate more covertly – behind closed doors, using more secure and sophisticated communication techniques, instead of operating in public through high street stalls or mosques.[17] Additionally, the MCB argued that the new Act was 'based on a number of false premises', and that it rendered the entire Muslim community 'liable to suspicion, censorship and persecution',[18] urging the government to exercise 'maximum restraint' in utilising the new legal powers, and warning that it would 'consider legal intervention' if the law was used to ban Muslim groups.[19]

Whilst the concerted efforts of this broad-based opposition to the new raft of speech-related offences did not succeed in preventing the Act from materialising, it has been argued that the widespread criticism of it served to 'undermin(e) its chances of being an effective tool'.[20] Indeed, while there have been some attempts to prosecute using the Act, they have been few in number, and verdicts have often been overturned on appeal. The remainder of this section will look at three high-profile cases in which the Terrorism Act 2006 was invoked, and ask whether the law can be judged to have fulfilled the government's aspirations of preventing terrorism through denying radical extremists and their organisations any form of public platform from which to preach, and in turn deterring others from being drawn to violent extremism through preventing the possibility of such ideas being expressed in the public domain.

Case study: Samina Malik – thought-criminal or potential terrorist?
This was the first case to be successfully prosecuted in which the new Terrorism Act 2006, which included the highly controversial clause that prohibited the encouragement or glorification of terrorist acts, was invoked. However, ultimately Malik was convicted specifically for 'possessing records likely to be useful in terrorism' (using Section 58 of the Terrorism Act 2000) and was handed a nine-month suspended sentence in December 2007. A shop assistant at a WH Smith outlet in Heathrow Airport, she had engaged in regular internet communications on *jihadi* websites and discussion forums. Using the screen-name 'Lyrical Terrorist' she fantasised through poetry, often graphically, her aspirations to engage in violent acts,

including beheadings, *'jihad'*, and to die as a martyr. In addition, she was found to have corresponded with Sohail Qureshi, a 30-year-old dentist who had been arrested at Heathrow Airport as he attempted to board a flight to Pakistan carrying weapons, cash and terror handbooks.

Her trial found no evidence that she had undertaken any concrete physical criminal actions, yet she was nonetheless found guilty on the basis that she had in her possession 'records likely to be useful for terrorism' – these included *jihadi* literature that was found on her computer and at her home, as well as her own writings and poetry. Representing perhaps the first time that the new 'rules of the game' on terrorism were tested through a real and hard case, the conviction provoked a great deal of public outrage. English PEN, the same group that had defended Salman Rushdie's publication of his *The Satanic Verses*, back in 1989, came out and spoke in defence of Samina Malik. Deputy President Lisa Appignanesi declared that the criminalisation of Malik merely for 'dreaming and writing behind a bookshop counter would have Byron and Shelley turning in their graves'.[21] In addition, numerous petitions and collectives sprung up online, variously defending Malik's 'freedom of expression', there were calls for a 'World Samina Malik Day'[22] and countless public figures wrote to denounce the 'draconian' nature of the anti-terror laws, which, it was argued, had effectively created thought crimes.[23] An interesting comparison was drawn between Section 58 of the Terrorism Act 2000 under which Malik was prosecuted and the recent experience of Gillian Gibbons, a British teacher in the Sudan who had been imprisoned for acquiescing to her pupils' choice of the name 'Muhammad' for their teddy bear, and was only released after international uproar and mediation from a delegation of British (Muslim) politicians.

Malik's conviction was later quashed in the wake of a successful appeal for the 'Bradford Five',[24] a test case in which a landmark ruling judged that Section 58 of the Terrorism Act 2000 could not reasonably be stretched to encompass 'propagandist or theological material'. Upon re-examining her case, judges ruled that the documents in Malik's possession and upon which her conviction had relied could fall under this category.

Case study: Abu Izzadeen – deterrence or the making of a martyr-figure?

Abu Izzadeen, also known as Trevor Brooks, rose to public prominence in his role as a leader and spokesperson for *Al Ghurabaa*.[25] He made several outspoken media appearances between 2001 and 2006, in which he brazenly flirted with anti-terror laws by praising specific acts of suicide bombing and even declaring his own aspiration to perform such actions.[26] In September 2006, he heckled and disrupted a meeting of the Muslim community in Leytonstone, east London, with the then-Home Secretary John Reid. Abu Izzadeen accused Reid of being an 'enemy' of Islam and decried the audience for listening to him, and 'let(ting) him come into a Muslim area', declaring that it was shameful for them to listen to his call for Muslim parents to 'spy' on their children and report any concerns to the authorities, while 'over 1,000 Muslims had been arrested' (in anti-terror raids). His outburst received keen media attention, to the point of raising suspicions that the clash had even been staged,[27] as a way of bolstering the message that Reid was trying to put across. Whatever the facts behind the incident – this was just the most prominent of what had by this stage become a catalogue of numerous statements which were arguably falling foul of the new anti-terror restrictions on speech.[28]

Eventually, Abu Izzadeen was prosecuted and found guilty in April 2008 of inciting terrorism and of fundraising for terrorism. His case was considered by critics of the Terrorism Act 2006 to be politically motivated and part of a 'knee-jerk reaction',[29] particularly since the comments which he was prosecuted for were actually made in 2004, before the London bombings had even prompted the government to introduce further anti-terror legislation. Moreover, his conviction was ultimately secured under the Terrorism Act 2000, since initial attempts to secure a conviction for the 'encouragement' of terrorism using the Terrorism Act 2006 fell through after a jury failed to reach a verdict, thus further cementing existing expectations that the Act was far too broad to be effective in any tangible sense.

As to Abu Izzadeen himself, he served one year of his four-and-a-half year sentence, and was then released early after an appeal, much to the joy of supporters who received him as a 'modern day Muslim hero'.[30] He was recalled to prison only months later in July for breaking the conditions of his release by allegedly assaulting a police officer. Finally, he was released again in October 2010. Upon release, he wasted no time in firing off strident and unrepentant accusations against the government and the judicial system for being biased and unduly harsh against Muslims.[31] If anything, the whole episode served to raise his profile and to cement his following, as evidenced by the warm and enthusiastic reception he received from his 'followers' upon his latest release from prison.[32] He was greeted at the gates of Pentonville Prison by a crowd of cheering supporters, saluting him as a 'Lion of *Tawheed*' (monotheism), and insisting that 'The British government's behaviour in silencing individuals whom (sic) oppose and expose the government's economic, social or more importantly foreign policies ... (will not) stop Muslim activists propagating the divine way of live (sic) of *Al-Islam*'.[33] Abu Izzadeen then proceeded to scale the prison walls and deliver a speech-cum-press statement to his assembled supporters and the media. Video recordings show that he was clearly relishing the moment, and when questioned about whether his spell in prison had made him reconsider his views or the nature of any future public statements, he responded with indignation: 'we have a right to speak out the truth, we have a right to expose the corruption that's going on, and if we're going to go to prison for it, we're more than willing to'.[34]

This case study suggests that the efforts of anti-terror legislation in deterring Abu Izzadeen from making comments in support of violence against British troops abroad, and from speaking approvingly of terrorist acts at home, were unsuccessful, and even counterproductive. Abu Izzadeen's trial, imprisonment and the high-level press coverage afforded to his outspoken views (this point being especially pertinent if his confrontation with John Reid was indeed staged) all contributed to maximising his audience. That the efforts to convict him under the 2006 Act fell through is in itself something of an indictment of the legislation. In addition, just as the entire situation must have swelled the ranks of his critics, it undoubtedly did the same for his admirers, for whom the efforts to silence him only made him and his rhetoric all the more appealing, particularly when considered in tandem with the negative impacts of other strands of the government's efforts in the areas of anti-terrorism and security, such as the Prevent programme, and high-profile blunders such as the botched police raid in Forest Gate of June 2006.[35]

Case study: Ahmed Faraz and the perils of state-endorsed religious interpretations

My final case study looks at Ahmed Faraz, a Birmingham bookseller convicted under Sections 1 and 2 of the Terrorism Act 2006. Faraz ran *Al-Maktabah*, an Islamic bookshop that was found to stock a number of texts that were used by, or found in the possession of, various convicted terrorists over the previous decade. His conviction for possessing and disseminating information 'likely to be useful to a person committing or preparing an act of terrorism'[36] bore some parallels with Samina Malik's case, in that the judge conceded that there was 'no indication ... Mr Faraz ever intended to carry out a terrorist attack'.[37] It was also similar in that Section 58 of the Terrorism Act 2000 had to be relied upon to secure the conviction. The books in question were annotated editions of classical volumes, or modern texts based on classical works. The majority of the books were written by three authors: Ibn Taymiyyah, a thirteenth/fourteenth-century scholar, whose writings have been associated with modern puritanical Islamic thought, including Wahhabism; and two twentieth-century authors: Sayyid Qutb, member and ideologue of the Egyptian Muslim Brotherhood, and Abdullah Azzam, a leader of the Afghan jihad against the Soviet Union. Both of the latter have been credited with inspiring Al Qaeda and modern *jihadi* thinking in general. Additionally, both have been hailed as martyrs to their causes – Qutb was executed by the Egyptian government and Azzam was assassinated, allegedly, by rival *jihadis* in Afghanistan, after the withdrawal of the Soviet Union.

The trial decided that by stocking editions of these books that were accompanied by extensive commentary and appendices of the sort that 'goaded' readers to engage in fighting, spoke of Christians and Jews in highly derogatory terms and provided footage of 'martyrdom' attacks, Faraz was guilty of incitement to terrorism.[38] Yet critics of the verdict pointed to the fact that most of the audio-visual footage of attacks that was relied upon by the prosecution was seized from a personal computer folder entitled 'PhD', and that Faraz had spoken of correspondence he had engaged in with a potential research supervisor, copies of which were also contained in the same folder.[39] They argued that the conviction of Faraz on the basis that the court deemed the books he stocked to be dangerous was more or less equivalent to the books themselves being banned. By sending a signal that these books were considered to be unacceptable, the courts were effectively criminalising other booksellers, as well as creating a chilling effect, whereby potential stockists would engage in self-censorship in order to avoid prosecution.

Faraz's conviction was later overturned by the Court of Appeal on 21 December 2012.[40] The court took the view that his earlier conviction had relied on a jury that was insufficiently informed about the complexities of the relevant aspects of Islamic theology, and that the controversial literature stocked at *Al-Maktabah* could not be assumed to have necessarily been responsible for encouraging terrorist activity. This development is yet further evidence of the confusing nature and ineffectiveness of the encouragement offences in the 2006 anti-terror legislation.

But perhaps the most worrying aspect of Faraz's conviction was the basis upon which the texts in question were classified by the court to be dangerous. This relied heavily on the account of an expert witness to the trial, whose arguments were built predominantly upon theological debates and differences.[41] Essentially what this meant was that the justice system, through this conviction, offered official legal approval and privilege to one religious interpretation over another. Naturally this outcome is deeply problematic from the perspective of freedom of expression and freedom of conscience, since it gives succour to the notion that the state can legitimately play a role in endorsing 'acceptable' schools of religious thought and, conversely, that it can legitimately reject 'unacceptable' schools of thought and religious interpretations. Britain is a nation whose constitutional history tells a story of struggle for freedom of conscience and, crucially, freedom of belief. Indeed, it has sheltered refugees from religious persecution abroad, notably the Huguenots and the Jews; and dissenters fought for, and won, the right to differ freely from the Church of England. For these reasons, the idea that the courts could indict a defendant using evidence based on theological interpretations is one that gives rise to deep misgivings about the potential extent to which these laws can be used to outlaw certain religious interpretations, or to criminalise those who are merely interested in reading about them, let alone actually being convinced of them.

This difficulty is especially potent when considered in conjunction with concurrent misgivings around the Prevent programme, and the Department for Communities and Local Government's (DCLG) proactive efforts in promoting an 'acceptable' Islam to defeat a more 'radical' or 'extremist' Islam in the battle for hearts and minds. These have all been important and ongoing security concerns, which I discuss in further detail in the following section.

STATE-INITIATED COMMUNITY-CENTRED RESPONSES: THE 'SOFT' APPROACH

In addition to the use of forceful rhetoric, the government set about putting initiatives into place with the aim of engaging with Britain's Muslim communities in a deeper and more meaningful manner, and thus providing genuine and authentic deterrents to what was increasingly termed 'violent extremism', based on the foundations of comprehensive community networks and supported by key individuals and institutions from within the communities themselves. This approach has often been referred to as 'community-policing',[42] a technique which sought both legitimacy *and* authenticity through actively seeking out and engaging with Muslim community representatives on a broader and deeper level than had been done in recent history. To this end, a 'Preventing Extremism Together' taskforce appeared in August 2005, consisting of seven 'working groups', comprised of handpicked 'experts' who were briefed to meet and discuss pertinent issues surrounding each of: Engaging with young people, Education, Engaging with Muslim women, Supporting regional and local initiatives and community actions, Imam training and accreditation and the role of mosques, Community security and Tackling extremism and radicalisation. These groups met regularly over a period of two months, at the end of which a summary of their discussions and subsequent recommendations were collated and presented to the government via the Home Office.[43]

The taskforce recommendations were extensive and ambitious. Yet they drew sharp criticism in the ensuing period as something of a superficial exercise, since the follow-up on their recommendations was remarkably sparse, giving rise to warnings of rising disillusionment among Muslims,[44] and to suggestions that they were conveniently shelved for the discomfort that their contents may have posed to government narratives and objectives on the causes of extremism and how to combat it.[45] It is interesting to note that the single recommendation (out of a list of 64) from the PET working groups that *was* promptly followed through by government was the facilitation of a 'scholars' road-show'.[46] This eventually materialised into the Radical Middle Way (RMW) project, which started off as a joint collaboration between Q *News* magazine, the Federation of Student Islamic Societies (FOSIS), the Young Muslim Organisation (YMO) and a new body by the name of Mahabba Unlimited.

According to the recommendation in the PET report, the thinking behind such a road-show was to make accessible to young British Muslims 'a group of international and national mainstream scholars … with credibility and influence … to disseminate effective intellectual and theological counter-arguments against extremist interpretations of Islam'.[47] This aspiration was fair enough, but the government's zeal in implementing this particular recommendation cannot be disconnected from its pre-existing plans to launch a very similar campaign, exposing 'moderate' Muslim voices to young British Muslims, which were first mooted in 2004.

In May 2004, the *Sunday Times* published leaked details of the initial blueprint for what was to become widely known as the Contest strategy.[48] Contest picked up with great energy in the wake of the 7/7 attacks, but according to the document leaked to the *Sunday Times*, after 9/11 plans had already begun to be discussed on how the government could 'win over' 'disaffected' young Muslims, specifically seeking ways to 'strengthen the hand of moderate Muslim leaders'.[49] In the light of this, government enthusiasm in backing the RMW is not surprising. Indeed it appears to suggest that the channelling of Foreign Office and Prevent funding towards the project was not much more than a convenient way of letting vetted Muslim groups execute and assume responsibility for a pre-conceived government strategy.[50] The road-shows were resented in some quarters as having 'an air of the colonial era about them', since the government's preference for its pre-approved scholars from overseas was made clear, sidestepping 'the talented expertise of home grown scholars'.[51] This in turn raised questions as to the level of independence of the RMW project, and the extent to which it was a government tool to channel community debates in a desired direction or to keep close tabs on community groups and individuals as a way of gathering information. This theme is an important one, since it was to regularly recur with respect to government-led or government-sponsored initiatives under the Prevent umbrella – often with good grounds for suspicion.

The Prevent Strategy and its use and abuse of Muslim communities' freedom of expression

A key ambition of the new community-based approach that was favoured by the Contest scheme was to engender 'collaborative partnerships' of trust, and good channels of communication between communities and the authorities. In this spirit, April 2007 saw the official launch of Prevent, a scheme claiming to embody many of the ideas put forward by the PET exercise. It was one of four 'workstreams' that together formed the Contest strategy, a multi-pronged approach to effectively deliver the government's counter-terrorism work. The four workstreams were described by the Home Office as:

- **Pursue**: to stop terrorist attacks.
- **Prevent**: to stop people from becoming terrorists or supporting terrorism.
- **Protect**: to strengthen our protection against terrorist attack.
- **Prepare**: where an attack cannot be stopped, to mitigate its impact.[52]

The Prevent workstream is of particular interest to this study because it was designed specifically to develop and promote ideological challenges to 'extremist ideas that are conducive to terrorism or are shared by terrorist groups'.[53] This aim was posited on the notion that extremism stemmed from a 'religio-cultural rejection of western modernity',[54] and that in order to prevent extremism from gaining any credence, the government had to spearhead a 'battle of ideas' – to 'win the hearts and minds' of those (mainly young, mainly Muslims) who were potential recruits to, or sympathisers with, extremist ideology. This preoccupation with ideology meant that the strategy would necessarily operate around the realm of speech acts (inasmuch as they were the expression of ideas) and, as such, it is of great relevance to this study as not only did it mark a new development in Muslim identity politics and government–Muslim relations, but it also presented a scenario in which speech and expression issues were intricately intertwined with securitisation and community cohesion concerns in such a way that proved problematic from both a liberal (theoretical) perspective and that of the practical implementation of policy.

Analysing these problems under three sub-headings: funding, intelligence-gathering and public relations, I show that the government proved unable to build a sufficiently genuine partnership of trust with Muslim communities through Prevent. This was because the approach that it adopted with respect of these three issues lacked transparency, openness to real dialogue and consultation, and relied on the imposition of its own agenda, one that was frequently rigid and pre-engineered. While the Prevent scheme did represent an unprecedented level of official recognition for Muslim communities, this was combined with an often patronising and instrumentalist attitude towards them in the way that the strategy was formulated. In addition, government displayed a remarkable intolerance, almost an allergy, towards the idea of giving space for feedback and the uninhibited airing of ideas, something which would seem to be a basic need for an endeavour which sought to win over the hearts and minds of troubled communities, and particularly young people.

Funding

An important aspect of Prevent was the funding of community-based initiatives in such a way that government provided the material support for them, but the community retained ownership. To this end, central government made available a generous fund,[55] to which applications could be made by groups and agencies for 'community-led' projects. While the idea was that Prevent's aims could be achieved through government-funded capacity-building projects, anecdotal evidence and recent research has found that a large number of community organisers felt disengaged and bypassed when it came to decision-making and maintained that major decisions were always made in advance, 'behind closed doors', and only later presented to them as a *'fait accompli'*.[56] This inconsistency was allegedly exacerbated by the poor grasp that central government decision-makers had of local issues and needs.[57] Other problems identified with this funding have included an expectation – often understated but sometimes openly expressed – by police or other official representatives that community workers 'toe the (central) government line' when it came to exploring opinions, from deeply emotive and controversial topics including foreign policy to day-to-day differences on what the priorities for local work and projects should be and how they should be implemented.[58] The message that many came away with was that government funding was being offered with one hand, and that central government was expecting to receive on the other hand loyalty and tacit obedience to a preconceived agenda of priorities that was put together by Whitehall mandarins and their think-tanks of preference.[59] Many community workers saw this funding arrangement to be especially manipulative since at a time when money for voluntary sector work was becoming increasingly difficult to secure, it was felt by some that they had little choice but to accept Prevent funding, and that if it was necessary to do so on government terms, then so be it.[60]

Allegations of surveillance and intelligence-gathering

Throughout the period of its operation, the Contest scheme, and specifically Prevent, have regularly been the subject of shocking allegations. Among these are that rather than being simply an empowering community education and development scheme, it was utilised as an intelligence-gathering tool used by the secret services to keep a close eye on Muslim communities, including surveillance and the collection of information such as religious and political views as well as on mental health, sexual activity and associates.[61] Whilst such allegations have been strenuously denied by the government,[62] a number of community and youth workers have given detailed reports of instances when they were explicitly asked to provide information about the individuals with whom they worked to the police or local authority with which they liaised.[63] Such allegations proved to be deeply problematic for government–community engagement, for two major reasons.

Firstly, even the smallest indication that Prevent was being used for information-gathering, profiling and mapping of Muslim communities shook the already-damaged trust between the state and its community partners. At a stage where recent milestones in official recognition for Britain's Muslims had been reached,[64] this proved to be a tremendous setback to the development of understanding and rapport between the state and Muslim community groups, as well as the grassroots. Unease about Prevent was exacerbated by a range of other surveillance-related concerns. There were complaints that young Muslim men were being accosted by members of the security services and attempts being made to recruit them as informers. A high-profile case reported by the *Independent* involved a group of five young Muslim men in Camden, North London, who had each been individually approached by members of the security services or undercover police officers, and 'intimidated' or 'blackmailed' to provide them with information and assistance, and that their refusal was met with specific threats against them and even their families.[65] The imposition of Information Sharing Agreements (ISAs) as a requirement for all Prevent funded projects and, furthermore, suggestions by prominent politicians that public sector employees keep a vigilant eye (widely understood to be code for 'spy') on the young people in their charge for any signs of 'radicalisation' all fed into a growing unease about any kind of community work that was linked with Prevent in particular, and with government in general. Indeed, some project leaders spoke of how they would deliberately avoid mentioning that they were using Prevent funding, or consciously rebrand the names of their projects, due to the increasingly negative connotations that the scheme began to carry.[66]

Secondly, repeated suggestions that responsible adults should report signs of extremism among the young people in their charge presented a major blow not only to trust between communities and the authorities, but among Muslim organisations,[67] and also more generally within institutions which traditionally had come to be regarded as safe havens for free expression and experimentation with new, contrasting and often radical ideas. Universities, schools, youth clubs and even (perhaps idealistically!) mosques should all be spaces where debates are conducted and ideas are explored. Yet for many young people this avenue for safe and supervised self-discovery fell into jeopardy, as they could never be sure whether confiding in their teachers or youth workers would result in their being referred to the authorities as potential extremists.[68] A motion passed at the National Union of Students conference in May 2008 affirmed that the MI5 and Special Branch had not only been 'actively spying, harassing and intimidating students on campus', but that they had even 'sought to recruit numerous members of Islamic societies on campus'. The motion expressed grave concerns that such activities were creating a climate of suspicion and distrust in which 'fewer Muslims (would become) involved in Islamic societies, Students' Unions or any political societies'.[69] For the motion to have passed as it did, it is clear that the concerns around spying and recruitment were very real and were restricting Muslim youth and students' sense of freedom of expression, affecting the kinds of circles that they mixed in and the everyday choices that they made.

Targeted consultations and public relations

Another venture that attracted a great deal of Prevent funding and publicity interest was the idea of targeted focus groups and slick promotional campaigns on issues that were identified as critical to the battle for hearts and minds. On a domestic level, this included the launch of two government advisory groups focusing on Muslim women and young people – the National Muslim Women's Advisory Group (NMWAG, est. 2007) and the Young Muslim Advisory Group (YMAG, est. 2008). In addition, there was the establishment of a mosques advisory board (MINAB). Although these were set up to be officially independent bodies, their reliance on funding from Prevent meant that in effect they were obliged to function within the parameters set by the DCLG.[70]

For the former two, their purported role was to advise ministers on issues pertinent to their respective groups on matters relating to integration and community cohesion as well as to act as positive role models for women and young people in the Muslim communities. With NMWAG, as with other aspects of Prevent, high-minded intentions ended up translating into less-than-agreeable realities. As the groups were basically hand-picked by civil servants,[71] their only mandate came from Communities Minister Hazel Blears and her team. This was hardly sufficient if they were to make real headway in winning over hearts and minds for the cause against radicalisation. In fact, it led many to question just how effective these groups could ever be, including a member of NMWAG, claiming to be the group's co-ordinator, who resigned in 2010 citing a refusal to be used as a 'political pawn'[72] and emphatically complaining that the linking of the initiative with the Prevent agenda was 'disempowering' and merely a 'political fad'. Other members of NMWAG echoed her objections, 'we thought we were going to be advisors, but found that (instead) we were project managers', complained one participant.[73]

YMAG seems to have been comparatively more successful than NMWAG. Members of the group have described how their relationship with government was honest and frank, and that they regularly gave advice and recommendations on sensitive issues such as extremism on university and college campuses. In fact, it was felt that the ministers with whom they met displayed a greater readiness to listen to blunt criticism *because* it was coming from young people, and it was almost expected that young people would adopt a more direct tone and 'tell it how it is'.[74] One member related how they had no qualms about telling ministers that such an advisory group under Prevent was 'pointless', and that 'we're only here to tell you that'.[75] YMAG was given a list of tasks to fulfil – a website, a national youth conference and civic participation projects. Yet while there was scope for the group to run these projects themselves, they were nonetheless made aware of set parameters within which they could work, and there were instances when their proposals were vetoed or decisions reprimanded.

Fundamentally, for both YMAG and NMWAG, although they were technically and officially independent, in practice their reliance on the state for funding meant that they were unavoidably compelled to operate in a manner that was acceptable to government strategy, and to work only on approved issues. Proof of the extent of this reliance is that when the general election of 2010 brought in a new coalition government, funding for YMAG was ended, and government support for the group was withdrawn. Consequently, the YMAG website, magazine and a yet-to-be-launched research paper were all either completely withdrawn or left in limbo as the group was forced to disband, despite the strong bonds that had grown between the members, and their sense of common cause. This situation suggests strongly that ultimate control of this advisory group was not in the hands of its members, but in the hands of its funders, who could 'pull the plug' on it, so to speak, at will.[76]

MINAB

The idea for a mosque regulatory body initially emerged from the PET Working Groups discussions.[77] However, its formation became somewhat delayed as there was disagreement between the government and Muslim community groups over its design. The Labour peer, Lord Ahmed, was initially tasked with the role of assembling a mosques board, but 'when he was unable to make any progress, it was entrusted to four community organisations'.[78] At the earlier discussions it was consistently emphasised that such a body should retain full independence and should be controlled and answerable to the community rather than to any government department. The finished product was unveiled in 2007 as the Mosques and Imams Advisory Board (MINAB). It differed from NMWAG and YMAG in that it was set up under the joint aegis of the MCB, the Al Khoei Foundation, the MAB and the British Muslim Forum, rather than being directly under the DCLG. Yet when it emerged that it was to be heavily Prevent-funded, the extent to which these community groups actually 'owned' MINAB was brought into question, especially since MINAB seemed reluctant to declare upfront the provenance of its main funding.[79] Disquiet was expressed among many imams and mosque officials as something of a power struggle ensued between community groups and the government for control of the fledgling body. MINAB's links with the government[80] were described by Iqbal Sacranie as 'excessive Home Office involvement, insufficient consultation and (giving) the perception that there was an attempt to marginalise the MCB'.[81] Despite this, the four founding bodies decided to back MINAB, perhaps seeing their continued involvement as the best way to keep government interference at bay. Yet these issues of funding and independence ultimately tainted MINAB's reputation in such a way that its ability to actually perform its declared functions was hampered.

Each of the founding bodies nominated representatives who then formed a board of trustees and sat in specialist committees within an organisational set-up that bore several close similarities to that of the MCB.[82] MINAB was to fulfil the role of a self-regulatory body and concentrate on setting and raising standards for the UK's diverse and hitherto disaggregated mosques and Islamic centres. This would be achieved through sharing best practice, and providing and facilitating training courses for imams and mosque staff, as well as through maintaining dialogue and communication links with government. These plans were broadly accepted across Muslim communities as being timely and welcome steps forward in community and institutional development.

Yet as time went on, senior figures from within MINAB's four founding organisations expressed substantial scepticism about its ability to have much impact.[83] Its election process proved unwieldy and problematic, and far too heavily reliant upon the four founding organisations, leaving it open to charges of cronyism, and severely watering down its powers of mandate or implementation. As one interviewee put it, 'MINAB doesn't have any power, it is only advisory',[84] and herein lay its main problem.

The nature of a very diverse and un-hierarchical organisational landscape within Britain's Muslim communities (and of the Islamic faith itself) dictates that an advisory body (rather than an instructive one) would be the most appropriate format for self-regulation.[85] Here

I must differentiate between the inevitable existence of an unofficial, organic hierarchy of relationships within and between *Muslim communities*, and the lack of structural, official or clergy-like hierarchy within the *Islamic faith*. While there do exist organic hierarchies in the form of the power, respect and patronage that are wielded by community leaders, elders, religious and spiritual figures within community networks, the faith of Islam does not endorse a hierarchy of clergy or religious institutions that is in any way comparable, say, to the hierarchies that are to be found in various denominations of the Christian faith. So, given this background, an advisory body seemed to be the best regulatory set-up for British mosques, and, naturally, such a body could only hope to be successful if it was able to win over the willing support and engagement of as many mosques as possible. MINAB's close links with Prevent, and its subsequent lack of transparency and openness regarding its funding and procedures, proved a serious blow to community confidence in it as an institution. This was reflected in the relatively low proportion of mosques and Islamic centres that joined MINAB. Although the 600-odd members did include among them the largest and most prominent mosque organisations in the UK, it was arguably the smaller, more obscure and perhaps far less well-resourced institutions which were more urgently in need of guidance, training, support and general raising of standards. With a total of around 1,200–1,500 mosques in the UK,[86] this left up to 60 per cent unattached to MINAB.

Ultimately, MINAB's role shifted to focus more on service-provision and training, and away from the notion of regulation, since a crucial pre-requisite for the latter was a strong, consensual and trust-based relationship with a sufficient proportion of the country's mosques and Islamic centres. Without this, MINAB instead offered training courses and consultation meetings on topical issues, to a limited range of participating institutions, largely those that were associated with the main groups at the centre of its administration. This is not to belittle the importance of the issues and skills that were addressed – transparency and democracy in mosque administration, the inclusion of women and young people in decision-making, the provision of training and leadership opportunities and engagement in interfaith and community initiatives were all laudable areas for MINAB to encourage mosques to focus on. However, with no significant outreach to the majority of smaller institutions – those without the benefit of basic infrastructure or the luxury of even the most preliminary of communication and networking capabilities that would have facilitated their participation in such initiatives, MINAB was left open to similar charges to those faced by NMWAG – that it was a tick-box exercise preaching to the converted. These are charges that were only bolstered by evidence of discord and difficulties among MINAB affiliates around the matter of elections and organisational processes.[87]

Public relations overseas

Efforts were also made to take the battle for hearts and minds beyond the shores of the UK. The Foreign Office ran a Prevent-funded campaign entitled 'Projecting British Muslims' (PBM).[88] Prominent British Muslims were selected to take part in whirlwind foreign visits to Muslim-majority countries where they would meet with government, civil society and community bodies and perform something of an ambassadorial role by extolling the positive aspects of life as a Muslim in Britain to their audiences. The FCO envisaged that the project would 'signal the UK's pride in its Muslim youth', and as well as providing the delegations with opportunities to 'challenge misconceptions about the reality of life for Muslims in Britain', also give them the chance to learn more about the British government's work in these areas, leading to stronger ties between British Muslims and communities overseas in addition to 'grassroots follow-up initiatives'.[89] Yet as genuine as the efforts of those who took part may have been, this was hardly a project of a grassroots nature. Since delegates were handpicked by the FCO, it is reasonable to deduce that they would hardly have included individuals with a propensity to take a line too disparaging of the government's own policies. Moreover, with the itineraries for each visit set and managed by the FCO, encounters would have been at best too closely supervised and at worst too staged for participants to engage deeply in the kinds of frank and honest exchanges of the sort that a *real* battle of ideas would produce. The above discussion on how surveillance and profiling featured in the Prevent workstream serves to underline this analysis. While participants in the PBM project have spoken of beneficial and fruitful engagement at their visits, they have also criticised the project for being intensely and exhaustively covered by the media, to the extent that it felt like an 'obvious propaganda campaign', and leaving many participants wondering what the visit was *actually* doing to prevent violent extremism.[90]

Also funded with Prevent money through the FCO were a number of projects run by non-governmental bodies. For instance, in 2009, 'Deen International', an organisation headed by Khurshid Ahmed, then of the British Muslim Forum, partnered with the FCO and was granted £500,000 to deliver a campaign entitled 'I am Muslim, I am British'.[91] This was by its own admission 'a major marketing and PR offensive'.[92] The project got as far as a pilot phase, which was based in Pakistan. It included a media campaign with advertisements on television, radio and in the print media as well as a website. There were debates, discussions and conferences and an extensive lecture tour of universities and colleges around Pakistan.[93] These efforts were aimed at utilising the services of prominent, successful British Pakistani Muslims to put across the message that 'British society was not *"anti-Islamic"'*, to demonstrate the extent of British Muslim integration in the UK, and to 'stimulate and facilitate constructive debate' on liberal values and Islam.[94] In doing so, the hope was that the extremist narrative against Britain (and 'The West') as 'enemies' of Islam and Muslims would be robustly challenged, that allies might be won from amongst 'ordinary' Muslims abroad, and thus that some headway would be made towards combating the threat to UK security from 'radical Islamism'.

Don't mention foreign policy

A final factor of great importance to the degeneration of trust between the government and Muslim communities in the period after 7/7 has been the dogged refusal of government to acknowledge that its foreign policy decisions may have played any role in increasing radicalisation among young Muslims, and thus threatening the nation's security. This was most acute during the Blair years. From the very first exercise in government–community engagement after 7/7, the PET Working Groups, UK foreign policy had been identified as a 'root cause' of terrorism, which needed to be 'interrogat(ed) and understood', along with other root causes, if terrorism was to be effectively tackled.[95] However, despite the government's declared intention to tackle the factors behind the appeal of violent extremism amongst young British Muslims, critics were quick and persistent in pointing out an almost pathological blindness to any sort of recognition that foreign policy may have played a role in this regard.[96] For these detractors, the idea that the road to violent extremism could be understood, and thus adequately tackled, without considering the discontent and anger at British involvement in Afghanistan and Iraq, not to mention historically in Palestine, was farcical at best, and deeply insulting at the very worst.[97] For the Blair government, admission that foreign policy played a role in increasing the terror threat was dismissed as giving in to the terrorists, or 'making excuses' for their horrific acts and thereby granting them the hope of some legitimacy, no matter how minimal.

To many Muslims, such a stance smacked of arrogance and was hugely frustrating. For those working on the ground with young Muslims, it was crystal clear that the offensives in Afghanistan and Iraq were viewed with resentment. With details emerging steadily of civilian deaths in these countries, of destruction, the mistreatment of prisoners in Abu Ghraib prison and others, it seemed remarkably myopic of the state to accuse critics of trying to excuse the terrorists' actions, or even to explain them away. Moreover, perhaps the single consistently recurrent theme in the speeches or testimonies of so many of those who attempted to, or indeed did carry out terrorist acts, was their citation of foreign policy in 'Muslim lands' as a major motivating factor.[98]

A prime example of dissonance between the government and Muslim communities on this issue took place in August 2006. At the height of the Israel–Hezbollah conflict, and in a rare gesture of unity bringing together otherwise disparate and rival sections of the Muslim community, an open letter was published urging Prime Minister Tony Blair to 'redouble his efforts to tackle terror and extremism and change our foreign policy to show the world that we value the lives of civilians wherever they live and whatever their religion.'[99] Signed by Sunni, Shi'i and Sufi groups from all areas of the UK as well as the majority of Muslim parliamentarians (Birmingham Perry Barr's Khalid Mahmood being the notable exception), it was a demonstration of unanimity in asserting to the government with one voice that engaging in 'policy risks' abroad 'not only increases the risk to ordinary people in that region (the Middle East), it is also ammunition to extremists who threaten us all'.[100] Despite the letter's broad-based support, and the painstaking efforts made by its signatories to condemn terrorism, a chorus of government figures roundly proceeded to write off the initiative as 'dangerous and foolish',[101] and 'the gravest possible error'.[102] Rather than a plea to understand the root causes of disillusionment and despair that might leave young people vulnerable to radicalisation, it was interpreted as an unacceptable attempt to allow terrorists to 'dictate' to the UK how to shape its foreign policy, and a call to engage in some kind of appeasement or concession.

Participants in YMAG and the PBM project have spoken of how they would be regularly sent 'fact-sheets' by the FCO whenever any aspect of foreign policy provoked controversy among Muslim communities. These documents would highlight 'all the positive aspects of UK involvement, say in Iraq or Afghanistan, and (they) were asked to "please share this with your communities"'.[103] This approach was seen to be patronising both in its tone and its expectations – after all, participants in these forums were chosen for their leadership and initiative, and were (at least officially) assured that they would be free to express their own independent views of government policy.

This sort of situation was to recur often, as Muslim groups became increasingly convinced of UK foreign policy's role in making extremism appealing and the government maintained its refusal to even countenance that its foreign policy decisions could provide an explanation for the appeal of radicalisation as a resort for frustrated and disillusioned young Muslims. With neither side willing to shift its position on this matter, the issue of foreign policy proved to be a major source of disconnect between advocates from Muslim communities and the government.

To sum up, there was obviously a pressing need for an initiative such as Prevent. Its declared ambitions: empowerment, capacity building and educating so as to combat the spread of violent extremism, were fair enough, and in principle had a great deal of willing support. However, a preoccupation with securitisation tainted the venture, as it resulted in a 'conflation between the security and counter-terrorism aspects, and community cohesion'[104]. Evidence of community profiling and the involvement of intelligence services, in addition to a bureaucratic preoccupation with meeting targets and the conducting of superficial consultations in order to tick boxes seriously damaged the level of trust between Muslim communities and government agencies. The extent to which the 'soft' approach to counter-terrorism, and specifically the Prevent programme, succeeded in stopping extremism in its tracks or safeguarding the UK from terror threats is difficult to measure in concrete terms. However, what is certain is that Prevent caused acute and lasting damage to the level of trust between the government and Muslim communities, and that this was exacerbated by stubborn intransigence from the government on the issue of foreign policy as a root cause of radicalisation. Whether this scar can be healed is yet to be seen, but neither the Labour government, nor the successive Conservative and Conservative-led administrations succeeding it since 2010, have shown signs of abandoning the Prevent approach.[105]

THE MCB, THE 'ISRAEL TEST' AND THE RISE OF 'APOLITICAL' ISLAM – THE MEDIA DIRECTLY INFLUENCING POLITICAL TRENDS?

Challenging the MCB in the media

From around August 2005, there began to appear a steady stream of voices in the media challenging the working arrangement under which the MCB and the government had been operating for most of the preceding decade. Led by a handful of journalists who were broadly aligned with the 'liberal left', these voices were likened by some to a 'campaign', since their efforts appeared to be co-ordinated and sources were often mutually shared.[106] In August 2005, the BBC's *Panorama* featured a programme presented by John Ware entitled 'A Question of

Leadership'. This documentary sought to argue that the Muslim community, and the MCB's leadership in particular, were in 'a state of denial' about the presence of extreme views among its affiliates, and that they were out of touch, and subsequently failing to take seriously the need to combat radical views. These were views that, although not necessarily espousing violence, did nonetheless promote separatism, 'contempt' towards non-Muslims, and acted as a 'slippery slope' towards extremism and eventually violence.[107] Central to Ware's argument was his search for authenticity and lack of equivocation in the MCB's condemnation of violence and specifically suicide bombing.

The 7/7 attacks were the first time that suicide bombing had taken place on UK soil. They had shocked the nation and prompted much soul-searching amongst Muslim groups that had previously preferred to focus on conspiracy theories and victimisation as easy scapegoats for the rise of Islamist terrorism. Ware argued that in the post-7/7 era, it was simply unacceptable for those claiming to lead the Muslim community to sustain a position where on one hand they had vowed to root out extremism and come down harshly upon it,[108] while on the other they were reluctant to denounce specific cases of sympathy for extremists or to distance themselves from affiliate organisations that held personalities with 'radical views' in high regard[109].

To make his argument, Ware persistently challenged leading MCB figures, including Secretary General Sir Iqbal Sacranie and Deputy Secretary General, Muhammad Abdul Bari, to clearly and directly condemn the tactic of suicide bombing by Palestinians in Israel. Ware, by his own admission, had set this as a sort of litmus test:

> The reason I focused on Israel ... is because I think the Israel-Palestine conflict presents the toughest test, in a way, for all the high-minded principles, including tolerance and peace, which political Islam claims to have

And, in response to accusations of bias in his questioning technique:

> I appreciate the Middle East conflict has a dynamic of its own, but there were people on the MCB who felt it was justifiable to support the targeting of civilians in Israel on theological grounds but not in London. I think those two positions must be incompatible, I really do.[110]

Ware also challenged the MCB on its non-attendance of the UK's Holocaust Memorial Day event,[111] as well as on Iqbal Sacranie's presence at a memorial service for Shaykh Ahmed Yasin, the spiritual leader of Hamas who was assassinated in a targeted strike by the Israeli military. In the meantime, an investigative article was published in the *Observer* newspaper to coincide with Ware's programme. Its findings overlapped with Ware's claims of double standards towards extremism within the MCB, drawing attention to sympathies with Pakistan's *Jamaat-e-Islami* (JI) among some of MCB's larger and more influential affiliates, and arguing that the JI and its founder, Sayyid Abul A'la Mawdudi, subscribed to extremist, separatist views that were incompatible with the liberal, secular democracy of modern Britain.[112] The *Observer* also suggested, as did Ware in his film, that the MCB was wielding its influence to stifle creativity and diversity in an upcoming Festival of Muslim Cultures, in the name of preserving religious orthodoxy.[113]

However, these efforts were received with suspicion, indignation and defensiveness by the MCB, who accused the BBC of succumbing to pressures from the 'pro-Israeli' lobby. Sacranie declared that he refused to pass the 'Israel Test',[114] which he considered to be a disingenuous ploy to de-legitimise the MCB and to portray their principled political stances in a negative light, thus undermining the entire notion of Muslim political engagement and therefore of Muslim identity politics itself. The MCB fired off furious press releases, and letters to the BBC and the *Observer*, charging them with poorly researched and agenda-driven journalism and arguing that the various journalists and commentators involved were engaged in a 'witch-hunt' against it, aiming to 'purposefully sabotage' British Muslim efforts at political participation.[115]

The following year, similar accusations were levelled by Martin Bright, in a *Dispatches* documentary[116] and an accompanying pamphlet, in which he argued that the government, and especially the Foreign and Commonwealth Office, were engaged in a 'love affair with radical Islamism'.[117] This, he elaborated, was a gravely mistaken policy of engaging with non-violent but 'reactionary' Muslim groups such as the Muslim Brotherhood abroad and its counterpart organisations in the UK, as a strategy with which to combat the spread of violent extremist ideas in the Muslim community. Bright relied on a series of leaked documents from a civil servant at the Foreign Office for his information,[118] which related to a number of occasions when officials in the FCO's Engaging with the Islamic World Group (EIWG) positively pushed for dialogue with and even the promotion of groups and individuals who were 'reactionary' and 'Islamist'. Bright contended that the EIWG's preferred stance of engagement with figures from abroad such as Shaykh Yusuf Al-Qaradawi and Delwar Hossain Sayeedi, as well as UK groups such as FOSIS and YMO,[119] rather than acting as a desired 'buffer' against violent extremism, instead served only to legitimise intolerant and illiberal views towards religions other than Islam, towards women, homosexuals and towards democracy itself. He accused many of these groups and figures of having inconsistent positions on violence, denouncing it in front of Western audiences only to then sanction it as an acceptable tactic in places such as Israel and Iraq. Furthermore, he concurred with John Ware's argument, which was basically a version of the 'conveyor belt' thesis. This was that even if these non-violent groups were deemed to be ready partners from within Islamism who were willing to work with the government in tackling and isolating violent extremism, they nonetheless (even if unintentionally) acted as stepping stones via which disaffected young Muslims could hop from 'moderate radicalism' to more extreme and violent versions of Islamism.

THE RISE OF 'APOLITICAL ISLAM'

This 'conveyor belt' understanding of the process of radicalisation was finding increasing favour within the liberal left. It insisted that truly moderate Islam did not concern itself with political ideologies or political affairs. The implication of this was that truly moderate Muslims needed to be either apolitical, or at least to be non-dissenting from the political status quo, since any dissent or vocal political activism from a Muslim would make them an Islamist, and thus place them at the start of the conveyor belt moving through radicalisation and towards violent extremism. In this context, a number of self-professed 'apolitical

Muslim' groups were indeed appearing on the Muslim representation scene.

These groups included the British Muslim Forum (BMF) and the
Sufi Muslim Council (SMC), both of whom were set up apparently to
fulfil alternative roles to that of the MCB – that of bringing together
Muslim groups across the country, representing British Muslims to
government, the media and other official arenas. The BMF, like the
MCB, was an umbrella group, but its affiliates consisted mainly of
Barelwi mosques.[120] The SMC on the other hand did not appear to
have an easily definable constituency as such, yet both of these
groups claimed to be speaking for the silent, apolitical majority of
British Muslims who apparently resented their religion being
hijacked for political purposes by the likes of the MCB. These new
groups contended that Islamism had kept a hold on British Muslim
community leadership for too long; and in regularly and painstak-
ingly arguing that there should be a clear and absolute demarcation
between Islam and Islamism, they sought to present a somewhat
polarised landscape of the Muslim community in which they were
the *bona fide* representatives of adherents to the former (the majority,
who were law abiding, everyday citizens) and in which the latter, the
Islamists, were holding disproportionate sway, often with self-serving
motives that were not aligned with the aspirations of the majority.

Also within this general trend were the more localised or specialist
voices of new quasi-intellectual groups and consultancies. These
included Dr Taj Hargey of the Muslim Education Centre of Oxford
(MECO), British Muslims for Secular Democracy (BMSD) founded by
the columnist Yasmin Alibhai-Brown, who acted as a trustee and
prominent spokesperson, Ed Husain and his Quilliam Foundation,
and Haras Rafiq (initially linked with the SMC), who set up CENTRI
(Counter Extremism Consultancy, Training Research and Interventions), but later moved on to Quilliam. As specialist groups, these
differed from the aforementioned representative bodies in that they
did not seek to directly represent the grassroots in the same way that
the BMF, SMC, MCB, or even radical voices such as HT and others did.
Instead they chose to engage with government and the media on the
basis of their expertise. This was largely derived from personal
experience, with many of these groups employing or relying on

former extremists who had denounced their pasts and embraced 'moderate' (effectively, quietist) Islam. Again, this was often a purportedly apolitical religiosity, centring around notions of spirituality. Yet what was most peculiarly consistent about these individuals and the groups within which they worked was their near-obsessive opposition to the use of Muslim identity in the political sphere.[121] The paradox of this position was that, on one hand, it was arguing that Muslims should leave their religion out of politics, and, on the other, these groups were engaging heavily in politics in contestation with the MCB and others, overwhelmingly on issues relating to Muslims. So while arguing that the 'silent majority' of authentic Muslims were apolitical, they were demonstrating themselves to be deeply engaged in politics, *as Muslims*, albeit ex-extremist ones. This attitude put them at odds with the more long-lived Muslim groups, primarily the MCB, which, as I have demonstrated, was founded on the very idea of Muslim political agency, with Muslim-ness as the primary marker of identity. Another notable consistency was a conspicuous acquiescence to the political status quo, or, at the very least, silence on foreign policy issues that were otherwise highly contentious among UK Muslims, namely Iraq and Afghanistan.

The official reception that such groups received from the state was warm and encouraging. Communities Secretary Ruth Kelly and her successor Hazel Blears each in turn made it clear that they were amenable to cooperation with newly formed bodies that better suited their agenda, and, moreover, that they were willing to end or freeze cordial relations with existing bodies that were not so readily enthusiastic about the direction of government policy.[122] For the MCB, this was seen as a direct threat,[123] and an affront to their right to differ with government on matters of principle.[124] They, and others responded by pointing out that these new government advisors were seriously lacking in credibility due to their detachment from grassroots Muslim institutions.[125] This did not seem to halt the progress of these new bodies. Led by individuals who were themselves very well connected in the media, government departments and quangos, they were able to secure prominent exposure and highly placed support in a relatively short time.[126]

Nonetheless, for some of these bodies, their heavy reliance on the sway of a handful of prominent individuals proved to be a cause for their swift descent into obscurity. Beyond sparse, intermittent activities centring around key personalities,[127] they have been largely absent from the day-to-day issues affecting ordinary Muslims. Activities have focused on denouncing terrorism and 'Islamism', yet there is no evidence of any real efforts to engage with 'bread and butter' issues concerning Muslim communities, such as education, employment, youth work, to mention a few. Indeed, the BMF has been virtually defunct since 2008 after issuing a statement in support of the government's highly controversial proposal to introduce 42-day detention without charge for terrorism suspects, which led to a split in its ranks.

Whilst the MCB has soldiered on, it has been weighed down by the complexity of its set-up, with committees and sub-committees galore, and no straightforward way for individuals to become involved except through membership of an affiliated organisation, or through personal connections.[128] Accusations that I have mentioned earlier regarding a lack of transparency, outreach and a broader representation of the UK's Muslim communities are not without foundation, and suggestions for improvement have regularly been put forward by well-wishers.[129] Despite these structural difficulties, the MCB's grassroots support level has gone up, as greater energy has been invested in community empower- ment schemes, work with young people in schools, mentoring initiatives, leadership development programmes, joining civic partnerships and coalitions and running health campaigns, to mention just a few.[130] None of the newer advocacy bodies have offered this level of service to the community, and certainly not with such consistency. In fact, it is doubtful whether they enjoy the commensurate level of grassroots support to be able to implement such schemes. With the most active of these groups being consultancy or think-tank-type bodies rather than community organisations with a membership or institutional base, their level of popular support is difficult to gauge. Yet, just as the MCB cannot claim to be fully representative of British Muslims, neither can it be said that the post-2005 'apolitical' set of Muslim groups do not represent anyone at all.

BRITISH MUSLIMS – A CHANGED IDENTITY POLITICS IN A CHANGING POLITICAL LANDSCAPE

By 2006/7 it had become increasingly clear that the future of British Muslim identity politics was in considerable flux. If one thing was for certain, it was that securitisation and the terror threat from extremism had come to dominate the relationship between the government and Muslim community groups in an unprecedented manner.

The arrival of a multitude of representative groups and the growth of an 'ex-extremist' advisory sector meant that each Muslim representative organisation was now open to greater scrutiny, and comparisons were regularly conducted between them. A natural consequence was that introspection ensued within existing groups, and steps were taken to become more relevant and engage with current issues and to deal with weaknesses in a productive manner. This was especially true of the MCB, which gradually become more reconciled to the presence of other ('competitor') umbrella and advocacy groups. For instance, it undertook to cooperate with the BMF on the matter of MINAB, in which both groups sat on the Board's steering committee.

Over time, the MCB has gradually shown itself to be more open to seeking common cause with others *despite* major differences. Whereas previously it had made little effort to shake off the reputation of being the exclusive preserve of orthodox Muslims, 2007 saw the MCB take steps to openly support the Equality Act, which included new laws against discrimination on the basis of sexual orientation.[131] Despite the inclusion of a firm addendum to its statement maintaining the Islamic theological opposition to homosexuality, this step was welcomed by gay rights campaigners and groups, some of whom had earlier invited the MCB to join hands with them to eradicate the 'twin hatreds of Islamophobia and Homophobia'.[132] Whilst the MCB didn't go as far as taking this invitation further, their statement, as short and precise as it was, marked a small but potentially significant shift in thinking. In expressing support for the law, it demonstrated a new maturity in its political approach, one that appreciated that in campaigning for 'Muslim interests' in a modern and pluralist Britain, it needed to understand and even empathise with the interests of other groups, even if they differed on fundamental issues. Therefore, that if it was to argue for a solution to the Equality Gap for Muslims, in terms of discrimination in employment, for instance, then it had to equally appreciate that other minorities and historically disadvantaged groups deserved the same recognition from the state, and the same level of parity under the law, despite fundamental theological or value-based differences that it might have with them.

Further, in January 2008, the MCB finally took the decision to participate officially in the national Holocaust Memorial Day, dropping its previous stance of 'staying away'[133] until the occasion became more generic and 'more inclusive of other genocides'. This step had been the result of persistent and divisive deliberations within the organisation, which pitted those who preferred not to participate until the condition of inclusivity had been met, against those who saw the MCB's absence as a 'self-inflicted wound', providing opponents with a 'stick with which to beat us'.[134] Again, this decision was a difficult one to make and still remains controversial among the MCB's affiliates. Indeed, senior MCB figures stayed away again in 2009, perhaps in protest against the belligerence of Israel's bombing campaign on Gaza during that time, and the UK government's muted response.

Still, no matter how painful these controversial decisions were for those who made them, they were transformative, both for the MCB and for Muslim communities. As much as the Council's influence and leverage has diminished over the years, its so-far unparalleled level of community support and its unmatched consistency of operation have served it well and have helped it to retain a (though often wobbly) *primus inter pares* position. Subsequently, difficult decisions such as these made perceptible if unassuming ripples further afield within Britain's Muslim communities and networks, and added legitimacy and weight to those who were already pushing for a less insular and more open understanding of civic cooperation.[135]

Additionally, recent structural reappraisals in the form of a constitutional review of the MCB were carried out in 2010 and 2011, with the aim of making the organisation's governance more streamlined and transparent.[136] Efforts to be more inclusive of diversity within the organisation's executive posts were made, with women and young people featuring in these positions regularly in recent years. However, with the results of its elections still being effectively pre-determined by the Council's main affiliates, the emergence of fresh blood, and the contribution of individuals who are not linked to any of the major affiliates, remains virtually impossible.

The case of Mohammed Amin, a Manchester accountant who put himself forward for the post of MCB Secretary General at its 2010 elections, is illustrative of this point. Here was an individual who had been involved in various sub-committees of the MCB for a good couple of years, had enjoyed a distinguished career and had been of service to his local community in various capacities. In putting himself forward for the post he went to great efforts to highlight his suitability and his goals and ambitions for the MCB by publishing a manifesto and acquiring endorsements from a handful of prominent Muslim figures. Yet the outcome of the election was a foregone conclusion – the main affiliate organisations[137] of the MCB had, as per tradition, decided well in advance to instruct their delegates to back Farooq Murad (then Chairman of Muslim Aid and a long-time community activist and leader) for the post. Murad was highly qualified too, and I am by no means arguing that Amin was necessarily a better candidate. The salient point here is that Amin's campaign was not given a fighting chance because he was a relative newcomer to the MCB and because he lacked the heavyweight backing from the main MCB affiliates that Murad enjoyed. In a sense, the election was over before it began.[138] This incident reflected cogently how the MCB was still a long way away from demonstrating a capacity for true inclusivity beyond the handful of groups to which it owed so much of its patronage, manpower and indeed its very foundation. It was almost as though these groups had invested so much hope and effort into the MCB that they had become obsessed with retaining control of its direction. Yet without giving genuine room for others to come forward, and without a fairer voting system, it remained impossible to see what a much more representative MCB would look like, and how its policy priorities and decisions might be affected.

To sum up, a brief comparison of the 2005–2010 period with the previous phase (2001–2005) is helpful. The period between 9/11 and 7/7 witnessed a peak in rapport between the state and the MCB. Despite their disagreements, the MCB enjoyed a pre-eminent and quasi-official position, as it was endorsed and promoted by the government in the wake of 9/11 as the voice of British Muslims. The then-MCB Secretary General Yousuf Bhailok talks of having daily phone conversations to co-ordinate with the Home Secretary in the months following the attacks.[139] Additionally, government ministers and even the Prime Minister himself were regular fixtures at MCB events, and MCB officials were regular guests at Downing Street, Parliament and the various government departments. For example, the MCB were invited to send a delegation to Downing Street for consultation with the Prime Minister in the run-up to the decision to send troops to Afghanistan in 2001.[140] This was a highly publicised event, to which the MCB was the only Muslim representative organisation to be invited. Contrast this with the aftermath of 7/7, when the net was cast much wider than the MCB, now only one of several groups to be consulted by the government.

This conferment of an 'official status' on the MCB symbolised a 'coming of age' for Muslim identity politics. It was a mutually beneficial arrangement for both the government and the MCB. The direct benefit for the MCB was that it had the ear of the government if it ever needed to raise an issue, and the government, for its part, was assured that it had direct lines of communication into the Muslim community. Of course, this is not to ignore that the MCB did not represent all components of Britain's diverse Muslim communities, but the channel of communication was there, it was prominent and 'above board', and those who wished to use it knew what they had to do.

The period between 2001 and 2005 also witnessed the Muslim community gradually adopting a far less insular attitude, and a new sense of being 'at ease' with aspects of wider society that shared values and ambitions. This was manifested through greater participation in civic campaigns on shared issues and a huge diversification of self-expression, using an ever-broader range of media.

By 2010, there had been regressions on a number of fronts. After July 2005, relations between the state and Muslim groups became progressively more strained, and more conditional, when it came to matters related to community cohesion and security. This was in spite of a far greater honesty and openness to introspection, self-criticism and difference between mainstream Muslim players. The main exception was that of new 'government-friendly' organisations, who now enjoyed cordial, supportive relationships with the state, but whose efficacy was questionable since they were less well established than the MCB and many of its affiliates. As we have seen, most of these organisations were either single-issue focused, had sporadic or short-lived activity, or eventually faded into some level of obscurity.

A major contributing factor to these strained relations was the Prevent strand of the Contest scheme, which contributed significantly to a loss of trust and a rise in suspicion between local Muslim groups, communities and the government. New and more stringent legal developments which sought to criminalise speech acts that were deemed harmful also fed into a growing atmosphere of distrust and resentment among Muslim communities, who felt that they were being unfairly targeted and that their highly cherished freedoms to criticise and speak openly on many aspects of politics and even religion were being unduly restricted. Many of the attempts that were made to implement these laws proved ultimately to be difficult to uphold in court and had the undesired attempt of creating martyr figures from among the outspoken, obnoxious and dangerous individuals that they targeted. Insofar as dialogue was concerned, the nature of government–community conversation had returned again to a far more abrupt nature. Rather than the flexible, almost empathetic approach that had been used post-9/11, there was now a 'take-it-or-leave-it style' characterised by a fair amount of public grandstanding and ultimatums being issued by the government.

On the other hand, positive developments have included greater steps towards transparency and openness in Muslim community groups, as a result of the more intense and often hostile public scrutiny that they faced, notably from quarters within the media. While the conditions for these developments may unquestionably have been difficult, they ultimately yielded community groups that have become more willing to reform and embrace progress and change. In addition, many of those lobbying for 'Muslim' causes have invested greater efforts into putting their message across through the media and through civil society campaigning, recognising that the state's preoccupation with securitisation meant that non-governmental avenues were more effective for their purposes.

For the MCB, this period was a case of 'two steps back' following the post-9/11 'one step forward'. As the following chapter shows, the Conservative–Liberal Democrat coalition government that came into power in 2010 did little to deeply or meaningfully engage with Muslim communities. Cameron's Conservatives were not known to be keen on the notion of identity politics, having regularly criticised it whilst in opposition. This stance marked it apart from Labour's long tradition of championing the causes of society's minority and disadvantaged groups. With the May administration continuing in this approach, indications are that the future of Muslim identity politics, if it is to survive beyond the coming phase, is necessarily at something of a crossroads. While some legal aspects of the Equality Gap have been substantively tackled, the religious hatred legislation remains something of an open wound, facing charges of being something of a dud law – one that, at best, fills a gap in technicalities rather than in equalities.[141]

The nature of the gap itself has also experienced a shift. On one hand, it has been narrowed through the abolition of blasphemy legislation in 2008, but on the other hand, issues of Islamophobia still persist, and are arguably worsening. Recent times have seen Britain First and the English Defence League (EDL) take on the mantle of the BNP, which in turn is ever more anxious to gain respectability, having enjoyed a short-lived spurt of electoral successes at the local council and European Parliament levels in 2008 and 2009. Education and awareness regarding Islamophobia is needed as much as ever, evidenced by the uproar in reaction to the speech of then Conservative Party Chairman, Baroness Warsi, in 2011, in which she warned that Islamophobia was the last remaining socially acceptable prejudice among British polite society. She argued that it had 'passed the dinner table test', and was seen by many as 'normal and uncontroversial'.[142] A whole host of public figures and commentators had recently taken issue with the very notion of Islamophobia, questioning the extent of its existence or arguing that it was disingenuously exaggerated. Others had indulged in casual anti-Muslim comments that were designed to positively test the boundaries of the acceptable, in ways that would have been roundly denounced if they had been made about other minority groups.[143] As Tariq Modood has noted:

> Muslims are frequently criticised in the comment pages of the respectable press in a way that few, if any, other minority groups are. Muslims often remark that if, in such articles, the words 'Jews' or 'blacks' were substituted for 'Muslims', the newspapers in question would be attacked as racist and, indeed, be vulnerable to legal proceedings. Just as the hostility against Jews, in various times and places, has been a varying blend of anti-Judaism (hostility to a religion) and anti-Semitism (hostility to a racialised group), so it is difficult to gauge to what extent contemporary British Islamophobia is 'religious' and to what extent 'racial'.[144]

As for Muslim advocacy groups, they learned a great deal during this period, emerging with greater confidence and resilience. On balance, the MCB's experience of 'detachment' from government, as painful as it may have been, was ultimately beneficial. It opened up possibilities for a serious reassessment of approach, but for their part, important strategic decisions need to be made as to whether civic partnerships and campaigns will be the way forward for Muslim political agency, or whether lobbying the government will regain its position as the main preoccupation of Muslim organisations.

CHAPTER 7

Current Debates

This chapter gives consideration to some of the issues and debates that have dominated British Muslim identity politics from 2010 onwards. After introducing the Conservative Party's approach to identity politics, and Muslim identity politics in particular, I consider some complex and overlapping themes that have emerged over recent years. I then move on to unpack how some of these challenges have affected the evolution of Muslim identity politics in the three areas of intra-community relations, Muslim communal organisations and the state, public political culture and the media. In doing so, I touch on two overlapping and interrelated themes that are at the core of today's Muslim identity politics landscape: Islamophobia and racism, and the Prevent strategy and wider CVE (countering violent extremism) agenda.

I consider how Muslim representative organisations, notably the MCB, have been responding to pressures for democratisation and reform from within Muslim communities. In a large part, this has been the result of the ongoing developments in the areas of identity and self-expression. Many of the changes that I discussed under this heading in Chapter 5 have since continued apace, and recent years have seen a proliferation of new and unconventional set-ups accommodating another type of 'equality gap' within Muslim communities. The marginalisation experienced by British Muslim communities does not preclude that privilege exists within them. Women, young people and unorthodox religious voices remain generally unaccounted for in the default 'community leader'-dominated identity politics that had been propped up and encouraged by the New Labour government.

Returning to earlier comparisons I have made with Jewish communal organisations, I show that although shared challenges are faced by community advocacy organisations for both faiths, the MCB and Muslim representative groups in general are confronted with many more challenges, both from within their communities and from several factors existing within the public political climate. I end by bringing together all of these strands and assessing how they have affected the Equality Gap, arguing that while the nature of Muslim identity politics in Britain has indisputably changed, the Equality Gap persists, albeit in a changed form.

THE FUTURE OF MULTICULTURALISM AND OF IDENTITY POLITICS: A CHANGING GAME

Multiculturalism in the balance

As we saw in Chapter 6, the aftermath of the 7/7 attacks ushered in much probing and reflection over the future of multiculturalism. Had multiculturalism as a policy been a contributory factor to a divisive climate in Britain, within which citizens could bring themselves to launch a terror attack in their own country? Had we 'focused far too much on the "multi" and not enough on the common culture'?[1] Was it time to now discard it, and for the state to take the lead in calling for a more forthright national unity, demanding more outward signs of loyalty and assimilation to a shared British culture from minority communities, while making less allowances for their specific needs or claims? These questions were being asked increasingly by voices in the centre-left of politics, and with the combined pressures of securitisation and the electoral threat from the rise of the far right, including anti-immigration parties such as the UK Independence Party (UKIP), and in line with elsewhere in Europe,[2] these thoughts soon began to find their home in day-to-day British politics.

In Chapter 6, we saw how the Labour government during the final months of Tony Blair's premiership and beyond began to shift its approach to identity politics by signalling that it would only be open to engagement and co-operation with any group that fulfilled the requisite requirements in 'tackling extremism and defending our shared values'.[3] The engagement of community representative organisations with the government was now firmly based upon conditionality. In addition to the veiled threat made by Ruth Kelly to the MCB on its history of absence from the Holocaust Memorial Day service,[4] another important example is the standoff that took place between the government and the MCB in 2009 over the position of its Deputy Secretary General, Dr Daud Abdullah. Abdullah had signed a declaration at a 'Global Anti Aggression Campaign' conference in Istanbul regarding the Israeli offensive on Gaza in January 2009. The eighth point within the declaration took the view that it was:

> The obligation of the Islamic Nation to regard the sending of foreign warships into Muslim waters, claiming to control the borders and prevent the smuggling of arms to Gaza, as a declaration of war, a new occupation, sinful aggression, and a clear violation of the sovereignty of the Nation. This must be rejected and fought by all means and ways.[5]

This point was interpreted by many observers, including the Communities Secretary Hazel Blears, as a call to arms against British troops, in view of the then-Prime Minister Gordon Brown's recent suggestion that the Royal Navy could be sent to the region to help enforce an arms blockade on Gaza. Blears' response was to 'suspend' engagement with the MCB, pending the outcome of an investigation, while stating in no uncertain terms that it expected the outcome of this investigation to result in the resignation of Dr Abdullah from the MCB, 'and for the MCB to confirm their opposition to acts of violent extremism'.[6] Events soon escalated as the MCB rejected Blears' correspondence as an 'unacceptable ... attempt to undermine the independence of the MCB',[7] and intervening talks held with the MCB by Muslim parliamentarians,[8] as well as diverse other representations,[9] proved fruitless in moving matters forward.[10]

While this approach from the government can be criticised as meddling and even 'dictatorial', recent times have also witnessed a sea-change within the structures of identity politics. This has partly been in response to governmental pressures, which ultimately forced the MCB into a position of complete self-reliance and self-sufficiency. Daud Abdullah himself argued that:

> If anything good is to emerge from this saga it should be the affirmation of the independence of MCB. However much Hazel Blears may dislike or disagree with its views she should respect this independence and deal with its representatives as equal citizens, just as it deals with the representatives of other communities.[11]

Such a position placed the onus on the MCB to demonstrate its credibility and worth solely on its own merit, without relying on connections, networks or support from government departments or agencies, as it may have done in its earlier years.

In the age of global terrorism and securitisation, and particularly after the 7/7 attacks in London, multiculturalism as state policy has come under immense scrutiny, as many have questioned whether it has been to blame for encouraging 'separateness' among Britain's minority communities, thus undermining the scope for loyalty and ultimately creating fertile conditions for the growth of radicalisation and extremism.[12] Successive government ministers have taken this thinking on board, and it was reflected more and more clearly in the communities policy of the Labour government in its later years, as conditionality for engagement with community groups became the norm, and greater emphasis was placed on promoting 'Britishness' and a shared national identity.

This line of thinking has been picked up even more strongly by the Conservative-led coalition government since 2010, as exemplified by Prime Minister David Cameron's speech to a Security Conference in Munich, where he declared that the 'doctrine of state multi-culturalism' had 'failed'.[13] Practical implications of this attitude for Muslim organisations became visible in the antagonistic approach that Cameron and his supporters in the cabinet (such as then Home and Education Secretaries, Theresa May and Michael Gove) main-tained towards 'Islamists', defining the term very broadly.[14] Examples include David Cameron's directive in 2010 that no Conservative politicians should attend the Islam Channel's Global Peace and Unity event,[15] causing his party's Co-Chairman, Baroness Warsi, to pull out after having already committed to attend.[16] Additionally, the fact that Theresa May issued an exclusion order as Home Secretary in 2010 to prevent a UK visit of the Indian Muslim 'televangelist' Dr Zakir Naik in response to concerted campaigns from right-wingers, while having earlier that year granted a visa to the far-right Dutch politician, Geert Wilders (despite his exclusion the previous year),[17] suggested double standards and victimisation to many Muslims.[18] And in 2011, a review of the Prevent strategy made it clear that community organisations who were deemed to support 'non-violent extremism' were no longer going to be considered eligible for funding or partnership.[19]

In 2014, the 'Trojan Horse' controversy in Birmingham brought to a head many distinct aspects of the Conservative-led government's approach to Muslim identity politics. The affair was ignited by the contents of an anonymous letter that was initially sent to Sir Albert Bore, then Leader of Birmingham City Council, and later leaked to the press. The letter purported to detail strategies through which the 'Islamisation' of a number of state schools in Birmingham was being achieved, as a model for potential emulation by an associate in Bradford. May and Gove both made public comments on the affair, although this was to take on its own momentum, revealing an internal rift between their two departments, centring on an accusation by the Home Office that the Department for Education had been aware of the allegations contained in the 'Trojan Horse' letter since 2010.[20] The authenticity of the letter itself has been brought into serious question on numerous occasions, hence the alternative reference to the affair as 'Trojan Hoax' rather than 'Horse'. However, it dominated national headlines for a considerable period of time, rapidly prompting interventions from senior politicians including the prime minister, who backed a succession of snap inspections from the education watchdog, Ofsted, and, ultimately, four separate national inquiries.[21] The MCB and other Muslim groups dubbed the snap school inspections a 'witch-hunt', reiterating its position that a conflation of concerns around governance and irregularity in these schools should not be conflated with the security agenda.[22] Ironically, the use of the term 'witch-hunt' ran the risk of feeding directly into the victimhood narrative that was regarded as one of the objectionable features of the worldview presented at some of these schools.

A common charge during this controversy was that Muslim teachers and governors had been engaged in 'entryism', a charge that echoed previous incidents, notably in the accusations that dogged the election of Lutfur Rahman as the first executive mayor of the London Borough of Tower Hamlets in 2010, in reference to his relationship with the IFE.[23] This charge of 'entryism' proved problematic in the case of the Birmingham schools since it seemed to suggest that parents and governors were 'outsiders' to the school communities, and were on a mission to infiltrate them. Many of the schools concerned were 'free schools', meaning that governors enjoyed a greater level of freedom and autonomy with regards to the curriculum. With the pupil populations in these schools being overwhelmingly Muslim, governors would have been within their rights to consider how their schools could best reflect the communities that they served (even if allegations of exclusionary practices and instances of hostility to pupils and staff who were considered not to be complying with a specific 'Islamic' ethos were clearly serious matters worthy of investigation). Viewed in this light, governors and parents were in one sense modelling community engagement and service, not only through direct involvement in their children's schooling but also through making it their mission to bring up these previously 'failing' or, at best, mediocre inner-city schools, to the point where they were being nationally recognised and applauded for their distinctive achievements.[24] This is an argument that was made by the 'Hands off our Birmingham Schools' campaign group that emerged in response to the controversy, conveying a sense that Muslims were facing double standards in public life and thus providing another example of how tensions around freedom of expression and how it impacts Muslims vis-à-vis society at large has influenced the nature of Muslim identity politics.[25]

One of the most lasting direct consequences of the affair was to be David Cameron's revisiting of the notion that the state should promote an official set of 'British values'.[26] During a speech in 2015 at Ninestiles Academy, one of the Birmingham schools caught up in the row, he stated that 'we must enforce our values', outlining specifically that they were: democracy, the rule of law, individual liberty and mutual respect and tolerance of different faiths and beliefs.[27] Cameron reinforced the argument he had made previously regarding the active promotion of 'muscular liberalism', and argued further that social cohesion was best achieved through the state's active encouragement of 'the reforming and moderate Muslim voices'.[28] This signified an intention not only to promote, through reward or incentive, a state-defined understanding of 'British values', but also, more critically, the explicit and unapologetic engagement of the state in the area of theological claims. Essentially through offering backing and endorsement to those Muslims 'who share our values', in the form of 'practical help, funding, campaigns, protection and political representation', and the open confrontation and public disparagement of those Muslim voices that it deemed to be at odds with said values, Cameron and, by extension, the state, was explicitly promulgating a definition of what 'good' and 'bad' Islam was.[29] We have seen in Chapter 6 how the Labour government had engaged in the active promotion of an 'acceptable' Islam through the funding of specific initiatives, and Cameron's speech indicated to many Muslims a ramping-up of this approach. The MCB responded furiously, claiming this approach could 'perpetuate further alienation of the community (and be) used to restrict freedom of thought and expression, or to conflate conservative views with violent extremism without any evidence base'.[30] This sentiment was expressed by other groups, including the tabloid-style Muslim news website *5 Pillars*, which commissioned a research exercise to report on what 'influential British Muslims' considered to be 'normative Islam', in an attempt to address the 'ambiguity' that it attributed partly to comments made by 'mainstream politicians'.[31]

A further announcement made in Cameron's 2015 speech was the commissioning of Dame Louise Casey to conduct a review of 'opportunity and integration'. This was to report back on how problems of segregation and isolation in communities could be addressed through policy. It was claimed that this, coupled with his announcement that a new 'Community Engagement Forum' (CEF) would be set up as part of the government's counter-extremism strategy signalled a desire to explore some of these challenges from a wider perspective than simply that of securitisation and of Islam.[32] Though the CEF did bring together individuals from a range of different faith and professional backgrounds, participants remained handpicked by the government, and a survey of those attending CEF meetings reveals a notable exclusion of voices that had been even vaguely critical of government counter-extremism policy or approaches to integration.[33] As for the Casey Review, this was eventually published in December 2016.[34] For a review that had been trumpeted by the government as an exercise in understanding the needs of all minority and deprived communities,[35] it received a critical reception for its overarching focus on Muslims. Suggestions in the report that 'regressive religious and cultural practices'[36] were to blame alongside socio-economic factors for holding back women's emancipation were received with indignation by those working within Muslim communities to address systemic discriminatory barriers to education and employment. Similarly, for a report that was to 'bring Britain together as one nation', the Casey Review was remarkably England-centric in its coverage.[37]

A final development that can be attributed at least in part to the fallout of the Trojan Horse affair was the introduction in 2015 of what has come to be known as the 'Prevent Duty'. Section 26 of the Counter Terrorism and Security Act 2015 places a statutory duty on public bodies across the UK to 'have due regard to the need to prevent people from being drawn into terrorism'.[38] This measure was rolled out in July 2015 to be implemented in particular at local authority level, in schools, institutions of further and higher education, and the health and prison sectors. For schools especially, the Prevent Duty has proved problematic, not least due to consternation around the nature of 'prevent training' that some members of staff would be expected to undergo, concerns that the statutorisation of this highly politically charged strategy, with a deeply divisive history, would affect the relationship of trust that teachers aim to maintain with their pupils. Additionally, the Prevent Duty introduced a requirement for schools to actively promote 'fundamental British values' – a set of state-defined values that, as we have seen above, are vaguely defined,[39] and the teaching of which is arguably impeded and even undermined by their introduction onto the curriculum in the context of a securitisation agenda.[40]

The introduction of the Prevent Duty can also be considered to have played a decisive role in polarising the existing debate around

Prevent within Muslim communities. Students in particular have organised in opposition to the Duty, arguing that it had led to the profiling of Muslim students and their victimisation on campuses, as well as restricting academic freedoms.[41] On the other hand, some of the most ardent supporters of Prevent have emerged from among the cohort of 'post-2005' counter-extremist organisations that I have profiled on pages 209–219.[42] As a result, support of or opposition to Prevent in general, and the Prevent Duty in particular, has come to influence and shape in specific ways the nature of Muslim political engagement and representation. This is a climate that has been endorsed and perpetuated by the state in its clear unwillingness to engage with dissenting views on Prevent, whether through the CEF or on other platforms. It is also a climate that has presented substantial difficulties for Muslim community institutions as they struggle to cope with perhaps the most urgent and terrifying challenge of recent years – the news of British Muslims travelling to Syria to join Daesh – some with aspirations to take part in fighting, and others 'making *hijra*', in an imagined emulation of the migration of the Prophet Muhammad and his followers to Medina, fleeing persecution in Mecca.[43]

Dealing with radicalisation and incidents of British Muslims travelling to Syria has been immensely testing, raw and traumatic at one and the same time for many Muslim organisations as they seek to provide support for affected families. They have had to try and make some sense of what has happened and work towards safeguarding their communities and young people from radicalisation on one hand and, on the other, cope with the hostility of a political environment exacerbated by the divisiveness, mistrust and suspicion that has grown around Prevent and counter-extremism. But the media interest in incidents such as these also places such Muslim organisations in an unfairly harsh and often unforgiving public spotlight. A good example here would be the way in which the East London Mosque became embroiled in the national media coverage around the unfolding story of three teenage girls from Bethnal Green who ran away from home in 2015 to Syria.[44] Suggestions in a number of media outlets that the mosque was implicated in the radicalisation of these girls meant that the mosque was compelled to focus its energies on clarifying its own position and responding to these allegations, at a time when its members of staff were also working hard to support the families of the girls in question.[45] As for the Trojan Horse controversy, its impacts continue to rumble on even in excess of two years after the initial allegations,[46] providing a vivid illustration of the state's changing approach to multiculturalism, and how this has impacted Muslim identity politics.

It is also fair to say that other circumstances have played a part in the evolution of Muslim identity politics in general, and the MCB in particular, over recent years. These include the growing involvement of the younger generations within communal organisational structures. For many of these individuals, the culturally infused norms and traditions of the older generations simply do not hold much purchase. So the notion of community representation that is run almost exclusively by a rotation of older men with links to the same group of organisations, even if convenient or effective, has been challenged far too many times for it to feasibly continue as the MCB's system of operation. In addition to this, the proliferation and ease of mass communication techniques through new media over the past few years has meant that the policy positions, actions, and indeed the inactions, of the MCB have been open to swifter and more intense circulation, commentary and scrutiny. On one hand, this has meant a greater workload for the (administratively stretched) organisation in managing these added challenges. But it has also provided new channels for communication and accountability with sections of Muslim and wider communities that it may never have otherwise reached. It proved imperative for the MCB to adapt to these new realities.

These challenges have been encountered in other communities as well and, along with the changing approach of the government, look set to have a strong bearing on the shape of identity politics among British minority faith groups, into the future. In the following section, I revisit the comparisons that I considered between Muslim and Jewish experiences of communal representation in Chapter 4, and cast a glance at some of the relevant developments that have taken placed within the MCB and the BOD.

Community representation: recent changes in both Muslim and Jewish identity politics

Today's largest British Jewish and Muslim representative organisations (the BOD and the MCB) have a substantial number of features
in common. While both maintain that they expend substantial effort
to bring together disparate sections of their respective communities,
their procedures for election and other routes to participation have
often been criticised as unwieldy and outdated. Both have been
regularly criticised for being unrepresentative, and for an undue
absence of women and young people from their leaderships.[47] Both
are accused of being out of touch and controlled by cliques, and
both regularly face charges of pandering to the government or the
establishment at the expense of authentically conveying community
concerns. Additionally, both the MCB and the BOD have had their
virtual monopoly on communal representation challenged and
weakened by the emergence of newer groups in recent times.

In a (perhaps pre-emptive) move, evidently in recognition of
the waning influence of the BOD, a Jewish Leadership Council
(JLC) was established in 2003.[48] This brought together leading
Jewish organisations such as the BOD, charities and prominent and
'well connected' personalities[49] to 'act as a coordinating body'.[50]
The JLC has since been growing in leverage and influence, but has
also been facing increased criticism. A notable example is that
of Jonathan Arkush, then a vice-president of the BOD, who
in 2012 severely criticised the JLC as 'unelected, unaccountable,
and ... therefore unacceptable' (as leader or representative of the
Jewish community).[51] Arkush proceeded to swiftly and unreservedly
apologise for his words, thus adding to the impression that he was
pressured into doing so by the JLC chairman, who had suggested a
reconsideration of its financial support for the BOD. Independent
Jewish Voices (IJV) was launched in 2007, taking issue with the pro-
Israel stance of the BOD and other leading communal organisations,
and seeking to democratise and diversify Anglo Jewish representation.[52]
The IJV argued that:

> ... the broad spectrum of opinion among the Jewish population of this
> country is not reflected by those institutions which claim authority to

represent the Jewish community as a whole (and) ... that individuals and groups ... should feel free to express their views on any issue of public concern without incurring accusations of disloyalty.[53]

Other signals of the Jewish communal establishment's recognition of the changing times include the formation of a JLC Committee on Women in Jewish Leadership. This committee produced a report in 2012, leading to the creation of two working groups on 'Personal Leadership Development' and 'Governance and Organisation', both with the aim of encouraging and assisting Jewish communal organisations to tackle the gender imbalance in participation and leadership.[54] Additionally, 'Changing the Board', a youth-initiated campaign to push for more young and female voices to be heard at the BOD, whether through facilitating the affiliation to the BOD of young people's groups, or encouraging women and young people to stand for election as deputies.[55] An integral part of this campaign has been pressuring the BOD to adopt greater transparency and communication with the wider Jewish community and young people in particular, for instance through organising pre-Board Election hustings events, and engagement in online social networks such as Twitter and Facebook. Two recent developments can at least partly be attributed to this campaign. The first of these is the now routine livestreaming of BOD meetings, making the discussions and proceedings more readily accessible to the public. The second is the recent election in 2015 of 30-year-old Richard Verber, the driving force behind 'Changing the Board', as Senior Vice President, making him the youngest person to hold honorary office in the BOD's history.

The MCB for its part has also long been under fire for having a stagnant, 'retrogressive' leadership.[56] The post-7/7 period has seen an abundance of Muslim organisations of all shades and structures seeking to speak for various sections of the Muslim community. Some have been more successful than others, as my discussion of them in Chapter 6 shows.[57] While the MCB leadership has gradually come to acknowledge the shortcomings in its structure and composition,[58] it has been slow to take any steps in rectification. After protracted internal debate and review, motions were finally passed at its annual general meeting in 2012 to create a 20-per cent quota for women in the organisation's National Council, and for the post of Secretary General to become directly elected by delegates to the AGM (rather than chosen by the newly elected National Council from amongst themselves, as had been the previous arrangement).[59] While these are clearly welcome developments for the cause of greater representation, democracy and transparency, they were not implemented until the 2014 elections for the Secretary General and National Council, begging the question of why the voting on these motions was not scheduled *ahead* of the elections at the 2012 AGM rather than *after* them. This would have allowed for the motions to be implemented straightaway, and thus for MCB to send out a far stronger message demonstrating its willingness to include more diverse and varied voices. Nonetheless, these changes meant that as of 2014, at least in theory, elections for the MCB's Secretary General have become necessarily a more competitive affair than they have ever been, since it is now harder for the main organisations among the MCB's affiliates to nominate and collectively back a preferred candidate in the manner that had hitherto been customary.[60] What has actually happened both in 2014 and 2016 is that the position of Deputy Secretary General has been contested by two male candidates, while a single candidate has stood for the Secretary General position, and in each instance was automatically elected unopposed. Whilst this overall situation represents something of an improve-ment on the status quo that had been in operation during the MCB's first 16 years, in which election results were generally forgone conclusions, it is clearly lacking, from the perspective of realising a genuinely inclusive and open competition for the Council's key leadership positions. Though the MCB seems to be making tantalising strides in the direction of gender parity, it will ultimately require bolder measures for this change to be lasting and more than skin-deep. Quotas and a more diverse leadership can only go so far when many of the MCB's affiliate organisations regularly display problematic attitudes, sometimes on a chronic scale, with regard to recognition and representation of women and young people.

In 2011, there were rumours of receptiveness in government circles towards the creation of a more pliant Muslim Leadership

Panel, which would perhaps overshadow and effectively replace the MCB, perhaps in a similar way to that in which some argue that the JLC is gradually overshadowing the BOD.[61] Importantly, both Jewish and Muslim representative groups have to deal with the reality of the multiple challenges facing multiculturalism in twenty-first-century Britain. What this has meant for organisations such as the BOD and the MCB is that both now face the shared challenge of adapting their terms of operation to a political landscape that is becoming increasingly uneasy with the notion of affording recognition to group identity. So, while these groups developed, with active encouragement and endorsement from the government, to speak for and represent the identity politics of religious minority communities, if they wish to continue to play a representative role in politics, they will need to become far more accessible, open and streamlined in their structure and operation. They will also need to reassess the premises upon which they justify their existence – for the MCB and other Muslim representative groups, this involves a resetting of agenda priorities (the Equality Gap) and the techniques through which their causes are furthered.

Anti-Semitism and Islamophobia – Jews and Muslims as both victims and perpetrators

The years following 2010 saw a dramatic rise in the prominence of the EDL, not least encouraged by the murder in May 2013 of a member of the armed forces in Woolwich by two men claiming to be acting in the name of Islam and in retaliation against British foreign policy in Muslim lands.[62] In 2014, Britain First (BF), another far-right movement and self-described 'street defence organisation'[63] that was formed by ex-members of the BNP, came to prominence after staging several 'mosque invasions' in a number of cities across the UK. It has since fielded candidates in elections, notably the London mayoral election of 2016, and calls have been made for it to be proscribed as a terrorist organisation in the wake of eyewitness claims that it was invoked by Thomas Mair, the murderer of Jo Cox MP in June 2016. Yet although the EDL remains an extremist fringe group, the BNP now suffers from infighting,[64] and BF's electoral fortunes have been marginal, all indicators –

from the divisive political campaigning around Brexit to the rise of the so-called 'alt-right' – nonetheless suggest that Islamophobia from the far-right is set to persist into the future period. This is only exacerbated by aspects of the media, including sensationalist stories that imply that Islam and Muslims are inherently insidious,[65] as well as irresponsible programming that gives extremists a wider audience than they would ever have reached otherwise, and one entirely disproportionate to the segment of the wider population who may share their views.[66] Further aggravation has been caused by misguided 'revenge' attacks, by equally fringe and extremist Muslims.[67]

There have been a number of recent academic comparisons made between current experiences of Islamophobia, and the anti-Semitism that the Jewish communities of Britain and Europe suffered in the nineteenth and twentieth centuries.[68] It has been argued that there is substantial similarity and overlap between the racism that Jewish communities experienced in the past and that which Muslim communities are currently experiencing.[69] This is evidenced by the invocation of 'cultural and biological discourses' to emphasise 'otherness', and to draw into question the suitability of the 'other' to adjusting or living peacefully in the UK. For instance, both Muslims and Jews have faced suggestions that they are culturally unfamiliar with democracy and democratic processes due to radical or fundamentalist tendencies.[70] And just as the loyalty of Jews to Britain was brought into question by sections of the press and politicians in the early twentieth century,[71] so Muslims today are often at the receiving end of the same suspicious, polarising question: are you British *or* Muslim?

Yet while the task of tackling Islamophobia might technically stand to benefit from the past experiences of British Jews in combating anti-Semitism, it is further compounded by attitudes and instances of Jewish Islamophobia on one hand, and Muslim anti-Semitism on the other. On the official level, both the MCB and the BOD have on separate occasions accused the other of engaging in or sanctioning prejudice against the communities that they represent.[72] Often these sentiments can be intertwined with the highly emotive ongoing Palestinian–Israeli conflict, and indeed such accusations have most commonly flared up in relation to moments of Israeli military aggression.[73] Yet expressions of prejudice are also wider and deeper than this, with instances of anti-Semitic discourse reported to have been expressed in mosques by religious leaders and publications,[74] as well as by political figures.[75] Jewish figures, for their part, have regularly conflated anti-Zionist political stances with anti-Semitism, and given succour to populist far-right discourses on an inherently illiberal and extremist Islam, whose followers, 'unlike other minorities ... expected their host culture to adapt to meet their requirements.'[76]

Having said this, away from political and theological conflicts between both communities, as influential as they might be, there are also signs that dialogue and collaboration between Muslim and Jewish institutions are helping to address Islamophobia on a practical level. In the same way that Muslim communal organisations have looked to the prior experience of British Jews, there have also been cases where Muslim efforts in addressing Islamophobia have turned towards Jewish endeavours in the area of anti-Semitism. One prominent recent example is the Tell MAMA Islamophobia monitoring helpline, which received guidance and advice from the Community Security Trust (CST), 'to establish and professionalise itself'.[77] Cases such as this can hold much promise of productive cooperation and solidarity, rather than a rivalry of victim mentalities that critics of identity politics have warned against.[78] Yet, at the same time, they can also draw attention to important discrepancies.

One case in point is the regular grant that, since 2010, has been allocated by the Department of Education to the CST, to cover the costs of hiring security services for government funded Jewish schools.[79] In 2015, it was announced that further funds would be allocated to extend this scheme beyond Jewish state schools, to cover Jewish private schools and other communal institutions.[80] Muslim institutions have never enjoyed similar government assistance, and indeed, the decision to temporarily deploy police protection to 'vulnerable Islamic sites' in response to a number of 'Woolwich revenge attacks', was seen as 'long overdue'.[81] Most recently, a scheme launched in the wake of rocketing levels of Islamophobia linked to an emboldened far-right that has benefited from divisive and populist politics that have been on display around the Brexit referendum offers the opportunity for places of worship to bid for security equipment.[82] After the first round of funding for this had been awarded, 12 Muslim places of worship (out of 59 'Muslim applications' to the scheme) have now been awarded funding for the installation of security equipment.[83] While undoubtedly this is an improvement, in the sense that some support is provided for security at places of worship for vulnerable communities at a time when they are facing regular and substantial hostility, including damage to buildings and sometimes lethal attacks,[84] the limiting of such funding to security equipment at places of worship, and its allocation by way of competition, compares poorly with the automatic entitlement that Jewish schools and communal institutions (including places of worship) have to security services. Most recently, a terror attack on Muslims in North London during the month of Ramadan during the summer of 2017, which appears to have been carried out by an individual motivated by the anti-Muslim far-right, has prompted the Home Office and police services nationwide to provide assurances that police presence at mosques would continue for the remainder of the holy month, but there have been no similar assurances relating to the long term. Rather, Prime Minister Theresa May has indicated an intention to categorise Islamophobia as a form of extremism – a move which has been positively received by some as a welcome departure from the Conservative Party's persistent blind eye towards it (and, arguably, its complicity).[85] However, as others have noted, the framing of Islamophobia as extremism, rather than as a hate-crime on a par with anti-Semitism, has the worrying consequence of placing it in the legal frame of securitisation, instead of the remit of equalities. Doing so exceptionalises Islamophobia and thus fails to capture the 'day-to-day manifestations and expressions of Islamophobia',[86] which are well-documented as having surged in recent years. Muslims for whom everyday experiences of Islamophobia have now become a fact of life will encounter inequality as a result of such a classification since these everyday experiences may well not be considered as acts of 'extremism' and thus not attract the attention of the law in the same way that everyday anti-Semitism quite rightly does. Such differential treatment brings us back to the Equality Gap. As I shall go on to argue in my concluding chapter, these discrepancies are best dealt with in the realm of civic activism by cross-community dialogues and alliances that promote the shared interests of communities with a view to narrowing the gap in all its manifestations.

CHAPTER 8

Epilogue: Equality and the Future of Muslim Identity Politics in Britain

This book has studied the development of Muslim identity politics in the UK since 1960, utilising the vantage point of freedom of expression. It has used recognition theory to explain the motivations and justifications behind the emergence of Muslim identity politics and claims-making over recent decades, and argued that the existence of an Equality Gap has been the main reason for the continuation of this type of identity politics. By examining case-studies related to the theme of freedom of expression, it has identified chronological phases in the development of Muslim identity politics, and highlighted important themes that have contributed to the path that this identity politics has followed. It has also considered and assessed some of the most recent developments, and their anticipated impact on the future.

For this concluding chapter, I use three main questions to summarise and bring together the argument in this book, as well as looking at the prospects for future work that it can lead to. The first question helps to provide a sense of chronology and summarisation of the time period covered by this book, while the other two correspond to the themes that I introduced in Chapter 2, namely free speech, equality and identity politics:

1. What were the main phases in the trajectory of Muslim identity politics over the past 50 years, including their defining features?
2. How has free speech fared and how does it help us to understand the trajectory of Muslim identity politics in the UK?
3. The Equality Gap – has it been filled?

1. WHAT WERE THE MAIN PHASES IN THE TRAJECTORY OF MUSLIM IDENTITY POLITICS OVER THE PAST 50 YEARS, INCLUDING THEIR DEFINING FEATURES?

During the 1960s, modern Muslim consciousness in Britain was only just beginning to lay down roots through the emergence of a range of organisations, which were linked to transnational Islamic movements. For these groups, Muslim identity was at the core of their mission and self-understanding. By the time that the first localised community campaigns and national unity initiatives were underway, there was already an express desire among many British Muslims for greater recognition from the government and official institutions. This was exemplified in many of the local and regional campaigns around education and schooling, as well as the calls by the UMO for the official recognition of Muslim holidays, provision for time off without penalty for Muslim employees for Friday prayers, and the recognition of Muslim family law.

Freedom of expression issues can serve as a prism through which we can appreciate how differences between Muslim immigrant communities and British public and political culture became apparent during this period – in the areas of history as well as social, cultural and political heritage. The Rushdie Affair drew polarised responses as it dealt with subjects that each side held in extremely high regard. Muslims could not countenance such perceived callous ridicule of their most revered personality going unchecked. They felt indescribable humiliation over the contents of a literary piece, one which portrayed the sources of their faith, and for many, their own self-worth, in terms so offensive that they could not even bring themselves to utter them. On the other hand, the British government and many in wider British society could not accept the call for censorship of a literary piece on the basis of merely (in their eyes) the offence it had happened to cause. Rather, it seemed that these Muslims needed to make progress in coming to terms with liberal ideas on freedom of expression, a stance which only accentuated the deep hurt felt by Muslims, who were then all the more frustrated at being misunderstood.

The Rushdie Affair was the first time that a national issue came to such a head, providing conditions that demanded from the existing array of Muslim community leaders and groups that they recognise the crucial value that creating a united front would add to the furtherance of their cause. It also compelled them to seriously think about how they could articulate their claims-making in such a way that was both accessible and persuasive to the government, the media and wider British society. This is not to say that they were successful at this stage, far from it. As I have shown in Chapter 4, the whole affair can be considered to have been more of a failure than a success in terms of dialogue between Muslim community representatives and the government. However, what did emerge from the legacy of the Rushdie Affair was a resolve on the part of both Muslim organisations and the government that it was best for a repeat of this situation to be avoided. Consequently, the UKACIA maintained relations with the government through to the early 1990s, and the government, for its part, encouraged community leaders towards the formation of an official unified body to facilitate its engagement with British Muslim political claims-making.

The mid-1990s up until 2001 can be regarded as the heyday of British Muslim identity politics. With the MCB up and running, we saw a coming together of British Muslim organisations and activists on the broadest platform yet. While the MCB was more inclusive than any of its predecessors had been, it was still at this stage functioning very much within the very limited sphere of community activism, and still predominantly male and controlled by those hailing from a reformist background. Positive encouragement and public promotion of the MCB by the Labour government went a long way, and it seemed as though the MCB was finally moving forward to gaining much-coveted status, and recognition that was on a par with that enjoyed by the BOD. Conversely, the Labour government was benefiting by enjoying a direct and influential channel into the

Muslim communities of Britain, including mosques and the largest Muslim national and regional organisations.

Two turning points then brought about changes that have seen Muslim identity politics take a path that could not have been envisaged during the early days. The terror attacks of 11 September 2001 threw the MCB into the limelight as never before. Its newfound role as official 'spokesman' for British Muslims gave it a huge reach and exposure, but also brought with it the considerable challenges of balancing the demands of credibly representing its extremely diverse constituency on the one hand, and maintaining good relations with a government whose foreign policy ambitions were fast becoming a source of anger and dismay among British Muslims. In facing this impossible situation, the MCB ultimately took the decision to oppose the government on matters relating to foreign policy and the war on terror. In doing so, it effectively had to forge a new path for its future, since its opposition to the Blair government's military engagement in Afghanistan and Iraq meant that it could no longer count on the same level, or the same exclusivity of support, from the government. The post-9/11 period saw Muslim identity politics diversify into seeking partnerships across other sections of civic society on common-interest issues, including opposition to the war and opposition to the rising Islamophobic tactics that were being employed by far-right groups such as the BNP. Additionally, with the coming of age of younger, British-born generations, creative and less conventional forms of self-expression utilising arts and technology were explored as alternatives or complements to the traditional methods of formal political protest and representation that had been preferred by the older generations.

The second turning point came after the terror attacks on London's public transport system that took place on 7 July 2005. These prompted serious introspection on the part of the government and Muslim community organisations alike, as they reconsidered their existing approaches towards radicalisation, extremism and security. A new raft of anti-terror legislation included 'encourage-ment clauses', which took terror offences into the realm of speech and expression by criminalising the encouragement or glorification of terrorism. The Prevent strand of the government's Contest scheme for tackling radicalisation at home also weighed heavily on themes of free expression, not only because of its self-declared mission to win the battle for 'hearts and minds', but also as it became associated in the eyes of many, particularly many Muslims, with surveillance and intelligence-gathering.[1]

At the same time, the increasingly anti-Muslim focus of the British far-right, as well as the growing national debate on the viability or otherwise of multiculturalism, contributed towards feeding an increasingly vocal and often threatening Islamophobia. The support that this Islamophobia regularly received in public discourse, was too often met with passive or lethargic responses from people in positions of power and influence, to the extent that its very existence was questioned by some, and derisively belittled by others. What was seen as a *laissez faire* approach to public discourse that was hostile to Islam and Muslims smacked of double standards when juxtaposed with the tough talk that was being employed by the government in relation to the encouragement and glorification of terrorism. This in turn fuelled further resentment among Muslims for the government's counter-radicalisation strategies – resentment which was only very margin-ally quelled, if at all, by the introduction of the largely inept Racial and Religious Hatred Act 2006.

By the close of the decade, relations between the MCB and the state had suffered immensely as a result of what had proved to be the toxic mix of securitisation with community cohesion. Multicultur-alism had become a scapegoat in many quarters for society's anxieties around security and immigration. This, combined with the far-right's focus on anti-Muslim discourse, pushed the government to revise the nature of its engagement with Muslim representative organisations. With the emergence of a host of new Muslim representative and advocacy bodies, each seeking to represent diverse voices from amongst British Muslim communities, the government realised it did not have to rely exclusively on the MCB to act as its interlocutor, and the MCB eventually came to appreciate that it was in no position to command such an exclusivity. Conditionality became a new feature of engagement, as talk of loyalty and British values was a key feature of this latest phase of the twenty-first-century critique of multiculturalism. Finally, voices within the Muslim community played an important role in pushing for modernisation and greater transparency of structure and operations within the MCB, as has been the case with the communal representation of other minority communities, such as the BOD. These factors, combined, have meant that the future of identity politics is set to take a new turn in priority and focus.

Since 2010, successive Conservative-led governments have continued to pursue a policy of conditional engagement with Muslim communal groups, a policy which remains at odds with their approach to Jewish groups, as the JLC and the BOD continue to enjoy regular audiences with ministers of state, regardless of their political stances.

2. HOW HAS FREE SPEECH FARED AND HOW DOES IT HELP US TO UNDERSTAND THE TRAJECTORY OF MUSLIM IDENTITY POLITICS IN THE UK?

The Rushdie Affair helped to rally together previously disparate Muslim community initiatives around a common cause, at the centre of which was freedom of expression, and the debate over the legitimacy or otherwise of calls to restrict it. Following this, speech-related causes always featured prominently in the articulation of Muslim claims to the government, as my first summary of the Equality Gap showed.[2]

By the close of 2001, freedom of expression was beginning to feature through a new dimension – as a component of civil liberties which were felt to be under increasing threat from the recently enacted anti-terrorism legislation. This was in addition to the more nuanced freedom for Muslim community groups, specifically the MCB, to maintain their right to a free and independent stance on current affairs, irrespective of government policy. The realities of the modern terror threat, the drive towards securitisation through anti-terror laws and the government's participation in the War on Terror all had implications for the government-MCB relationship. While there were significant efforts made by both sides to coordinate responses to the attacks, there were also several points of sore disagreement and divergence. These included increasingly draconian aspects of the new anti-terror legislation, and the widespread opposition among British Muslims (as part of strong opposition in the wider public) to military involvement in Afghanistan and Iraq.

Out of this scenario, there emerged increasingly confident voices from within Britain's Muslim communities that were keen to express themselves and communicate their experiences, perspectives and values by building partnerships with others and exploring more creative means of communication. This trend went some way in generating significant progress from the near-stalemate in inter-cultural dialogue and the sense of communicative dissonance which had been such a notable feature of the discourse around the Rushdie Affair.

Yet elements of this dissonance have remained, and are exemplified by the attitudes of relative tolerance by the political establishment towards the regular appearance of anti-Muslim bigotry in mainstream press, despite pleas from Muslims and supporting anti-Islamophobia activists for acknowledgement of this problem, for restraint and for shows of solidarity.[3] From a legal perspective, consistent calls from Muslim organisations for legislative reform to criminalise incitement to religious hatred ignited heated debate around the future of free speech in the UK, and the role, if any, that the state had in limiting it to protect vulnerable groups. One consequence of this debate was that while a law was eventually passed in 2005, extensive objections and amendments in parliament meant that it did not deliver the even-handedness (in relation to the Race Relations Act) that Muslim groups had so long called for.

In the area of security, the introduction of the controversial 'encouragement clauses' in the Terrorism Act 2006, even though they proved largely unenforceable in the courts, had the consequence of feeding the perception that Muslims were being unduly singled out, regulated and suspected. This view was only bolstered by the impression that a similar suspicion was being planted upon any Muslim who had the gall to express misgivings or frustration, let alone opposition, to the UK's foreign policy, lest this expression fall foul of the new laws. Additionally, the case of Ahmed Faraz prompted substantial fears that the courts would be prepared to criminalise certain extreme or archaic theological positions by prosecuting for the possession or distribution of the texts upon which they were based. Coupled with this was the troubled reception of the Prevent scheme within Muslim communities, its reputation varying from being an intelligence-gathering exercise at worst to an extensive PR project at best. All of these factors combined served in one way or another to diminish freedom of expression within Muslim communities, whether in real terms, or in people's perceptions of the extent of this freedom that they enjoyed. So, whether it was self-censorship precipitated by a 'chilling effect' or actual experiences of harassment, surveillance or arrest, the general sense was that freedom of expression was being severely limited in the name of security, with far less qualms than had been expressed over calls to restrict incitement to religious hatred.

To return to the 2005 Religious Hatred Act; with its introduction, and the abolition of the long-defunct blasphemy laws in 2008, the Equality Gap (as described in Chapter 4), seems to have narrowed considerably. Indeed, with significant progress having been made in terms of background concerns relating to recognition and respect for Britain's Muslims, is it now time to take stock and ask if the Equality Gap still exists? I address this and related issues in the following section.

3. THE EQUALITY GAP – HAS IT BEEN FILLED?

In order to answer this question, it is useful to revisit the early days when the notion of Muslim identity politics on a UK level was gathering momentum and the Equality Gap was beginning to be seriously articulated. During the Rushdie Affair, this was happening for the first time, and, as I described in Chapter 4, the Equality Gap to which the UKACIA and others appealed consisted of a speech component and an action component. To re-cap, the speech component included the continued existence of blasphemy legislation in English law to which the Church of England had recourse, to the exclusion of other faiths, significantly Islam. It also included the shortcomings of current legislation in proscribing incitement to religious hatred. As for the action component, this related to the inadequacy of anti-discrimination legislation in appreciating the complexity of the British Muslim experience as an 'ethno-religious' group. The clearest way to illustrate this gap was to refer to the inclusion of Jews and Sikhs under race-discrimination legislation, but the exclusion of other faiths. Again, this anomaly was most significant with respect to Muslims, as the largest minority faith in Britain. Together, these components represented the central claims around which the UKACIA was framing its representations to the government by 1993, when it made a submission to the Home Secretary on this matter.[4]

By 2010, Muslim identity politics in Britain had weathered an intense and often complex course. Formal relations and lobbying combined with willingness from the government had yielded recognition on various levels; the religion question in the national census has helped to provide the best demographic snapshot of Britain's Muslim community so far, making coordination with local authorities on needs, services and the articulation of claims easier, more accurate and more credible. There were strides made in political representation both in parliament and on a local level. Government departments took greater steps to cater for the specific needs of British Muslims in different areas of life, for example, by establishing the British Hajj delegation, and instituting a Muslim advisor to work in Her Majesty's Prisons.

Global politics, terrorism at home, the resurgence of the far-right and the rise of divisive populism have all played important parts in igniting fears around immigration and feeding into a 'crisis of multiculturalism'. This has witnessed introspection and speculation within government, among policy-makers and in public commentary about whether it is conducive for society to continue to recognise identity politics or whether the notion of minority group representation has had its day. Detractors will protest that Muslim identity politics is little more than a ploy used by self-important and self-appointed community leaders to cultivate a grievance culture and bask in the 'perks' of the victim-status that they feed with exaggerated claims of Islamophobia.[5] Yet there are others who refuse to 'see identity politics as antithetical to political perspectives focused on the good of society as a whole.'[6] Modood argues that there remains a place for identity politics, and that for many, the sense of Muslim identity that they feel, 'has nothing to do with religiosity'.[7] Rather, 'Muslimness' can, and does, mean different things to different people. Additionally, he notes that Muslim feelings of community, and especially affinity with the *ummah*, do not have the luxury of being supported or celebrated by the British government. Rather, these relationships are often the subject of suspicion and a questioning of loyalties. I would add that as long as significant elements within society, be they the press, public political culture or institutions, continue to express hostility, distaste or hatred towards Muslims, there will be no end in sight for Muslim identity politics, since it is these experiences that often serve to make people far more deeply conscious, defensive and even proud of their identities.

So rather than seeing its end in the coming era, I would argue that Muslim identity politics faces new challenges, and that these challenges call for an adjustment in the way that identity politics is conducted. Modood argues that this is already happening.[8] On the other hand, Sir Iqbal Sacranie has in the past called for the Muslim community to enter a new phase, one of 'greater engagement as individuals in the civil society around us', which would replace the age of identity politics that, he argued, although it 'has been psychologically satisfying, and allowed socio-economic inequalities to be addressed, also nurtures community self-interest'.[9] Modood disagrees, and I have also discussed in Chapters 5 and 6 how new forms of creativity and expression are on the rise within British Muslim communities, and that conventional and traditional ways of organising and representation are being questioned, as calls to democratise these organisations further and make them more transparent and accessible are, slowly but surely, making gains, whether with the support of or in spite of the old guard of community leaders. Indeed, as the discussion in Chapter 7 has shown, these developments are happening within other minority communities as well, specifically in Jewish identity politics, suggesting that the tired but frustratingly persistent binary of 'group' identity politics vs. community cohesion and 'national' identity, one that is too often imposed from above by leaders and gatekeepers from within the political arena and the establishment or from within communities, can be slowly but steadily challenged from the grassroots.

I propose that we are at a stage, not where the Equality Gap has become less significant, but where we are in a position to revise its articulation. I submit that it can now be described as follows:

- **Legal** – primarily this relates to the limitations of the Racial and Religious Hatred Act 2006 and the case for its potential strengthening.
- **Applicative** – this relates to the application of security measures in post-9/11 and post-7/7 Britain, which have been shown to contribute to the victimisation of Muslims as a community. This feeds into the third category:
- **Cultural** – this relates to the persistence and growth of cultural anti-Muslim sentiment and Islamophobia. Modern concerns surrounding terrorism and security, the war against terrorism and debates on multiculturalism and immigration have all fed into the anti-Muslim rhetoric of the far-right. That anti-religious hatred legislation has been a weak weapon against Islamophobia has given room for its spread to go comparatively unchecked. Official indifference towards, and even complicity in, Islamophobic discourse has contributed towards this trend. And although this problem is not one that can be appropriately solved by hard legislation, it nonetheless provides a strong reason for the continuation of Muslim identity politics into the future.

These three categories together sum up the basis on which Muslim representative organisations can continue to call for greater recognition and respect in the public and political domain. The methods that they utilise to further this are clearly already under revision, as is the government's approach to engagement with representative groups. I want to suggest here that lobbying in the traditional sense does not have to be the primary role of representative groups. While it can and must surely still play a role, there are plenty of avenues for partnerships, networks and coalitions that can be explored within the paradigm of identity politics. These can involve cross-community ventures that campaign for matters of common interest, while at the same time breaking down cultural barriers and building bridges. Such partnerships have the advantage of drawing attention to the legal and applicative aspects of the Equality Gap, while also, in practice, targeting the cultural aspect.

There remains a strong preference among many British Muslims to continue to identify publicly with their faith – a preference in no small part sustained by the rise in populist politics that has utilised divisive nativist rhetoric to foster another type of identity politics, one that has increasingly portrayed Muslims at worst as a threat to be eliminated, or at best, a parasitic drain on society's resources. Alliances in response to this have taken on a momentum of their own, and Muslim engagement within them has been a demonstration of the growing shift among British Muslim activists who are jaded by the identity politics of lobbying towards a more upbeat approach that is consciously rooted *in* Britain, *for* Britain. Whether Muslim identity politics remains best pursued under the heading of a 'British Muslim' identity is a question worth considering, particularly as the past few years have seen a plethora of Muslim identities come to the forefront of the British Muslim 'scene'. Black British Muslims, feminists and inclusive Muslim spaces of worship are all examples of this natural diversification of British Muslimness,[10] which signifies a Muslim population at home and at ease with its place in Britain, such that it is no longer defined by the characteristic impulse common to many minorities or diasporas to organise politically purely under an exclusive and unified banner.

Additionally, these schemes, often with diversity as their main strength, have the potential of allaying the concerns of critics who perceive identity politics as necessarily fostering attitudes of victimhood and competitiveness between minority communities, as well as the possibility of reification hampering accurate and authentic understanding between communities, and between communities and the state. Civic partnerships that connect people across the lines of faith, culture and socio-economic factors in support of issues of shared interest can provide ample opportunities for Muslim communities and individuals of all shades to come forward and make their voices heard, rather than simply leaving this role exclusively to representative organisations. Some of these have already been taken up, as I have shown in Chapter 6, but I believe that these have the potential to play a far more central role in raising awareness of the (revised) Equality Gap, and working to narrow it.

Hope not Hate is one campaign organisation which has been a location of such activism, where Muslims have engaged with a spectrum of others to mobilise against racism and Islamophobia, and provide support for refugees by offering 'a positive antidote to the politics of hate'.[11] Another example is Brendan Cox's *The Great Get Together*, an initiative to commemorate the life of his late wife Jo Cox MP, which he hopes will

> give us a chance to reassert what unites us as a country, as a nation – the values of community, of tolerance … People are sick of the emphasis placed upon our divisions, along with political extremism and the nastiness of the public debate at this time.[12]

The declared aims of this campaign resound closely with the state's rhetoric around 'British values' (see Chapter 7). But whereas the latter has often been met with resentment for its lecturing tone that assumes British Muslims need to 'learn' these values, and 'unlearn' those 'un-British' aspects of conservative Islam, the former can credit its far wider appeal to its starting point that everyone (Muslims and others) has 'more in common', to use Cox's widely cited phrase. It can be understood as something of a bottom-up response to government rhetoric by presenting common values as a feature that transcends and is enriched by cultural and religious difference, as distinct to the perception that this difference is something of a barrier to the goal of civic integration. Julie Siddiqi, the Muslim activist coordinating *The Great Get Together*'s partnership with her own annual *Big Iftar* project, articulates this perspective in her response in an online discussion to the publication of 'Muslim manifestos' by representative groups in the context of the 2017 General Election:

> How long will that narrow thinking carry on for? Yes, we know there are issues [around representation and portrayal in politics and the media], we need to get smart at lobbying, smart at holding media and politicians to account but there is SO much more we also need to be doing around engagement, building partnerships and allies. THOSE [our allies and partners] are the people that then effectively speak out about Islamophobia better than we ever can. [We need] to really see the

people of this country as 'our people' not just on the odd document or in a speech here and there but to really feel it in our bones, sincerely from the heart. This is not 'the Muslim manifesto' because it is so narrow and ignores how beautifully diverse British Muslims are who do not want to be viewed through the lens of terrorism the whole time.[13]

The 'Muslims for Change' crowdfunding campaign for a 'British Muslim election war chest' (2017) is another expression of this outward-looking activism. In contrast to the traditional 'Muslim manifesto' lobbying documents that have regularly been produced by representative groups in the run-up to general elections,[14] this is a campaign that is self-consciously Muslim but grounds its objectives in an articulation of Britishness that goes beyond serving the interests of Muslims only. By soliciting donations from Muslims, it is 'harnessing the capacity of Britain's Muslim communities to produce positive change'[15] for society as a whole. Indeed, the very method being utilised here marks a departure from the tradition of putting demands on the table, towards positively offering a contribution (in this case financial) to those who are considered to be allies in the political sphere (prospective parliamentary candidates). Moreover, the scheme sees the funding element as the start of a relationship, whereby they will 'follow-up with candidates once they are elected to ensure continued visibility around the issues we care about'.[16]

These two examples can be critiqued for emerging from a more elite or privileged section of the Muslim population, namely those in a position to be able to make political donations, or with the national connections and networks to organise street parties. However, the spontaneous and extensive Muslim response to the Grenfell Tower disaster in June 2017 demonstrated that this shift in activism also holds deep resonance in local community institutions and grassroots. The range of Muslim reponses included organisation of immediate relief and shelter via the Muslim Cultural Heritage Centre (AlManaar) in Ladbroke Grove, to the development of a legal support hub,[17] the provision of free counselling, befriending and funeral services,[18] and also financial aid through the National Zakat Foundation, in collaboration with the *London Evening Standard*'s Dispossessed Fund.[19] What they all had in common was the same outward-looking appetite for collaboration with diverse partners with a shared goal, and the desire to organise collectively for the benefit of the affected community broadly understood. So while this was a 'Muslim response', in that it was led by Muslim civil society, it was anything but exclusively Muslim in its outlook, contributors or intended reach.

It is an exciting time of great change and development for Muslim identity politics in Britain, and the trend towards opening-up that I discuss above also prompts me to consider ways in which the research in this book can be built upon in the future. The concept of an Equality Gap that I have discussed at length in this book could be explored with reference to inequalities *within* Britain's Muslim communities. Identity politics as experienced by Muslim women's organisations or female Muslim community leaders would be a good way of exploring the extent to which there might be a gender equality gap among British Muslims. Such research would complement some of the recent literature on challenges to gender inclusivity in mosques and Muslim spaces of worship.[20] The comparisons and contrasts that I have drawn between British Muslim and British Jewish communal organisations can also provide avenues for further research. The role of both the MCB and the BOD is under close scrutiny within their respective communities, and it would be interesting to follow and examine how they each respond and evolve in light of considerable shared challenges, including calls for greater democratisation and transparency and the inevitability of younger leaders taking on greater leadership roles. Additionally, there is scope for further research into British Muslim identity politics that takes into account the political engagement of communities of different Muslim theological denominations. Here I have focused on organisations with a (majority) *sunni* background as well as some *shi'i* organisations insofar as they have been involved with collective Muslim communal efforts (such as the Al-Khoei Foundation's involvement with the MCB and MINAB). Further studies could look more deeply at the range of diverse organisations within British *shi'a* communities and the differences between them and their approaches towards political engagement.

This book has traced the development of contemporary Muslim identity politics in Britain, from the formative years through to the present. It offers a fresh way with which we can understand the motivations and the methods by which British Muslims have mobilised *qua* Muslims in the political domain. By articulating this through the notion of an Equality Gap, it has problematised the justifications that have been offered by Muslim activists for their claims over time, and offered analysis of the directions in which Muslim identity politics in Britain is heading, based on deep engagement with the range of factors as they have shifted and changed at different junctures over the past 50-or-so years. I believe that although both internal and external pressures have caused the role of lobbying to decline within Muslim identity politics, it will not disappear completely. So long as the public and political culture in Britain continues to struggle with the Muslim question, be it through Islamophobia or through legal channels and in particular securitisation, there will always be a role for communal representation. The changing religious landscape of Britain – a combination of non-religious British citizens increasing demographically with time, a general decline in Christian affiliation and a notably increased diversity of people who have a religious faith[21] – presents challenges for the state and for Muslim communities and activists alike. The present context is one in which the state has all but disengaged with Muslim representative groups, but also failed to forcefully challenge a veritable tide of populist xenophobia, while pursuing an agenda of austerity that has hit the socio-economically most disadvantaged (among whom Muslims are significantly over-represented) the hardest. Muslim activism within broad-based alliances has found common cause with a range of other minorities and disadvantaged groups, and, crucially, is at ease with championing others' causes on the basis of shared values and the pursuit of equality, rather than group interests.

APPENDIX

Profiles of Muslim Representative and Advocacy Groups in the UK

Earliest Unity Initiatives

Name	Established	Constituency	Key figures	Notes
FOSIS – Federation of Student Islamic Societies	1963	Muslim students in the UK and Ireland – through affiliated student Islamic societies in universities and colleges.	High turnover of membership as it is a student organisation.	Key alumni have gone on to lead other Muslim organisations including some of those profiled below and international alumni have also taken up leadership roles in government, NGOs and international business. Some examples include: former Turkish President Abdullah Gul; Anwar Ibrahim, former Prime Minister of Malaysia; and in the UK Dr Hany El-Banna, founder of Islamic Relief.
UMO – Union of Muslim Organisations	1972	UK and Ireland. A number of member organisations as well as individual volunteers.	Dr Syed Aziz Pasha (d. 2011).	Was at its most active in the 1970s and 1980s. Beyond that, limited presence or impact.

Post-Rushdie Affair

Name	Established	Constituency	Key figures	Notes
Muslim Parliament UK	1989	Constituted of 'Muslim Members of Parliament (MMPs)' and various committees, but no clear election procedure, or identifiable electorate.	Kalim Siddiqui (d. 1996); Ghayasuddin Siddiqui (1996–present).	Suffered from infighting and a split after the death of Kalim Siddiqui. Now largely dormant, bar irregular topical public statements from Ghayasuddin Siddiqui – although leanings have shifted markedly from Khomenite, heavy, confrontational and aggrieved rhetoric to conciliatory tones embracing civic participation, secularism and democracy, and opposing extremism and foreign-influenced Islam. Participated in the Stop the War Coalition in the early 2000s and also launched a 'model Muslim marriage contract' in 2008, for British Muslims wishing to marry under Muslim law, claiming to uniquely secure equality between men and women, while appreciating the realities of modern British Muslim family life, and remaining faithful to the Islamic tradition. Ghayasuddin Siddiqui has also been involved with British Muslims for Secular Democracy (see below).
UKACIA – UK Action Committee on Islamic Affairs	1989	Representatives from a range of Muslim organisations.	Iqbal Sacranie.	Now defunct with its mantle having been taken up by the MCB.

Name	Established	Constituency	Key figures	Notes
MCB – Muslim Council of Britain	1997	Affiliated local, regional and national Muslim organisations and mosques.	Secretaries General: Iqbal Sacranie (1997–2000 and 2002–2006); Yousuf Bhailok (2000–2002); Muhammad Abdul Bari (2006–2010); Farooq Murad (2010–2014); Shuja Shafi (2014–2016); Harun Khan (2016–present).	Established to be the main Muslim representative body in 1997. Remained largely so through to 2005, after which the establishment of a range of alternative organisations coupled with a tense relationship with the government weakened the MCB's position as the primary community representative body. It has nonetheless continued to function and develop, and while it hasn't re-established the close rapport with government that it enjoyed during its 'honeymoon' years, it still does liaise with various government departments, run pan-community initiatives and speak on Muslim issues in the press. The MCB elected its first British-born secretary-general in 2016.

Post-2005 Representative Bodies

Name	Established	Constituency	Key figures	Notes
MINAB – Mosques and Imams National Advisory Board	2006	Jointly founded by the Al-Khoei Foundation, British Muslim Forum, Muslim Association of Britain and the MCB. Each of these organisations is represented in the board and its various committees.	Positions rotate between representatives of the various founding bodies.	There are signs that government made cautious forays into regulating mosques, through the publication of a consultation paper in 2005 entitled 'Preventing extremism – places of worship', which proposed potential powers for 'controllers' of mosques to exclude persons or groups, and for courts to have the power to close places of worship where deemed necessary. However, swift and

adamant opposition was put forward both by the MCB and a large number of major mosques to any insinuation that there could be any sort of 'state-control' over mosques.[1]

There were numerous calls from politicians and in the media for greater regulation of imams and mosques, particularly in light of concerns that some mosques were effectively functioning as extremist headquarters. The most high-profile case being the North London Central Mosque, which was controlled by Abu Hamza and his supporters until a police raid in 2003. The MCB commissioned a study, 'Voices from the Minarets',[2] which interviewed imams and mosque committee members on a range of topics including mosque governance, structure, remit and the role of imams. This study then laid the foundations for the establishment of MINAB, however, the degree to which MINAB can command legitimacy to regulate mosques is debatable.

| BMI – British Muslim Initiative | 2005 | Lobby group – no defined membership. Sought to represent the 'Muslim community' in general. | Mohammed Sawalha; Fida Alaeddin; Azzam Tamimi; Anas Altikriti. | An organisation spearheaded by previous members and associates of the MAB. Came into being after a strategic decision was made by the MAB to divert its focus and resources away from the Stop the War Coalition alliance and international affairs, and towards more domestic British Muslim community issues such as community development and youth work. Mainly motivated by a desire to put forward views on international issues, regarding which they criticised the MCB for maintaining a weak stance. Also vocal on matters relating to security and counter-terrorism as well as Islamophobia. After 2008, activity became intermittent and largely reactive since 2008, though there was a notable spurt in activity in the wake of the Arab uprisings of 2011. |

Organisation	Date	Constituency	Key figures	Description
BMF – British Muslim Forum	March 2005	Largely sufi-oriented (*barelvi*) mosques and imams across the UK.	Khurshid Ahmed; Zareen Roohi Ahmed.	Launched in 2005 with 500 affiliated mosques and support from parliamentarians. It sought to become 'a co-ordinating platform that aspires to provide a focus reflecting the hopes, fears and aspirations of the grassroots … to complement and enhance the work and achievement of other national platforms of the Muslim community.'[3] Between 2008 and 2010, the BMF apparently went through a period of reform, after its decision to come out in support of the government's 42-day detention plans for terror suspects caused major divisions in the organisation. It quietly re-launched in 2010 and has since had a low national profile.
SMC – Sufi Muslim Council	June 2006	No defined constituency.	Haras Rafiq; Azhar Ali; Shaykh Hisham Kabbani (spiritual figure).	Apparent paradox of seeking to 'represent' (presumably politically?!) the 'silent majority' of 'apolitical' Muslims.
BMSD – British Muslims for Secular Democracy	April 2008	No defined constituency.	Founded by Yasmin Alibhai-Brown.	Aims to raise awareness within Muslims about secular democracy, and to encourage religious understanding, harmony and a celebration of the 'variety of Muslim cultures, values and traditions which are present in British society.'[4]

Name	Established	Remit	Key figures	Notes
Progressive British Muslims	November 2005	No defined constituency.	Farmida Bi.	A group of self-described 'liberal Muslims', who emphasised 'cultural identity', and felt unrepresented by existing faith-based Muslim groups.[5] The group dissolved in 2012, with at least one former member becoming active in the BMSD.

Post-2005 Research and Consultancy Bodies

Name	Established	Remit	Key figures	Notes
Quilliam Foundation	2007	Counter-extremism think-tank	Ed Husain (Until 2009); Maajid Nawaz; Haras Rafiq; Adam Deen.	Founded by former Islamists providing research, training and consultation on counter-extremism and claiming unique expertise and insight drawn from the personal experiences of its staff inside various Islamist groups. Gained widespread interest and acclaim, courting celebrity, political and media figures, but also the subject of strong criticisms. Since 2014 has expanded its 'theology and outreach' team by recruiting a number of new staff, and in 2016 announced that Haras Rafiq had become its CEO while Adam Deen took the role of Managing Director (UK).
Cage (formerly Cageprisoners, Stop Political Terror, Stop Police Terror)	2003	Advocacy group for communities impacted by the 'war on terror'.	Moazzam Begg; Asim Qureshi; Adnan Siddiqui.	Set up initially to campaign for the rights of prisoners held at Guantanamo Bay and others who were affected by British counter-terrorism, including terror suspects held without

Organisation	Date	Type	Key figures	Description
				charge in British prisons. In recent years (especially post-2005) has broadened out to engage in campaigns relating to the erosion of civil liberties and due process as a result of counter-terrorism legislation. Has been at the centre of considerable controversy relating to its representation of terrorist suspects, but particularly of individuals who have gone on to join Daesh in Syria – most prominently Mohammed Emwazi (AKA 'Jihadi John').
CENTRI – Counter Extremism Consultancy, Training, Research and Interventions	Circa. 2008	Counter-extremism consultancy.	Haras Rafiq (now at Quilliam); Rashad Ali.	Offers commentary, training, consultancy and interventions on matters relating to extremism.
Muslim Institute	Dates back to the 1980s but revived and relaunched in 2010 after a long spell of dormancy.	Research institute.	Merryl Wynne Davies.	Aims to 'promote and support the growth of thought, knowledge, research, creativity and open debate within the Muslim community and wider society.' Activities include conferences, events, debates and a newsletter publication, 'Critical Muslim', as well as a dynamic website, www.musliminstitute.org (accessed 20 May 2017).

Organisation	Year	Type	Key figure	Description
Cordoba Foundation	2005	Research and public relations organisation.	Anas Altikriti.	A research and public relations organisation 'committed to dialogue and rapprochement between Islam and the west'[6] – provides an opposing perspective to the 'ex-extremist' narrative which favours the promotion of 'apolitical Islam', by championing political and civic engagement on the basis of Islamic values.
MEMO – Middle East Monitor	Circa. 2008	Research organisation.	Daud Abdullah.	Seeks to provide reporting on the Middle East, particularly the Palestinian question. While this body is clearly focused on foreign affairs, much of its interest centres on British foreign policy in the Middle East, and it has proved to be a useful forum for Dr Daud Abdullah to put forward perspectives in this field that had been too controversial for his former role at the MCB.
Inspire	2009	Women's empowerment and counter-extremism consultancy.	Sara Khan.	Organises leadership training for Muslim women, runs campaigns for gender equality and human rights as well as consultancy work on 'tackling extremism and the Prevent agenda', community cohesion and integration. Website: www.wewillinspire.com (accessed 20 May 2017)

New Horizons in British Islam	2014	Research, education and public engagement.	Dilwar Hussain; Rabiha Hannan.	Self-described as a 'forward-looking organisation that will work for reform in Muslim thought and practise. Promotes a integrationist message often by attempting to apply reformist solutions to difficult or taboo issues.' Website: www.nhorizons.org (accessed 20 May 2017).

1 MCB press release 'Muslim community rejects inference that mosques foment or encourage terrorism' (22 November 2005); available at http://www.mcb.org.uk/muslim-community-rejects-inference-that-mosques-encourage-or-foment-terrorism/ (accessed 22 May 2017).

3 C3ube Training and Consultancy, *Voices from the Minarets* (London: MCB, 2006).

BMF Secretary-General Gul Muhammed speech, quoted in the official account of the BMF opening conference in Walthamstow, London, 11 March 2005: 'British Muslim Forum: Sufis Rise'; available at: http://web.archive.org/web/20050427133635/ http://www.britishmuslimforum.org/view_press_release.php?id 12 (accessed 23 June 2016).

5 http://bmsd.org.uk/index.php/about-us/ (accessed 23 June 2016).

Website no longer active, but archived at: https://web.archive.org/web/20080828181845/ http://www.pbm.org.uk/ (accessed 23 June 2016).

http://www.thecordobafoundation.com/about_us.php (accessed 23 June 2016).

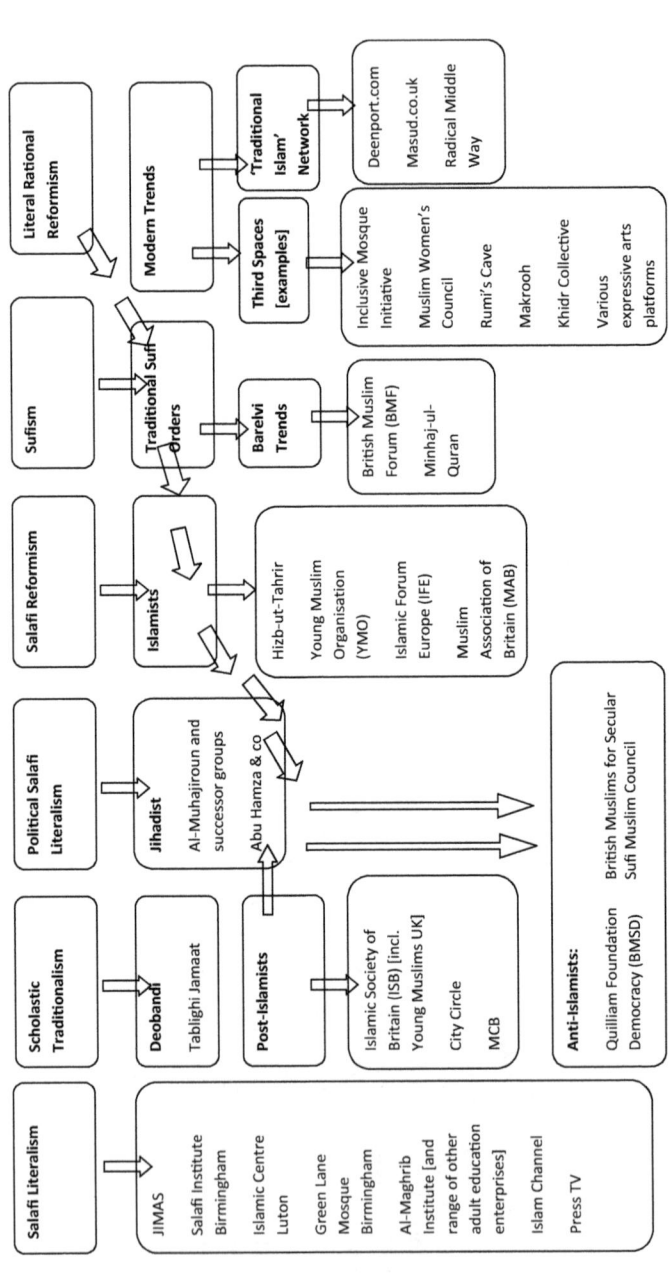

FIGURE 1 Adaptation of Sadek Hamid's 'Applying Ramadan's six major Islamic tendencies to the British Muslim context'.

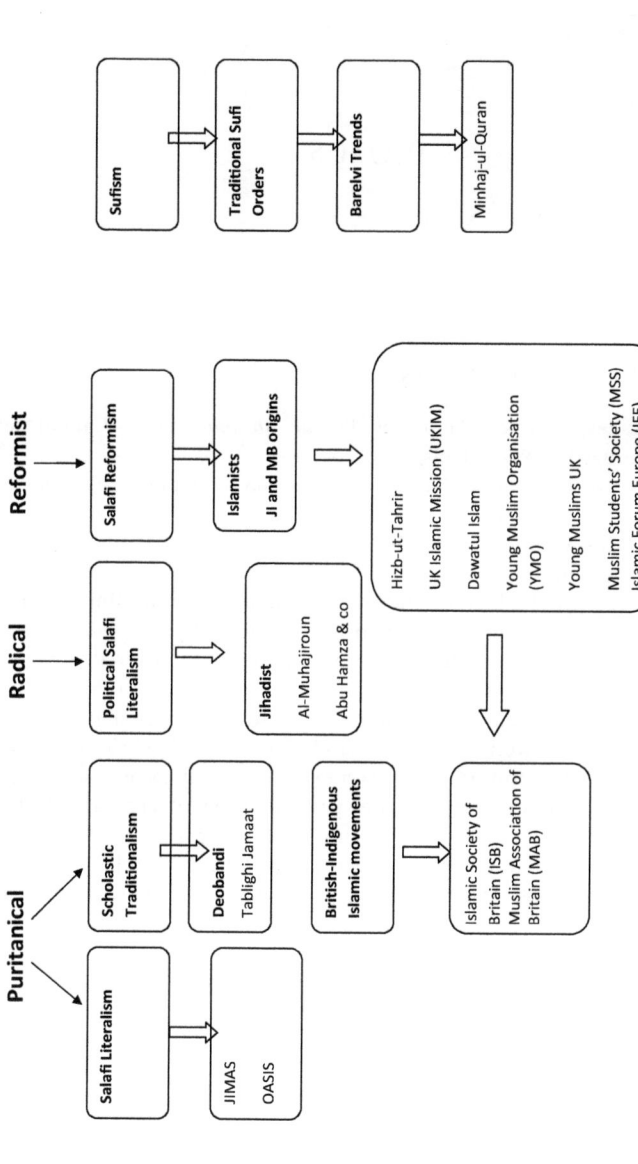

FIGURE 2 Historical version of Sadek Hamid's 'Applying Ramadan's six major Islamic tendencies to the British Muslim context', based on landscape of Muslim organisations/trends between 1960 and the 1990s.

Notes

CHAPTER 1   INTRODUCTION

1. Gilliat-Ray, Sophie, *Muslims in Britain: an introduction* (Cambridge: Cambridge University Press, 2010), pp. 6–7.
2. Matar, Nabil, *Islam in Britain – 1558–1685* (Cambridge: Cambridge University Press, 2008).
3. I use 'Muslim world' advisedly in this book, as shorthand for Muslim-majority countries, but acknowledge the problematic nature of the term as 'a Western idea built on the faulty racial logic that Muslims live in a world of their own – that Islam is an eastern, foreign religion that properly belongs in a distant, faraway, dusty place.' Grewal, Zareena, 'The "Muslim World" Does Not Exist', *The Atlantic*, 21 May 2017; available at: https://www.theatlantic.com/international/archive/2017/05/the-muslim-world-is-a-place-that-does-not-exist/527550/ (accessed 28 May 2017). Indeed, a key argument of this book is that British Muslim activism is now in a large part expressive of Islam as a British religion, thus prompting us to consider whether Britain can also be regarded in one way or other as part of the 'Muslim world'.
4. Ali, Sundas, *British Muslims in Numbers: a demographic, socio-economic and health profile of Muslims in Britain drawing on the 2011 Census* (London: Muslim Council of Britain, 2015).
   Elshayyal, Khadijah, *Scottish Muslims in Numbers: understanding Scotland's Muslims through the 2011 Census* (Edinburgh: The Alwaleed Centre, 2016).
5. Ansari, Humayun, *The Infidel Within: Muslims in Britain since 1800* (London: C. Hurst, 2004); Gilliat-Ray, *Muslims in Britain*.
6. Visram, Rozina, *Ayahs, Lascars and Princes: Indians in Britain 1700–1947* (London: Pluto Press, 1986), pp. 97–102; Ansari, Humayun, 'Introduction' in *The Making of the East London Mosque 1910–1951 – minutes of the London Mosque Fund and the East London Mosque Trust Ltd.* (Cambridge:

Cambridge University Press, 2011), pp. 6–9. Ali was a British-educated Indian lawyer who became the first Indian to be appointed to the Privy Council. His earliest political activity was focused on the Muslims of India, co-founding the All-India Muslim League to promote educational and economic 'advancement' among Muslims. But by 1904 he had retired and settled in Britain, and in due course became chairman of the Committee of the Woking Mosque, as well as the London Mosque Fund, campaigning enthusiastically for a mosque in central London (which became the East London Mosque).

7. Khwaja Kamaluddin is credited with having revived the Woking Mosque after a period of dormancy, and establishing the Woking Muslim Mission, cf. Ansari, *The Infidel Within*, pp. 88 and 126.

8. Geaves, Ron, *Islam in Victorian Britain: the life and times of Abdullah Quilliam* (Leicester: Kube, 2010).

9. Klausen, Jytte, *The Islamic Challenge: politics and religion in Western Europe* (Oxford: Oxford University Press, 2005); Laurence, Jonathan, *The Emancipation of Europe's Muslims: the state's role in minority integration* (Princeton, NJ: Princeton University Press, 2012), as well as edited volumes including Cesari, Jocelyne and Sean McLoughlin (eds), *European Muslims and the Secular State* (Aldershot: Ashgate, 2005) and Modood, Tariq, Anna Triandafyllidou and Ricard Zapata-Barrero, *Multiculturalism, Muslims and Citizenship: a European approach* (London: Routledge, 2006).

10. Vertovec, Steven, 'Islamophobia and Muslim recognition in Britain', in Yvonne Yazbeck Haddad (ed.), *Muslims in the West: from sojourners to citizens* (New York: Oxford University Press, 2002), pp. 19–35. Peace, Timothy (ed.), *Muslims and Political Participation in Britain* (Abingdon: Routledge, 2015) is a notable exception – a volume devoted to the study of Muslim participation in the UK.

11. Lewis, Philip, *Islamic Britain: religion, politics and identity among British Muslims* (London: I.B.Tauris, 1994).

12. Mustafa, Asma, *Identity and Political Participation among Young British Muslims: believing and belonging* (Basingstoke: Palgrave, 2015); Lewis, Philip, *Young, British and Muslim* (London: Continuum, 2007); Kabir, Nahid Afrose, *Young British Muslims: identity, culture, politics and the media* (Edinburgh: Edinburgh University Press, 2010).

13. Halstead, Mark J., *Education, Justice and Cultural Diversity: an examination of the Honeyford affair, 1984–85* (London: Falmer, 1988); Weller, Paul, *A Mirror for our Times: the Rushdie affair and the future of multiculturalism* (London: Continuum, 2009).

14. Examples include: Modood, Tariq, *Multiculturalism: a civic idea* (Cambridge: Polity, 2007); Modood, Tariq, *Multicultural Politics: racism, ethnicity and Muslims in Britain* (Edinburgh: Edinburgh University Press, 2005b); Modood, Tariq, 'Muslims and the Politics of Difference', *Political Quarterly* 74/S1 (August 2003), pp. 100–115.

15. A term used by *Newsweek* in the cover of its 24 September 2012 edition, which was swiftly reclaimed as a focus of satirical parodies by users of Twitter and other social media sites across the world. See Alexander Hotz, 'Newsweek "Muslim rage" cover invokes a rage of its own', US News Media Blog, *Guardian* (17 September 2012). 'Muslim rage' was used as early as 1990 by Bernard Lewis in his *From Babel to Dragomans: Interpreting the Middle East* (New York: Oxford University Press, 2nd edition, 2004), where he describes it as the 'irrational but surely historic reaction of an ancient rival against our Judeo-Christian heritage, our secular present, and the worldwide expansion of both', p. 330.

16. They were originally published in late 2005, although worldwide protests only really gained momentum by January 2006.

17. Aaronovitch, David, 'Is this the reaction of a grown-up religion?', *The Times*, 20 September 2012.

18. Cf. the Samina Malik and Ahmed Faraz cases, discussed in Chapter 6.

19. This concept is one that I have developed to summarise the justifications presented by Muslim activists in the UK for their engagement in identity politics over the years, and shall hereinafter be referred to as the Equality Gap.

20. See Chapter 4.

21. Amartya Sen, *Identity and Violence: the illusion of destiny* (London: Allen Lane, 2006).

22. Amartya Sen, 'The uses and abuses of Multiculturalism', *The New Republic*, 27 February 2006.

23. By this I mean the dominant stereotype of minority community leaders – male, middle-aged, self-appointed, self-inflated, out of touch and unrepresentative of his community. This image has been recently caricatured in popular culture by the BBC TV sitcom *Citizen Khan*, which features a Mr Khan who self-identifies as a 'community leader – they all know me!', but is barely recognised in public and is out of touch with even his own immediate family's concerns.

24. See for instance Okin, Susan Moller, 'Is multiculturalism bad for women?', in Joshua Cohen et al. (eds), *Is Multiculturalism Bad for Women?* (Princeton, NJ: Princeton University Press, 1999), pp. 7–24, and, specifically on Muslims in Britain, Manea, Elham, *Women and Shari'a Law* (London: I.B.Tauris, 2016).

25. Phillips, Anne, *Multiculturalism without Culture* (Princeton, NJ: Princeton University Press, 2007) presents one such argument where she makes the case for a multiculturalism that is focused on individuals and individual rights, rather than one with groups and cultures as its primary concern.

26. For instance, a 2006 poll found that less than 4 per cent of British Muslims felt that the MCB represented them, and 12 per cent felt that it represented their political views – NOP/Channel 4, 'Dispatches Muslim Survey', results broadcast on 'What Muslims Want' *Dispatches*, Channel 4, 7 August 2006.

CHAPTER 2 SETTING THE SCENE: HISTORICAL AND THEORETICAL CONTEXTS

1. Elmarsafy, Ziad, *The Enlightenment Qur'an: the politics of translation and the construction of Islam* (Oxford: Oneworld, 2009) draws our attention to a number of (often sympathetic) European translations of the Qur'an that were written during the early modern period. Accompanying commentary and critiques also expressed high regard for the 'achievements' and leadership of the Prophet Muhammad.

2. See also Garcia, Humberto, *Islam and the English Enlightenment, 1670–1840* (Baltimore: Johns Hopkins University Press, 2012).

3. On this cf. Asad, Talal, 'Multiculturalism and British identity in the wake of the Rushdie affair', in *Politics and Society* 18/4 (1990), pp. 455–480.

4. Mondal, Anshuman, *Islam and Controversy: the politics of free speech after Rushdie* (Basingstoke: Palgrave, 2014), pp. 13–22.

5. Of course, it was as a reply to Sir Robert Filmer's *Patriarcha* that Locke wrote his *First Treatise of Government*. However, Locke was obviously aware of the work of Hobbes and his work since the two were contemporaries.

6. Hampsher-Monk, Iain, *A History of Modern Political Thought: major political thinkers from Hobbes to Marx* (Oxford: Blackwell, 1992), pp. 69–72.

7. Gough, J.W., *John Locke's Political Philosophy: eight studies* (Oxford: Clarendon Press, 1973), pp. 27–28.

8. Tuckness, Alex, 'Rethinking the intolerant Locke', in *American Journal of Political Science* 46/2 (2002), pp. 288–298.

9. Ibid.

10. Mill, John Stuart, *Utilitarianism, Liberty, Representative Government* (London: Dent, 1972), p. 92.

11. Brown, Alex, 'The Racial and Religious Hatred Act: a Millian response', *Critical Review of International Social and Political Philosophy (CRISPP)* 11/1 (March 2008), p. 7.

12. Op. cit., p. 78.

13. Brown, 'The Racial and Religious Hatred Act', p. 7.

14. More will be said about blasphemy laws, the historical background to them and their relation to this debate in Chapter 4.

15. Slaughter, M.M., 'The Salman Rushdie Affair: Apostasy, Honor and Freedom of Speech', *Virginia Law Review* 79/1 (February 1993), pp. 153–204. Also Akhtar, Shabbir, *Be Careful with Muhammad: the Salman Rushdie affair* (London: Bellew Publishers, 1989).

16. Kamali, Muhammad Hashim, *Freedom of Expression in Islam* (Cambridge: Islamic Texts Society, 1997), p. 8.

17. I am aware that 'the West' is a hugely generalised term, and my use of inverted commas here and later on is to indicate appreciation that just as Islam and Muslims are not monolithic entities, neither is 'the West'.

18. In this instance I am referring to *shari'a* as a legal framework, as potentially the basis for authority in a political community, and not to its meaning on the more day-to-day level, as a personal path informing an individual's citizenship as inspired by her faith.

19. Hasan, Usama, *No Compulsion in Religion: an Islamic case against blasphemy laws* (London: Quilliam Foundation, 2012).

20. It is worth pointing out here Talal Asad's observation that Muslims objecting to the Danish 'Muhammad cartoons' published in 2005 did not use the Arabic equivalent of 'blasphemy' (*tajdif*), rather they preferred the term *isa'ah*, meaning insult, harm or offence – Asad, Talal, 'Free speech, blasphemy and secular criticism', in Talal Asad et al., *Is Critique Secular? Blasphemy, Injury and Free Speech* (Berkeley, CA: University of California Press, 2009), p. 38.

21. Op. cit.

22. Ramadan, Tariq, *Faith and Free Speech: defamation of religions and freedom of expression,*speech delivered at PEN America Conference, UN Headquarters, New York, 16 September 2010.

23. Modood, Tariq, 'The liberal dilemma: integration or vilification?', *Open Democracy*, 8 February 2006; available at: http://www.opendemocracy. net/faith-terrorism/liberal_dilemma_3249.jsp (accessed 13 June 2016).

24. Asad, Talal, 'Freedom of speech and religious limitations', in Craig Calhoun, Mark Jurgensmeyer and Jonathan Van Antwerpen (eds), *Rethinking Secularism* (New York: Oxford University Press, 2011), pp. 282–297.

25. Ibid.

26. Kamali, *Freedom of Expression in Islam*, p. 213.

27. Akhtar, *Be Careful with Muhammad*, Ch.1. More recently the international furore in the wake of Danish newspaper *Jyllands Posten*'s publication in 2005 of satirical cartoons depicting the Prophet Muhammad, is demonstrative of how the Prophet remains highly revered and respected by Muslims worldwide. Granted, the escalation of both this and the Rushdie Affair were given substantial impetus by political forces, but nonetheless, they both drew highly charged and indignant protest from Muslims from all backgrounds across the world who expressed a sense of deeply felt offence and grievance.

28. Shabbir Akhtar quoted in Ahsan, M.M. and A.R. Kidwai, *Sacrilege Versus Civility: Muslim perspectives on the Satanic Verses affair* (Markfield: Islamic Foundation, 1993), pp. 52–53. Akhtar links every Muslim's personal *'ird* with the reputation of the Prophet Muhammad and thus argues that insulting the prophet is enough of a deep and hurtful affront to each and every Muslim who aspires to his example and leadership, for it to be banned.

29. Tariq Modood and Bhikhu Parekh each make a case for understanding a notion of 'group libel' with respect to this issue: Modood, Tariq, 'Muslims, incitement to hatred and the law', in John Horton (ed.),

Liberalism, Multiculturalism and Toleration (Basingstoke: Macmillan, 1993), pp. 139–156; Parekh, Bhikhu, *Rethinking Multiculturalism: cultural diversity and political theory* (Basingstoke: Macmillan, 2000).

30. Siddiqui, Kalim, *Generating Power without Politics: Speech by Kalim Siddiqui at a One-Day Conference on the Future of Muslims in Britain, London, 14 July 1990* (London: Muslim Institute, 1992).

31. Asad, 'Multiculturalism and British identity in the wake of the Rushdie affair', pp. 456–457.

32. Cf. *Sacrilege versus Civility*; UK Action Committee on Islamic Affairs, *Muslims and the Law in Multi-Faith Britain: need for reform* (London: UK Action Committee on Islamic Affairs, 1993).

33. A good overview of the features and challenges of this adjustment experience is found in 'Mind the gap', Chapter 2 in Lewis, *Young, British and Muslim.*

34. Malik, Zaiba, *We are a Muslim, please* (London: William Heinemann, 2010), pp. 197–199.

35. Ibid., p. 198.

36. Allen, Chris and Arshad Isakjee, 'Controversy, Islam and politics: an exploration of the "Innocence of Muslims" affair through the eyes of British Muslim elites', *Ethnic and Racial Studies* 38/11 (2015), pp. 1852–1867.

37. Francois-Cerrah, Myriam, 'Demonstrating for dignity: why are Muslims so enraged?', *Huffington Post* 18 September 2012; available at: http://www.huffingtonpost.co.uk/myriam-francois/demonstrating-for-dignity_b_1885020.html (accessed 13 June 2016).

38. Ibid.

39. Although a wave of protest and revolution had brought about the fall of dictatorships in the Muslim world in 2010/11 in countries such as Tunisia, Egypt and Libya, the political landscape in these countries is still very unstable. While some of their populations may gradually be experiencing greater political freedoms, the effects of decades-long authoritarian regimes are still present.

40. Honneth, Axel, 'Recognition and moral obligation', *Social Research* 64/1 (1997), pp. 16–35; Taylor, Charles, *Multiculturalism and the Politics of Recognition* (Chichester: Princeton University Press, 1994).

41. Honneth, Axel, *The Struggle for Recognition: the moral grammar of social conflicts* (Cambridge: Polity, 1996), p. 134.

42. Ibid., pp. 131–135.

43. See McKinnon, Catriona, *Toleration: a critical introduction* (London: Routledge, 2006), Ch.1. Also Deveaux, Monique, *Cultural Pluralism and Dilemmas of Justice* (Ithaca, NY: Cornell University Press, 2002), pp. 67–72 discusses the origins of and connections between the liberal principles of neutrality and toleration.

44. Galeotti, Anna E., *Toleration as Recognition* (Cambridge: Cambridge University Press, 2002), pp. 10–12.

45. Fraser, Nancy with Axel Honneth, *Redistribution or Recognition? A political-philosophical exchange* (London: Verso, 2003), p. 34. Although this argument itself has also been criticised for being unduly rigid and failing to appreciate other dimensions to justice such as questions of political inclusion and exclusion, cf. Phillips, Anne, *The Politics of Presence* (Oxford: Clarendon Press, 1995).

46. Parekh, Bhikhu, 'Redistribution or Recognition? A misguided debate', in Tariq Modood, Stephen May and Judith Squires (eds), *Ethnicity, Nationalism and Minority Rights* (Cambridge: Cambridge University Press, 2004), p. 208.

47. Meer, Nasar et al., 'Misrecognition and ethno-religious diversity', *Ethnicities* 12/2 (January 2012), pp. 131–141.

48. Martineau, Wendy, 'Misrecognition and cross-cultural understanding: shaping the space for a "fusion of horizons"', *Ethnicities* 12/2 (January 2012,) p. 166.

49. Ibid., p. 162.

50. Ibid., p. 173. Author's own emphasis.

51. This type of system, one which largely lives on until today, has been regularly criticised for being prone to domination by cliques of self-appointed, older, male 'community leaders'.

52. Ibid., pp. 167–171.

53. In Chapter 4, I discuss how consecutive Conservative and Labour governments supported the establishment of a Muslim umbrella group, and effectively made it something of a prerequisite for engagement. Representative organisations for other minority religions such as the Hindu and Sikh faiths have since also been established.

54. Barry, Brian, *Culture and Equality: an egalitarian critique of multiculturalism* (London: Polity, 2001).

55. Fraser, Nancy, 'From redistribution to recognition? Dilemmas of justice in a "post-socialist" age', *New Left Review* I/212 (July–August 1995), pp. 68–93.

56. Heyes, Cressida, 'Identity politics', in Edward N. Zalta (ed.), *The Stanford Encyclopedia of Philosophy* (Spring 2012) https://plato.stanford.edu/entries/identity-politics/ (accessed 26 June 2017).

57. Brown, Wendy, *States of Injury: power and freedom in late modernity* (Princeton, NJ: Princeton University Press, 1995).

58. Young, Iris Marion, *Justice and the Politics of Difference* (Princeton, NJ: Princeton University Press, 1990), pp. 54–55.

CHAPTER 3   THE BIRTH OF MODERN BRITISH MUSLIM IDENTITY POLITICS: IDENTITY PRESERVATION IN THE 1960S–1980S

1. Modood, Tariq, 'Being somebody and being oppressed: catching up with Jesse Jackson', in Tariq Modood, *Not Easy Being British: colour, culture and*

citizenship (London: Runnymede Trust and Trentham Books, 1992), pp. 47−59.

2. I look at areas of similarity and overlap with experiences of African-Caribbean communities in this chapter, and will give more attention to those with Jewish communities in Chapter 4.

3. Hussain, Dilwar, 'British Muslim identity', in Seddon, Mohammed Siddique, Dilwar Hussain and Nadeem Malik, *British Muslims between Assimilation and Segregation: historical, legal and social realities* (Leicester: Islamic Foundation, 2004), pp. 83−118.

4. The most comprehensive include Tariq Ramadan's in his *Western Muslims and the Future of Islam* (New York: Oxford University Press, 2004), pp. 24−30; more empirically Jytte Klausen's in *The Islamic Challenge: politics and religion in Western Europe* (Oxford: Oxford University Press, 2005), pp. 87−94; and more historically, Sean McLoughlin's in 'The state, "new" Muslim leaderships and Islam as a "resource" for public engagement in Britain', in Jocelyn Cesari and Sean McLoughlin (eds), *European Muslims and the Secular State* (Aldershot: Ashgate, 2005), pp. 55−70.

5. Lewis, Philip, *Young, British and Muslim* (London: Continuum, 2007), p. 23.

6. Ansari, Humayun, *The Infidel Within: Muslims in Britain since 1800* (London: C. Hurst, 2004), pp. 41−44; Halliday, Fred, *Britain's First Muslims: portrait of an Arab community* (London: I.B.Tauris, 2010).

7. Ansari, *The Infidel Within*, pp. 98−103.

8. Ibid., Ch. 4.

9. See Halliday, *Britain's First Muslims*.

10. Op.cit., pp. 35−36.

11. Quilliam and many of the endeavours with which he was associated are often cited as among the first British Muslim communities which organised and identified collectively on the basis of their shared faith; including among them prominent numbers of (native) converts. An Abdullah Quilliam Society has been active in Liverpool since 1998, with the aim of restoring and making functional once again the site of 'England's first historical mosque and Islamic institution', cf. the society's website: www.abdullahquilliam.com (accessed 13 June 2016). From an altogether different perspective, Quilliam's name has been adopted by the Quilliam Foundation (est. 2008) which on its establishment claimed to see him as a figurehead emblematic of a 'genuine British Islam, ... free from the bitter politics of the Arab and Muslim world', cf. http://www.quilliamfoundation.org/about-us.html (accessed 15 September 2008), this last assertion drawing some objection from those pointing to Abdullah Quilliam's quite overt affiliations with politics and political leaders in the Arab and Muslim world, and his moments of open criticism of the British Empire and support for the Khilafa. For example, Geaves, Ron, *Islam in Victorian Britain: the life and times of Abdullah*

Quilliam (Leicester: Kube, 2010), devotes two chapters to Quilliam's international politics and activism. Geaves argues that 'Quilliam is being reinvented in some circles to provide narratives of integration', and that far from eschewing Arab and Muslim politics: 'when it came to conflict between the West and the Islamic Majority world, ... He (Quilliam) was not beyond threatening the British governments of his time with the prospect of inciting the Muslims of the Empire to rise up in the cause of injustices inflicted upon fellow Muslims. It is unlikely that his fatwa could have achieved this but he was ready to do it. Such behaviour, if undertaken by a Muslim leader today, would be labelled extremism', pp. 306–307. Interestingly, an observation of website archives via archive.org demonstrates how the Foundation's website underwent gradual editing over the course of 2008–9 whereby references to Quiliam himself were toned down and eventually removed altogether. See also Birt, Yahya, 'Preachers, patriots and Islamists: contemporary British Muslims and the afterlives of Abdullah Quilliam', in Ron Geaves and Jamie Gilham (eds), *Victorian Muslim: Abdullah Quilliam and Islam in the West* (London: Hurst, 2017), pp. 133–150 for the range of ways in which contemporary British Muslims have related to and engaged with the story of Quilliam and his legacy.

12. Lengthy articles in the *Islamic Review* (archives at: www.wokingmuslim. org) are devoted to debating the rights and wrongs of the empire's policies abroad and the nature of loyalty to the *ummah*.

13. A collection of archives relating to Lord Headley is available at the website of the Woking Muslim Mission: http://wokingmuslim.org/pers/ headley/ (accessed 13 June 2016).

14. Lord Headley to Austin Chamberlain, 23 March 1916, quoted in Ansari, Humayun, 'Introduction' in *The Making of the East London Mosque 1910– 1951 – minutes of the London Mosque Fund and the East London Mosque Trust Ltd.* (Cambridge: Cambridge University Press, 2011), p. 11.

15. Sherif, M.A., *Searching for Solace: a biography of Abdullah Yusuf Ali, interpreter of the Qur'an* (Kuala Lumpur: Islamic Book Trust, 1994), p. 45.

16. Ibid., for instance cf, p. 46, which mentions Yusuf Ali's lavish praise for 'the admirable manner' in which accommodations had been made, and care taken of the welfare of Indian soldiers on the European fronts.

17. Ansari, *The Infidel Within*, p. 103.

18. Lawless, Richard, *From Ta'izz to Tyneside: an Arab community in the North East of England in the early twentieth century* (Exeter: University of Exeter Press, 1995), pp. 167–168.

19. Op. cit., p. 113.

20. Ibid.

21. There have been numerous definitions put forward for the term 'identity politics', as discussed by Mary Bernstein, 'Identity politics', *Annual Review of Sociology* 31 (2005), pp. 47–74.

22. Gutmann, Amy, *Identity in Democracy* (Princeton, NJ: Princeton University Press, 2003), p. 9.

23. Kymlicka, Will, *Multicultural Citizenship* (Oxford: Clarendon Press, 1995).

24. Of course, there is a whole debate to be had as to whether, and if so the extent to which, beliefs and belonging to religious or cultural groups are 'chosen'. The question is addressed in some detail by Susan Mendus in 'The tigers of wrath and the horses of instruction', in John Horton (ed.), *Liberalism, Multiculturalism and Toleration* (Basingstoke: Macmillan, 1993), pp. 193–206; Parekh, Bhikhu, 'The Rushdie affair: research agenda for political philosophy' *Political Studies* 38/4 (1990), pp. 695–709 and Modood, Tariq, *Multiculturalism: a civic idea* (Cambridge: Polity, 2007), Ch. 2.

25. Phillips, Anne, *Multiculturalism without Culture* (Princeton, NJ: Princeton University Press, 2007).

26. I take this terminology from Jones, Peter, 'Bearing the consequences of belief', in Robert Goodin and Philip Pettit (eds), *Contemporary Political Philosophy: an anthology* (Oxford: Blackwell, 2006), pp. 607–620. Jones draws a distinction between *burdens* of belief and *consequences* of belief. The former comprising 'demands intrinsic to a belief system', invariably personal in nature, and ones for which the bearer would not suggest/ request assistance from others in society. Consequences, in contrast, are more far-reaching in their impact (e.g., faith schools or time off work for prayer/ (minority) religious holidays) and arise more clearly (although not always) as a result of the bearer's belief system being that of a minority whose practices/preferences differ from those of the majority.

27. Young, Iris Marion, *Justice and the Politics of Difference* (Princeton, NJ: Princeton University Press, 1990), p. 158.

28. Bleich, Erik, *Race Politics in Britain and France: ideas and policymaking since the 1960s* (Cambridge: Cambridge University Press, 2003), Ch. 4.

29. This point being relevant to the understanding of historical connections between these newly arrived communities and their home in the UK, their reasons for settlement there (postwar labour market) and the relationships and perceptions of power between them and the UK.

30. Favell, Adrian, *Philosophies of Integration: immigration and the idea of citizenship in France and Britain* (Basingstoke: Palgrave, 2001), p. 111.

31. Ibid., and pp. 115–116.

32. The Race Relations Act 1968 describes its task as 'the establishment of harmonious community relations', 'The Community Relations Commission', *Race Relations Act 1968*, Part III, 25.

33. Sooben, Philip N., *The Origins of the Race Relations Act* (Coventry: Centre for Research in Ethnic Relations, 1990).

34. The first Race Relations Act of 1965 was a very weak piece of legislation, covering only discrimination in 'places of public resort', so it was soon followed up by the Race Relations Act 1968, which further expanded on the definition of settings in which discrimination was to be outlawed.

But it was the Race Relations Act 1976 that made real headway by covering indirect as well as direct discrimination, and establishing the Commission for Racial Equality.

35. Op. cit., p. 5.

36. Cesarani, David, 'The changing character of citizenship and nationality in Britain', in David Cesarani and Mary Fulbrook (eds), *Citizenship, Nationality and Migration in Europe* (London: Routledge, 1996), pp. 57–73.

37. See Ramamurthy, Anandi, *Black Star: Britain's Asian youth movements* (London: Pluto Press, 2013) for the best historical account of the AYMs.

38. The categories of discrimination specified were those on the grounds of 'colour, race, or ethnic or national origins'. However, none of these categories were defined in the legislation, leaving judges to define how they would be understood in the courts. *Race Relations Act 1968.*

39. Sooben, *The Origins of the Race Relations Act*, pp. 9–10.

40. Modood, Tariq, *Multicultural Politics: racism, ethnicity and Muslims in Britain* (Edinburgh: Edinburgh University Press, 2005b), Introduction pp. 1–26.

41. Favell, *Philosophies of Integration*, pp. 111–116.

42. Macpherson, Sir William et al., *The Stephen Lawrence Inquiry* (London: Stationery Office, 1999).

43. Ibid.

44. Trevor Phillips, giving evidence to the Home Affairs Committee of the House of Commons on 28 April 2009, said that the term 'institutional racism' 'was absolutely critical in shaking police forces up and down the country out of their complacency'. Great Britain. Parliament. House of Commons. Home Affairs Committee, 'The Macpherson Report – ten years on' (14 July 2009); available at: http://www.publications.parliament.uk/pa/cm200809/cmselect/cmhaff/427/42702.htm#evidence (accessed 5 August 2013).

45. Rob Evans, Rob and Paul Lewis, 'Police "smear" campaign targeted Stephen Lawrence's friends and family', *Guardian*, 23 June 2013.

46. Phrase taken from Favell, *Philosophies of Integration*, p. 116.

47. I use the term 'communities' wherever possible throughout this book, in preference to 'community', which gives an inaccurate impression of artificial homogeneity. However, I am also conscious of the possible connotations of 'communities' as plural monolithic blocs, and of the fact that there will be many Muslim individuals relevant to my discussion who will not want to associate with any 'community' at all.

48. Nielsen, Jørgen S., *The Impact of Islam in Contemporary Western Europe* (Bracknell: Centre for the Study of Religious and Cultural Diversity, Newbold College, 2004), pp. 1–3.

49. I refer here to their needs as immigrants/newcomers to the UK. Muslim/Asian or any other specific identity is not necessarily of significance at this point.

50. Such as France and Germany, where incentives and specific 'guest-worker' programmes were instituted.

51. Hansen, Randall, *Citizenship and Immigration in Post-war Britain* (Oxford: Oxfor University Press, 2004), pp. 4–5.

52. For instance, campaigns by lascars (seamen) and other manual workers in the early twentieth century against the discrimination they experienced in working and living conditions. Cf. Ansari, *The Infidel Within*, Ch. 4. Note that the chosen names for workers' societies and organisations more commonly reflected ethnic rather than religious identities – e.g., the Somali and Arab Clubs and the Indian Workers Association. Ibid., pp. 115–117.

53. See Werbner, Pnina, *Imagined Diasporas among Manchester Muslims: the public performance of Pakistani transnational identity politics* (New Mexico: School of American Research Press, 2002), and Shaw, Alison, *A Pakistani Community in Britain* (Oxford: Basil Blackwell, 1988) for in-depth studies of micro-political engagement of Pakistani Muslim communities in the cities of Manchester and Oxford respectively.

54. The importance accorded especially to both of these primarily religious (although functionally more than 'just' religious) features is demonstrated in the urgency with which new immigrants set about making arrangements for securing them, even before the arrival of family members.

55. For instance, the right to withdraw children from religious education lessons/assemblies, or to request adjustments to school uniform in compliance with Islamic dress.

56. Sarwar, Ghulam M.A., *Muslims and Education in the UK* (London: Muslim Educational Trust, 1983).

57. 'Bradford Muslims' 5-point plea on children's schools', *The Times*, 7 January 1974 and Rahman, Afzal, 'Muslim girls' schooling' (letter to the editor), *The Times*, 18 January 1974.

58. Of course, there were self-conscious 'Muslim communities' in various parts of the UK during the nineteenth century, as evidenced by the Liverpool Muslim Institute (1887) and the Woking Mosque (1889). Additionally, a glance at any early copy of the Woking Muslim Mission's *Islamic Review* (first published in 1913) will demonstrate how the idea of an Islamic community and indeed of a wider *ummah* were popularised and widely used concepts, that had been functioning for the preceding decades.

59. Halstead, J.M., *Education, Justice and Cultural Diversity: an examination of the Honeyford affair, 1984–85* (London: Falmer, 1988). Cf, pp. 56–71 especially for fuller details of the contents of Honeyford's articles.

60. Ibid., In fact, Honeyford had been writing articles in various publications on the topic of multiculturalism and education since 1982, and the offending *Salisbury Review* article did not provoke protest until it was

picked up by the press two months after its publication (cf. Halstead, *Education, Justice and Cultural Diversity*, pp. 237–247).

61. Ibid., p. 169.

62. The *Daily Mail* published a three-part series of Honeyford's account, 'The Hounding of Honeyford', *Daily Mail*, 16–19 December 1985. Honeyford himself continued to write extensively.

63. National Muslim Education Council, *Religious Education: a Muslim perspective* (London: NMEC, 1997) and Sarwar, Ghulam, *British Muslims and Schools: proposals for progress* (London: Muslim Educational Trust, 1991).

64. Halstead, *Education, Justice and Cultural Diversity*.

65. Dr Hany El-Banna, founder of Islamic Relief and early FOSIS alumnus, quoted in 'Taking a Smile to the World', an interview with him in *emel* 5, May/June 2004.

66. *The Muslim* December 1969.

67. *The Muslim* June 1970.

68. *The Muslim* March and April 1970.

69. *The Muslim* April 1970.

70. While FOSIS (est. 1963) technically preceded the UMO as an umbrella/unity group, its remit has officially been limited to student Islamic societies. Although, as I illustrate above, its interests did often extend beyond this, to family issues, education and international politics for instance, nonetheless, its reach and ambitions did not seek to concentrate on community leadership and representation in the same way that the UMO and its successors did. If anything, it has become more focused and specialised over time on its student constituency, even though it continues to engage with government and other stakeholders, it has done so with a student remit.

71. Cf. 'A Propaganda Exercise' in *The Muslim* (October 1969) p. 24, where claims are made that plans were in place to establish a Muslim unity organisation with Dr Pasha as its head, modelled on the Cairo-based Young Men's Muslim Association. Also cf. 'Changing schemes for unity: "leaders" left groping', *The Muslim* (October 1970), pp. 22–23, on the eventual withdrawal of Egyptian officials, and of initial support from the London Central Mosque for the scheme. The position of Secretary General then went to Dr Pasha, who proceeded to establish the organisation along with a handful of other individuals.

72. Nielsen, Jørgen S., Muslims in Western Europe (Edinburgh: Edinburgh University Press, 2004), p. 49.

73. Union of Muslim Organisations of UK and Ireland, *Union of Muslim Organisations of UK and Ireland, 1970–1995: a record of achievement* (London: Union of Muslim Organisations of UK & Ireland, 1995).

74. These included requests for official annual public holidays for Muslims on the two '*Eid* festivals. Cf. ibid., p. 22.

75. Cf. correspondences with the three main political parties reproduced in Union of Muslim Organisations of UK and Ireland, *Union of Muslim Organisations of UK and Ireland, 1970–1995*, pp. 29–39.

76. For a more in-depth survey and discussion of British Islamic activist trends during this period, see Hamid, Sadek, *Sufis, Salafis and Islamists: the contested ground of British Islamic activism* (London: I.B.Tauris, 2016).

77. Ramadan's typology is found in Ramadan, Tariq, *To be a European Muslim* (Leicester: Islamic Foundation, 1999), and Hamid's application of it to the British Muslim context is made in Hamid, Sadek, 'British Muslim young people: facts, features and religious trends', *Religion, State and Society* 39:2/3 (2011), pp. 247–261.

78. Hamid, 'British Muslim young people'.

79. See page 220–221 of this book.

80. Hamid, Sadek, 'The attraction of "authentic" Islam: Salafism and British Muslim Youth', in Roel Meijer (ed.), *Global Salafism: Islam's new religious movement* (London: Hurst & Co., 2009), pp. 386–387.

81. A network with its origins in nineteenth-century India, which (through settlement in the UK) had established mosques and headquarters in Birmingham. In keeping with Salafi norms, the Ahle Hadith placed emphasis on reforming 'innovated' 'Sufi practices and beliefs common among British Pakistanis'. Cf. Birt, Jonathan, 'Wahhabism in the United Kingdom – manifestations and reactions', in Madawi Al-Rasheed (ed.), *Transnational Connections and the Arab Gulf* (Abingdon: Routledge, 2005), pp. 168–171.

82. Inge, Annabel, *The Making of a Salafi Muslim Woman: paths to conversion* (Oxford: Oxford University Press, 2016).

83. Hamid, 'The attraction of "authentic" Islam'. Exception was made for the Arabic language, which, as the language of traditional scholarship, was given great reverence since it conveyed authenticity and a feeling of closeness to the *salaf* – as demonstrated in the Arabic name in the acronym JIMAS, and the adoption by its members of *kunyas* – in emulation of the early generations of Muslims – e.g., *Abu Muntasir* (Father of Muntasir).

84. Birt, 'Wahhabism in the United Kingdom', pp. 171–172.

85. Inge, *The Making of a Salafi Muslim Woman*.

86. Op. cit, p. 172, and Inge, *The Making of a Salafi Muslim Woman*.

87. Hamid, 'The attraction of "authentic" Islam', pp. 384–403.

88. Ibid., p. 361.

89. Lambert, Robert, 'Empowering Salafis and Islamists against Al-Qaeda: a London counterterrorism case study', *Political Science and Politics* 41/1 (2008), pp. 31–35.

90. Ibid., Such as the Muslim Association of Britain's role in working with the police to 'purge' the North London Central Mosque of the influence of Abu Hamza and his associates.

91. It should be noted that *Deobandi* mosques in other parts of South Asia are independent of the TJ, even though the TJ utilise *Deobandi* mosque networks to further their missionary activities.
92. Geaves, Ron, 'The reproduction of Jamaat-i Islami in Britain', *Islam and Christian-Muslim Relations* 6/2 (1995), pp. 187–210.
93. Ibid.
94. Garbin, David, 'A diasporic sense of place: dynamics of spatialization and transnational political fields among Bangladeshi Muslims in Britain', in M.P. Smith and J. Eade (eds), *Transnational Ties: cities, identities and migrations* (London: Transaction Publishers, 2009), pp. 1–10.
95. Ibid.; Ansari, Humayun, 'Introduction' in Humayun Ansari (ed.), *The Making of the East London Mosque: 1910–1951* (Cambridge University Press, 2011), pp. 65–67.
96. *Dawatul Islam* now functions from a new headquarters, Darul Ummah, in Shadwell; YMO has since broken affiliation with *Dawatul Islam* and joined with the IFE as its youth wing, thus also functioning with the East London Mosque as its hub, and all three of these groups have since gained branches and followings in various parts of the UK.
97. JI was roughly set up as the counterpart of the Muslim Brotherhood (est. 1928 in Egypt and with a presence across the Middle East and beyond).
98. Geaves, 'The reproduction of Jamaat-i Islami in Britain'.
99. Pargeter, Alison, *The Muslim Brotherhood: the burden of tradition* (London: Saqi, 2010), pp. 150–153.
100. Hamid, Sadek, 'Islamic political radicalism in Britain: the case of Hizb-ut-Tahrir', in Tahir Abbas (ed.), *Islamic Political Radicalism: A European Perspective* (Edinburgh: Edinburgh University Press, 2007), pp. 147–148; Taji-Farouki, Suha, *A Fundamental Quest: Hizb al-Tahrir and the search for the Islamic caliphate* (London: Grey Seal, 1996), p. 171.
101. Husain, Ed, *The Islamist: why I joined Radical Islam in Britain, what I saw inside and why I left* (London: Penguin, 2007), pp. 149–153.
102. Kaashif Nawaz, a former HT member, brother of Quilliam, co-founder and current chairman Maajid Nawaz and contemporary of Husain states: 'The murder at East Ham College was not of a man who was a Christian, but of a man who was high on drugs, and carrying two knives with intent on attacking one of the students on campus, he was intercepted by a gang of Muslims – nothing to do with Islamism or HT, but more to do with gang wars.' Source: Booso, Andrew, 'Review of *The Islamist*', *The Translators*, 21 May 2007, available at: http://thetranslators1.wordpress.com/2007/05/21/review-of-%E2%80%9Cthe-islamist%E2%80%9D-ust-andrew-booso-complete/ (accessed 13 June 2016).
103. For example, Muslims Against Crusades have in the past carried out high profile 'poppy burning' stunts around Remembrance Day, where they chanted slogans such as 'British soldiers burn in hell!'. Additionally, in 2016 Anjem Choudary and Mohammed Rahman, both leading figures in these groups, were convicted of inviting support for a proscribed terrorist

organisation see *R. v. Choudary and Rahman* (2016), T20150301, CCC, and at least one of the three perpetrators of the London Bridge attack of June 2017 had a known connection with the individuals around *Al Muhajiroun* and its successor groups.

104. Here, and elsewhere in this book, I follow Nasar Meer's use of this term, cf. Meer, Nasar, *Citizenship, Identity and the Politics of Multiculturalism: the rise of Muslim consciousness* (Basingstoke: Palgrave Macmillan, 2010), in which Meer uses 'Muslim-consciousness' to describe Muslim political identification and assertiveness.

105. Hamid, 'The attraction of 'authentic' Islam', pp. 352–371. For a personal account, see Husain, *The Islamist*, Chapters 6, 7 and 8, in which he describes his experiences of Muslim-consciousness in 1990s college and university campuses.

106. Hamid, 'The attraction of 'authentic' Islam', p. 359.

107. Ibid., p. 360.

108. McLoughlin, Sean, 'The state, new Muslim leaderships and Islam as a resource for public engagement in Britain', in Jocelyne Cesari and Sean McLoughlin (eds), *European Muslims and the Secular State* (Aldershot: Ashgate, 2005), pp. 55–70; Lewis, Philip, *Islamic Britain: religion, politics and identity among British Muslims* (London: I.B.Tauris, 1994), pp. 102–112.

109. Cf. Chapter 4 of this book.

110. 'Our Story', *Islam Awareness Week website*: www.iaw.org.uk (accessed 13 June 2016).

111. Hamid, 'Islamic political radicalism in Britain: the case of Hizb-ut-Tahrir', p. 148.

112. Ibid.

CHAPTER 4   THE FORMALISATION OF MUSLIM IDENTITY POLITICS: RESPONSES TO HATE SPEECH, DISCRIMINATION AND THE EQUALITY GAP (1980s–2001)

1. For instance: Vertovec, Steven, 'Muslims, the state, and the public sphere in Britain', in Gerd Nonnemann, Tim Niblock and Bogdan Szajkowski (eds), *Muslim Communities in the New Europe* (London: Ithaca, 1996), pp. 169–185; Nielsen, *Muslims in Western Europe* (2004); Seddon, Mohammad Siddique, 'Muslim communities in Britain: a historiography', in Seddon, Hussain and Malik, *British Muslims Between Assimilation and Segregation*, pp. 1–42; Lewis, *Islamic Britain* (1994).

2. It is important to stress here that my account of the development of Muslim identity politics in the wake of the Rushdie Affair and beyond focuses primarily upon the public articulation of grievances by individual and group actors in the political arena – these were largely framed in the discourse of recognition and equality. This is not to ignore the very real

(and perhaps at times far more vocal) expressions of outrage and hurt which were grounded in a feeling that blasphemy had been committed. Of course, this was widely felt and expressed, but of more direct relevance to the discussion at hand is the way in which this experience triggered off both an awareness of the Equality Gap, and a momentum for a Muslim identity politics as a way of tackling this gap.

3. Although the existence of Muslim political groupings and organisations in the UK much preceded the Rushdie Affair (some of the earliest dating back to the early 1960s), these were more localised in focus, and characterised by a preoccupation with social and intra-community issues, rather than political affairs. While several political standpoints were being articulated at this time, these were predominantly informed and coloured by 'back home' perspectives and allegiances. For many of these the Rushdie Affair served to force an earnest effort to engage with the political landscape of the UK and to seek to formulate arguments that were located with a view to a permanent future in the UK, the most notable being the UK Action Committee on Islamic Affairs (UKACIA) followed to a lesser degree by the more 'radical' Muslim Parliament. Both continue to exist (albeit in changed and diminished forms) to this day.

4. An illustration of this kind of concerted action can be found in UK Action Committee on Islamic Affairs, *Muslims and the Law in Multi-Faith Britain: need for reform* (London: UK Action Committee on Islamic Affairs, 1993), which also includes exchanges with the government including Home Office Minister John Patten.

5. Lord Scarman, as quoted in McKinnon, Catriona, *Toleration: a critical introduction* (London: Routledge, 2006), p. 130.

6. UK Action Committee on Islamic Affairs, *Muslims and the Law in Multifaith Britain*. Also Parekh, Bhikhu, *Rethinking Multiculturalism* (Basingstoke: Macmillan, 2000), Chapter 10, and Modood, Tariq, 'Muslims, incitement to hatred and the law', in John Horton (ed.), *Liberalism, Multiculturalism and Toleration* (Basingstoke: Macmillan, 1993), pp. 139–156.

7. Letter from UKACIA to John Patten, 19 July 1989, reproduced in UK Action Committee on Islamic Affairs, *Muslims and the Law in Multifaith Britain*.

8. *Seide v. Gilette Industries Ltd.* (1980) IRLR 427; *Mandla v. Dowell Lee* (1983) 2 AC 548 (HL), 565.

9. Meer, Nasar, 'The politics of voluntary and involuntary identities: are Muslims in Britain an ethnic, racial or religious minority?', *Patterns of Prejudice* 42/1 (2008), pp. 61–81.

10. See Malik, Nadeem, 'Equality? The treatment of Muslims under the English legal system', in Seddon, Hussain and Malik, *British Muslims Between Assimilation and Segregation*, pp. 43–82 for detail on the legal loophole, also Modood, Tariq, 'British Muslims and multiculturalism', in Tariq Modood et al. (eds), *Multiculturalism, Muslims and Citizenship:*

a European approach (London: Routledge, 2005a), pp. 42–46 situates it in the context of EU human rights regulations – noting that the Amsterdam Treaty of 1999 expects member states to outlaw religious discrimination, further highlighting the gap in the law. See Allen, Christopher, 'From race to religion: the new form of discrimination', in Tahir Abbas (ed.), *Muslim Britain: Communities under Pressure* (London: Zed Books, 2005) on the far-right's exploitation of it.

11. Modood, Tariq, 'Muslims, race and equality in Britain: some post-Rushdie affair reflections', *Third Text* 4/11 (1990), pp. 127–134.

12. This viewpoint is supported by research into negative public portrayals of Islam and Muslims. For instance, Richardson, John E., *(Mis)representing Islam: the racism and rhetoric of British broadsheet newspapers* (Amsterdam: John Benjamins, 2004), who sees racism as a 'shifting and changing concept' which is not limited to colour or ethnic differences but defined more by hierarchical and unjust social relations. See also the distinction that Bhikhu Parekh makes between racism grounded in 'physical' difference and racism grounded in 'cultural' difference: 'over the centuries all racisms have had – and continue to have – two separate but intertwining strands. One uses physical or biologically derived signs as a way of recognising difference – skin colour, hair, features, body type, and so on. The other uses cultural features such as ways of life, customs, language, religion and dress [...] most Muslims are recognised by physical features as well as by their culture and religion, and the biological and cultural strands in anti-Muslim racism are often impossible to disentangle.' Runnymede Trust and Bhikhu Parekh, *Report of the Commission on The Future of Multi-ethnic Britain* (London: Profile, 2000), p. 62.

13. Modood, Tariq, *Multicultural Politics: racism, ethnicity and Muslims in Britain* (Edinburgh: Edinburgh University Press, 2005b), pp. 104–108 and p. 114.

14. This is discussed in Choudhury, Tufyal, 'Comparative perspectives on discrimination law', in Yunas Samad and Kasturi Sen (eds), *Islam in the European Union: transnationalism, youth and the War on Terror* (Karachi: Oxford University Press, 2007), pp. 187–188.

15. The offences of blasphemy and blasphemous libel were finally repealed by the Criminal Justice and Immigration Act 2008.

16. Werbner, Pnina, 'Islamophobia: Incitement to religious hatred – legislating for a new fear?', *Anthropology Today* 21/1 (February 2005), pp. 5–9. Also, Modood, 'British Muslims and multiculturalism'.

17. 'Religious hatred law perpetuates inequality After Commons vote', MCB press release, 1 February 2006; available at: http://www.mcb.org.uk/religious-hatred-law-perpetuates-inequality-after-commons-vote/ (accessed 13 June 2016).

18. McLoughlin, Sean, 'The state, new Muslim leaderships and Islam as a resource for public engagement in Britain', in Jocelyne Cesari and Sean

McLoughlin (eds), *European Muslims and the Secular State* (Aldershot: Ashgate, 2005), pp. 55–70. See also Forum Against Islamophobia and Racism (FAIR), *The Religious Offences Bill 2002: a response* (October 2002).

19. Sherif, Jamil, A Census chronicle – reflections on the campaign for a religion question in the 2001 Census for England and Wales, *Journal of Beliefs & Values* 32/1 (2011), pp. 1–18.

20. *The Muslim Manifesto* (London: Muslim Parliament of Great Britain, 1990).

21. Ghayasuddin Siddiqui has in recent times joined the British Muslims for Secular Democracy (BMSD, cf. Table 1). He has also undergone a rather dramatic shift in his opinions, now being a vocal opponent of Islamism and a proponent of 'liberal' Islam. He has also been involved in the rebirth of the Muslim Institute, which was re-established in December 2009 with a new structure, staff, and a revised outlook aiming 'to promote and support the growth of thought, knowledge, research, creativity and open debate within the Muslim community and wider society.' Cf. www.musliminstitute.org (accessed 13 June 2016).

22. Cf. http://www.icit-ca.org/ (accessed 13 June 2016).

23. *Crescent International* can be read online at www.crescenticit.com (accessed 13 June 2016).

24. Cf. Sacrilege versus Civility: Muslim perspectives on the Satanic Verses affair (Markfield: Islamic Foundation, 1993), p. 342.

25. 'Muslims, the law and multi-faith Britain', *British Muslims Monthly Survey* I/8 (August 1993), pp. 5–6.

26. Ahsan and Kidwai, *Sacrilege versus Civility*, p. 363.

27. Malik, Kenan, From Fatwa to Jihad: the Rushdie affair and its legacy (London: Atlantic: 2009), p. 123.

28. The Rushdie Affair 1988–1991; available at: http://www.salaam.co.uk/themeofthemonth/september03/events.html (accessed 13 June 2016).

29. Cf. the numerous documents in Chapter 5, 'The Muslim Argument' in Ahsan and Kidwai, *Sacrilege versus Civility*.

30. Faruqi, M.H., 'Muslims and Britain', in Ahsan and Kidwai, *Sacrilege versus Civility*, pp. 193–199 (reprinted from *Impact International* 10–23 March 1989, pp. 5–8).

31. Ibid.,

32. Malik, From Fatwa to Jihad.

33. Ibid. Also Al-Rasheed, Madawi, 'Saudi religious transnationalism in London', in Madawi Al-Rasheed (ed.), *Transnational Connections and the Arab Gulf* (Abingdon: Routledge, 2005), pp. 155–156.

34. Cf. https://www.icit-digital.org/articles/a-short-introduction-to-the-the-muslim-parliament under the heading: 'The decline of the Muslim Parliament' (accessed 13 June 2016).

35. Cf. the two separate publications: National Muslim Education Council, *Religious Education: a Muslim perspective* (London: NMEC, 1997); and

Muslim Educational Trust, *Issues in Islamic Education* (London: MET, 1996).

36. 'UMO Vigilance Committee', in Union of Muslim Organisations of UK and Ireland, *Union of Muslim Organisations of UK and Ireland, 1970–1995: a record of achievement* (London: Union of Muslim Organisations of UK & Ireland, 1995), p. 15.

37. Source: 'Was the MCB founded by the government of the day?' in *Frequently asked questions*, http://www.mcb.org.uk/about-mcb/faqs/ (accessed 13 June 2016) and 'S for Surveys'; available at http://www.salaam.co.uk/maktabi/survey.html (accessed 13 June 2016).

38. Siddiqui, Kalim, Generating Power without Politics: Speech by Kalim Siddiqui at a One-Day Conference on the Future of Muslims in Britain, London, 14 July 1990 (London: Muslim Institute, 1992); letter from UKACIA to John Patten (19 July 1989) reproduced in UK Action Committee on Islamic Affairs, Muslims and the Law in Multi-faith Britain: the need for reform, pp. 31–33.

39. By the time of its election into government in May 1997, the Labour Party was already in communication with Muslim groups (UKACIA and then the MCB) about the introduction of religious discrimination legislation and the state funding of Muslim schools. See *British Muslims Monthly Survey* from June 1997 through to January 1998.

40. During the Rushdie Affair, Shabbir Akhtar had not been alone in arguing that had Muslims 'been a powerful, well-organised lobby like the Jews, Rushdie's outrages would never have got into print', quoted in Malik, *From Fatwa to Jihad*, p. 126, and calls to emulate the 'Jewish model' were made regularly. Iqbal Sacranie is also reported to have once said: 'We are going to model ourselves on the Jewish Board of Deputies. See how much power they have in this country when we have none.' Quoted by Yasmin Alibhai-Brown, 'Muslims can learn from this new Jewish group', *Independent*, 12 February 2007.

41. Cf. Letter to *The Times* 'Support for UK Grand Mufti', 4 February 2011, and 'Announcement by scholars of *Al-Azhar Al-Sharif* concerning the declaration of "*Banu Ibrahim* – Children of Abraham" on dialogue between Muslims, Jews and Christians, and the establishment of the Office of Grand Mufti of the United Kingdom', released 7 October 2010; available at the www.deenport.com message board (accessed 15 June 2016).

42. Binyon, Michael, 'Grand Mufti claim highlights the pros and cons of Islam's lack of ecclesiastical hierarchies', *The Times*, 28 January 2011.

43. Langham, Raphael, 250 Years of Convention and Contention: a history of the Board of Deputies of British Jews, 1760–2010 (Edgware: Vallentine Mitchell, 2010), pp. 8–10.

44. Extracted from the minute books of the London Committee of Deputies of British Jews, and quoted in Emmanuel, C., *A Century and a Half of Jewish History* (London: Routledge, 1910), p. 1.

45. Clark, Michael, Albion and Jerusalem: the Anglo-Jewish community in the post-emancipation era, 1858–1887 (Oxford: Oxford University Press, 2009), p. 110; Langham, 250 Years of Convention and Contention, pp. 21–75.

46. Clark, *Albion and Jerusalem* (2009), pp. 113–116.

47. Endelman, Todd, *The Jews of Britain, 1656 to 2000* (Berkeley, CA: University of California Press, 2002), p. 51.

48. 'United Kingdom legislation concerning Jews', in Massil, Stephen W (ed.), *The Jewish Year Book 1999* (Essex: Vallentine Mitchell, 1999).

49. Benjamin Disraeli, who preceded him, although Jewish by descent, had converted to Anglicanism at the age of 12.

50. Maughan, Philip, 'Rowan Williams: Sharia law question "still pertinent"', *New Statesman*, 5 June 2013. This remains a sore point for many Muslim commentators and advocacy groups who have taken umbrage at the current government's independent review into 'the application of *shari'a* in England and Wales', a review understood to be in a large part focused on 'misuse' of *shari'a* by Shari'a Councils. Among the objections to the review is that no similar exercise is being carried out for *Beth Din.*

51. Endelman, *The Jews of Britain*, p. 68.

52. There is a debate to be had about whether the respective authors intended to indulge in or endorse anti-Semitism through creating these characters, or whether they simply sought to reflect and portray the tragedy of real ethnic prejudices as they were lived in the society of their time. However, the images are telling of the type and nature of Jewish stereotypes that existed in society.

53. See Chapter 1 for a discussion of this.

54. Such as the *Jamaat-e-Islami* and *Deobandi* movements in the Indian Subcontinent, and various branches of the Muslim Brotherhood in the Middle East.

55. Cesarani, David, *The Jewish Chronicle and Anglo Jewry, 1841–1991* (Cambridge: Cambridge University Press, 1994), p. 86.

56. Cesarani, David, 'The transformation of communal authority in Anglo-Jewry 1914–1940', in David Cesarani (ed.), *The Making of Modern Anglo-Jewry* (Oxford: Blackwell, 1990), pp. 115–140.

57. Paul Goodman, *Zionism in England* (London: English Zionist Federation, 1929), p. 48.

58. Endelman, *The Jews of Britain*, pp. 2–5.

59. Ibid., pp. 183–184.

60. There have been 'twice-migrant' instances of Muslim immigration to Britain – notably East African Asians during the 1970s. However, although some individuals from this group have played leadership roles in Muslim communal representation (the most prominent example perhaps being Sir Iqbal Sacranie who headed UKACIA and later the MCB), my analysis here refers to the overall profile of Britain's Muslim population, within which East African Asians constitute a small, though

not insignificant, minority. Moreover, being largely comprised of business and professional classes, the economic circumstances of East African Asian arrivals to the UK in the 1970s were significantly different to those of Jewish postwar refugees.

61. Ansari, *The Infidel Within*, pp. 147–153.
62. Anwar, Muhammad, *The Myth of Return: Pakistanis in Britain* (London: Heinemann Educational, 1979).
63. Rozin, Mordechai, The Rich and the Poor: Jewish philanthropy and social control in nineteenth century London (Brighton: Sussex Academic Press, 1999).
64. Newman, Aubrey, The Board of Deputies of British Jews 1760–1985 – a brief survey (London: Vallentine Mitchell, 1987), p. 5.
65. Clark, Albion and Jerusalem, p. 110.
66. Cf. Section 3.1 in this chapter.
67. Ibid., pp. 196–198.
68. Ibid., p. 199.
69. Livshin, R., 'The acculturation of the children of immigrant Jews in Manchester, c.1890–1920', in David Cesarani (ed.), *The Making of Modern Anglo-Jewry* (Oxford: Basil Blackwell, 1990), p. 82. See also Kahn-Harris, Keith and Gidley, Ben, *Turbulent Times: The British Jewish Community Today* (London: Continuum, 2010), p. 20.
70. Endelman, *The Jews of Britain*, p. 146.
71. Parker-Jenkins, Marie, 'Equal access to state funding: the case of Muslim schools in Britain', paper presented at the British Educational Research Association Annual Conference, Queen's University of Belfast, Northern Ireland 27–30 August (1998); available at: http://www.leeds.ac.uk/educol/documents/000000911.htm (accessed 13 June 2017).
72. Lewis, *Islamic Britain*, pp. 70–71.
73. Akhtar, Shabbir, The Muslim Parents' Handbook: what every Muslim parent should know (London: Ta Ha Publishers, 1993); Sarwar, Muslims and Education in the UK.
74. Laurence, *The Emancipation of Europe's Muslims*, pp. 160–162. There has, thus far, been hardly any academic literature devoted to the MCB, its history and development. Studies I have identified are Radcliffe, Liat, 'A Muslim lobby at Whitehall? Examining the role of the Muslim minority in British foreign policy making', *Islam and Christian-Muslim Relations* (2010), pp. 365–386, Pedziwiatr, Konrad, 'Creating new discursive arenas and influencing the policies of the state: the case of the Muslim Council of Britain', *Social Compass* 54/2 (2007), pp. 267–280, and an unpublished MSc dissertation at Birkbeck College, University of London, entitled 'The Muslim Council of Britain and the participation of Islam focused interest groups in British politics' (2010).
75. Ansari, *The Infidel Within*, p. 364.
76. Cf. Chapter 2 on the distance in understanding between government/establishment and community representatives.

77. Author's personal conversation with Dr Abdul Bari, October 2011. Also see www.islamicforumeurope.com (accessed 17 April 2012 – link appears to be broken, June 2016) for more information about the IFE and its activities.
78. Lewis, Philip, 'British *'ulama* and the politics of social visibility', in Gerdien Jonker and Valérie Amiraux (eds), *Politics of Visibility: young Muslims in European public spaces* (London: Transaction Publishers, 2006), p. 170.
79. See Figure 2, p. 220.
80. 'Religious Discrimination Legislation' *British Muslims Monthly Survey* V/6 (June 1997), p. 1, and 'New Blasphemy Law?' *British Muslims Monthly Survey* V/7 (July 1997), p. 3.
81. Lord Henry Stanley of Alderley (d. 1903) was the first Muslim peer, having converted to Islam in 1862. He received a Muslim burial, attended by diplomats from the Ottoman Embassy in London, and a *janaza* prayer was performed for him by Abdullah Quilliam at the Liverpool Mosque. Later on, Lord Rowland Headley (d. 1935) and Lady Evelyn Cobbold (d. 1963) were both hereditary peers who converted to Islam during the inter-war period, however, Labour's appointed Muslim peers were marked out by their appointment not only as Muslim peers, but with an implicit understanding that they would communicate and represent Muslim community interests – which they did.
82. *British Muslims Monthly Survey* V/1 (January 1997), p. 7, and V/5 (May 1997), p. 4.
83. 'First Muslim advisor to Prison Service', *The Common Good* 1/ 2, December 1999.
84. Runnymede Trust, *Islamophobia: a challenge for us all* (London: Runnymede Trust, 1997). Only two years later, in 1999, the Macpherson Inquiry's report into the murder of Stephen Lawrence was published, which, aside from crucial recommendations to the Metropolitan Police, also prompted enormous soul-searching in matters relating to race-relations and discrimination in politics and society on a more general level. Notably, Dr Richard Stone, a member of the commission which produced the report was also an advisor to the Macpherson Inquiry.
85. The Runnymede definition of Islamophobia has not gone uncontested; cf. Ansari, Humayun and Farid Hafez, 'Islamophobia: an introduction', in Humayun Ansari and Farid Hafez (eds), *From the Far Right to the Mainstream: Islamophobia in party politics and the media* (Campus, 2012), esp. pp. 14–20. Among the main criticisms are that the definition is too simplistic, describing the features of Islamophobia in binary, black and white terms. For instance, that 'Islam is seen as separate and other, rather than similar and interdependent', or 'Islam is seen as an enemy – violent, threatening and terroristic, rather than as a partner'. Runnymede Trust, *Islamophobia*. Chris Allen argues that such a definition is problematic because it overlooks the reality that many manifestations

of Islamophobia in everyday life will be of a more 'grey' variety. In other words, the Runnymede definition does not tackle arguments about the face-veil being a 'barrier' to social cohesion or those about the 'death' of multiculturalism. These, he argues, are fertile ground from which the likes of the BNP have been making gains. Cf. 'K.I.S.S – Keeping Islamophobia Simple and Stupid', available at www.drchrisallen.uk (28 April 2008) (accessed 15 June 2016). Such a view is not dissimilar to the arguments made by Baroness Warsi in her 2011 speech on 'dinner table Islamophobia' (see Chapter 6). Another weakness, argue Nasar Meer and Tariq Modood, is the use of the term 'unfounded hostility', since this would be open to interpretation in the courts. They additionally express concern that the term 'Islamophobia' has itself been overused, producing a 'victimology' and potentially providing ammunition to those critics who might like to deny its significance or claim it has been exaggerated. See Meer, Nasar and Tariq Modood, 'Refutations of racism in the "Muslim question"', *Patterns of Prejudice* 43:3/4 (2009) pp. 335–354. So while the report itself was definitely a step forward in official recognition of how widespread Islamophobia was, it nevertheless left substantial outstanding unresolved issues of definition.

86. Allen, Christopher, 'The "first" decade of Islamophobia', 5 July 2007; available at www.drchrisallen.uk (accessed 13 June 2016); Birt, Yahya, 'Defining Islamophobia today: the state of the art', 15 September 2009; available at: https://yahyabirt1.wordpress.com/2009/09/15/defining-islamophobia-today-the-state-of-the-art (accessed 13 June 2016).

87. Crime and Disorder Act 1998, Part II, Racially or religiously aggravated offences: England and Wales.

88. Extract from a speech by Sarah Joseph, then of the MCB's Social Welfare and Regeneration Committee, quoted in Versi, Ahmed, 'Cabinet Minister accepts Muslim lunch invitation', *The Muslim News*, 25 December 1998.

89. As I go on to discuss in Chapter 5, the Act was strongly contested, and the form in which it was ultimately passed was considerably amended in places so that it could get past the House of Lords. Yet while it was welcomed, the extent to which it has the power to forcefully prosecute racists, and specifically anti-Muslim racists, has been held in serious doubt. Still, it was seen as progress, albeit limited.

CHAPTER 5   IDENTITY POLITICS IN THE AFTERMATH OF 9/11 (SEPTEMBER 2001–JULY 2005)

1. For instance, Jonathan Birt reports on the preferred dress of a local salafi meeting-group of young men. I quote: 'Some members of the group had developed a "look": Pakistani-style *shalwar kameez* in camouflage, an Afghan hat alongside the obligatory Doctor Martin boots or Nike trainers.

This was recognized among local Muslims as the "jihadi" style.' From Birt, Jonathan, 'The radical nineties revisited: jihadi discourses in Britain' in Madawi Al-Rasheed and Marat Shterin (eds), *Dying for Faith: religiously motivated violence in the contemporary world* (London: I.B.Tauris, 2009), p. 106. Also see Imtiaz, Atif, 'A marcher's song', in his anthology *Wandering Lonely in a Crowd* (Kube, Leicester: 2011), esp. pp. 64–76, which recounts his own personal experiences of activism in British Muslim youth organisations (specifically FOSIS and YMUK), and highlights the intricacies of inter-group rivalries and debates during the 1990s: 'I think most of these inter-group debates, if we were to talk about them with non-Muslims, they'd think we've lost it. We have a highly developed internal or private language ... between ourselves, and a hardly-developed public language'.

2. Hussain, Dilwar, 'Councillors and caliphs: Muslim political participation in Britain', in Seddon, Hussain and Malik, *British Muslims between Assimilation and Segregation*, pp. 173–200; and Anwar, Muhammad, 'Issues, policy and practice', in Tahir Abbas (ed.), *Muslims in Britain* (2005), pp. 38–39.

3. Ibid., and the IPB website www.islamicparty.com (accessed 13 June 2016).

4. See Chapter 1 of this book, on British-Muslim cultural disorientations.

5. For a window into British historical perceptions of Islam and Muslims see works by Nabil Matar, including his chapter: 'Britons and Muslims in the early modern period: from prejudice to (a theory of) toleration', in Maleiha Malik (ed.), *Anti-Muslim Prejudice: past and present* (Abingdon: Routledge, 2010), pp. 7–25, in which he shows how Muslims and Islam typically suffered prejudice and negative stereotypes in their portrayals in literature and theology, while actual interactions by diplomats and traders with Muslims led to less hostile and more tolerant perspectives of Muslims and Muslim cultures.

6. 'Shutting the door in the face of Islam's bogeymen', *Guardian*, 27 May 1995.

7. 'Militants in the line-up for conference season', *Guardian*, 5 August 1995.

8. Modood, Tariq, '"Difference", cultural racism and anti-racism', in Tariq Modood and Pnina Werbner (eds), *Debating Cultural Hybridity: multi-cultural identities and the politics of anti-racism* (London: Zed Books, 1997), pp. 154–172.

9. McRoy, Anthony, *From Rushdie to 7/7: the radicalisation of Islam in Britain* (London: Social Affairs Unit, 2006), pp. 15–22.

10. Ibid.

11. See 'Concern for Bosnia', *British Muslims Monthly Survey* III/7 (July 1995), pp. 1–2.

12. *The Muslim News*, 24 November 1995, reporting on speeches at Islamic Convention held in September 1995 at the London Arena by the Islamic Society of Britain.

13. See Chapter 3 for a summary of HT's origins in Britain during the 1990s.

14. For a useful overview of HT during this period cf. Hamid, 'Islamic political radicalism in Britain: the case of Hizb-Ut-Tahrir', pp. 145–159.

15. Taji-Farouki, Suha, *A Fundamental Quest: Hizb al-Tahrir and the search for the Islamic caliphate* (London: Grey Seal, 1996), pp. 172–176.

16. A sketchy personal account of the build-up for this conference and of the event itself is given by Ed Husain in his memoir – Husain, Ed, *The Islamist: why I joined Radical Islam in Britain, what I saw inside and why I left* (London: Penguin, 2007), pp. 134–138. Another (observer's) account of the conference features in 'Much Ado About Nothing', *Q News* (12 August 1994).

17. Op. cit., p. 145.

18. Examples include: 'Muslim body accused of racism: Muslim rally angers Jews', *Independent* (7 August 1994); Kelsey, Tim, 'Fundamentalist gathering seeks political overthrow of Western democracies: Muslims call for Israeli state to be destroyed', *Independent* (8 August 1994); and 'Wembley survives the Muslim call to arms', *Daily Telegraph* (8 August 1994).

19. I use both of these terms as they would generally be used in day to day parlance. The *salafi* trend, referring to a preoccupation with a strict and often puritanically literalist interpretation of original sources and texts, coupled with a deep suspicion of any 'innovation' in religion. The *jihadi* trend, which often attracts sympathisers from *salafi* circles, is broadly descriptive of a support for violence/armed fighting in the name of Islam – during this period, still very much confined to the international (rather than domestic) arena.

20. Birt, 'The radical nineties revisited', pp. 107–109.

21. Arabic for 'realm of Islam' and 'realm of disbelief', respectively.

22. Jon Ronson recalls his shadowing of Omar Bakri Mohammad and his *Al Muhajiroun* throughout 1997 in his article: 'My Night of Jihad', *Guardian*, 30 April 2007 http://www.guardian.co.uk/commentisfree/2007/apr/30/mynightofjihad (accessed 13 June 2016).

23. Hamid, 'Islamic political radicalism in Britain: the case of Hizb-ut-Tahrir', p. 148.

24. Cf. 'In the eye of the storm: The MCB – fulfilling its responsibilities', in Muslim Council of Britain, *The Quest for Sanity: reflections on September 11 and the aftermath* (Wembley: Muslim Council of Britain, 2002), Section 2, pp. 29–37, for documentation of the kind of anti-Muslim hostility that took place in the wake of 9/11. Other reports include 'September 11 and its aftermath'; available at: http://www.salaam.co.uk/themeofthemonth/september03_index.php?l=34 (accessed 13 June 2016). Also a log of Islamophobic incidents in the UK as reported to the Forum Against Islamophobia and Racism (FAIR) between 11 September 2001 and 18 January 2005; available at: http://www.fairuk.org/research/FAIRuk-ResearchData-IslamophobicIncidentLog.pdf (accessed 13 June 2016).

25. This sort of gesture became a regular feature of government-community conversation, used by Tony Blair and other prominent politicians both domestically and internationally. Stephen Lyon describes it as 'the rise of universal values' in his chapter: 'The shadow of September 11: multiculturalism and identity', in *Muslim Britain* ed. by Tahir Abbas (London: Zed Books, 2005), pp. 79–84.

26. Respectively parts 4, 9, 10 and 11 of the *Anti-Terrorism, Crime and Security Act 2001*.

27. The full text of Blair's statement is available at: http://www.guardian.co.uk/politics/2001/sep/12/politicalnews.september111 (accessed 13 June 2016).

28. Speech by Tony Blair to House of Commons on 14 September 2001. Full text available at: http://www.guardian.co.uk/politics/2001/sep/14/houseofcommons.uk1 (accessed 13 June 2016).

29. 'Muslims and Christians share values – Blair', *BBC Website*, 27 September 2001; available at: http://news.bbc.co.uk/1/hi/uk_politics/1567187.stm (accessed 13 June 2016); 'Blair condemns racist attacks – PM stresses shared heritage', *Guardian*, 28 September 2001.

30. Richardson, John E., *(Mis)representing Islam: the racism and rhetoric of British broadsheet newspapers* (Amsterdam: John Benjamins, 2004); Poole, Elizabeth, *Reporting Islam: media representations of British Muslims* (London: I.B.Tauris, 2002).

31. The only exceptions to this were extremist elements such as *Al Muhajiroun* who (often provocatively) expressed praise and approval of the attacks, and eventually held an 'anniversary' event celebrating the 'Magnificent 19', a reference to the 19 hijackers who carried out the three attacks on 9/11. See 'Rallies will highlight "Magnificent 19" of Sept 11', *Daily Telegraph*, 10 September 2003. Also Akhtar, Parveen, '"(Re)turn to religion" and radical Islam', in Tahir Abbas (ed.), *Muslim Britain: communities under pressure* (London: Zed Books, 2005), p. 164. However, even these were lone, marginal voices that were given very little serious attention by the mainstream within Muslim communities.

32. See Islam Awareness Week blogsite: https://iaw2012.wordpress.com/previous-years/ (accessed 13 June 2016).

33. Abbas, Tahir, 'British South Asian Muslims: before and after September 11', in Abbas, *Muslim Britain*, p. 15.

34. Birt, Jonathan, 'Lobbying and marching: British Muslims and the state', in Abbas, *Muslim Britain*, p. 95; Bodi, Faisal, 'Opportunistic cronies', *The Guardian*, 13 November 2001.

35. Ibid., Birt, pp. 93–99.

36. Abbas, 'British South Asian Muslims', p. 16.

37. Op.cit.

38. According to Matthew Goodwin at the University of Nottingham, this campaign was launched 'in the hours following the terrorist attacks of September 11th 2001'. 'The BNP and Islam' at the election blog of the

University's School of Politics and International Relations; available at: http://electionblog2010.blogspot.co.uk/2010/04/bnp-and-islam.html (accessed 13 June 2016).

39. Allen, Christopher, 'From race to religion: the new face of discrimination' in Abbas, *Muslim Britain*, esp. pp. 55–63.

40. The BNP under the leadership of Nick Griffin has been at pains to portray itself as respectable, patriotic and wholly un-racist. In doing so, it describes its struggle as that of the native or indigenous white population of the British Isles, whose culture, language, religion and other norms are being threatened by immigration and multiculturalism. In the words of Griffin: 'Towns and cities all over our beautiful country now resemble parts of Africa or Asia. British people have become a minority in many areas already, and within a few decades, we will become a minority across the country as a whole.' 'A Message from BNP Leader Nick Griffin MEP', Archived page available at: https://web.archive.org/web/20140725200638/https://bnp.org.uk/ introduction (accessed 13 June 2016). See also Goodwin, Matthew J., 'In Search of the winning formula: Nick Griffin and the "modernisation" of the British National Party', in R. Goodwin and M.J. Eatwell (eds), *The New Extremism in 21st Century Britain* (Abingdon: Routledge, 2010), pp. 169–190.

41. Transcript of BBC documentary 'The Secret Agent', aired on 15 July 2004; available at: http://news.bbc.co.uk/1/hi/programmes/newsnight/ 3896921. stm (accessed 13 June 2016).

42. Ibid. Also see Taylor, Matthew, 'BNP leaders may face charges after TV exposé of racism', *Guardian*, 15 July 2004.

43. Allen, Christopher, *Islamophobia* (Farnham: Ashgate, 2010), pp. 88–89.

44. 'What they said about ... The BNP', *Guardian*, 17 July 2004; available at: http://www.guardian.co.uk/uk/2004/jul/17/race.thefarright (accessed 13 June 2016).

45. Goodall, Kay, 'Incitement to religious hatred: all talk and no substance?' *Modern Law Review* 70/1 (2007), p. 89.

46. Ibid., pp. 93–94, in which Goodall documents (now purged) online statements from the BNP website in which party leader Nick Griffin provides guidance for contributors. To quote directly: 'Emotive words, however justified they may be, must be avoided. Truth hurts, so words like 'alien', 'vermin', 'gang' instead of 'group', and such like must be avoided. A white rapist may be described as a 'beast' or an 'animal', but a black one must be merely a 'criminal'.

47. Goodwin, 'In search of the winning formula', p. 178; the broadcast itself can be viewed at: http://www.youtube.com/watch?v=2epLm34iNok (accessed 13 June 2016).

48. Op. cit. Also Allen, 'From race to religion'. A high-profile public campaign against the religious hatred legislation was led by the comedian Rowan Atkinson, cf. Atkinson, Rowan, 'Every Joke Has a

Victim', speech delivered at the House of Commons, 30 January 2006; transcript available at: http://www.guardian.co.uk/politics/2006/jan/30/immigrationpolicy.religion (accessed 13 June 2016).

49. For example, 'Muslims laud Tony Blair's stand on faith schools, but concerned over rise in Islamophobia', MCB press release, 20 May 2002; available at: http://www.mcb.org.uk/muslims-laud-tony-blairs-stand-on-faith-schools-but-concerned-over-rise-in-islamophobia/ (accessed 13 June 2016).

50. Forum Against Islamophobia and Racism (FAIR): 'The Religious Offences Bill 2002: a response' (October 2002) emphatically makes the case for policy changes to criminalise incitement against religious identity, along with discrimination on the grounds of religion.

51. Commission on British Muslims and Islamophobia,'Islamophobia: issues, challenges and action' (London: Runnymede Trust, 2004), p. 75.

52. Ibid.

53. Labour Party Manifesto, 'Forward not Back' (2005), pp. 111–112.

54. Meer, Nasar, *Citizenship, Identity and the Politics of Multiculturalism*, pp. 163–164.

55. *Racial and Religious Hatred Act 2006*, Part 3A: 'Acts intended to stir up religious hatred', in Schedule: Hatred against persons on religious grounds.

56. Goodall, 'Incitement to religious hatred', p. 11.

57. 'Religious hatred law perpetuates inequality after Commons vote', MCB press release, 1 February 2006; available at: http://www.mcb.org.uk/religious-hatred-law-perpetuates-inequality-after-commons-vote/ (accessed 13 June 2016).

58. *Daily Telegraph*, 23 October 1997.

59. Goodall, 'Incitement to religious hatred', p. 91.

60. Forum Against Islamophobia and Racism (FAIR), 'The Religious Offences Bill 2002'; and 'MCB calls for an end to misrepresentation of proposed incitement law', MCB press release, 13 January 2005; available at: http://www.mcb.org.uk/mcb-calls-for-an-end-to-misrepresentation-of-proposed-incitement-law/ (accessed 13 June 2016).

61. Ibid.

62. Richardson, John E., '"Get shot of the lot of them": election reporting of Muslims in British newspapers', in Maleiha Malik (ed.), *Anti-Muslim Prejudice: past and present* (Abingdon: Routledge, 2010), pp. 146–168; and Bowen, John R., *Blaming Islam* (Cambridge, MA: MIT Press, 2012).

63. Eatwell, Roger, 'Responses to the extreme right in Britain', in Roger Eatwell and Matthew J. Goodwin (eds), *The New Extremism in 21st Century Britain* (Abingdon: Routledge, 2010), pp. 213–220.

64. Phillips, Richard, 'Standing together: The Muslim Association of Britain and the anti-war movement', *Race and Class* 50/2 (2008), pp. 101–113.

65. Classic critiques of the Muslim-Left anti-war alliance can be found in Cohen, Nick, *What's Left?: how liberals lost their way* (London: Fourth Estate, 2007) and Anthony, Andrew, *The Fallout: how a guilty liberal lost his innocence* (London: Jonathan Cape, 2007).
66. Wavell, Stuart, 'Putting a good glossy on the Muslim lifestyle', *The Sunday Times*, 9 October 2005.
67. 'Sami Yusuf hopes music helps Muslim image', *Arab News*, 19 August 2007; available at: http://www.arabnews.com/node/302261 (accessed 20 June 2016).
68. Rahman, Samia, 'The biggest star in the Middle East is a Brit', *Guardian*, 27 April 2006.
69. The Cordoba Foundation – Who we are? http://www.thecordoba foundation.com/about_us.php?load=20 (accessed 20 June 2016).

CHAPTER 6   IDENTITY POLITICS AND TERRORISM AT HOME
(7 JULY 2005–JUNE 2010)

1. On the Bradford riots see: Allen, Christopher, *Fair Justice: The Bradford Disturbances, the Sentencing and the Impact* (London: FAIR, 2003).
2. For a personal account of the 'Diversity and Inclusion' remit of the London Organising Committee of the Olympic and Paralympic Games (LOCOG) see Bari, Muhammad Abdul, 'London 2012: a celebration of Britain's diversity', *Huffington Post UK*, 21 February 2012, available at: http://www.huffingtonpost.co.uk/muhammad-abdul-bari/olympics-london-2012-a-celebration_b_1292015.html (accessed 14 June 2016).
3. From a government perspective, cf. Trevor Phillips's speech of 22 September 2005: 'After 7/7: Sleepwalking into Segregation', delivered at Manchester University, 22 September 2005; available at: https://www.jiscmail.ac.uk/cgi-bin/webadmin?A3=ind0509&L=CRONEM&E=quoted-printable&P=60513&B=----_%3D_NextPart_001_01C5C28A.09501783&T=text%2Fhtml;%20charset=iso-8859-1&pending= (accessed 14 June 2016) – in which he remarked that the nature of British multiculturalism needed to be reviewed in the light of 7/7, and that too much emphasis had been placed on respecting and making space for the various differences among Britain's minorities, at the expense of developing a common and unifying shared culture. Modood, Tariq, 'Remaking Multiculturalism after 7/7', *Open Democracy*, 28 September 2005; available at: http://www.opendemocracy.net/conflict-terrorism/multiculturalism_2879.jsp (accessed 14 June 2016) summarises the range of commentary on the debate about the viability of multiculturalism as policy in Britain post-7/7.
4. Gove, Michael, *Celsius 7/7* (London: Weidenfeld and Nicolson, 2006).

5. Rai, Milan, *7/7, the London bombings, Islam and the Iraq War* (London: Pluto Press, 2006), p. 31.
6. Vallely, Paul, 'So what turned Sid Khan into a bomber?', *Independent*, 18 November 2005.
7. Gove, *Celsius 7/7*.
8. Milan Rai provides extensive profiles of each of the bombers, their backgrounds, family circumstances and childhoods in Rai, *7/7, the London bombings, Islam and the Iraq war*, pp. 21–48.
9. Of course, comparisons can be made with other instances when similar social detachment has been displayed – such as perpetrators of a number of school/workplace shooting sprees that have occurred in the USA in recent times, as well as most recently the Oslo/Utoeya massacres of July 2011 which were carried out by Anders Behring Breivik, a Norwegian far-right extremist. Such examples show how high levels of personal/ emotional detachment from society can come about as a result of a feeling of being 'under attack'.
10. Mohammed Siddique Khan's 'martyrdom' video, broadcast on *Al Jazeera Satellite Channel*, 1 September 2005.
11. Briggs, Rachel, Catherine Fieschi and Hannah Lownsbrough, 'Bringing it home: community-based approaches to counterterrorism' (London: Demos, 2006).
12. Blair, Tony, 'Prime minister's statement on anti-terror measures', 5 August 2005; available at: http://www.guardian.co.uk/politics/2005/ aug/05/uksecurity.terrorism1 (accessed 14 June 2016).
13. Sections 2, 6 and 8 of the Terrorism Act 2006.
14. 'New Anti-Terror Bill Published', Liberty press release, 15 September 2005; available at http://www.liberty-human-rights.org.uk/media/ press/2005/new-anti-terror-bill-published.php (accessed 14 June 2016).
15. Article 19, 'Submission to the 91st Session of the UN Human Rights Committee on Respect for Freedom of Expression in the UK and Northern Ireland' (October 2007), p. 8.
16. Barendt, Eric, 'Incitement to, and glorification of, terrorism', in Ivan Hare and James Weinstein (eds), *Extreme Speech and Democracy* (Oxford: Oxford University Press, 2009), pp. 445–462, and Choudhury, Tufyal, 'The Terrorism Act 2006: discouraging terrorism', in Hare and Weinstein, *Extreme Speech and Democracy*, pp. 463–487. Also Kundnani, Arun, *The End of Tolerance: racism in 21st century Britain* (London: Pluto Press, 2007), p. 179.
17. Police and security working group feedback, Warraich, Shaukat and Ifath Nawaz (eds), *'Preventing Extremism Together' Working Groups Report* (London: Home Office, 2005). Also cf. Gledhill, Ruth, 'Muslim task force attacks Government anti-terror plans', *The Times*, 10 November 2005; Travis, Alan and Patrick Wintour, 'Terror bill chilling for Muslims, Blair warned', *Guardian*, 11 November 2005.

18. 'Muslim community opposes new anti terror legislation and urges government to exercise maximum restraint and caution', MCB press release, 13 April 2006; available at: http://www.mcb.org.uk/muslim-community-opposes-new-anti-terror-legislation-and-urges-government-to-exercise-maximum-restraint-and-caution/ (accessed 14 June 2016).

19. This moment represents an interesting point in the development of British Muslim political identities. The threat of proscription for UK Muslim groups was quite clearly aimed at the separatist, radical and increasingly violence-endorsing trend which included groups such as *Al Muhajiroun*, The Saviour Sect and *Al Ghurabaa* – all of whom openly praised acts of terrorism, and often spoke contemptuously and provocatively of Britain, its government and its population, as well as of other religions. Tony Blair and many of his advisors became persuaded of the 'conveyor belt' theory – that groups like the (also separatist but avowedly non-violent) *Hizb-ut-Tahrir* were also eligible for proscription (David Cameron and the Conservatives have also incorporated this thinking into their government's approach to national security – cf. Cameron's security speech at Munich in March 2011). Even though it was officially non-violent, HT was regarded as a 'breeding ground' from which many members 'graduated' on to violent extremism. Blair's admission that he wished to ban HT sparked off a number of heated defences from various quarters in the Muslim community who genuinely feared that with the criteria for 'radical' and 'extremist' firmly in the government's grip, it would only be a matter of time before a whole range of other UK Muslim groups could be criminalised – whether for loose/historic international links with Islamist groups abroad (as I demonstrate in Chapter 2, there are plenty of these!), or for favouring ultra-conservative religious views (for instance on homosexuality or the role of women in society), or indeed for simply differing with the government on major foreign policy issues (see previous chapter for discussion on the MCB's rift with government on the 2001 invasion of Afghanistan).

20. Parker, Ellen, 'Implementation of the UK Terrorism Act 2006 – the relationship between counterterrorism law, free speech and the Muslim community in the United Kingdom versus the United States', *Emory International Law Review* 21/2 (Fall 2007), p. 756.

21. 'Don't jail "lyrical terrorist", writers' group tells judges', *Guardian*, 6 December 2007.

22. 'World Samina Malik Day December 6th', http://clatterymachinery.wordpress.com/2007/11/18/world-samina-malik-day-december-6th/ (accessed 14 June 2016).

23. Parris, Matthew, 'Think no evil? Are you serious?', *The Times*, 17 November 2007; Liddle, Rod, 'Free speech and the lyrical terrorist', *The Spectator*, 21 November 2007, in which he pens a short poem mocking the situation.

24. The case of four Bradford University students and a school pupil from Ilford, Essex, who had engaged in internet conversations fantasising about *jihad*, including communicating with individuals in Pakistan and downloading propaganda materials. Their initial conviction was quashed in February 2008.

25. *Al Ghurabaa* (Arabic for 'The Strangers') was a successor group to *Al Muhajiroun*, which was proscribed in the wake of 7/7 under the Terrorism Act 2006. In January 2010, the then home secretary, Alan Johnson, issued a banning order: 'The Proscribed Organisations (Name Changes) Order 2010' (London: Home Office, January 2010), extending the proscription for *Al Muhajiroun* to *Al Ghurabaa*, Islam4UK, London School of Sharia and the eclectic host of other names that the group's members had taken to operating under.

26. For example, in an interview with BBC Newsnight in August 2005 he described the 7/7 attacks as 'completely praiseworthy', and refused to refer to them negatively as 'suicide attacks', preferring instead the term '*mujahideen* activity'. He also told Channel 4 News that: 'For Muslims there (referring to Iraq and Afghanistan), they have a duty to fight occupiers, whether they are American soldiers or British soldiers', quoted at 'Radicals warned of treason risk', *BBC News Website*; available at: http://news.bbc.co.uk/1/hi/uk/4129502.stm (accessed 14 June 2016), prompting calls for him to be prosecuted for treason or incitement to treason.

27. Allen, Christopher, *Islamophobia* (Farnham: Ashgate, 2010), p. 94; Howe, Darcus, 'John Reid's dirty little one-act play', *New Statesman*, 6 October 2006.

28. Nikkhah, Roya and Adam Lusher, 'Police accused of "cowardly failure" to prosecute militant', *Daily Telegraph*, 24 September 2006.

29. Letter from George Galloway MP, 'Alarm bells over terror conviction', *Guardian*, 24 April 2008.

30. 'Radical preacher Abu Izzadeen freed from jail early', *Daily Telegraph*, 6 May 2009.

31. *Press TV* interview with Abu Izzadeen on his release from prison, 28 October 2010.

32. 'Abu Izzadeen released', *Salafi Media* website (website no longer available); archive available at: http://web.archive.org/web/20110228225427/http://www.salafimedia.com/component/k2/item/1092-abu-izzadeen-released.html (accessed 14 June 2016).

33. Ibid.

34. 'Abu Izzadeen released from prison' video; available at: https://www.youtube.com/watch?v = aR8tIOprMKI (accessed 21 June 2016).

35. A dawn raid carried out on a home in Forest Gate, east London, targeted two brothers – Abdul Kahar and Abul Koiyar – and was based on what turned out to be false intelligence. The raid was widely criticised for the apparently gung-ho and heavy-handed attitude of the officers. One of

the brothers was shot in the shoulder and there was huge community outcry regarding why and how such an intensive raid could have been carried out on the basis of such weak intelligence, and of course how it was that the police officer in charge of the raid could have shot Abdul Kahar so readily, when he showed no signs of resistance.

36. Section 58, Terrorism Act 2000.
37. Justice Calvert-Smith, quoted in Brittain, Victoria and Asim Qureshi, 'Banning books in Britain, fifty years after Lady Chatterley', *Open Democracy*, 17 December 2011; available at: http://www.opendemocracy.net/ourkingdom/victoria-brittain-asim-qureshi/banning-books-in-britain-fifty-years-after-lady-chatterley (accessed 14 June 2016).
38. Cf. the account of the prosecution's expert witness: Wilkinson, Matthew Tariq, 'This bookseller deserved his incitement to terrorism conviction', *Guardian*, 18 May 2012.
39. Brittain and Qureshi, 'Banning books in Britain'. Also Qureshi, Asim, 'Conviction of thought: How Islamic concepts are ruled on in UK Courts', *Arches Quarterly* 5/9 (Spring 2012), pp. 171–176.
40. *R. v. Faraz* (2012), Crim 2820, EWCA (201200251, C5).
41. Cf. *R. v. Faraz – Testimony of Matthew 'Tariq' Wilkinson for the prosecution*; transcript available at: https://web.archive.org/web/20150102003123/http:/www.cageprisoners.com/learn-more/legal-issues/item/2922-r-v-faraz-testimony-of-matthew-tariq-wilkinson-for-the-prosecution-day-1 (accessed 20 May 2017).
42. Klausen, Jytte, 'British Counter-Terrorism after 7/7: adapting community policing to the fight against domestic terrorism', *Journal of Ethnic and Migration Studies* 35/3 (2009), pp. 403–420.
43. Warraich and Nawaz, *'Preventing Extremism Together' Working Groups*.
44. Sadiq Khan MP in his speech 'Being a British Muslim' to the Fabian Society and the City Circle, in London, on 3 July 2006; archived at: http://web.archive.org/web/20091123163018/http://fabians.org.uk/events/event-reports/missing-a-positive-vision-for-british-muslims (accessed 14 June 2016).
45. Sadiq Khan MP quoted in Malik, Kenan, *From Fatwa to Jihad: the Rushdie affair and its legacy* (London: Atlantic: 2009), p. 120.
46. Warraich and Nawaz, *'Preventing Extremism Together' Working Groups*, pp. 12–14.
47. Ibid., p. 14.
48. Great Britain. Foreign and Commonwealth Office and Great Britain. Home Office, 'Draft Report on Young Muslims and Extremism' (April 2004); available at: http://www.globalsecurity.org/security/library/report/2004/muslimext-uk.htm (accessed 14 June 2016). Also see: 'Britain's secret plan to win Muslim hearts and minds', *The Sunday Times*, 30 May 2004.
49. The document made particular mention of Amr Khaled, an Egyptian 'televangelist' who had recently moved to the UK, Hamza Yusuf and

Suhaib Webb – both US imams with widespread international followings, and Tariq Ramadan – a Swiss/Egyptian academic who's appeal to English speaking audiences was rising substantially at this time, also coinciding with his move to settle in the UK.

50. Briggs, Fieschi and Lownsbrough, 'Bringing it home'.
51. Iqbal Sacranie's valedictory speech to the MCB Annual General Meeting, London, 4 June 2006; available at: http://web.archive.org/web/20140307045227/http://www.mcb.org.uk/uploads/SECGEN.pdf (accessed 21 June 2016).
52. Great Britain. Home Office, 'The Counter-terrorism strategy', available at: http://www.homeoffice.gov.uk/counter-terrorism/uk-counter-terrorism-strat/ (accessed 3 November 2011).
53. Ibid.
54. Kundnani, Arun, 'Spooked: how not to prevent violent extremism' (London: Institute of Race Relations, 2009), p. 39.
55. Between 2007 and 2010 various Prevent budgets totalled up to several hundred million pounds, see HM Government 'Pursue, Prevent, Protect, Prepare: the UK strategy for countering international terrorism', *Annual Report* (March 2010), p. 13; Kundnani, 'Spooked', pp. 11–12.
56. Kundnani, 'Spooked', p. 15.
57. Ibid., p. 15.
58. Ibid., p. 17.
59. Thomas, Paul, 'Failed and friendless: the UK's "Preventing Violent Extremism" programme', *British Journal of Politics and International Relations* 12/3 (August 2010), pp. 442–458.
60. Op. cit., pp. 26–27.
61. Dodd, Vikram, 'MPs investigate anti-extremism programme after spying claims', *Guardian*, 18 October 2009.
62. Rimmer, Stephen, 'Allegations made in the *Panorama* programme "Muslim First – British Second" on Monday 16th February', statement from the Office for Security and Counter Terrorism, 17 February 2009. In response to the *Guardian* investigation of October 2009, a Home Office spokesman said: 'Any suggestion that Prevent is about spying is simply wrong. Prevent is about working with communities to protect vulnerable individuals and address the root causes of radicalisation.', quoted in Hough, Andrew, 'Anti-extremism scheme "spying on Muslims"', *Daily Telegraph*, 17 October 2009. A more recent denial that Prevent was a 'tool' for spying came from Rudd, Amber, 'Safeguarding our young people from becoming radicalised should not be a controversial aim', *The Sun*, 9 August 2017. However, shortly before this piece, commenting on BBC Question Time on 25 May 2017, Home Secretary Amber Rudd's claim that 'We get the intelligence much more from the Prevent strategy, which engages with local community groups, not through the police', was swiftly taken by many activists to be

something of an admission from the government that Prevent was, and remained, an intelligence-gathering exercise.

63. Kundnani, 'Spooked', p. 28.

64. For instance, through legislation against discrimination in employment and against incitement to religious hatred, and long-fought-for victories in equal recognition such as the funding for Muslim faith schools and the inclusion of a religion question in the national census. Cf. previous chapters.

65. Verkaik, Robert, 'Exclusive: how the MI5 blackmails British Muslims', *Independent*, 21 May 2009. One of these men has since been identified as Mahdi Hashi, a British Somali who claims to have been regularly harassed when travelling. He was deported from Somalia on the instructions of British authorities, and is reported to have later been transferred to a US military base in Djibouti with the acquiescence of the British authorities. In 2012, his family was informed that he had been stripped of his British citizenship on the grounds of alleged extremism, making him one of only a handful of Britons to have had his citizenship revoked in modern times. Hashi has since been held in solitary confinement in the US, and was finally tried in 2015 where he pleaded guilty (arguably under coercion) to the charge of providing support to the Somalia terrorist group, Al Shabaab. For more on Hashi's case see: Qureshi, Asim, 'The UK counter-terrorism matrix: structural racism and the case of Mahdi Hashi', in Massoumi, Narzanin, Tom Mills and David Miller (eds), *What is Islamophobia? Racism, social movements and the state* (London: Pluto Press, 2017), pp. 74–96.

66. Kundnani, 'Spooked', p. 17; O'Toole, Therese, Stephen H. Jones and Daniel Nilsson Dehanas, 'The new Prevent: will it work? Can it work?', *Arches Quarterly* 5/9 (Spring 2012), pp. 56–62.

67. To mention one such controversy: Ed Husain of the Quilliam Foundation was roundly opposed by other Muslim groups when he insisted that 'it is good and it is right' for Prevent to conduct intelligence-gathering amongst Muslims, even if they were not suspected of committing any crimes. Husain argued that intelligence gathering should trump concerns around civil liberties, since: 'It's not about doing the right thing by Islamists or by liberal do-gooders, it's about creating a society where liberal do-gooders survive freely.' Condemnation of his comments was so strong that Quilliam later issued a rather vague statement to moderate the tone of Husain's earlier comments: 'Allegations of government spying on UK Muslims – a statement from Quilliam directors', 20 October 2009; available at: http://www.quilliamfoundation.org/press/allegations-of-government-spying-on-uk-muslims-a-statement-from-quilliam-directors/ (accessed 14 June 2016).

68. O'Toole, Jones and Dehanas, 'The new Prevent'.

69. Full text of the motion 'Spying on Campus' available at: http://fosis.org.uk/images/stories/blogs/spyingoncampusmotion.pdf (accessed 14 June 2016). For some anecdotal background see Derfoufi, Zin, 'MI5: leave young Muslims alone', *Guardian*, 26 May 2009.

70. Shaista Gohir's open resignation letter to Home Secretary John Denham, 6 April 2010; available at: http://wallscometumblingdown.wordpress.com/2010/04/08/founder-quits-national-muslim-womens-advisory-group-in-protest/ (accessed 14 June 2016). Author's interview with a member of YMAG, 2008-present, wishing to remain anonymous, 30 November 2011.

71. While NMWAG members were handpicked from the start, there was an applications process for YMAG membership, but applicants were short-listed and eventual group members were then selected by the government. After it became apparent that the initial intake of NMWAG members 'didn't have a good enough cross-section of ages, ethnicities and backgrounds', a competition round was held for a second intake of members to apply for positions on the group. Source: Author's interview with Julie Siddiqi, second-round entrant to NMWAG, 20 June 2012.

72. Ibid,. Also see Gohir, Shaista, 'Muslim women are not political pawns' *Guardian: Comment is Free*, 9 April 2009; available at: http://www.guardian.co.uk/commentisfree/2010/apr/09/government-failed-muslim-women?INTCMP=ILCNETTXT3487 (accessed 14 June 2016). Shaista Gohir's position as co-ordinator of NMWAG has been disputed by two other former members in their conversations with me. Both recall that there was no position of co-ordinator in the group. The existence of this dispute demonstrates that there were tensions between the group members which contributed towards hindering its potential. See also Chris Allen and Surinder Guru, 'Between political fad and political empowerment: a critical evaluation of the National Muslim Women's Advisory Group (NMWAG) and governmental processes of engaging Muslim women', *Sociological Research Online* 17/3 (2012); available at http://www.socresonline.org.uk/17/3/17.html (accessed 26 June 2017).

73. Author's interview with former NMWAG member, wishing to remain anonymous, 9 January 2012.

74. Author's interview with former YMAG member, wishing to remain anonymous, 30 November 2011.

75. Ibid.

76. YMAG briefly re-launched (2011–2012) as an independent social enterprise with the aim of 'acting as a bridge between young people and policy makers'. Website archived at: http://web.archive.org/web/20130322042214/http://ymag.org.uk/ (accessed 27 June 2016).

77. Warraich and Nawaz, *'Preventing Extremism Together' Working Groups*, p. 6.

78. Author's interview with MCB official wishing to remain anonymous, conducted on 17 October 2011.

79. Bunglawala, Inayat, 'MINAB: community initiative, or quango?', *Guardian: Comment is Free*, 15 May 2009; available at: http://www. guardian.co.uk/commentisfree/belief/2009/may/15/minab-mosques-imams-islam?INTCMP=ILCNETTXT3487 (accessed 14 June 2016).

80. Author's interview with Yousuf Bhailok, MCB Secretary General 2000–2002, conducted on 10 October 2011. Also see: 'MINAB: autonomy or acquiescence?' *The Saga of Home Office Working Groups and its projects – Salaam.co.uk*; available at: http://www.salaam.co.uk/themeofthemonth/september03_index.php?l=60#ccc2 (accessed 14 June 2016).

81. Sacranie, Iqbal, valedictory speech to the MCB Annual General Meeting, London, 4 June 2006; available at: http://www.mcb.org.uk/uploads/SECGEN.pdf (accessed 24 July 2012).

82. The main architect of MINAB's structure, Khurshid Drabu, was also a key figure in formulating the MCB's constitution.

83. Author's interview with Yousuf Bhailok, 10 October 2011. Also, author's conversation with senior MAB official wishing to remain anonymous, December 2011.

84. Author's interview with former MCB official, wishing to remain anonymous, conducted on 17 October 2011.

85. Laurence, *The Emancipation of Europe's Muslims* (2012), p. 194.

86. Gilliat-Ray, *Muslims in Britain: an introduction* (2010), p. 158.

87. Ibid., p. 171.

88. From June 2010, the project was discontinued by the Coalition government. A general archive of the project with details of various international visits is available at: http://web.archive.org/web/20100107003231/http://www.projectingbritishmuslims.com/. Additionally, the YouTube page with video interviews and footage from the visits is still available at: https://www.youtube.com/user/britishislam (both accessed 27 June 2016).

89. Correspondence from Lucy Hughes, Head, Prevent Team CTD at the FCO to Graeme Breen, in response to the latter's freedom of information request regarding FCO involvement with the Quilliam Foundation and the PBM project.10 May 2010, Reference 0238-10; available at: http://www.whatdotheyknow.com/request/30412/response/85454/attach/html/5/0238%2010Breen%20letter%20final.doc.html (accessed 14 June 2016).

90. Author's interview with past PBM delegate wishing to remain anonymous, 29 November 2011.

91. Lords Hansard 30 March 2009; available at: http://www.publications.parliament.uk/pa/ld200809/ldhansrd/text/90330w0002.htm (accessed 14 June 2016).

92. 'I am the West – project synopsis'; archived at: http://web.archive.org/web/20090411052702/http://www.deeninternational.co.uk/downloads/i-am-the-west.pdf (accessed 27 June 2016) ('I am the West' was the initial

title given to the project, before it was changed to 'I am Muslim, I am British' – see previous footnote).

93. Ibid.

94. Ibid., p. 3. Emphasis in original.

95. Warraich and Nawaz, *'Preventing Extremism Together' Working Groups*, p. 75.

96. Rai, *7/7, The London bombings*, pp. 145–152 compiles the perspectives of a range of figures from the worlds of policy, politics (both the Labour and Conservative parties) as well as from within Muslim communities who have all taken the view that the Iraq war in particular, and foreign policy in general, have played an important role in driving young Muslims to extremism and increasing the threat of terrorism.

97. Yaqoob, Salma, 'Government's PVE agenda is failing to tackle extremism', *The Muslim News*, 28 November 2008.

98. Mohammed Siddique Khan's 'martyrdom' video, broadcast on *Al Jazeera Satellite Channel*; *Press TV* interview with Abu Izzadeen on his release from prison; and most recently expressed by Michael Adebolajo, one of two suspects in the murder in Woolwich of British serviceman Lee Rigby in May 2013. In an amateur video filmed at the scene of the murder and aired by ITV News on 22 May 2013, he said: 'The only reason we have killed this man today is because Muslims are dying daily by British soldiers. And this British soldier is one. It is an eye for an eye and a tooth for a tooth.' Full text at: 'Woolwich attack: the terrorist's rant', *The Telegraph website*; available at: http://www.telegraph.co.uk/news/uknews/terrorism-in-the-uk/10075488/Woolwich-attack-the-terrorists-rant.html (accessed 14 June 2016). Successive Labour and Conservative-led British Governments have continuously and consistently denied any connection between foreign policy and radicalisation.

99. Full text of the letter, entitled 'Protect citizens, wherever they are', is reproduced at: Birt, Yahya, 'An unprecedented letter', 13 August 2006; available at: https://yahyabirt1.wordpress.com/2006/08/13/an-unprecedented-letter/ (accessed 14 June 2016).

100. Ibid.

101. Transport Secretary, Douglas Alexander, speaking to Channel 4 News on 12 August 2006.

102. Foreign Secretary, Margaret Beckett, to the BBC, quoted in Temko, Ned, 'Beckett rejects link between foreign policy and terrorism', *The Observer*, 13 August 2006.

103. Author's interview with YMAG member, wishing to remain anonymous, 30 November 2011.

104. Dr Muhammad Abdul Bari, former Secretary General of the MCB, in an interview on BBC HARDtalk, *BBC News Channel*, 13 December 2010.

105. Although the Coalition government (2010–2015) gave the Prevent programme less significance than its Labour predecessors, notably by cutting back funding, Prevent was later shored up by being placed on a

statutory footing in 2015, and Theresa May's Conservatives have pledged to create a Commission for Countering Extremism.

106. Bunting, Madeleine, 'Throwing mud at Muslims', *Guardian*, 22 August 2005.

107. Ware, John, 'A Question of Leadership', Panorama, BBC1, broadcast on 21 August 2005 at 22.20 BST. Transcript available at: http://news.bbc.co.uk/2/hi/programmes/panorama/4171950.stm (accessed 14 June 2016).

108. The MCB organised a meeting of Muslim leaders and scholars on 19 July 2005 at which a declaration was issued condemning the 7/7 attacks and pronouncing that 'It is incumbent upon all of us, Muslims and non-Muslims – to help the authorities with any information that may lead to the planners of last week's atrocity being brought to justice.' The full text of the statement is available at: Muslim leaders' declaration on 7/7 bombings; available at: http://news.bbc.co.uk/1/hi/uk_politics/4696969.stm (accessed 14 June 2016).

109. Op. cit. Also Robinson, Mike, Editor, BBC Panorama, 'Response to MCB complaints', 30 September 2005; available at: http://news.bbc.co.uk/2/hi/programmes/panorama/4297490.stm (accessed 13 February 2017).

110. Silver, James, 'Interview: John Ware. "It's the last chance for Panorama"', *Guardian*, 21 August 2006.

111. Echoed in an editorial in the *Observer*: 'Muslim leaders in feud with BBC', 14 August 2005.

112. Bright, Martin, 'Radical links of UK's "moderate" Muslim group', *Observer*, 14 August 2005.

113. Ibid., and Ware, 'A question of leadership', Panorama, BBC1, 21 August 2005.

114. Cf. 'MCB responds to The Observer's "investigation"', MCB press release, 14 August 2005; available at: http://www.mcb.org.uk/mcb-responds-to-the-observers-investigation/ (accessed 14 June 2016), and Sacranie, Iqbal, 'British Muslims are judged by 'Israel test"', *Observer*, 21 August 2005.

115. 'John Ware's Panorama programme – a witch-hunt against British Muslims', MCB press release, 20 August 2005; available at http://www.mcb.org.uk/john-wares-panorama-programme-%C2%96-a-witch-hunt-against-british-muslims/ (accessed 14 June 2016). It is worth noting here that what the MCB will have considered to be self-defence on its own part, has led to charges of double standards on free speech. So attempts by the MCB to respond to what it perceived as attacks from the media have been rebutted as intolerance towards the exercise of free speech by those who would criticise the MCB, while at the same time demanding that they maintain the right to express offensive criticisms of those with whom they disagree. A prominent example would be Iqbal Sacranie's description of homosexuality as 'harmful', and 'not acceptable' on the PM Programme, BBC Radio 4, 3 January 2006.

116. Bright, Martin, 'Who speaks for Muslims?', Dispatches, Channel 4. Broadcast in July 2006.

117. Bright, Martin, *When Progressives Treat with Reactionaries: the British state's flirtation with radical Islamism* (London: Policy Exchange, 2006).

118. Later revealed to be a Mr Derek Pasquill, who subsequently faced a court case (eventually dropped) and suspension from his job at the FCO. Cf. Malik, *From Fatwa to Jihad*, pp. 127–128.

119. See Table 1 'Glossary of UK Muslim representative/lobby groups'.

120. Ibid., for more information on these organisations.

121. Nawaz, Maajid, 'How the government should handle the "Muslim Question"', *New Statesman* (5 December 2011).

122. 'Minister backs new Muslim group', *BBC News*, 19 July 2006; available at: http://news.bbc.co.uk/1/hi/uk/5193402.stm (accessed 14 June 2016); Kelly, Ruth, 'Britain: our values, our responsibilities', speech to Muslim organisations on working together to tackle extremism, London, 11 October 2006; archived at: http://webarchive.nationalarchives.gov. uk/+/ http:/www.communities.gov.uk/staging/index.asp?id = 1503690 (accessed 26 June 2017).

123. MCB, 'MCB responds to Ruth Kelly's speech', 15 October 2006. Full text of letter available at: http://www.mcb.org.uk/mcb-responds-to-ruth-kellys-speech/ (accessed 14 June 2016).

124. Author's interview with MCB official, wishing to remain anonymous, October 2011.

125. See 'Martin Bright's C4 documentary: part of a campaign to divide and rule', MCB press release, 13 July 2006; available at: https://web.archive. org/web/20130123171203/http://mcb.org.uk/media/presstext.php? ann_id = 214 (accessed 14 June 2016), in which an SMC representative is described as 'discredited' and it is queried 'what level of support – if any – he actually had within the Muslim communities across the UK which he is now claiming to represent.' See also Khan, Shehla, 'New Sufis for New Labour', *The Muslim News*, 25 August 2006. Additionally, former British Ambassador to Uzbekistan, Craig Murray, has claimed that the SMC was funded by the CIA, cf. Murray, Craig, 'Sufi Muslim Council a CIA/Karimov front', 23 March 2009; available at: http://www.craigmur-ray.org.uk/archives/2009/03/sufi_muslim_cou/ (accessed 14 June 2016).

126. Sjternholm, Simon, 'Sufi politics in Britain: the Sufi Muslim Council and the "silent majority" of Muslims', *Journal of Islamic Law and Culture* 12/3 (October 2010), pp. 215–226.

127. The SMC's most recent project was a five-venue tour with Shaykh Hisham Kabbani in July 2010, their apparent spiritual leader, who had also featured prominently in all their previous activities. Its youth magazine, *Spirit The Mag*, did not survive beyond its inaugural issue; see Sjternholm, 'Sufi politics in Britain'.

128. Cf. Muslim Council of Britain, *The Muslim Council of Britain – its structure, history and workings* (London: MCB, 2002), p. 6, for an outline of the organisation's structure, its various specialist committees and office-bearers.

129. For examples: Birt, Yahya, 'The next ten years: an open letter to the MCB', *emel magazine* 46 (July 2008); Amin, Mohammed, 'The Muslim Council of Britain's need for constitutional reform', 20 January 2011; available at: http://www.mohammedamin.com/Community_issues/ MCB-constitutional-reform.html (accessed 14 June 2016).

130. Some examples include: Footsteps – a mentoring scheme for young Muslim schoolchildren; the MCB Leadership Development Programme (run annually since 2004); the Young Muslim Beacon Awards (run annually since 2008); regular partnerships with Citizens UK, a grassroots campaigns alliance working to promote proactive political engagement in diverse communities; and a dedicated Muslim Spiritual Care project run in partnership with the National Health Service.

131. 'MCB statement on SORs', 30 April 2007; available at: https://web.archive. org/web/20130123172444/http://mcb.org.uk/media/presstext.php? ann_id=250 (accessed 14 June 2016). It is arguable that the MCB's opposition, along with a host of other faith groups, to the introduction of same-sex marriage in 2013 was a regression from this. See 'Same-sex marriage bill – act now!' MCB press release, 4 February 2013, available at: http://www.mcb.org.uk/index.php?option=com_content&view= article&id=2268 (accessed 10 August 2013). However, I would argue that it is unfair to make such a deduction, since all major faiths made representations to some effect on this matter before the law was finally passed. Additionally, an important part of the MCB's objection was its call for an exemption for mosques from being required to conduct same-sex marriages, on a par with the exemption granted to churches, demonstrating its by now characteristic approach in calling for even-handed treatment for Muslims by the law. See 'MCB calls for equal gay marriage exemption for mosques', i*Engage website*, 18 December 2012, available at: http://web.archive.org/web/20151201004234/http://iengage. org.uk/news/2270-mcb-calls-for-equal-gay-marriage-exemption-for- mosques (accessed 14 June 2016).

132. Extract of a letter from Peter Tatchell of OutRage! to Sir Iqbal Sacranie, quoted in: 'Muslim leader urged: drop homophobia. Gay group calls for solidarity against intolerance'; available at: http://www.petertatchell. net/religion/muslimleader.htm (accessed 14 June 2016).

133. Detractors of the MCB position preferred to call it a boycott.

134. Dodd, Vikram and Hugh Muir, 'Senior Muslims tried to reverse Holocaust Memorial Day snub', *Guardian*, 27 January 2007.

135. For example, prominent Muslim figures have since (at least) as early as 2006 been in occasional discussion with gay rights groups regarding the potential for cooperation in tackling homophobia among Muslims and in tackling Islamophobia together. Cf. minutes of Equality and Diversity Forum (EDF) meeting, 18 January 2006, which records such discussions between Mohammed Aziz and Alan Wardle of Stonewall. Aziz is cited to have been representing the MCB at this meeting, although the MCB later

disowned his comments, nonetheless, his approach is representative of a growing approach among leading British Muslim figures. See Equality and Diversity Forum, minutes of meeting held on 18 January 2006 in London; available at: www.edf.org.uk/publications/MinsJan06Mtg.doc (accessed 14 June 2013).

136. Author's interviews with Yousuf Bhailok (MCB Secretary General 2000–2002), and other (anonymous) MCB officials, 10 and 17 October 2011.

137. Here I refer specifically to the main British Muslim organisations of the reformist strand (see Chapter 2), or of reformist heritage. Specifically, the national bodies of the UKIM, *Dawatul Islam*, IFE, YMO, MAB, ISB, YMUK and all their local branches and affiliated mosques, the delegates of which, together, form a sizeable voting bloc within the MCB.

138. Bunting, Madeleine, 'The MCB's wonderland election', *Guardian*, 18 June 2010. Bunglawala, Inayat, 'Mohammed Amin resigns from the MCB'; available at: http://inayatscorner.wordpress.com/2010/06/22/mohammed-amin-resigns-from-the-mcb/ 22nd June 2010 (accessed 14 June 2016).

139. Author's interview with Yousuf Bhailok, 10 October 2011.

140. 'Muslim delegation meets with Prime Minister', *The Muslim News*, 28 September 2001.

141. Goodall, 'Incitement to religious hatred'; Thompson, Simon, 'Freedom of expression and hatred of religion', *Ethnicities* 12/2 (January 2012), pp. 215–232.

142. Warsi, Sayeeda, 'My Faith', *Sir Sigmund Sternberg Interfaith Lecture* delivered at Leicester University, 20 January 2011; available at: https://sayeedawarsi.com/2011/01/20/university-of-leicester-sir-sigmund-sternberg-lecture/ (accessed 26 June 2017).

143. Warsi cited Polly Toynbee, 'I am an Islamophobe and proud of it', *Independent*, 23 October 1997, as well as Rod Liddle who delivered a speech entitled 'Islamophobia? Count me in!' (Warsi, 'My Faith'). Other examples include Martin Amis who, commenting in an interview on the 2006 foiled transatlantic aircraft terror plot opined that: 'The Muslim community will have to suffer until it gets its house in order.' What sort of suffering? Not letting them travel. Deportation – further down the road. Curtailing of freedoms. Strip-searching people who look like they're from the Middle East or from Pakistan … Discriminatory stuff, until it hurts the whole community and they start getting tough with their children.' Dougary, Ginny, interview with Amis in *The Times Magazine*, 9 September 2006. See also Oborne, Peter, 'The shameful Islamophobia at the heart of Britain's press', *Independent*, 7 July 2008.

144. Modood, Tariq, 'Muslims and the politics of difference', in Peter Hopkins and Richard Gale (eds), *Muslims in Britain: race, place and identities* (Edinburgh: Edinburgh University Press, 2009), p. 204.

CHAPTER 7   CURRENT DEBATES

1. Phillips, Trevor, 'After 7/7: Sleepwalking into Segregation', delivered at Manchester University, 22 September 2005; available at: https://www.jiscmail.ac.uk/cgi-bin/webadmin?A3 = ind0509&L = CRONEM&E = quoted-printable&P = 60513&B = - - - -_%3D_NextPart_001_01C5C28A.09501783&T=text%2Fhtml;%20charset=iso-8859-1&pending= (accessed 14 June 2016).
2. O'Brien, Peter, *The Muslim Question in Europe: political controversies and public philosophies* (Philadelphia: Temple University Press, 2016), pp. 92–94.
3. Kelly, Ruth, 'Britain: our values, our responsibilities', speech to Muslim organisations on working together to tackle extremism, London, 11 October 2006; archived at: http://webarchive.nationalarchives.gov.uk/+/ http:/www.communities.gov.uk/staging/index.asp?id=1503690 (accessed 26 June 2017).
4. See Chapter 6.
5. Point 8, 'A statement by the religious scholars and proselytisers (*du'at*) of the Islamic Nation (*ummah*) to all rulers and peoples concerning events in Gaza' (commonly referred to as The Istanbul Declaration); available at: https://www.hurryupharry.org/wp-content/uploads/2009/03/istpdf.pdf (accessed 15 June 2016).
6. Hazel Blears' letter to Dr Abdul Bari, MCB Secretary General, dated 13 March 2009. A copy is available at: http://image.guardian.co.uk/sys-files/Guardian/documents/2009/03/23/blears__letter.pdf (accessed 15 June 2016).
7. Inayat Bunglawala, then spokesman for the MCB, quoted in: Dodd, Vikram, 'Muslim Council accuses government of undermining independence', *Guardian*, 26 March 2009.
8. Ibid.
9. Two such examples are: Whitaker, Brian, 'Alienating British Muslims', The *Guardian Comment is Free*, 24 March 2009; and Alderman, Geoffrey, 'Hazel Blears must back down', *Guardian: Comment is Free*, 25 March 2009.
10. The government later resumed relations with the MCB in January 2010, after more successful mediation between Muslim parliamentarians and the Council's leadership, and a written assurance from Muhammad Abdul Bari to Communities Secretary, John Denham, undertaking that the attendances of MCB office bearers of international conferences would, in future, be subject to set protocols. However, a number of MCB officials I have interviewed (all requesting anonymity) have said that government–MCB relations have not returned to the same levels of familiarity and trust that they had enjoyed previously.
11. Abdullah, Daud, 'My reply to Hazel Blears', *Guardian*, 26 March 2009.

12. For an example of this type of argument see: Mirza, Munira, Abi Senthilkumaran and Zein Ja'far, *Living Apart Together: British Muslims and the paradox of multiculturalism* (London: Policy Exchange, 2007).

13. David Cameron, speech at Munich Security Conference, 5 February 2011. Full transcript available at: http://www.number10.gov.uk/news/pms-speech-at-munich-security-conference/ (accessed 15 June 2016).

14. The contents of this speech resonated with thinking that had been present within the Conservative Party during its time in opposition. A policy report produced by the Conservative Party's Group on National and International Security for Dame Pauline Neville Jones took the line that almost all British Muslim organisations and trends had links with Islamism, and argued that the government had been 'mistaken (to) conduct business or take such organisations or members of them as dialogue partners, the effect of this being to give them status while diminishing that of organisations and individuals sharing our values'. Instead, it recommended that government 'patronage' should only be offered to those organisations conforming to 'our values'. Conservative Party Group on National and International Security, *Uniting the Country* (2007), p. 37.

15. A then annual Muslim gathering which had regularly been attended by politicians from all parties in the past.

16. Townsend, Mark, 'Baroness Warsi told by David Cameron not to appear at Islamic conference', *Guardian*, 24 October 2010. Warsi recounts this incident in her book, where she attributes it to 'the paranoid state' Warsi, Sayeeda, *The Enemy Within: a tale of Muslim Britain* (London: Allen Lane, 2017), p. 125.

17. Ansari, Humayun, 'The multiculturalism backlash and the mainstreaming of Islamophobia post-9/11', in J Wolffe (ed.), *Catholics, Protestants, and Muslims: Irish 'Religious' Conflict in Comparative Perspective* (Basingstoke: Palgrave, 2014), pp. 169–190.

18. 'Zakir Naik Exclusion Order a Serious Error of Judgement', MCB press release, 18 June 2010; available at: http://www.mcb.org.uk/zakir-naik-exclusion-order-a-serious-error-of-judgement/ (accessed 15 June 2016).

19. HM Government, 'Prevent Strategy', July 2011, p. 50.

20. This rift became public after it was leaked to the press, and eventually led to the transferral of Michael Gove from his Education brief to the position of Secretary of State for Justice – widely interpreted as a demotion.

21. The full text of the 'Trojan Horse' letter is included in the report of the government inquiry into the affair: Clarke, Peter, 'Report into allegations concerning Birmingham schools arising from the "Trojan horse" letter' (House of Commons, 22 July 2014).

22. 'We need clarity and consistency in our education standards: British Muslims respond to the Ofsted reports of schools in Birmingham', MCB

Press Release, 9 June 2014; available at: http://www.mcb.org.uk/we-need-clarity-and-consistency-in-our-education-standards-british-muslims-respond-to-the-ofsted-reports-of-schools-in-birmingham/ (accessed 4 March 2017).

23. See Hill, Dave, 'The rise and fall of Lutfur Rahman', *Guardian*, 10 June 2015, for a comprehensive overview of the saga relating to Rahman's election and subsequent removal from office, including an account of claims made by the Labour MP Jim Fitzpatrick that the IFE was 'acting almost as an entryist organisation, placing people within political parties'.

24. For instance, Park View Academy, the school at the centre of this controversy, had received an 'outstanding' Ofsted rating in an inspection carried out in 2012. During a personal visit to the school, it received direct praise from Sir Michael Wilshaw, the Chief Inspector of Schools, for 'get(ting) the best' out of children 'from tough backgrounds'. He even went as far as declaring that 'all schools should be like this', and in a *Guardian* report of the visit, Wilshaw is pictured flanked by Tahir Alam, then chair of the Park View Trust, observing a lesson approvingly – see: Vasagar, Jeevan, 'An inspector calls: the day the head of Ofsted visited one school', *Guardian*, 27 March 2012.

25. See Tahir Alam's account of the affair in Abbas, Tahir, 'The "Trojan Horse" plot and the fear of Muslim power in British state schools', *Journal of Muslim Minority Affairs* (pre-print, published online 17 April 2017).

26. The first articulation of 'British values' put forward by the state during recent times was by the Labour Home Secretary Jacqui Smith in 2008.

27. Cameron, David, Speech on extremism, Ninestiles Academy, Birmingham, 20 July 2015; available at: https://www.gov.uk/government/speeches/extremism-pm-speech (accessed 15 June 2016).

28. Ibid.

29. Ibid., In the speech, Cameron specifically mentions Cage, which has been something of a regular thorn in the side of the political establishment through its persistent interrogation of counter-extremism policy, which has involved leaking of classified information from Prevent, and the exposure of non-transparent relationships between government agencies and ostensibly grassroots Muslim counter-extremism initiatives.

30. '"One Nation Counter-Extremism Strategy" risks further undermining fight against terrorism', MCB press release, 19 October 2015; available at: http://www.mcb.org.uk/one-nation-counter-extremism-strategy-risks-fight-against-terrorism-191015/ (accessed 15 June 2016).

31. Pickersgill, Peter, 'Normative Islam report' (London: *5 Pillars*, 2016).

32. Prime Minister's Office, 'Prime Minister: "I want to build a national coalition to challenge and speak out against extremism"', press release, 13 October 2015; available at: https://www.gov.uk/government/news/

prime-minister-i-want-to-build-a-national-coalition-to-challenge-and-speak-out-against-extremism (accessed 15 June 2016).

33. Correspondence from the Cabinet Office in response to a freedom of information request from Yahya Birt regarding the Community Engagement Forum; available at: https://www.whatdotheyknow.com/request/296826/response/735065/attach/3/FOI321889%20Reply.pdf (accessed 4 March 2017). Also: House of Commons written question asked by Greg Mulholland MP and answered by Karen Bradley MP, 'Community Engagement Forum October 2015, list of attendees'; Commons Hansard 22 October 2010, available at: http://www.parliament.uk/business/publications/written-questions-answers-statements/written-question/Commons/2015-10-22/13090/ (accessed 4 March 2017).

34. Casey, Louise, 'The Casey Review: a review into opportunity and integration' (Department for Communities and Local Government, December 2016).

35. Cameron, Speech on extremism, 20 July 2015.

36. Op cit, pp. 15 and 101.

37. Perhaps the two points are related, since 95.5 per cent of British Muslims reside in England.

38. Counter Terrorism and Security Act 2015, Section 26.

39. There has been a proliferation of primary school and early years curriculum resources visually representing 'British values' as plates of fish and chips, images of the Queen and as red pillar boxes – perhaps not the most inclusive or critical of approaches to citizenship education.

40. Davies, Lyn, 'Security, extremism and education: safeguarding or surveillance', *British Journal of Educational Studies* 64/1 (2016), pp. 1–19.

41. An example of this organising is the 'Students not Suspects' campaign led by FOSIS, the National Union of Students and the University and College Union: www.studentsnotsuspects.com (accessed 6 March 2017). Alison Scott-Baumann unpacks how the increasingly dominant 'Prevent narrative' on British universities is, through self-censorship and no-platforming, leading to a climate of fear and severely limiting freedom of expression among many students in her 'Ideology, utopia and Islam on campus: How to free speech a little from its own terrors' Education, Citizenship and Social Justice 12/2 (2017), pp.159–176.

42. See, for example, Khan, Sara with Tony McMahon, *The Battle for British Islam: reclaiming Muslim identity from extremists* (London: Saqi, 2016), which puts forward a passionate defence of Prevent and, by extension, a scathing attack on (rather brusquely defined) 'salafi-Islamist' oriented groups that are fervently opposed to it.

43. Daesh continually makes reference to 'hijra' in its literature, including in its English language magazine, *Dabiq*, which features articles such as: 'A call to hijrah', *Dabiq* 3 (September 2014).

44. For example, see: Blundy, Rachel, 'London schoolgirl who recruited three classmates to join IS in Syria "was radicalised at east London mosque"', *Evening Standard* (2 August 2015); Wahid, Omar, 'Britain's jihadi bride groomer: schoolgirl radicalised in London mosque recruited her three classmates to join ISIS in Syria', *The Mail on Sunday*, 1 August 2015.

45. 'Response to the Mail on Sunday'; available at: www.eastlondonmosque. org.uk/news/response-mail-sunday/ (accessed 24 February 2017); and 'Statement from the families of Amira Abase, Shamima Begum and Khadiza Sultana'; available at: www.eastlondonmosque.org.uk/sites/ default/files/documents/Statement%20of%20families%2002_08_2015. pdf (accessed 24 February 2017).

46. A recent Birmingham high court ruling overturned a previous judgement imposed by the Department for Education that had given lifetime bans from the profession to two teachers implicated in the 'plot', see 'Prohibition Orders imposed on teachers at "Trojan Horse" school quashed by High Court', Doughty Street Chambers press release, 21 October 2016; available at: http://www.doughtystreet.co.uk/news/ article/prohibition-orders-imposed-on-teachers-at-trojan-horse-school- quashed-by-hi (accessed 13 February 2017). As of May 2017, the ongoing hearing has been dropped after an independent panel deemed the failure of lawyers acting for the Department of Education to disclose witness transcripts 'an abuse of process' – see Busby, Eleanor, 'Disciplinary cases against five "Trojan Horse" teachers thrown out', *Times Educational Supplement*, 30 May 2017.

47. Alderman, Geoffrey, 'Disband this body of (un)representatives', *The Jewish Chronicle*, 1 March 2002; Alibhai-Brown, Yasmin, 'Muslims can learn from this new Jewish group', *Independent*, 12 February 2007.

48. Declaration, Independent Jewish Voices; available at: http://ijv.org.uk/ declaration/ (accessed 15 June 2016).

49. Initially the Jewish Community Leadership Council, the word 'Community' was soon dropped. Cf. http://www.thejlc.org/about-us/history/ (accessed 15 June 2016).

50. Geoffrey Alderman has referred to individual members of the JLC as the 'funding fathers' of the Jewish community – in a nod to the considerable financial backing that they provide to various communal institutions. Cf. Alderman, Geoffrey, *The Communal Gadfly* (Brighton: Academic Studies Press, 2009), Section 1.

51. Op. cit.

52. Kahn-Harris and Gidley, *Turbulent Times*, pp. 154–159.

53. Rocker, Simon, 'Board vice-president's attack on JLC prompts open warfare', *The Jewish Chronicle*, 23 February 2012.

54. Commission on Women in Jewish Leadership, 'Inspiring women leaders: advancing gender equality in Jewish communal life' (JLC, 2012). It was announced in February 2017 that the Women in Jewish Leadership

270 *Notes to Pages 186–188*

project was now complete and it would be incorporated into the Board's work – see https://www.bod.org.uk/board-of-deputies-to-integrate-work-on-women-in-the-community-following-completion-of-women-in-jewish-leadership-project/ (accessed 13 February 2017).

55. Changing the Board, 'Mission statement'; available at: www.changing theboard.wordpress.com/about/ (accessed 15 June 2016).
56. Alibhai-Brown, Yasmin, 'The cloak of darkness is no exercise of civil liberties', *Independent*, 25 January 2010.
57. Muslim organisations in Britain are also profiled in pages 209–219 of this book.
58. Author's interviews with several MCB officials, all choosing to remain anonymous, October and November 2011, and with Harun Khan, current MCB Secretary General, August 2016.
59. 'Muslim Council re-elects leader, promotes female quotas', MCB press release, 11 June 2012; available at: https://web.archive.org/web/20130123165526/http://mcb.org.uk/media/presstext.php?ann_id=490 (accessed 15 June 2016).
60. See Chapter 6.
61. Goodman, Paul, 'Pickles and Warsi wrestle for control of Government strategy on anti-Muslim hatred', *Conservative Home*; available at: http://web.archive.org/web/20111121213958/http://conservativehome.blogs.com/thetorydiary/2011/11/who-is-in-charge-of-the-governments-strategy-on-anti-muslim-hatred.html (accessed 13 February 2017). Introductory correspondence between the MLP and Eric Pickles (Secretary of State for Communities and Local Government) states: 'The impetus for the formation of the MLP is the absence of a constituted body that the Government, the European Parliament and established organisations (for example, the Church of England) are able to constructively converse with on matters relating to the British Muslim community.' Letter from Iftikhar Awan, MLP Co-ordinator to Eric Pickles (3 November 2011), included in correspondence from Keith Harrison, Tackling Extremism and Hate Crime Division, DCLG to Yahya Birt, in response to the latter's freedom of information request regarding the MLP. 28 November 2012, Reference FO006322; available at: http://www.whatdotheyknow.com/request/remitmembership_of_the_muslim_le_2#incoming-336750 (accessed 15 June 2013).
62. Michael Adebolajo, one of the alleged perpetrators of the attack, is recorded to have said: 'we must fight them as they fight us ... I apologise that women had to witness this today, but in our lands our women have to see the same'. Mentioning women brought in a new dimension, as responses from EDL supporters on social media began to call for the targeting of Muslim schools and mosques, and attacks on women and children.
63. BF leader Paul Golding interviewed on the BBC's *Daily Politics* show, 15 May 2014.

64. Goodwin, Matthew, 'Forever a false dawn? Explaining the electoral collapse of the British National Party', *Parliamentary Affairs* 66/2 (April 2013), pp. 887–906.

65. Harker, Joseph, 'This is how racism takes root', *Guardian*, 22 July 2012.

66. National media outlets have been widely criticised for providing the oxygen of publicity to extremists from Muslim communities as well as the far-right. For instance, Anjem Choudary (formerly of *Al Muhajiroun*) was a guest on BBC *Newsnight* the day after the Woolwich incident (23 May 2013), and EDL leader Tommy Robinson appeared on BBC Radio 4's *Today* programme following a suspected arson attack on a mosque in Muswell Hill, London that is widely suspected to have been carried out as 'revenge' against the Woolwich killing (11 June 2013).

67. Cf. the 2013 case of six Muslim men who were convicted of plotting to carry out a gun and bomb attack on an EDL rally in Dewsbury, West Yorkshire. Peachey, Paul, 'Islamist gang of six jailed for at least 18 years each for plotting bomb attack on EDL rally', *Independent*, 10 June 2013.

68. Bunzl, Matti, *Anti-Semitism and Islamophobia: Hatreds old and new in Europe* (Chicago: Prickly Paradigm Press, 2007); Meer, Nasar and Tehseen Noorani, 'A sociological comparison of anti-Semitism and anti-Muslim sentiment in Britain', *Sociological Review* 56/2 (May 2008), pp. 195–219; Firestone, Reuven, 'Islamophobia and anti-Semitism: history and possibility', *Arches Quarterly* 4/7 (Winter 2010), pp. 42–53; Malik, Maleiha, 'Muslims are now getting the same treatment Jews had a century ago', *Guardian*, 2 February 2007.

69. Ansari, Humayun and Farid Hafez, 'Islamophobia: an introduction', in Humayun Ansari and Farid Hafez (eds), *From the Far Right to the Mainstream: Islamophobia in party politics and the media* (Frankfurt: Campus, 2012), pp. 7–28.

70. Meer and Noorani, 'A sociological comparison of anti-Semitism and anti-Muslim sentiment in Britain'.

71. Malik, 'Muslims are now getting the same treatment Jews had a century ago'.

72. See Chapter 6 on the 'Israel test', which was not the first time that the MCB protested that it was being pressured to tone down its criticism of Israel on account of appearing to condone anti-Semitism. Also, Rocker, Simon, 'Muslim Council of Britain must be boycotted until reform', *The Jewish Chronicle*, 24 September 2009, in reference to rapprochement between the government and MCB after the Daud Abdullah incident.

73. See as an example the exchange of correspondence between the MCB and the Board regarding the Jenin Massacre in 2002: Sacranie, Iqbal, 'Critics of Israel not anti-Semitic' (letter to the Editor), *The Times*, 13 May 2002, and Wagerman, Jo, 'Impact of the Middle East on Britain' (letter to the Editor), *The Times*, 22 May 2002.

74. 'Undercover Mosque', *Dispatches*, Channel 4. Broadcast on 15 January 2007. It is important to note here that anti-Semitism expressed by Muslims in a religious context is apparently far less ambiguous to detect than the Islamophobia by Jews for the simple reason that, chronologically, the Jewish faith preceded Islam, thus there are numerous historic references to Jews in the Qur'an, many of which are disingenuously or ignorantly taken as commentary on a contemporary context. Jewish scriptures do not, of course, contain references to Islam or Muslims, thus there is no possibility of the converse. However Jewish figures and groups have been accused of unduly victimising Muslims or Muslim causes on matters of political stance as well as calling into question or belittling their experiences of Islamophobia. See, for example, Julius, Anthony, *Trials of the Diaspora: a history of anti-Semitism in England* (New York: Oxford University Press, 2010), p. 536, where he accuses the MCB of Holocaust denial.

75. Cf. Lord Ahmed's recent resignation from the Labour Party on account of alleged anti-Semitic comments he made in a Pakistani television interview. Dutta, Kunal, 'Labour peer Lord Ahmed resigns from party over alleged anti-Semitic comments', *Independent*, 14 May 2013.

76. Phillips, Melanie, 'My immigrant family were proud to assimilate. I despair that too many today expect Britain to adopt THEIR culture', *Daily Mail*, 7 May 2013.

77. This relationship has been referred to several times by the CST. For example: 'Tell MAMA launched today', *CST Blog*, 21 February 2012; available at: https://cst.org.uk/news/blog/2012/02/21/tell-mama-measuring-anti-muslim-attacks-launched-today, and 'Tell MAMA – first annual report', *CST Blog*, 11 March 2013; available at: https://cst.org.uk/news/blog/2013/03/11/tell-mama-first-annual-report (both accessed 15 June 2016).

78. Malik, Maleiha, 'How can British Muslim groups better protect themselves?', *Guardian*, 11 June 2013.

79. Department for Education, 'Funding for tighter security to protect Jewish schools from anti-Semitism', press release, 8 December 2010; available at: https://www.gov.uk/government/news/funding-for-tighter-security-to-protect-jewish-schools-from-anti-semitism (accessed 15 June 2016).

80. Cameron, David, Speech to the Community Security Trust Annual Dinner, London, 18 March 2015; available at: https://www.gov.uk/government/speeches/community-security-trust-cst-prime-ministers-speech (accessed 15 June 2016).

81. 'Muslim Council of Britain welcomes steps to increase police patrols for vulnerable Islamic sites', MCB press release, 10 June 2013; available at: http://www.mcb.org.uk/muslim-council-of-britain-welcomes-steps-to-increase-police-patrols-for-vulnerable-islamic-sites/ (accessed 15 June 2016).

82. Places of Worship: Security funding scheme; available at: https://www. gov.uk/guidance/places-of-worship-security-funding-scheme (accessed 20 January 2017).

83. Correspondence from Home Office Information Rights team in response to a Freedom of Information request from the author regarding the 'Places of Worship Security Funding Scheme', 2 February 2017, available at: https://www.whatdotheyknow.com/request/384463/ response/931308/attach/html/3/42633%20response.pdf.html (accessed 13 February 2017).

84. Tell MAMA, 'Seven Infographics reflecting on 7/7/'; available at: https:// www.tellmamauk.org/wp-content/uploads/pdf/Anti-Muslim%20Hate% 20Ten%20Years%20After%207-7.pdf (accessed 13 February 2017).

85. Sayeeda Warsi recently claimed that there was a 'simmering underbelly of Islamophobia in the Conservative Party', *Nihal* BBC Asian Network, 12 May 2016.

86. Allen, Chris, 'Why Theresa May is wrong to suggest that Islamophobia is a form of extremism', *Huffington Post*, 20 June 2017; available at: http:// www.huffingtonpost.co.uk/dr-chris-allen/islamophobia_b_17214242. html (accessed 27 June 2017).

CHAPTER 8   EPILOGUE: EQUALITY AND THE FUTURE OF MUSLIM IDENTITY POLITICS IN BRITAIN

1. Parallels have been drawn between today's Muslim communities and Irish communities between the 1970s and 1990s, with both perceiving that they are viewed by the state and media, and thus segments of the public, as 'suspect' communities. As such, they feel that they are being expected to 'prove' their loyalty and 'Britishness' in a way that is not expected of others. Cf. Hickman, Mary J., '"Suspect populations": Irish communities, Muslim communities and the British justice system', in Kjartan Pal Sveinsson (ed.), *Criminal Justice v. Racial Justice: minority ethnic overrepresentation in the criminal justice system* (London: Runnymede Trust, 2012), pp. 27–29. Muslim responses to this have included the *Kafa* (Enough) Islamophobia campaign (2009), which was jointly led by the Stop the War Coalition and the BMI. Its launch statement said: 'We call for a broad-based campaign to confront the growth of racist attitudes towards Muslims and rising governmental and state harassment of Muslim citizens.' Source: 'Stop attacks on the Muslim community', available at: https://web.archive.org/web/20160120024836/http://stop-war.org.uk/images//kafa_statement.pdf (accessed 22 May 2017). Also 'Schedule 7 stories', a website run by the advocacy group, Cage, to document and raise awareness around 'the experiences of suspect communities at UK ports', see: http://schedule7stories.com/ (accessed 15 June 2016).

2. See Chapter 4.
3. For example, see the Alternative Leveson Inquiry into the practise and reporting of Muslim and Islamic affairs. This was launched as a response to the ongoing Leveson Inquiry into the culture, practice and ethics of the press, which was initiated in the wake of the phone-hacking scandal of July 2011. The Alternative Leveson argues that 'The Leveson Inquiry has failed to adequately address the negative media coverage relating to Muslims and Islam. The reason an alternative inquiry is necessary to investigate what many regard as widespread and systematic discriminatory practises in reporting on Muslims and Islam in the British media.' Source: 'Background', *The Alternative Leveson*; available at: http://web.archive.org/web/20120324163906/http://www.alternativeleveson.org.uk/?page_id = 13 (accessed 15 June 2016). Also, Hasan, Mehdi, 'We mustn't allow Muslims in public life to be silenced', *Guardian*, 8 July 2012.
4. UK Action Committee on Islamic Affairs, *Muslims and the Law in Multi-Faith Britain: need for reform* (London: UK Action Committee on Islamic Affairs, 1993).
5. Malik, Kenan, *From Fatwa to Jihad: the Rushdie affair and its legacy* (London: Atlantic: 2009). This is a view which was given extensive airing in the press by Andrew Gilligan, e.g., Gilligan, Andrew, 'The truth about the "wave of attacks on Muslims" after Woolwich murder', *Daily Telegraph*, 1 June 2013, in which he refers to an 'Islamophobia industry', for whom 'the narrative of British Muslims under attack, increasingly hated and feared by their fellow citizens, is essential for recruitment' (to Islamism).
6. Modood, Tariq, *Multiculturalism: a civic idea* (Cambridge: Polity, 2007), p. 136.
7. Ibid.
8. Ibid., pp. 139–142.
9. Sir Iqbal Sacranie's valedictory speech to the MCB AGM in 2006.
10. There are countless examples, including among others: The Black Muslim Times: https://theblackmuslimtimesuk.org/; Making Herstory: www.makingherstory.org.uk; the Muslim Women's Collective; and the Inclusive Mosque Initiative: www.inclusivemosqueinitiative.org (all links accessed 30 June 2017).
11. 'About us – Hope not Hate'; available at: http://hopenothate.org.uk/about-us/ (accessed 22 May 2017).
12. Cox, Brendan, 'Jo Cox always loved a good party. Let's honour her with a massive celebration of Britain's diversity and unity', *The Telegraph*, 22 February 2017.
13. Julie Siddiqi, comment in a Muslim women's Facebook discussion group, 16 May 2017, reproduced here with permission.
14. For examples relating to the 2017 General Election see: MEND, *Muslim Manifesto 2017* (London: MEND, May 2017), and MCB, *Fairness not*

Favours: British Muslim perspectives at the 2015 General Election (London: MCB, March 2015, reissued in May 2017). It is worth noting here that these manifestos are not a unique feature of Muslim communal organisations – the Board of Deputies of British Jews also regularly publishes similar documents, see Board of Deputies of British Jews, *The Jewish Manifesto* (London: BOD, June 2016).

15. Muslims for Change, *Make your voice heard in the 2017 UK elections* https://www.launchgood.com/project/make_your_voice_heard__2017_uk_elections#/ (accessed 22 May 2017).

16. Ibid.

17. See Grenfell Legal Support; available at: www.grenfell-legalsupport.org (accessed 30 June 2017), which offers 'support on a universal, multi-ethnic, multi-faith basis'.

18. See Eden Care, London Grenfell Tower Fire update; available at: http://www.edencareuk.com/london-grenfell-tower-fire/ (accessed 30 June 2017).

19. See Grenfell Tower Disaster; available at: https://www.nzf.org.uk/News/ViewArticle/4209 (accessed 30 June 2017).

20. Shannahan, Dervla Sara, 'Gender, inclusivity and UK mosque experiences', *Contemporary Islam* 8/1 (2014), pp. 1–16.

21. Commission on Religion and Belief in British Public Life (CORAB), *Living with Difference: community, diversity and the common good* (Cambridge: Woolf Institute, 2015).

Bibliography

CORRESPONDENCE

Correspondence from the Cabinet Office in response to a Freedom of Information request from Yahya Birt regarding the Community Engagement Forum; available at: https://www.whatdotheyknow.com/request/296826/ response/735065/attach/3/FOI321889%20Reply.pdf (accessed 4 March 2017).

Correspondence from Home Office Information Rights team in response to a Freedom of Information request from the author regarding the 'Places of Worship Security Funding Scheme', 2 February 2017; available at: https:// www.whatdotheyknow.com/request/384463/response/931308/attach/ html/3/42633%20response.pdf.html (accessed 13 February 2017).

Correspondence from Lucy Hughes, Head, Prevent Team CTD at the FCO to Graeme Breen, in response to the latter's Freedom of Information request regarding FCO involvement with the Quilliam Foundation and the PBM project. 10 May 2010, Reference 0238–10; available at: http://www.whatdotheyknow. com/request/30412/response/85454/attach/html/5/0238%202010Breen%20 letter%20final.doc.html (accessed 14 June 2016).

Butler, Judith, *et al* 'The government is hijacking LGBT+ sex education to bolster its counterterrorism strategy – it must stop now' Letters, *Independent*, 5 September 2019.

Letter from George Galloway MP, 'Alarm bells over terror conviction', *Guardian*, 24 April 2008.

Letter from Harun Khan to Brandon Lewis, Chairman of the Conservative Party, 30 May 2018. Available at: https://mcb.org.uk/wpcontent/uploads/2018/06/ BrandonLewis_ConservativeChair-Islamophobia_30May2018.docx.pdf (accessed 10 September 2019).

Letter from Iftikhar Awan, MLP Co-ordinator to Eric Pickles (3 November 2011), included in correspondence from Keith Harrison, Tackling Extremism and

Hate Crime Division, DCLG to Yahya Birt, in response to the latter's freedom of information request regarding the MLP.28 November 2012, Reference FO006322; available at: http://www.whatdotheyknow.com/request/remitmembership_of_the_muslim_le_2# incoming-336750 (accessed 15 June 2013).

Letter from Peter Tatchell of Out Rage! to Sir Iqbal Sacranie, quoted in: 'Muslim leader urged: drop homophobia. Gay group calls for solidarity agains intolerance' available at: http://www.petertatchell.net/religion/muslim-leader.htm (accessed 14 June 2016).

Open letter to Prime Minister Tony Blair from Muslim parliamentarians and community leaders: 'Protect Citizens, wherever they are' text available at: http://www.yahyabirt.co.uk/?p=120 (accessed 15 June 2013).

Robinson, Mike, Editor, BBC Panorama, 'Response to MCB complaints', 30 September 2005; available at: http://news.bbc.co.uk/2/hi/programmes/panorama/4297490.stm (accessed 13 February 2017).

Rt Hon Hazel Blears MP's letter to Dr Abdul Bari, MCB Secretary General, dated 13 March 2009.

Shaista Gohir's open resignation letter to Home Secretary John Denham, 6 April 2010; available at: http://wallscometumblingdown.wordpress.com/2010/04/08/founder-quits-national-muslim-womens-advisory-group-in-protest/ (accessed 14 June 2016).

DOCUMENTS, PAMPHLETS AND REPORTS

Article 19, 'Submission to the 91st Session of the UN Human Rights Committee on Respect for Freedom of Expression in the UK and Northern Ireland' (October 2007).

'A call to hijrah', *Dabiq* (3 September 2014).

Board of Deputies of British Jews, *The Jewish Manifesto* (London: BOD, June 2016).

C3ubeTrainingandConsultancy, Voices from the Minarets (London: MCB, 2006).

Casey, Louise, 'The Casey Review: a review into opportunity and integration' (London: Department for Communities and Local Government, December 2016).

Changing the Board, 'Mission statement'; available at: www.changingtheboard.wordpress.com/about/ (accessed 15 June 2016).

Clarke, Peter, 'Report into allegations concerning Birmingham schools arising from the "Trojan horse letter"' (House of Commons, 22 July 2014).

Commission on British Muslims and Islamophobia, *Islamophobia: issues, challenges and action* (London: Runnymede Trust, 2004).

Commission on Religion and Belief in British Public Life (CORAB), *Living with Difference: community, diversity and the common good* (Cambridge: Woolf Institute, 2015).

Commission on Women in Jewish Leadership, *Inspiring Women Leaders: advancing gender equality in Jewish communal life* (London: JLC, 2012).

Conservative Party Group on National and International Security, *Uniting the Country* (2007).

Deen International, 'I am the West – project synopsis'; available at: http://www.deeninternational.co.uk/downloads/i-am-the-west.pdf (accessed 21 November 2011).

Doughty Street Chambers, 'Prohibition Orders imposed on teachers at "Trojan Horse" school quashed by High Court', press release, 21 October 2016; available at: http://www.doughtystreet.co.uk/news/article/prohibi- tion-orders-imposed-on-teachers-at-trojan-horse-school-quashed-by-hi (accessed 13 February 2017).

East London Mosque, 'Response to the *Mail on Sunday*'; available at: www.eastlondonmosque.org.uk/news/response-mail-sunday/ (accessed 24 February 2017).

Equality and Diversity Forum, minutes of meeting held on 18 January 2006 in London; available at: www.edf.org.uk/publications/MinsJan06Mtg.doc (accessed 14 June 2013).

Forum Against Islamophobia and Racism (FAIR), Log of reported Islamophobic incidents in the UK between 11 September 2001 and 18 January 2005; available at: http://www.fairuk.org/research/ FAIR uk-Research Data-Islamophobic Incident Log.pdf (accessed 16 June 2013).

———, *The Religious Offences Bill 2002: a response* (October 2002).

Great Britain Foreign and Common wealth Office and Great Britain Home Office, 'Draft Report on Young Muslims and Extremism' (April2004); available at: http://www.globalsecurity.org/security/library/report/2004/ muslimext-uk.htm (accessed 17 June 2017).

Great Britain. Home Office, 'The Counter-terrorism strategy 'available at: http://www.homeoffice.gov.uk/counter-terrorism/uk-counter-terrorism- strat/ (accessed 3 November 2011).

Great Britain. Parliament. House of Commons. Home Affairs Committee, 'The Macpherson Report–ten years on' (14July2009); available at: http:// www.publications.parliament.uk/pa/cm200809/cmselect/cmhaff/427/42702.htm#evidence (accessed 5 August 2013).

Independent Jewish Voices, *Declaration*; available at: http://ijv.org.uk/declaration/ (accessed 15 June 2016).

Labour Party, *Forward not Back* (General Election Manifesto) (2005). HM Government, 'Prevent Strategy' (July 2011).

———, 'Pursue, Prevent, Protect, Prepare: the UK strategy for countering international terrorism', *Annual Report* (March 2010).

MCB *Fairness not Favours: British Muslim perspectives at the 2015 General Election* (London: MCB, March 2015, reissued in May 2017). MEND, *Muslim Manifesto 2017* (London: MEND, May 2017).

Muslim Council of Britain, The Muslim Council of Britain–its structure, history and workings (London: MCB, 2002).

Muslim Educational Trust, *Issues in Islamic Education* (London: MET, 1996).

Muslim leaders' declaration on 7/7 bombings; available at: http://news.bbc.co.uk/1/hi/uk_politics/4696969.stm (accessed 14 June 2016).

Muslim Parliament of Great Britain, *White Paper on Muslim Education in Great Britain* (London: Muslim Parliament of Great Britain, 1992).

———, *The Muslim Parliament of Great Britain: Structure and Procedures of a Minority Political System* (London: Muslim Parliament of Great Britain, 1991).

———, *The Muslim Manifesto* (London: Muslim Parliament of Great Britain, 1990).

National Muslim Education Council, *Religious Education: a Muslim perspective* (London: NMEC, 1997).

National Union of Students, 'Spying on Campus', motion passed at NUS Conference, May 2008.

Pickersgill, Peter, *Normative Islam Report* (London: 5 Pillars, 2016).

Rimmer, Stephen, 'Allegations made in the *Panorama* programme "Muslim First – British Second "on Monday16thFebruary',statement from the Office for Security and Counter Terrorism, 17 February 2009.

Siddiqui, Kalim, *The Muslim Parliament of Great Britain: Political Innovation and Adaptation* (London: Muslim Parliament of Great Britain, 1992).

'A statement by the religious scholars and proselytisers (*du'at*) of the Islamic Nation (*ummah*) to all rulers and peoples concerning events in Gaza' (commonly referred to as The Istanbul Declaration); available at: http:// www.hurryupharry.org/wpcontent/uploads/2009/03/istpdf.pdf (accessed 15 June 2016).

'Statement from the families of Amira Abase, Shamima Begum and Khadiza Sultana';availableat:www.eastlondonmosque.org.uk/sites/default/files/ documents/Statement%20of%20families%2002_08_2015.pdf (accessed 24 February 2017).

Tell MAMA, Normalising Hatred', Tell MAMA Annual Report 2018

UK Action Committee on Islamic Affairs, *Muslims and the Law in Multi-Faith Britain: need for reform* (London: UK Action Committee on Islamic Affairs, 1993).

Warraich, Shaukat and Ifath Nawaz (eds), *'Preventing Extremism Together'* Working Groups Report (London: Home Office, 2005).

LEGAL SOURCES

Mandla v. Dowell Lee (1983) 2 AC 548, HL, 565.

R. v. Choudary and Rahman (2016) T20150301, CCC.

R. v. Faraz (2012), Crim 2820, EWCA 201200251, C5.

R. v. Faraz – Testimony of Matthew 'Tariq' Wilkinson for the prosecution; transcript available at: http://web.archive.org/web/20150102003123/http://www. cageprisoners.com/learn more/legal-issues/item/2922-r-v-faraz-testimony-of-matthew-tariq-wilkinson-for-the-prosecution-day-1 (accessed 20 May 2017).

Seide v. Gilette Industries Ltd. (1980) IRLR 427.

Anti-Terrorism, Crime and Security Act 2001.

Crime and Disorder Act 1998.

The Proscribed Organisations (Name Changes) Order 2010.

Race Relations Act 1968. Race
Relations Act 1976.

Racial and Religious Hatred Act 2006.

Terrorism Act 2000.

Terrorism Act 2006.

SPEECHES

Atkinson, Rowan, 'Every Joke Has a Victim', speech delivered at the House of Commons, 30 January 2006, transcript available at: http://www.guardian.co.uk/politics/2006/jan/30/immigrationpolicy.religion (accessed 13 June 2016).

Blair, Tony, 'Prime minister's statement on anti-terror measures', 5 August 2005; available at: http://www.guardian.co.uk/politics/2005/aug/05/uksecurity.terrorism1 (accessed 14 June 2016).

——, Speech to House of Commons, 14 September 2001; available at: http://www.guardian.co.uk/politics/2001/sep/14/houseofcommons.uk1 (accessed 13 June 2016).

——, Statement on9/11,12September2001; available at: http://www.guardian.co.uk/politics/2001/sep/12/politicalnews.september111 (accessed 13 June 2016).

Cameron, David, Speech on extremism, Ninestiles Academy, Birmingham, 20 July 2015; available at: https://www.gov.uk/government/speeches/extremism-pm-speech (accessed 15 June 2016).

——, Speech to the Community Security Trust Annual Dinner, London, 18 March 2015; available at: https://www.gov.uk/government/speeches/community-security-trust-cst-prime-ministers-speech (accessed 15 June 2016).

——, Speech at Munich Security Conference, 5 February 2011; available at: http://www.number10.gov.uk/news/pms-speech-at-munich-security-conference/ (accessed 15 June 2016).

Kelly, Ruth, 'Britain: our values, our responsibilities', speech to Muslim organisations on working together to tackle extremism, London, 11 October 2006; archived at: http://webarchive.nationalarchives.gov.uk/+/http:/www.communities.gov.uk/staging/index.asp?id=1503690 (accessed 26 June 2017).

Khan, Sadiq, 'Being a British Muslim', speech delivered to the Fabian Society, in London, 3 July 2006; archived at: http://web.archive.org/web/20091123163018/http://fabians.org.uk/events/event-reports/missing-a-positive-vision-for-british-muslims (accessed 14 June 2016).

Khan Sara, speech delivered at Coin Street Community Centre, London, 19 July 2019. Transcript available at: https://www.gov.uk/government/speeches/lead-commissionners-speech-on-a-positive-vision-for-countering-extremism (accessed 9 September 2019).

Phillips, Trevor, 'After7/7: Sleep walking into Segregation', speech delivered at Manchester University, 22 September 2005; available at: https://www.jiscmail.ac.uk/cgi-bin/webadmin?A3=ind0509&L=CRONEM&E=quoted printable&P=60513&B=——_%3D_NextPart_001_01C5C28A.09501783&T=text%2Fhtml; %20charset=iso-8859-1&pending= (accessed 14 June 2016).

Ramadan, *Tariq, Faith and Free Speech: defamation of religions and freedom of expression*, speech delivered at PEN America Conference, UN Headquarters, New York, 16 September 2010; available at: https://www.youtube.com/watch?v=E7DC0spr5Gg (accessed 26 June 2017).

Sacranie, Iqbal, valedictory speech to the MCB Annual General Meeting, London, 4 June 2006; available at: http://www.mcb.org.uk/uploads/ SECGEN.pdf (accessed 24 July 2012).

Siddiqui, Kalim, *Generating Power without Politics: Speech by Kalim Siddiqui at a One-Day Conference on the Future of Muslims in Britain, London, 14 July 1990* (London: Muslim Institute, 1992).

Warsi, Sayeeda, 'My Faith', *Sir Sigmund Sternberg Interfaith Lecture* delivered at Leicester University, 20 January 2011; available at: https://sayeedawarsi.com/2011/01/20/university-of-leicester-sir-sigmund-sternberg-lecture/ (accessed 26 June 2017).

ARTICLES, BOOKS, AND RADIO & TV TRANSCRIPTS

Aaronovitch, David, 'Is this the reaction of a grown-up religion?' *The Times*, 20 September 2012.

Abbas, Tahir, 'The "Trojan Horse" plot and the fear of Muslim power in British state schools', *Journal of Muslim Minority Affairs* (pre-print, published online 17 April 2017).

——, *Islamic Radicalism and Multicultural Politics* (London: Routledge, 2011).

——, 'British South Asian Muslims: before and after September 11, in Tahir Abbas (ed.), *Muslim Britain: communities under pressure* (London: Zed Books, 2005), pp. 3–17.

——, ed., *Muslim Britain: communities under pressure* (London: Zed Books, 2005).

Abdul Bari, Muhammad, 'London 2012: a celebration of Britain's diversity', *Huffington Post UK*, 21 February 2012; available at: http://www.huffingtonpost.co.uk/muhammad-abdul-bari/olympics-london-2012-a-celebration_b_1292015.html (accessed 14 June 2016).

Abdullah, Daud, 'My reply to Hazel Blears', *Guardian*, 26 March 2009.

Ahsan, M.M. and A.R. Kidwai, *Sacrilege versus Civility: Muslim perspectives on the Satanic Verses affair* (Mark field: Islamic Foundation, 1993).

Akhtar, Parveen, '"(Re)turn to religion" and Radical Islam', in Tahir Abbas (ed.), *Muslim Britain: communities under pressure* (London: Zed Books, 2005), pp. 164–176.

Akhtar, Shabbir, *The Muslim Parents' Handbook: what every Muslim parent should know* (London: Ta-Ha Publishers, 1993).

——, *Be Careful with Muhammad: the Salman Rushdie affair* (London: Bellew, 1989).

Alderman, Geoffrey, *The Communal Gadfly* (Brighton, MA: Academic Studies Press, 2009).

——, 'Hazel Blears must back down', *Guardian: Comment is Free*, 25 March 2009.

——, 'Disband this body of (un)representatives', *The Jewish Chronicle*, 1 March 2002.

Ali, Sundas, *British Muslims in Numbers: a demographic, socio-economic and health profile of Muslims in Britain drawing on the 2011 Census* (London: Muslim Council of Britain, 2015).

Alibhai-Brown, Yasmin, 'The cloak of darkness is no exercise of civil liberties', *Independent*, 25 January 2010.

———, 'Muslims can learn from this new Jewish group', *Independent*, 12 February 2007.

Allen, Chris, 'Why Theresa May is wrong to suggest that Islamophobia is a form of extremism', Huffington *Post*, 20 June 2017; available at: http://www.huffingtonpost.co.uk/dr-chris-allen/islamophobia_b_17214242. html (accessed 27 June 2017)

———, *Islamophobia* (Farnham: Ashgate, 2010).

———, 'K.I.S.S–Keeping Islamophobia Simple and Stupid', available at www.drchrisallen.uk (28 April 2008) (accessed 15 June 2016).

———, 'The first decade of Islamophobia', available at www.drchrisallen.uk (5 July 2007).

———, 'From race to religion: the new form of discrimination', in Tahir Abbas (ed.), *Muslim Britain: communities under pressure* (London: Zed Books, 2005), pp. 49–65.

———, *Fair Justice: the Bradford Disturbances, the Sentencing and the Impact* (London: FAIR, 2003).

Allen, Chris and Arshad Isakjee, 'Controversy, Islam and politics: an exploration of the "Innocence of Muslims" affair through the eyes of British Muslim elites', *Ethnic and Racial Studies* 38/11 (2015), pp. 1852–1867.

Allen, Chris and Surinder Guru, 'Between political fad and political empowerment: a critical evaluation of the National Muslim Women's Advisory Group (NMWAG) and governmental processes of engaging Muslim women', *Sociological Research Online* 17/3 (2012); available at http://www.socresonline.org.uk/17/3/17.html (accessed 26 June 2017).

Al-Rasheed, Madawi, 'Saudi religious transnationalism in London', in Madawi Al-Rasheed (ed.), *Transnational Connections and the Arab Gulf* (Abingdon: Routledge, 2005), pp. 149–167.

Amin, Mohammed, 'The Muslim Council of Britain's need for constitutional reform', 20 January 2011; available at: http://www.mohammedamin.com/Community_issues/MCB-constitutional-reform.html (accessed 14 June 2016).

Ansari, Humayun, 'The multiculturalism backlash and the mainstreaming of Islamophobia post-9/11', in J. Wolffe (ed.), *Irish Religious Conflict in Comparative Perspective: Catholics, Protestants, and Muslims* (Basingstoke: Palgrave, 2014), pp. 169–190.

———, ed., *The Making of the East London Mosque 1910–1951–minutes of the London Mosque Fund and the East London Mosque Trust Ltd.* (Cambridge: Cambridge University Press, 2011).

———, *The Infidel Within: Muslims in Britain since 1800* (London: C. Hurst, 2004).

Ansari, Humayun and Farid Hafez, 'Islamophobia: an introduction', in Humayun Ansari and Farid Hafez (eds), *From the Far Right to the Mainstream: Islamophobia in party politics and the media* (Frankfurt: Campus, 2012), pp. 7–28.

Anthony, Andrew, *The Fallout: how a guilty liberal lost his innocence* (London: Jonathan Cape, 2007).

Anwar, Muhammad, 'Issues, policy and practice', in Tahir Abbas (ed.), *Muslim Britain: communities under pressure* (London: Zed Books, 2005), pp. 31–46.

———, The *Myth of Return: Pakistanis in Britain* (London: Heinemann Educational, 1979).

Asad, Talal, 'Freedom of speech and religious limitations', in Craig Calhoun, Mark Jurgensmeyer and Jonathan Van Antwerpen (eds), *Rethinking Secularism* (New York: Oxford University Press, 2011), pp. 282–297.

———, 'Free speech, blasphemy and secular criticism', in Talal Asad et al., Is Critique Secular? Blasphemy, Injury and Free Speech (Berkeley, CA: University of California Press, 2009), pp. 14–57.

———, 'Multiculturalism and British identity in the wake of the Rushdie Affair', *Politics and Society*, 18/4 (1990), pp. 455–480.

Atkinson, Nathan, 'Bradford Literature Festival has 15 withdrawals over fund source' *Telegraph and Argus*, 26 June 2019.

Barendt, Eric, 'Incitement to, and glorification of, terrorism', in Ivan Hare and James Weinstein (eds), *Extreme Speech and Democracy* (Oxford: Oxford University Press, 2009), pp. 445–462.

Barry, Brian, *Culture and Equality: an egalitarian critique of multiculturalism* (London: Polity, 2001).

BBC HARD*talk*, BBC News Channel, 13 December 2010.

BBC *Question Time*, BBC 1, 25 May 2017.

Bernstein, Mary, 'Identity politics', Annual *Review of Sociology* 31(2005), pp. 47–74.

Binyon, Michael, 'Grand Mufti claim highlights the pros and cons of Islam's lack of ecclesiastical hierarchies', *The Times* (28 January 2011).

Birt, Jonathan, 'The radical nineties revisited: Jihadi discourses in Britain', in Madawi Al-Rasheed and Marat Shterin (eds), *Dying for Faith: religiously motivated violence in the contemporary world* (London: I.B. Tauris, 2009), pp. 105–110.

———, 'Wahhabism in the United Kingdom–manifestations and reactions', in Madawi Al-Rasheed (ed.), *Transnational Connections and the Arab Gulf* (Abingdon: Routledge, 2005), pp. 168–184.

———, 'Lobbying and marching: British Muslims and the state', in Tahir Abbas (ed.), *Muslims in Britain: communities under pressure* (London: Zed Books, 2005), pp. 92–106.

Birt, Yahya, 'Astroturfing and the rise of the secular security state in Britain' Medium, 17 August 2019, available at: https://medium.com/@yahyabirt/astroturfing-and-the-rise-of-the-secular-security-state-in-britain-cd21c5005d43 (accessed 28 August 2019).

———, 'Preachers, patriots and Islamists: contemporary British Muslims and the afterlives of Abdullah Quilliam', in Ron Geaves and Jamie Gilham (eds), *Victorian Muslim: Abdullah Quillliam and Islam in the West* (London: Hurst, 2017), pp. 133–150.

———, 'Defining Islamophobia today: the state of the art' (15 September 2009); available at http://www.yahyabirt.co.uk/?p=175 (accessed 13 June 2016).

————, 'The next ten years: an open letter to the MCB', *emel magazine* 46 (July 2008).

Bleich, Erik, *Race Politics in Britain and France: ideas and policymaking since the 1960s* (Cambridge: Cambridge University Press, 2003).

Blundy, Rachel, 'London schoolgirl who recruited three classmates to join IS in Syria "was radicalised at east London mosque"', *Evening Standard* (2 August 2015).

Bodi, Faisal, 'Opportunistic cronies', *Guardian* (13 November 2001).

Booso, Andrew, *'Review of The Islamist'*, *The Translators* (21 May 2007); available at: http://thetranslators1.wordpress.com/2007/05/21/review-of-%E2%80%9Cthe-islamist%E2%80%9D-ust-andrew-booso-complete/ (accessed 15 June 2013).

Bowen, John R, *Blaming Islam* (Cambridge, MA: MIT Press, 2012).

'Bradford Muslims' 5-point plea on children's schools', *The Times*, 7 January 1974.

Breen, Damian and Nasar Meer, 'Securing whiteness?: Critical Race Theory (CRT) and the securitization of Muslims in education' *Identities* 26:5 (2019) pp. 595-613.

Briggs, Rachel, Catherine Fieschi and Hannah Lownsbrough, *Bringing It Home: community-based approaches to counter-terrorism* (London: Demos, 2006).

Bright, Martin, *When Progressives Treat with Reactionaries: the British state's flirtation with radical Islamism* (London: Policy Exchange, 2006).

————, 'Radical links of UK's "moderate" Muslim group', *Observer* (14 August 2005).

Brittain, Victoria and Asim Qureshi, 'Banning books in Britain, fifty years after Lady Chatterley', *Open Democracy* (17 December 2011); available at: http://www.opendemocracy.net/ourkingdom/victoria-brittain-asim-   qureshi/banning-books-in-britain-fifty-years-after-lady-chatterley(accessed 14 June 2016).

Brown, Alex, 'The Racial and Religious Hatred Act: a Millian response', *Critical Review of International Social and Political Philosophy* (CRISPP) 11/1 (March 2008), pp. 1–24.

Brown, Wendy, *States of Injury: power and freedom in late modernity* (Princeton, NJ: Princeton University Press, 1995).

Bunglawala, Inayat, Mohammed Amin resigns from the MCB' available at: http://inayatscorner.wordpress.com/2010/06/22/mohammed-amin- resigns-from-the-mcb/ 22nd June 2010 (accessed 14 June 2016).

————, 'MINAB:Communityinitiative,orquango?' *Guardian:CommentisFree*(15May 2009); availableat: http://www.guardian.co.uk/commentisfree/belief/2009/may/15/minab-mosques-imams-islam?INTCMP=ILCNETTXT3487(accessed 14 June 2016).

Bunting, Madeleine, 'The MCB's wonder land election', *Guardian* (18June 2010).

————, 'Throwing mud at Muslims', *Guardian* (22 August 2005).

Bunzl, Matti, *Anti-Semitism and Islamophobia: hatred sold and new in Europe* (Chicago: Prickly Paradigm Press, 2007).

Busby, Eleanor, 'Disciplinary cases against five "Trojan Horse" teachers thrown out', *Times Educational Supplement* (30 May 2017).

Cameron, David, 'British values aren't optional, they' revital', *The Mail on Sunday* (14 June 2014).

Cesarani, David, 'The changing character of citizenship and nationality in Britain', in David Cesarani and Mary Fulbrook (eds), *Citizenship, Nationality and Migration in Europe* (London: Routledge, 1996), pp. 57–73.

——, *The Jewish Chronicle and Anglo-Jewry, 1841–1991* (Cambridge: Cambridge University Press, 1994).

——, *The Making of Modern Anglo-Jewry* (Oxford: Basil Blackwell, 1990).

Cesari, Jocelyne and Sean McLoughlin, *European Muslims and the Secular State* (Aldershot: Ashgate, 2005).

Choudhury,Tufyal,'Comparative perspectives on discrimination law',in Yunas Samad and Kasturi Sen (eds), *Islam and the European Union: transnationalism, youth and the War on Terror* (Karachi: Oxford University Press, 2007), pp. 186–197.

——, 'The Terrorism Act 2006: discouraging terrorism', in Ivan Hare and James Weinstein (eds), *Extreme Speech and Democracy* (Oxford: Oxford University Press, 2009), pp. 463–487.

Clark, Michael, *Albion and Jerusalem: the Anglo-Jewish community in the post-emancipation era, 1858–1887* (Oxford: Oxford University Press, 2009).

Cohen, Nick, *What's Left?: how liberals lost their way* (London: Fourth Estate, 2007).

Commission for Countering Extremism, 'Our academic papers on extremism' *CCE Blog*, 7 October 2019, available at: https://extremismcommission.blog.gov.uk/2019/10/07/our-academic-papers-on-extremism/ (accessed 7 October 2019).

Cox, Brendan, 'Jo Cox always loved a good party. Let's honour her with a massive celebration of Britain's diversity and unity', *The Telegraph* (22 February 2017).

Davies, Lyn, 'Security, extremism and education: safeguarding or surveillance', *British Journal of Educational Studies* 64/1 (2016), pp. 1–19.

Department for Education, 'Funding for tighter security to protect Jewish schools from anti-Semitism', press release, 8 December 2010; available at: https://www.gov.uk/government/news/funding-for-tighter-security-to-protect-jewish-schools-from-anti-semitism (accessed 15 June 2016).

Derfoufi, Zin, 'MI5: leave young Muslims alone', *Guardian* (26 May 2009).

Deveaux, Monique, *Cultural Pluralism and Dilemmas of Justice* (Ithaca, NY: Cornell University Press, 2000).

Dispatches, 'Undercover Mosque', Channel 4, 15 January 2007.

Dispatches, 'What Muslims want', Channel 4, 7 August 2006.

Dispatches, 'Who speaks for Muslims?', Channel 4, July 2006.

Dodd, Vikram, 'MPs investigate anti-extremism programme after spying claims', *Guardian*, 18 October 2009.

——, 'Muslim Council accuses government of undermining independence', *Guardian*, 26 March 2009.

Dodd, Vikram and Hugh Muir, 'Senior Muslims tried to reverse Holocaust Memorial Day snub', *Guardian*, 27 January 2007.

Dougary, Ginny, Interview with Martin Amis, *The Times Magazine*, 9 September 2006.

Dutta, Kunal, 'Labour peer Lord Ahmed resigns from party over alleged anti-Semitic comments', *Independent*, 14 May 2013.

Eatwell, Roger, 'Responses to the extreme Right in Britain', in Eatwell, R. and M.J. Goodwin (eds), *The New Extremism in 21st Century Britain* (Abingdon: Routledge, 2010), pp. 211–231.

Elmarsafy, Ziad, *The Enlightenment Qur'an: the politics of translation and the construction of Islam* (Oxford: Oneworld, 2009).

Elshayyal, Khadijah, *Scottish Muslims in Numbers: understanding Scotland's Muslims through the 2011 census* (Edinburgh: The Alwaleed Centre, 2016).

Emmanuel, C., *A Century and a Half of Jewish History* (London: Routledge, 1910).

Endelman, Todd M., *The Jews of Britain, 1656 to 2000* (Berkeley, CA: University of California Press, 2002).

Evans, Rob and Paul Lewis, 'Police "smear" campaign targeted Stephen Lawrence's friends and family', *Guardian*, 23 June 2013.

Faruqi, M.H., 'Muslims and Britain', in M. Manazir Ahsan and Abdur Raheem Kidwai (eds), *Sacrilege versus Civility* (Markfield: Islamic Foundation, 1993), pp. 193–199.

Favell, Adrian, *Philosophies of Integration: immigration and the idea of citizenship in France and Britain* (Basingstoke: Palgrave, 2001).

Firestone, Reuven, 'Islamophobia and anti-Semitism: history and possibility', *Arches Quarterly* 4/7 (Winter 2010), pp. 42–53.

Francois-Cerrah, Myriam, 'Demonstrating for dignity: why are Muslims so enraged?', *Huffington Post*,18 September 2012; available at: http:// www. huffingtonpost.co.uk/myriam-francois/demonstrating-for-dignity_b_1885020.html (accessed 13 June 2016).

Fraser, Nancy, 'From redistribution to recognition? Dilemmas of justice in a "post-socialist" age', *New Left Review* I/212 (July–August 1995), pp. 68–93.

Fraser, Nancy and Axel Honneth, *Redistribution or Recognition? A Political-Philosophical Exchange* (London: Verso, 2003).

Galeotti, Anna E., *Toleration as Recognition* (Cambridge: Cambridge University Press, 2002).

Garbin, David, 'A diasporic sense of place: dynamics of spatialization and transnational political fields among Bangladeshi Muslims in Britain', in M.P. Smith and J. Eade (eds), *Transnational Ties: cities, identities and migrations* (London: Transaction Publishers, 2009), pp. 1–10.

Garcia, Humberto, *Islam and the English Enlightenment, 1670–1840* (Baltimore, MD: Johns Hopkins University Press, 2012).

Geaves, Ron, *Islam in Victorian Britain: the life and times of Abdullah Quilliam* (Leicester: Kube, 2010).

———, 'The reproduction of Jamaat-I Islami in Britain',*Islam and Christian- Muslim Relations* 6/2 (1995), pp. 187–210.

Gilliat-Ray, Sophie, *Muslims in Britain: an introduction* (Cambridge: Cambridge University Press, 2010).

Gilligan, Andrew and Richard Kerbaj, 'Muslim advisers hit by anti-Semitism row' *The Sunday Times*, 5 May 2019.

Gilligan, Andrew,'The truth about the "wave of attacks on Muslims" after Woolwich murder', *Daily Telegraph*, 1 June 2013.

Gledhill, Ruth, 'Muslim task force attacks Government anti-terror plans', *The Times*, 10 November 2005.

Gohir, Shaista, 'Muslim women are not political pawns', *Guardian: Comment is Free*, 9 April 2009; available at:http://www.guardian.co.uk/commentisfree/2010/apr/09/government-failed-muslim-women?INTCMP=ILC-   NETTXT3487 (accessed 14 June 2016).

Goodall, Kay, 'Incitement to religious hatred: all talk and no substance?', *Modern Law Review* 70/1 (2007), pp. 89–113.

Goodman, Paul, 'Pickles and Warsi wrestle for control of Government strategy on anti-Muslim hatred', *Conservative Home*, 19 November 2011; available at: http://web.archive.org/web/20111121213958/http://conservativehome.blogs.com/thetorydiary/2011/11/who-is-in-charge-of-the-governments-strategy-on-anti-muslim-hatred.html (accessed 13 February 2017).

Goodman, Paul, *Zionism in England, 1899–1929*(London: English Zionist Federation, 1930).

Goodwin, Matthew 'What lies behind the spectacular collapse of the British far-right' *New Statesman*, 10 February 2014.

Goodwin, Matthew J., 'Forever a false dawn? Explaining the electoral collapse of the British National Party', *Parliamentary Affairs* 66/2, April 2013, pp. 887–906.

———, 'In Search of the winning formula: Nick Griffin and the "modernisation" of the British National Party', in R. Goodwin and M.J. Eatwell (eds), *The New Extremism in 21st Century Britain* (Abingdon: Routledge, 2010), pp. 169–190.

———, 'The BNP and Islam' Elections 2010 blog hosted by the University of Nottingham School of Politics and International Relations; available at: http://electionblog2010.blogspot.co.uk/2010/04/bnp-and-islam.html (accessed 26 June 2017).

Gough, J.W., *John Locke's Political Philosophy: eight studies* (Oxford: Clarendon Press, 1973).

Gove, Michael, *Celsius 7/7* (London: Weidenfeld and Nicolson, 2006).

Grewal, Zareena, 'The "Muslim World" Does Not Exist', *The Atlantic*, 21 May 2017; available at: https://www.theatlantic.com/international/ archive/2017/05/the-muslim-world-is-a-place-that-does-not-exist/527550/ (accessed 28 May 2017).

Griffin, Nick, 'A message from BNP Leader Nick Griffin MEP' archived page available at: https://web.archive.org/web/20140725200638/https://bnp.org.uk/introduction (accessed 13 June 2016).

Gutmann, Amy, *Identity in Democracy* (Princeton, NJ: Princeton University Press, 2003).

Halliday, Fred, *Britain's First Muslims: portrait of an Arab community* (London: I.B.Tauris, 2010).

Halstead, J.M., Education, *Justice and Cultural Diversity: an examination of the Honeyford affair, 1984–85* (London: Falmer, 1988).

Hamid, Sadek, *Sufis, Salafis and Islamists: the contested ground of British Islamic activism* (London: I.B.Tauris, 2016).

——, 'British Muslim young people: facts, features and religious trends', *Religion, State and Society* 39/2–3 (2011), pp. 247–261.

——, 'The attraction of "authentic" Islam: Salafism and British Muslim youth', in Roel Meijer (ed.), *Global Salafism: Islam's new religious movement* (London: Hurst & Co., 2009), pp. 384–410.

——, 'Islamic political radicalism in Britain: the case of Hizb-Ut-Tahrir', in Tahir Abbas (ed.), *Islamic Political Radicalism: a European perspective* (Edinburgh: Edinburgh University Press, 2007), pp. 145–159.

Hampsher-Monk, Iain, *A History of Modern Political Thought: major political thinkers from Hobbes to Marx* (Oxford: Blackwell, 1992).

Hansen, Randall, *Citizenship and Immigration in Post-war Britain* (Oxford: Oxford University Press, 2004).

Harker, Joseph, 'This is how racism takes root', *Guardian*, 22 July 2012.

Hasan, Mehdi, 'We mustn't allow Muslims in public life to be silenced', *Guardian*, 8 July 2012.

Hasan, Usama *et al.*, 'Mainstreaming Islamism: Islamist institutions and civil society organisations' (September 2019), available at: https://assets.publishing. service.gov.uk/government/uploads/system/uploads/attachment_data/ file/836965/mainstreaming-islamism-islamist-insitutions-and-civil-society-organisations.pdf (accessed 7 October 2019).

Hasan, Usama, *No Compulsion in Religion: an Islamic case against blasphemy laws* (London: Quilliam Foundation, 2012).

Heyes, Cressida, 'Identity politics', in Edward N.Zalta (ed.), *The Stanford Encyclopedia of Philosophy* (Spring 2012) https://plato.stanford.edu/entries/ identity-politics/ (accessed 26 June 2017).

Hickman, Mary J., '"Suspect populations": Irish communities, Muslim communities and the British justice system', in Kjartan Pal Sveinsson (ed.), *Criminal Justice v. Racial Justice: minority ethnic overrepresentation in the criminal justice system* (London: Runnymede Trust, 2012), pp. 27–29.

Hill, Dave, 'The Rise and Fall of Lutfur Rahman', *Guardian*, 10 June 2015.

Holmwood, John, 'Fundamental British Values, Religion and Inequalities' *Discover Society*, 4 September 2019, available at: https://discoversociety. org/2019/09/04/fundamental-british-values-religion-and-inequalities/ (accessed 5 September 2019).

Honneth, Axel, 'Recognition and moral obligation', *Social Research* 64/1 (1997), pp. 16–35.

——, *The Struggle for Recognition: the moral grammar of social conflicts* (Cambridge: Polity, 1996).

Hotz, Alexander, 'Newsweek "Muslim rage" cover invokes a rage of its own', US News Media Blog, *Guardian* (17 September 2012).

Hough, Andrew, 'Anti-extremism scheme "spying on Muslims"', *Daily Telegraph*, 17 October 2009.

Howe, Darcus, 'John Reid's dirty little one-act play', *New Statesman*, 6 October 2006.

Husain, Ed, *The Islamist: why I joined Radical Islam in Britain, what I saw inside and why I left* (London: Penguin, 2007).

Hussain, Dilwar, 'British Muslim identity', in Seddon, Mohammed Siddique, Dilwar Hussain and Nadeem Malik, *British Muslims between Assimilation and Segregation* (Leicester: Islamic Foundation, 2004), pp. 83–118.

———, 'Councillors and caliphs: Muslim political participation in Britain', in Seddon, Mohammed Siddique, Dilwar Hussain and Nadeem Malik, *British Muslims between Assimilation and Segregation* (Leicester: Islamic Foundation, 2004), pp. 173–200.

Imtiaz, Atif, *Wandering Lonely in a Crowd* (Leicester: Kube, 2011).

Inge, Annabel, *The Making of a Salafi Muslim Woman: paths to conversion* (Oxford: Oxford University Press, 2016).

ITV News, interview with Jacob Rees Mogg MP, 13th June 2019

Johnson, Boris, 'Denmark has got it wrong. Yes, the burka is oppressive and ridiculous – but that's still no reason to ban it' *The Telegraph* 5 August 2018.

Jones, Peter, 'Bearing the consequences of belief', in Robert Goodin and Philip Pettit (eds), *Contemporary Political Philosophy: an anthology* (Oxford: Blackwell, 2006), pp. 607–620.

Julius, Anthony, *Trials of the Diaspora: a history of anti-Semitism in England* (New York: Oxford University Press, 2010).

Kabir, Nahid Afrose, *Young British Muslims: identity, culture, politics and the media* (Edinburgh: Edinburgh University Press, 2010).

Kahn-Harris, Keith and Ben Gidley, *Turbulent Times: The British Jewish Community Today* (London: Continuum, 2010).

Kamali, Mohammad Hashim, *Freedom of Expression in Islam* (Cambridge: Islamic Texts Society, 1997).

Kelsey, Tim, 'Fundamentalist gathering seeks political overthrow of Western democracies: Muslims call for Israeli state to be destroyed', *Independent*, 8 August 1994.

Khan, Sara with Tony McMahon, *The Battle for British Islam: reclaiming Muslim identity from extremists* (London: Saqi, 2016)

Khan, Shehla, 'New Sufis for New Labour', *The Muslim News*, 25 August 2006.

Klausen, Jytte, 'British Counter-Terrorism after 7/7: adapting community policing to fight against domestic terrorism', *Journal of Ethnic and Migration Studies* 35 (2009), pp. 403–420.

———, *The Islamic Challenge: politics and religion in Western Europe* (Oxford: Oxford University Press, 2005).

Kundnani, Arun, *Spooked: how not to prevent violent extremism* (London: Institute of Race Relations, 2009).

———, *The End of Tolerance: racism in 21st century Britain* (London: Pluto Press, 2007).

Kymlicka, Will, *Multicultural Citizenship: a liberal theory of minority rights* (Oxford: Clarendon Press, 1995).

———, *The Rights of Minority Cultures* (Oxford: Oxford University Press, 1995).

Lambert, Robert, 'Empowering Salafis and Islamists against Al-Qaeda: a

London counterterrorism case study', *Political Science and Politics* 41/1 (2008), pp. 31–35.

Langham, Raphael, *250 Years of Convention and Contention: a history of the Board of Deputies of British Jews, 1760–2010* (Edgware: Vallentine Mitchell, 2010).

Laurence, Jonathan, *The Emancipation of Europe's Muslims: the state's role in minority integration* (Princeton, NJ: Princeton University Press, 2012).

Lawless, Richard, *From Ta'izz to Tyneside: an Arab community in the North East of England in the early twentieth century* (Exeter: University of Exeter Press, 1995).

Lewis, Bernard, *From Babel to Dragomans: interpreting the Middle East* (New York: Oxford University Press, 2004).

Lewis, Philip, *Young, British and Muslim* (London: Continuum, 2007).

———, 'British *'ulama* and the politics of social visibility', in Gerdien Jonker and Vale´rie Amiraux (eds), *Politics of Visibility: young Muslims in European public spaces* (London: Transaction Publishers, 2006), pp. 169–190.

———, *Islamic Britain: religion, politics and identity among British Muslims* (London: I.B.Tauris, 1994).

Liddle, Rod, 'Free speech and the lyrical terrorist', *The Spectator*, 21 November 2007.

Livshin, R. 'The acculturation of the children of immigrant Jews in Manchester, c.1890–1920', in David Cesarani (ed.), *The Making of Modern Anglo-Jewry* (Oxford: Basil Blackwell, 1990).

Lyon, Stephen, 'The shadow of September 11: multiculturalism and identity', in Tahir Abbas (ed.), *Muslim Britain* (London: Zed Books, 2005), pp. 78–91.

MacPherson, William et al., *The Stephen Lawrence Inquiry* (London: Stationery Office, 1999).

Malik, Kenan, *From Fatwa to Jihad: the Rushdie affair and its legacy* (London: Atlantic, 2009).

Malik, Maleiha, 'How can British Muslim groups better protect themselves?', *Guardian*, 11 June 2013.

———, ed., *Anti-Muslim Prejudice: past and present* (London: Routledge, 2010).

———, 'Extreme speech and liberalism', in I. Hare and J. Weinstein (eds), *Extreme Speech and Democracy* (Oxford: Oxford University Press, 2009), pp. 96–122.

———, 'Muslims are now getting the same treatment Jews had a century ago', *Guardian*, 2 February 2007.

Malik, Nadeem, 'Equality? The treatment of Muslims under the English legal system', in Hussain Dilwar, Nadeem Malik and Mohammed Siddique Seddon, *British Muslims between Assimilation and Segregation* (Markfield: Islamic Foundation, 2004), pp. 43–82.

Malik, Nesrine, *We Need New Stories: challenging the toxic myths behind our age of discontent* (Weidenfield and Nicolson, 2019).

Malik, Zaiba, *We are a Muslim, Please* (London: William Heinemann, 2010).

Manea, Elham, *Women and Shari'a Law* (London: I.B.Tauris, 2016).

Martineau, Wendy, 'Misrecognition and cross-cultural understanding: shaping the space for a "fusion of horizons"' *Ethnicities* 12/2(January 2012), pp. 161–177.

Massil, Stephen W (ed.), *The Jewish Year Book 1999* (Essex: Vallentine Mitchell, 1999).

Matar, Nabil, 'Britons and Muslims in the early modern period: from prejudice to (a theory of) toleration', in Maleiha Malik (ed.), *Anti-Muslim Prejudice: past and present* (Abingdon: Routledge, 2010), pp. 7–25.

———, *Islam in Britain–1558–1685* (Cambridge: Cambridge University Press, 2008).

Maughan, Philip, 'Rowan Williams: Sharia law question "still pertinent"', *New Statesman*, 5 June 2013.

May, Stephen, Tariq Modood and Judith Squires, *Ethnicity, Nationalism and Minority Rights* (Cambridge: Cambridge University Press, 2004).

McKinnon, Catriona, *Toleration: a critical introduction* (London: Routledge, 2006).

McLoughlin, Sean, 'The state, new Muslim leaderships and Islam as a resource for public engagement in Britain', in Jocelyne Cesari and Sean McLoughlin (eds), *European Muslims and the Secular State* (Aldershot: Ashgate, 2005), pp. 55–70.

McRoy, Anthony, *From Rushdie to 7/7: the radicalization of Islam in Britain* (London: Social Affairs Unit, 2006).

Meer, Nasar, *Citizenship, Identity and the Politics of Multiculturalism: the rise of Muslim consciousness* (Basingstoke: Palgrave Macmillan, 2010).

———, 'The politics of voluntary and involuntary identities: are Muslims in Britain an ethnic, racial or religious minority?', *Patterns of Prejudice* 42/1 (2008), pp. 61–81.

Meer, Nasar and Tariq Modood, 'Refutations of racism in the "Muslim question"', *Patterns of Prejudice* 43/3–4 (2009), pp. 335–354.

Meer, Nasar and Tehseen Noorani, 'A sociological comparison of anti- Semitism and anti-Muslim sentiment in Britain', *Sociological Review* 56/2 (May 2008), pp. 195–219.

Mendus, Susan, 'The tigers of wrath and the horses of instruction', in John Horton (ed.), *Liberalism, Multiculturalism and Toleration* (Basingstoke: Macmillan, 1993), pp. 193–206.

Mill, John Stuart, *Utilitarianism, Liberty, Representative Government* (London: Dent, 1972).

Mirza, Munira, Abi Senthilkumaran and Zein Ja'far, *Living Apart Together: British Muslims and the paradox of multiculturalism* (London: Policy Exchange, 2007).

Modood, Tariq, 'Muslims and the politics of difference', in Peter Hopkins and Richard Gale (eds), *Muslims in Britain: race, place and identities* (Edinburgh: Edinburgh University Press, 2009), pp. 193–209.

———, *Multiculturalism: a civic idea* (Cambridge: Polity, 2007).

———, 'The liberal dilemma: integration or vilification?', Open Democracy, 8 February 2006; available at: http://www.opendemocracy.net/faith-terrorism/liberal_dilemma_3249.jsp (accessed 13 June 2016).

———, 'Remaking multiculturalism after 7/7', *Open Democracy*, 28 September 2005; available at: http://www.opendemocracy.net/conflict-terrorism/multiculturalism_2879.jsp (accessed 14 June 2016).

———, 'British Muslims and multiculturalism', in Tariq Modood et al. (eds), *Multiculturalism, Muslims and Citizenship: a European approach* (London: Routledge, 2005a), pp. 37–56.

————, *Multicultural Politics: racism, ethnicity and Muslims in Britain* (Edinburgh: Edinburgh University Press, 2005b).

————, 'Muslims and the Politics of Difference', *Political Quarterly* 74/S1 (August 2003), pp. 100–115.

————, '"Difference", cultural racism and anti-racism', in Tariq Modood and Pnina Werbner (eds), *Debating Cultural Hybridity: multicultural identities and the politics of anti-racism* (London: Zed Books, 1997), pp. 154–172.

————, 'Muslims, incitement to hatred and the law', in John Horton (ed.), *Liberalism, Multiculturalism and Toleration* (Basingstoke: Macmillan, 1993), pp. 139–156.

————, 'Being somebody and being oppressed: catching up with Jesse Jackson', in Tariq Modood, *Not Easy Being British: colour, culture and citizenship* (London: Runnymede Trust and Trentham Books, 1992), pp. 47–59.

————, 'Muslims, race and equality in Britain: some post-Rushdie affair reflections', *Third Text* 4/11 (1990), pp. 127–134.

Modood, Tariq, Anna Triandafyllidou and Ricard Zapata-Barrero, *Multi-culturalism, Muslims and Citizenship: a European approach* (London: Routledge, 2006).

Mondal, Anshuman, *Islam and Controversy: the politics of free speech after Rushdie* (Basingstoke: Palgrave, 2014).

Muir, Hugh, Laura Smith and Robin Richardson, *Islamophobia, Issues, Challenges and Action: a report* (Stoke on Trent: Trentham Books, in association with the Uniting Britain Trust, London, 2004).

Murray, Craig, 'Sufi Muslim Council a CIA/Karimov front', 23 March 2009; available at: http://www.craigmurray.org.uk/archives/2009/03/sufi_muslim_cou/ (accessed 14 June 2016).

Muslim Council of Britain, *The Quest for Sanity: reflections on September 11 and the aftermath* (Wembley: Muslim Council of Britain, 2002).

Muslims for Change, *Make your voice heard in the 2017 UK elections* https://www.launchgood.com/project/make_your_voice_heard__2017_uk_ elections#/ (accessed 22 May 2017).

Mustafa, Asma, *Identity and Political Participation among Young British Muslims: believing and belonging* (Basingstoke: Palgrave, 2015).

Nawaz, Maajid, 'How the government should handle the "Muslim Question"', *New Statesman*, 5 December 2011.

Newman, Aubrey, *The Board of Deputies of British Jews 1760–1985: a brief survey* (London: Vallentine Mitchell, 1987).

Nielsen, Jørgen S., *The Impact of Islam in Contemporary Western Europe* (Bracknell: Centre for the Study of Religious and Cultural Diversity, Newbold College, 2004).

————, *Muslims in Western Europe*(Edinburgh: Edinburgh University Press, 2004).

Nihal, BBC Asian Network, 12 May 2016.

Nikkhah, Roya and Adam Lusher, 'Police accused of "cowardly failure" to prosecute militant', *Daily Telegraph*, 24 September 2006.

Oborne,Peter,'TheshamefulIslamophobiaattheheartofBritain'spress', *Independent*, 7 July 2008.

O'Brien, Peter, *The Muslim Question in Europe: political controversies and public philosophies* (Philadelphia: Temple University Press, 2016).

Okin, Susan Moller, 'Is multiculturalism bad for women?', in Joshua Cohen et al.(eds),*Is Multiculturalism Bad for Women?* (Princeton, NJ: Princeton University Press, 1999), pp. 7–24.

O'Toole, Therese, Stephen H. Jones and Daniel Nilsson Dehanas, 'The new Prevent: will it work? Can it work?', *Arches Quarterly* 5/9 (Spring 2012), pp. 56–62.

Panorama 'Sex Education: the LGBT debate in Schools' BBC 1, 15 July 2019.

Panorama, 'A question of leadership', BBC1, 21 August 2005.

Panorama, 'The secret agent', BBC1, 15 July 2004.

Pantucci, Raffaello, *We Love Death as you Love Life: Britain's suburban terrorists* (London: Hurst, 2015).

Parekh, Bhikhu, 'Redistribution or recognition? A misguided debate', in Tariq Modood, Stephen May and Judith Squires (eds), *Ethnicity, Nationalism and Minority Rights* (Cambridge: Cambridge University Press, 2004), pp. 199–213.

———, *Rethinking Multiculturalism: cultural diversity and political theory* (Basingstoke: Macmillan, 2000).

———, 'The Rushdie affair: research agenda for political philosophy', *Political Studies* 38/4 (1990), pp. 695–709.

Pargeter, Alison, *The Muslim Brotherhood: the burden of tradition* (Saqi, London: 2010).

Parker, Ellen, 'Implementation of the UK Terrorism Act 2006 – the relationship between counter terrorism law, free speech and the Muslim community in the United Kingdom versus the United States', *Emory Law Review* 21/2 (Fall 2007), pp. 711–757.

Parker-Jenkins, Marie, 'Equal access to state funding: the case of Muslim schools in Britain', paper presented at the British Educational Research Association Annual Conference, Queen's University of Belfast, Northern Ireland August 27th to August 30 (1998); available at: http://www.leeds.ac. uk/educol/documents/000000911.htm (accessed 13 June 2017).

Parris, Matthew, 'Think no evil? Are you serious?', *The Times*, 17 November 2007.

Peace, Timothy (ed.), *Muslims and Political Participation in Britain* (Abingdon: Routledge, 2015).

Peachey, Paul, 'Islamist gang of six jailed for at least 18 years each for plotting bomb attack on EDL rally', *Independent*, 10 June 2013.

Pedziwiatr, Konrad, 'Creating new discursive arenas and influencing the policies of the state: the case of the Muslim Council of Britain', *Social Compass* 54/2 (2007), pp. 267–280.

Phillips, Anne, *Multiculturalism without Culture* (Princeton, NJ: Princeton University Press, 2007).

———, *The Politics of Presence* (Oxford: Clarendon Press, 1995).

Phillips, Melanie, 'My immigrant family were proud to assimilate. I despair that too many today expect Britain to adopt THEIR culture', *Daily Mail*, 7 May 2013.

Phillips, Richard, 'Standing together: the Muslim Association of Britain and the anti-war movement', *Race and Class* 50/2 (2008), pp. 101–113.

PM Programme, BBC Radio 4, 3 January 2006.

Poole, Elizabeth, *Reporting Islam: media representations of British Muslims* (London: I.B.Tauris, 2002).

Prime Minister's Office, 'Prime Minister: 'I want to build a national coalition to challenge and speak out against extremism' press release, 13 October 2015; available at: https://www.gov.uk/government/news/prime-minister-i-want-to-build-a-national-coalition-to-challenge-and-speak-out-against-extremism (accessed 15 June 2016).

Qureshi, Asim, 'The UK counter-terrorism matrix: structural racism and the case of Mahdi Hashi', in Massoumi, Narzanin, Tom Mills and David Miller (eds), *What is Islamophobia? Racism, social movements and the state* (London: Pluto Press, 2017), pp. 74–96.

———, 'Conviction of thought: how Islamic concepts are ruled on in UK courts', *Arches Quarterly* 5/9 (Spring 2012), pp. 171–176.

Rahman, Afzal,'Muslim girls' schooling'(letter to the editor),*The Times*, 18 January 1974.

Rahman, Samia, 'The biggest star in the Middle East is a Brit', *Guardian*, 27 April 2006.

Rai, Milan, 7/7, *the London Bombings, Islam and the Iraq War* (London: Pluto Press, 2006).

Ramadan, Tariq, *Western Muslims and the Future of Islam* (New York: Oxford University Press, 2004).

———, *To be a European Muslim* (Leicester: Islamic Foundation, 1999).

Ramamurthy, Anandi, *Black Star: Britain's Asian youth movements* (London: Pluto Press, 2013).

Radcliffe, Liat, 'A Muslim lobby at White hall? Examining the role of the Muslim minority in British foreign policy making', *Islam and Christian- Muslim Relations* (2010), pp. 365–386.

Richardson, John E., '"Get shot of the lot of them": election reporting of Muslims in British newspapers', in Maleiha Malik (ed.), *Anti-Muslim Prejudice: past and present* (Abingdon: Routledge, 2010), pp. 146–168.

———, *(Mis) representing Islam: the racism and rhetoric of British broadsheet newspapers* (Amsterdam: John Benjamins, 2004).

Rocker, Simon, 'Board vice-president's attack on JLC prompts open warfare', *The Jewish Chronicle*, 23 February 2012.

———, 'Muslim Council of Britain must be boycotted until reform', *The Jewish Chronicle*, 24 September 2009.

Ronson, Jon, 'My night of Jihad', *Guardian*, 30 April 2007; available at: http://www.guardian.co.uk/commentisfree/2007/apr/30/mynightofjihad (accessed 13 June 2016).

Rozin, Mordechai, *The Rich and the Poor: Jewish philanthropy and social control in nineteenth-century London* (Brighton: Sussex Academic Press, 1999).

Rudd, Amber, 'Safe guarding our young people from becoming radicalised should not be a controversial aim', *The Sun*, 9 August 2017.

Runnymede Trust and Bhikhu Parekh, *Report of the Commission on the Future of Multi-Ethnic Britain* (London: Profile, 2000).

———, *Islamophobia: a challenge for us all* (London: Runnymede Trust, 1997).

Sacranie, Iqbal, 'British Muslims are judged by "Israel test"', *The Observer*, 21 August 2005.

————, 'Critics of Israel not anti-Semitic'(letter to the editor), *The Times*, 13 May 2002.

Sarwar, Ghulam M.A., *Issues in Islamic Education* (London: Muslim Educational Trust, 1996).

————, *British Muslims and Schools: proposals for progress* (London: Muslim Educational Trust, 1991).

————, *Muslims and Education in the U.K.* (London: Muslim Educational Trust, 1983).

Scott-Baumann, Alison, 'Ideology, utopia and Islam on campus: How to free speech a little from its own terrors' Education, Citizenship and Social Justice 12/2 (2017), pp. 159–176.

Seddon, Mohammed Siddique, 'Muslim communities in Britain: a historiography', in Seddon, Mohammed Siddique, Dilwar Hussain and Nadeem Malik, *British Muslims between Assimilation and Segregation* (Leicester: Islamic Foundation, 2004), pp. 1–42.

Seddon, Mohammed Siddique, Dilwar Hussain and Nadeem Malik, *British Muslims between Assimilation and Segregation: historical, legal and social realities* (Leicester: Islamic Foundation, 2004).

Sen, Amartya, *Identity and Violence: the illusion of destiny* (London: Allen Lane, 2006).

————, 'The uses and abuses of Multiculturalism', *The New Republic*, 27 February 2006.

Shah, Naz,'Dear Sajid Javid, Denouncing Accusations Of Islamophobia In The Tory Party Doesn't Mean It Doesn't Exist' *Huffington Post*, 3 June 2018, available at: https://www.huffingtonpost.co.uk/entry/dear-sajid-javid-denouncing-islamophobia-in-the-tory-party-doesnt-make-it-untrue_uk_5b1428d1e4b0d5e89e209832 (accessed 10 September 2019).

Shannahan, Dervla Sara, 'Gender, inclusivity and UK mosque experiences', *Contemporary Islam* 8/1 (2014), pp. 1–16.

Shaw, Alison, *A Pakistani Community in Britain* (Oxford: Basil Blackwell, 1988).

Sherif, Jamil, A Census chronicle–reflections on the campaign for a religion question in the 2001 Census for England and Wales, *Journal of Beliefs & Values* 32/1 (2011), pp. 1–18.

Sherif, M.A., *Searching for Solace: a biography of Abdullah Yusuf Ali, interpreter of the Qur'an* (Kuala Lumpur: Islamic Book Trust, 1994).

Sian, Katy, 'Spies, surveillance and stakeouts: monitoring Muslim moves in British state schools', *Race Ethnicity and Education* 18:2 (2015) pp. 183-201.

Silver, James, 'Interview: John Ware. "It's the last chance for Panorama"', *Guardian*, 21 August 2006.

Slaughter, M.M., 'The Salman Rushdie affair: apostasy, honor and freedom of speech', *Virginia Law Review* 79/1 (February 1993), pp. 153–204.

Sooben, Philip N., *The Origins of the Race Relations Act* (Coventry: Centre for Research in Ethnic Relations, University of Warwick, 1990).

Stjernholm, Simon. 'Sufi politics in Britain: the Sufi Muslim Council and the "silent majority" of Muslims', *Journal of Islamic Law and Culture* 12/3 (October 2010), pp. 215–226.

Taji-Farouki, Suha, *A Fundamental Quest: Hizbal-Tahrir and the search for the Islamic caliphate* (London: Grey Seal, 1996).

Taylor, Charles, *Multiculturalism and the Politics of Recognition* (Chichester: Princeton University Press, 1994).

Taylor, Matthew, 'BNP leaders may face charges after TV exposé of racism', *Guardian*, 15 July 2004.

Temko, Ned, 'Beckett rejects link between foreign policy and terrorism', *The Observer*, 13 August 2006.

Thomas, Paul, 'Failed and friendless: the UK's "Preventing Violent Extremism" programme', *British Journal of Politics and International Relations* 12/3 (August 2010), pp. 442–458.

Thompson, Simon, 'Freedom of expression and hatred of religion', *Ethnicities* 12/2 (January 2012), pp. 215–232.

Townsend,Mark, 'Baroness Warsi told by David Cameron not to appear at Islamic conference', *Guardian*, 24 October 2010.

Travis, Alanand Patrick Wintour, 'Terror bill chilling for Muslims, Blair warned', *Guardian*, 11 November 2005.

Tuckness, Alex, 'Rethinking the intolerant Locke', *American Journal of Political Science* 46/2 (2002), pp. 288–298.

Union of Muslim Organisations of UK and Ireland, *Union of Muslim Organisations of UK and Ireland, 1970–1995: a record of achievement* (London: Union of Muslim Organisations of UK & Ireland, 1995).

Vallely, Paul, 'So what turned Sid Khan into a bomber?', *Independent*, 18 November 2005.

Vasagar, Jeevan, 'An inspector calls: the day the head of Ofsted visited one school', *Guardian*, 27 March 2012.

Verkaik, Robert, 'Exclusive: how the MI5 blackmails British Muslims', *Independent*, 21 May 2009.

Vertovec, Steven, 'Islamophobia and Muslim recognition in Britain', in Yvonne Yazbeck Haddad (ed.), *Muslims in the West: from sojourners to citizens* (New York: Oxford University Press, 2002), pp. 19–35.

———, 'Muslims, the state, and the public sphere in Britain', in Gerd Nonnemann, Tim Niblock and Bogdan Sjakowski (eds), *Muslim Communities in the New Europe* (London: Ithaca, 1996), pp. 169–185.

Visram, Rozina, *Ayahs, Lascars and Princes: Indians in Britain 1700–1947* (London: Pluto Press, 1986).

Wagerman, Jo, 'Impact of the Middle East on Britain' (letter to the editor) *The Times*, 22 May 2002.

Wahid, Omar, 'Britain's jihadi bride groomer: schoolgirl radicalised in London mosque recruited her three classmates to join ISIS in Syria', *The Mail on Sunday*, 1 August 2015.

Warsi, Sayeeda, *The Enemy Within: a tale of Muslim Britain* (London: Allen Lane, 2017).

Wavell, Stuart, 'Putting a good glossy on the Muslim lifestyle', *The Sunday Times*, 9 October 2005.

Weller, Paul, *A Mirror for our Times: the Rushdie affair and the future of multiculturalism* (London: Continuum, 2009).

Werbner, Pnina,'Islamophobia: incitement to religious hatred – legislating for a new fear?', *Anthropology Today* 21/1 (2005), pp. 5–9.

———, *Imagined Diasporas among Manchester Muslims: the public performance of Pakistani transnational identity politics* (New Mexico: School of American Research Press, 2002).

Werbner, Pnina and Tariq Modood (eds), *Debating Cultural Hybridity: multicultural identities and the politics of anti-racism* (Atlantic Highlands, NJ: Zed Books, 1997).

Whitaker, Brian, 'Alienating British Muslims', *Guardian: Comment is Free*, 24 March 2009.

Wilkinson, Matthew Tariq, 'This bookseller deserved his incitement to terrorism conviction', *Guardian*, 18 May 2012.

Yaqoob, Salma, 'Government's PVE agenda is failing to tackle extremism', *The Muslim News*, 28 November 2008.

Young, Iris Marion, *Justice and the Politics of Difference* (Princeton, NJ: Princeton University Press, 1990).

MEDIA SOURCES

Numerous online and print articles and publications have been consulted and are referenced throughout the book. Here I list only the publication title or main homepage for each source.

Broadcast media:
Al Jazeera Satellite Channel
British Broadcasting Corporation
Channel 4
Press TV

Magazines, periodicals and newspapers:

Arab News
British Muslims Monthly Survey
The Common Good
Crescent International
Daily Mail
Daily Telegraph
emel
Guardian
Hansard
Independent
Islamic Review

The Jewish Chronicle
The Mail on Sunday
The Muslim
The Muslim News
The New Republic
New Statesman
Newsweek
Observer
Q-News
Spectator
The Times

Online media and websites:

Abdullah Quilliam Society: www.abdullahquilliamsociety.org.uk

Alternative Leveson: www.alternativeleveson.org.uk (no longer available)

BBC News Website: www.bbc.co.uk/news

The Black Muslim Times: www.theblackmuslimtimesuk.org/

Board of Deputies of British Jews: www.bod.org.uk

Britain First: www.britainfirst.org

BNP: www.bnp.org.uk

Cage: www.cage.ngo

Changing the Board: www.changingtheboard.wordpress.com

Commission for Women in Jewish Leadership: http://www.thejlc.org/portfolio/commission-for-women-in-jewish-leadership/

DeenPort: www.deenport.com

Eden Care: www.edencareuk.com

Engage: www.iengage.org.uk

FOSIS: www.fosis.org.uk

Grenfell Legal Support: www.grenfell-legalsupport.org

Hope Not Hate: www.hopenothate.org.uk

Huffington Post: www.huffingtonpost.co.uk

Inclusive Mosque Initiative: www.inclusivemosqueinitiative.org/

Independent Jewish Voices: www.ijv.org.uk

Institute of Contemporary Islamic Thought: www.islamicthought.org

Islam Awareness Week: www.iaw.org.uk

Islamic Forum Europe: www.islamicforumeurope.com (no longer available)

Islamic Party of Britain: www.islamicparty.com

Jewish Leadership Council: www.thejlc.org

Liberty: www.liberty-human-rights.org.uk

Making Herstory: www.makingherstory.org.uk

MCB: www.mcb.org.uk

MEND: www.mend.org.uk

Middle East Eye: www.middleeasteye.net

The Muslim Institute: www.musliminstitute.org

National Zakat Foundation: www.nzf.org.uk

Open Democracy: www.opendemocracy.net

PBM: www.projectingbritishmuslims.co.uk (no longer available)

Peter Tatchell: www.petertatchell.net

Salaam: www.salaam.co.uk

Salafi Media: www.salafimedia.com (no longer available)

Schedule 7 Stories: www.schedule7stories.com

Stop the War Coalition: www.stopwar.org.uk

Students Not Suspects: www.studentsnotsuspects.com Woking Muslim Mission: www.wokingmuslim.org

YMAG: www.ymag.org.uk (no longer available)

Youtube: www.youtube.com

Index